RECORDS

OF THE

Courts of Quarter Sessions and Common Pleas

OF

BUCKS COUNTY PENNSYLVANIA

1684-1700

PUBLISHED BY THE COLONIAL SOCIETY OF PENNSYLVANIA

PRINTED BY
THE TRIBUNE PUBLISHING COMPANY
MEADVILLE, PA.
1943

Southern Historical Press, Inc.
Greenville, South Carolina

This volume was reproduced from
An 1943 edition located in the
Publisher's private Library

Please direct all correspondence and orders to:

www.southernhistoricalpress.com
or
SOUTHERN HISTORICAL PRESS, Inc.
PO BOX 1267
375 West Broad Street
Greenville, SC   29601
southernhistoricalpress@gmail.com

Originally published: Meadville, PA. 1943
ISBN #0-89308-907-9
All rights Reserved.
Printed in the United States of America

AN HISTORICAL NOTE

Previous to the granting of the charter for the Province of Pennsylvania to William Penn there were few inhabitants in the region comprising what is now Bucks County, and they were located near the "Falls of the Deleware." All matters at law which they had came under the jurisdiction of the Court of New Sweden prior to 1655, and after that date under the jurisdiction of the Court at New York.

In 1667, Governor Lovelace organized three judicial districts, that of Upland extending up the Delaware to the "Falls", and embracing the country of Bucks County to that point. Until the time of William Penn, the inhabitants had to go to Upland, the present Chester, to transact their legal business. The earliest court there was held in 1672. Under Governor Sir Edmond Andross the English system of jurisprudence was introduced on the Delaware. His courts at Upland, Newcastle and Hoornkill had powers of courts of sessions and could decide all matters under £20 without appeal and under £5 without a jury. Previous to 1677, all wills had to be proved and letters of administration granted at New York. The Upland Court petitioned Governor Andross for this power on the ground that the estates were too small to bear the expense and inconvenience of going to New York. The Court was then given authority to grant letters on estates under £30, but for those of greater amount the Court in New York retained jurisdiction.

The first action to recover a debt, brought by an inhabitant of what became Bucks County, was on November 12, 1678, when James Sanderlins of Bensalem, entered suit against John Edmunds of Maryland, for the value of 1200 pounds of tobacco, and the case was decided in his favor.[1] In 1679, Edmund Draufton, also of Bensalem, brought suit against Dunck Williams to recover for his services in teaching the latter's children to read the Bible within a year for 200 guilders. At the expiration of that time he refused to pay. The Upland Court decided in favor of Draufton.[2] On June 14, 1681, Claes Jansen brought to the session of the Upland Court held at Kingsesse the ear marks of his cattle and hogs and asked to have them recorded, which was accordingly done.[3]

1 *Memoirs of the Historical Society of Pennsylvania*, Vol. II, p. 111.
2 *Ibid*, p. 131.
3 *Ibid*, p. 190.

The first court held in Bucks County of which there is record, was at "ye new seate towne" on the Delaware below the "Falls", not far from where Morrisville stands. The place was called Crewcorne and the court the "Court of Crewcorne (Creekhorne) at the Falls." This Court was functioning prior to 1680, but how much earlier appears to be unknown. On April 12, 1680, the Court sent to the Governor of New York the names of four persons for magistrates, according to order, but their names are not given.[4]

After the granting of the Charter to William Penn, on March 4, 1681, he formulated a preliminary constitution and set of laws for the government of the province, which were known under the title "The FRAME of the Government of the Province of Pennsylvania in America: Together with certain LAWS agreed upon in England, by the Governor and divers Freemen of the aforesaid Province. To be Further explained and confirmed there, by the first Provincial Council that shall be held, if they see meet." Under the "Frame", the Governor and Provincial Council were authorized to erect from time to time standing Courts of Justice in such places and numbers as they should judge convenient for the good government of the Province.[5]

All courts were to be open, and justice neither sold, nor delayed: all persons of all persuasions could freely appear in their own way and according to their own manner and there personally plead their own cause themselves, or if unable, by their friends; all pleadings, processes and records in courts were to be short and in *English*, and in an ordinary and plain character, that they could be understood and justice speedily administered. All trials were to be by twelve men, and, as near as might be, peers or equals, and of the neighborhood, and men without just exception.

In cases of life the Sheriff was required first to return twenty-four men for a Grand Inquest, of whom twelve at least should find the complaint to be true; and then the twelve men or peers, to be likewise returned by the Sheriff had the final judgment. Reasonable challenge was always to be admitted against the twelve men, or any of them.

All fees in all cases were to be moderate, and settled by

4 Davis, *History of Bucks County*, Vol. II, p. 228.
5 *The Frame* etc., Section XVII.

the Provincial Council and General Assembly, and be hung up in a table in every respective court, and any one who should be convicted of taking more was required to pay two-fold, and be dismissed from his employment, one moiety going to the party wronged. Before the complaint of any person could be received, he had to solemnly declare in court that "he believes in his conscience his cause is just."[6]

In 1683 an act was passed for the establishment of County Courts, and the first court for Bucks County organized under that act, was erected at Crewcorne on the old road leading from Tullytown to the landing at Bordentown Ferry.[7] In recording the minutes of the sessions of this Court, Phineas Pemberton stated that the meetings were held at the Court House of the County, but did not mention the place of its location. Frequently he mentioned that the Court adjourned to or met at Gilbert Wheelers. This public house, at the old Ferry, Gilbert Wheeler called "Crewcorne." This was the seat of justice until 1705, when it was moved to Bristol, where it remained until 1725, when it was again moved to Newtown, and finally located at Doylestown in 1813, where it has since remained.

The oldest records of the courts of Bucks County, Pennsylvania, are those of the Orphans' Court. This Court was held at Gilbert Wheelers, on the 4th day of the first month, 1683, "to inspect and take an account of the improvements and usages of the Estates of Orphans." Those present were "the Governor William Penn, Justices James Harrison, Jon Otter, Wm yardley, Wm. Beakes, Thomas Fitzwater and Phineas Pemberton Cl:." The first case for consideration of the court was that of the two sons of John Spencer who died on the 22nd day of the 10th month 1683.

The next oldest court records are those contained in a volume entitled "Records of the Courts of Quarter Sessions and Common Pleas of Bucks County, 1684-1730." The minutes of the first session therein recorded are those of a court held on the 11th of the 10th month, 1684. The date of the organization of this Court appears to be unknown, but that there was a court functioning before that time is shown in the minutes of a meeting of the Provincial Council, held at Phila-

6 *Laws agreed upon,* etc., sections V - IX.
7 MacReynolds, *Place Names in Bucks County,* p. 60.

delphia, the 20th of the fourth month, 1683, when the following appeal was brought before it:

"Richard Noble, P1; on an apeal, Abra. Man, Def^t.

The Jugem^t of ye County Court against Richard Noble was reade, wth the reason of ye Apeale, and soe they proceeded to Tryall.

But for as much as ye apeal of Richd Noble before this board, is upon a Jugemt given by ye County Court of Philadelphia, concerning a Title of Land in ye County of Bucks, and that ye Law saith That all Causes shall be first Tryed where they arise, It is ye opinion of this board that ye apeal Lyes not Legally nor regularly before us and therefore doe refer ye Business to the proper County Court, and doe fine ye County Court of Philadelphia forty pounds for giving ye said Judgment against Law."[8]

A Provincial Circular Court was created by an act passed by the General Assembly on the 10th day of the third month, 1684, "to try all Criminalls & Titles of Land, and be a Court of Equity, to decide all Differences upon appeals from the County Courts."[9]

The Proprietor divided the Province into three counties but the lines of separation were not clearly defined. This soon led to confusion and uncertainty as to jurisdiction and the Provincial Council on the 8th of the second month, 1685, after considering the matter at two previous meetings, directed the following notice to be sent to the Sheriffs of the Counties concerned:—

"By the Presdt & Provil Councill of the Province of Pennsilvania & Territories thereunto belonging.

Whereas, there is a Necessity to ascertain the Bounds of ye severall Countyes of Pennsilvania, in Order to ye raising and Collecting of Taxes, publick Monys, and Otherways to adjust the Limitts of the respective Sheriffs for ye pforming of their Power and Duty: and also, that ye People might know unto what County they belong & appertaine to answer their dutys and places: and wheras the Govr. in presence of Tho. Janney & Phin. Pemberton, was pleased to say and Grant that

8 *Colonial Records*, Vol I, p. 76.
9 *Ibid*, p. 98; *Pa. Archives, 8th Series*, Vol. 1, p. 50.

yᵉ Bounds of yᵉ County of Bucks and Philadelphia should begin as followeth, Vizt.

To begin at yᵉ Mouth of Poctquesink Creek, on Delaware, and soe by yᵉ sd Creek, and to take in the Townships of Southampton and Warminster: in Obedience thereto and Confirmation thereof, The President and Councill have Seriously Weighed and Considered yᵉ same, have & doe hereby agree and Order that the bounds between the said Countys shall be thus: to begin at yᵉ Mouth of Poctquesink Creek on Delaware River, and to goe up thence a long yᵉ said Creek by yᵉ severall Courses thereof, to a S. W. & N. E. Line, which said Line devides the Land belonging to Jos. Growdon & Compa:, from yᵉ Southampton Township; from thence by a Lyne of Marked Trees along the said Line 120 Perches more or less, from thence N. W. by a Line of marked Trees, which said Line impart devided the Land belonging to Nich. Moor from Southampton & Warminster Townships, Contermeing the said Line as far as yᵉ said County shall Extend."[10]

The Courts having been organized and the jurisdictions defined, the administration of justice proceeded under the government of the Proprietor until the time of the revolution in England when King James II was succeeded by their Majesties King William III and Queen Mary. Penn had the misfortune to be suspected of treason and conspiracy and too great an attachment through correspondence with the late King. His failure to provide military assistance to the King went strongly against him with William, who was then engaged on the battlefields of Europe. An order in Council, dated March 10, 1692, was issued depriving Penn of his province and annexing it to the government of New York. By this the Province and Territories came under the authority and direction of Governor Benjamin Fletcher who took charge. A number of those whom the governor wished to continue in office declined to serve, among whom were Thomas Lloyd[11] and Phineas Pemberton. In the meantime Penn and his friends put forth their efforts to have the charges of treason and disloyalty disproved and having convinced the King and Queen of his innocence, finally on August 9th, 1694, thirty months after having been ousted, the government was restored to him by an order in Council. During the administration of Gover-

10 *Ibid*, p. 130.
11 *Ibid*, p. 364.

nor Fletcher the County Clerk was Robert Cole, who was present at a meeting of the Provincial Council on May 13, 1693, and "took the oath and test, and oath of Clark of the County of Bucks."[12]

Following the return of the Proprietor to his government, Phineas Pemberton was restored and confirmed as Clerk of the County Courts of Bucks, in full and ample manner, by William Markham, on September 20, 1695.[13]

Phineas Pemberton was born January 30, 1649-50, in Bolton-le-Moor, Lancashire, England, where he was engaged in the business of a grocer previous to his coming to America. He left Liverpool on June 6, 1682, and with his father, mother, wife, son and daughter, together with James Harrison and his family, arrived on the ship Submission, at Choptank, on the Patuxent River, in Maryland. Leaving their families there for the time being, they came by horseback to Philadelphia and then made the rest of the journey by water to the "Falls of the Delaware," where they stayed for a time to look over the region with a view of locating there. Harrison came as the agent and steward of the Proprietor, and Pemberton being well impressed with the country decided to settle in that locality. He purchased three hundred acres of land and later brought his family from Maryland and built a house which he called "Grove Place." While in England he married Phoebe, daughter of James Harrison, also of Bolton. Of their ten children, two married and left issue. In his new home he soon became prominent and active in the social and political affairs of the community, and the remainder of his life was devoted to public service which he performed with satisfaction to the Proprietor, and with distinction to himself.

Besides holding the office of Clerk of all the Courts of the county from their organization, he was commissioned the first Deputy Register of Wills, 1686, five months later becoming Register; appointed Receiver of the Proprietary Quit Rents for the county, 1689, and Master of the Rolls in 1695. He kept the records of the arrivals of settlers coming into the county and the marriages, births and deaths, as well as the Ear Marks for the owners of cattle and swine as required by law. At one time he was Surveyor General and was directed to survey and lay out roads. He served three terms in the Provincial Coun-

12 *Ibid*, p. 375.
13 Pemberton Papers, Hist. Society of Pennsylvania, Vol. 1, p. 57.

cil,[14] and for four terms in the General Assembly,[15] and was President[16] of that body during the latter half of the third term. These offices together with the great mass of writing which he left behind him are a testimonial of a very busy and useful life. In a letter dated at Pennsbury, 19th of June, 1686, John Saxby, writing to Patrick Robinson stated that the Council told him that P. Pemberton did all the writing for Bucks County.[17] In his minutes of the Court he wrote his name as Phinehas up to the time of the Court held on the 10th day of the fourth month, 1696, when he made an entry dropping the second h and thereafter wrote it Phineas. His useful career was terminated by a fatal illness on March 1st, 1701-02, in the 52nd year of his age, and he was buried in the old graveyard where also rest his wife and five of their children with members of the Harrison family. This graveyard four miles south of Morrisville, on the mainland near the Delaware River, opposite Biles' Island, is regarded as the oldest graveyard in Bucks County, if not the oldest in Pennsylvania.

Writing to James Logan on September 8, 1701, the Proprietor said "Poor Phineas Pemberton is a dying man, and was not at the election, though he crept (as I may Say) to meeting yesterday. I am grieved at it: for he has not his fellow, and without him this is a poor country indeed."[18] Samuel Carpenter wrote to Penn "Phineas Pemberton died the 1st mo last and will be greatly missed, having left few or none in these parts or adjacent like him for wisdom, integrity and general service, and he was a true friend to thee and the government. It is a matter of sorrow when I call to mind and consider that the best of our men are taken away, and how many are gone and how few to supply their places."[19] In a letter from the Proprietor to James Logan, dated at London, 21st, 4 mo., 1702, he wrote "I mourn for poor Phin. Pemberton the ablest as well as one of ye best men in the Province."[20]

The records which follow in this volume are those of the Courts of Quarter Sessions and Common Pleas of Bucks County, Pennsylvania, from 1684 to 1700. They are the minutes

14 *Colonial Records*, Vol. 1, p. 125.
15 *Ibid*, p. 570.
16 *Ibid*, pp. 547, 548.
17 Pemberton Papers, Vol. 1, p. 16.
18 *Memoirs of the Historical Society of Pennsylvania*, Vol. IX, p. 55; Logan Papers, Vol. I, p. 56, American Philosophical Society.
19 Jordan, *Colonial Families of Philadelphia*, Vol. 1, p. 281.
20 Logan Papers, Vol. I, p. 40, Historical Society of Pennsylvania.

complete, no omissions or eliminations have been made. By reason of its great age the volume has been subjected to the wear and tear of time. It was not begun as a book, but on loose sheets of folded paper the pages averaging 8 by 12. As the minutes of the sessions of the Court increased in number they were chronologically arranged, and at a later date all in *fasciculi* were bound into the present volume. Various makes of paper compose its pages, some thin and others of better quality and more durable. Because of this lack of uniformity some of the pages have been torn, with fragments missing along the margins as well as in the inner portions. Wherever such instances occur they have been indicated by * * * . The pages were not numbered originally but done by another hand at a later period. In the present volume this pagination has been maintained. Pages 50-54 are written in reverse in the original and have been so reproduced.

Because of time's habit, interlineations often requiring the use of the reading glass, and the peculiar script letters common to the period in which it was written, the book is a difficult one to read. Outstanding features of the handwriting are the use of the long letter s, indifferent spelling and use of capital letters, and frequent indications of a tired hand. In the reproduction every effort has been made to have a *vera copia, verbatim, literatim, et punctatim,* page for page and line for line transcript, as far as typography can make it, with the duplications and other peculiarities of the original maintained.

The transcription begun during the incumbency of the writer as President of the Colonial Society of Pennsylvania encountered so many unforseen obstacles that it has taken a long time for its completion. Notwithstanding, it has been of much personal interest and afforded great satisfaction in its accomplishment, and carries the hope that it may be of the same value to scholars as have been the previous publications of the Society.

J. E. Burnett Buckenham.

Somerhousen in the German Township
    and County of Philadelphia,
June 15th, 1943.

RECORDS

OF THE

Courts of Quarter Sessions and Common Pleas of Bucks County, Pennsylvania

The iith $\dfrac{io}{mo}$ 84

Robt Lucas declared in

this Court that   agt he did

    lieve in his contionce the Caufe
was Juft

The iith $\dfrac{io}{mo}$ i684

Robt Lucas plt agt Thomas Bowman deft in an
    action of the Cafe for wth holding Seven pounds wch was
    due to the fd plt in the 3 month Laft paft
       Summonc granted for Tho Bowman —
    County of Bucks in the provinc of Pennfilvania
Thefe are to Require thee to Summonc Thomas Bowman
if he Shall be found in thy Balywick that he be and
appeare att the next Court to be held in Bucks County
afforefd on the 19th $\dfrac{ii}{mo}$ next enfueing then and there to
    Anfwer
to the Complt of Robt Lucas for wth holding of feven
pounds wch will be made appeare to be due to the faid
Robt Lucas in open Court & hereof Thou art not
to faile given undr my hand & Seale the iith day
of the $\dfrac{io^{th}}{mo}$ being the 36 yeare of the kings Raine
& the 4th of the propriatorys govrmt 1684
To the Sherrif of the fd   Willm Beakes
County or his Deputy Thefe
       The Sherrifs Returne
    This Summonce was executed according to direction
      The iith $\dfrac{io}{mo}$ 1684
    p Luke Brindley deputy Sherrife
   The declaration of the Said Robt Lucas plt

Robt Lucas plt agt   ⎫   The iith io month 1684
Thomas Bowman defdt ⎰ Robt Lucas of the County of Bucks
in the Provinc of Pennfilvania makes Complt agt Tho:
Bowman of weft new Jarfey, that he the Said Thomas
Bowman detaines from him the Sum of Seven pounds w^{ch}
he the fd Robt Lucas will make appeare in open Court
to be due Sinc Spring laft therefore the fd plt prays
(3)

Judgmt of Court agt the Said deft for his faid   * * *
yᵉ: damages he has Suftained for the want th   * * *
was due, & Coft of Suite

   iiᵗʰ $\frac{io}{mo}$ i684   John Ackerman Conftable prfents Daniel
       Brinfon of Bucks
County for keeping unlawfull Cattle

[2]

    The 16ᵗʰ day of $\frac{io}{mo}$ i684

   gilbert wheeler plt agt walter pomferet deft in
an acction of Cafe for with holding of five pounds 10ˢ
wᶜʰ was due to the Said plt

      An Arreft for the goods of the fd walter pomferet
County of Bucks in the Provinc of Pennfilvania
   Thefe are by the kings Authority in the name of the
propriatory & govrnr to require thee that thou
Attach if found within thy Balywick of the goods & Chattles
    of walter pomferet
(of Burlington in weft new Jarfey) so much as thou in thy
difcretion Shall Judge by Reafonable Apprizement will amount
to & yeild as well the Sum of five pounds   ═════════
as allfo Coft of Suite, & the Same So Attached in Cuftody
   keepe untill further ordr from the Comr of the Court
   except
the Said Walter pomferet Shall give Sufitient fecurity
for his Appearanc att the next Court to be holden in Bucks
County on the 14ᵗʰ day of the iiᵗʰ month next enfueing to
Anfwer unto gilbert Wheeler in an acction of Cafe —
or that he Render to him the full and Juft Sum of five
pounds ═══ wᶜʰ to him he oweth & unjuftly detaineth
as its Said hereof faile not & have thou there this writ
given under my hand & Seale the 17ᵗʰ day of the $\frac{io}{mo}$ in
the 36 yeare of the kings Raigne & yᵉ: 4ᵗʰ of the ppria
═torys govrmt i684
To the Sherrife of the County
of Bucks or his deputy Thefe
     The Sherrifs Return
The firft day of the iiᵗʰ month i684
By vertue of this writ I have Attached of the goods of

Walter pomſeret one mare one horſe one yearling hors Colt
Luke Brindley deputy Sherrife

gilbert Wheeler plt –⎫
       agt   ⎬gilbert Wheeler makes Complt agt
walter pomſeret deft ⎭walter pomſeret how that the ſd deft
                  under

tooke to work for him about 4 yeares Agoe for wch the
* * * him his full due but the ſd deft after he had
* * * to his hands unjuſtly necglected Such A pte of
* * * is to the value of 5 £ to the great damage
* * * therefore the ſd plt prays Judgmt of Court * * *
for damage & Coſt of Suite

The firſt day of the iith month i684

                                       3

The i6th day of the $\frac{io}{mo}$ 1684

Willm Biles plt agt Walter pomſeret deft in A plea
of Caſe ══ for wth holding of five pounds ───
wch was due to the Said plt

An Arreſt granted for the goods of the ſaid Walter
    Pomſeret

County of Bucks in the Provinc of Pennſilvania

Theſe are by the kings Authority in the name of the propriatory
& govrnr to Require thee to Attach if found wthin thy
Balyweeke of the goods & Chattles of Walter pomſeret (of
Burlington in weſt new Jarſsey) So much as thou in thy
diſcretion Shall Judge by Reaſonable appriſement will amont
to & yeild as well the Sum of five pounds ════
as allſo Coſt of ſuit & the Same So Attached in Cuſtody keepe
untill further ordr from the Commiſſioners of the Court
Except the Said Walter pomſeret Shall give Suffitiont ──
Security for his Appearanc att the next Court to be holden

in Bucks County on the 14th day$\frac{ii}{mo}$next enſueing to Anſwer unto

Willm Biles in A plea of Caſe or y^t
he Render to him the full & Juſt Sum of five pounds
════wch to him he oweth & unjuſtly detaineth
as its Said hereof faile not & have thou there this writt

given under my hand & Seale the 17th day of the $\frac{io}{mo}$ in

the 36 yeare of the kings Raigne & the 4th of the propriatorys
govrmt i684

To the Sherrife of the County of
Bucks or his deputy Thefe
       The Sherrifs Return
The firſt of the ii[th] mo 1684 by vertue of this writ I
have attached of the goods of walter pomſeret one
horſe one mare & one yearling hors Colt
                Luke Brindly deputy Sherrif

Willm Biles plt ——— ⎰ Willm Biles makes Complt agt Walter
      agt   ⎱
Walter pomſeret deſt ⎰ pomſeret of weſt new Jarſey for that
the ſaid walter pomſeret unjuſtly detaines from him the
Sum of five pounds w[ch] is due to the ſd plt upon acct
as the ſd plt will make appeare in Court there fore
the ſaid plt prays Judgmt of Court agt the ſd
deſt for his ſd monys & Coſt of ſuite
The firſt day of the ii[th] month i684

$$\text{The i8}^{\text{th}}\ \frac{\text{io}}{\text{mo}}\ \text{1684}$$

(4)   Samuel Dark plt agt Walter Pomſeret deſt in A
plea of Caſe ===== for with holding of three pounds ten
Shillings w[ch] was due to the Said plt

     An Arreſt for the goods of the ſd Walter Pomſeret
County of Bucks in the Provinc of Pennſilvania
Theſe are by the kings Authority in the name of the
           Propriatory and
govrnr to Require thee that thou Attach if found wth in thy
balywicke the goods & Chattles (of Walter pomſeret (of
          Burling
=ton in weſt new Jarſey) So much as thou in thy diſcretion
Shall Judg by Reaſonable apprizement will amount to and
yeild as well the Sum of three pounds ten Shillings =====
as allſo Coſt of ſuite & the Same So Attached in Cuſtody
keepe untill further ordr from the Comrs of the Court Except
the Said Walter Pomſeret Shall give Suffitiont Se
=curity for his appearance att the next Court to be holden
in Bucks County the 9th of the $\frac{\text{ii}}{\text{mo}}$ next enſueing to Anſwer
unto Samuel Darke in A plea of Caſe or that he Render
to him the full & Juſt Sum of three pounds ten shillings
w[ch] to him he oweth & unjuſtly detaines (as its Said) hereof
faile not & have thou there this writ given under my
hand & Seale the 17th day of the io[th] month in the 36

yeare of the kings Raigne & the 4th of the propriatorys
govrmt 1684

To the Sherrife of the County
   of Bucks or his deputy Thefe
         The Sherrifs Return

(5)

Ann milcome plt agt Edward Smith & Willm Smith deft
   in A plea of Cafe for wth holding of one pound
     Nine Shillings three penc wch was due to the
       Said plt above 3 months Agoe
             A
     Summonc granted for Edward & Willm Smith

Ann milcome plt ⎫ The declaration of the fd Ann milcome plt
    agt | Ann milcome of the County of Bucks In the
Edward Smith— | Provinc of Pennfilvania makes Compt agt
    &   ⎬   Edward
Willm Smith— | Smith & Willm Smith of the County
   deft———— ⎭   afforefd that they owe to her the
              Sum of one pound Nine Shillings three
                pence
            wch was due to her in ye
firft month laft as She will make appeare in Court & that
they the faid defts unjuftly detaines her monys from her there
fore the Said plt prays Judgmt of Court agt them
for her fd monys & Coft of fuite

(6)   The 29th day of the $\frac{ii}{mo}$ i684
    Samuel overton of the County of Bucks plt agt
    John Clows of the fd County deft in an acct of Cafe
for wth holding of Seven pounds which is due to ye
Said plt
        The declaration of Samuel overton
       The 29th day of the $\frac{ii}{mo}$ i684

Samuel Overton plt⎫
     agt   ⎬ Samuel overton makes Complt agt
John Clows deft—⎭ the Said John Clows how that the
Said deft about 4 months ago Sent for the fd plt, to Come

to his houſe for that Joſeph Chorley ſervant to the Said deft
was Shot into the legg & that if the ſd plt wold Come
& Cure the ſd Servant the ſd deft wold Content
him whereupon the ſd plt wrought A Cure upon the ſd –
Servant of the ſd deft & that now the ſd deft refuſes to
pay the ſd plt, & unjuſtly detaines the Sum of Seven pounds
wch is due to the ſd plt from the ſd deft for working the
ſd Cure wherefore the ſd plt prays Judgmt of Court agt
the ſd deft for his monys & Coſt of ſuite

                A Summonc granted for the ſd John Clows
      County of Bucks in the provinc of Pennſilvania
Theſe are by the kings Authority in the name of the
      Propriatory & govr
to require thee to Summonce John Clows of
the ſaid County & Provinc that he be & appeare att the next

Court to be held in this County on the iith day of the $\frac{12^{th}}{mo}$

next Enſueing then & there to Anſwer the Complt of Sam:
overton for wth holding of Seven pounds wch is Said will
be made appeare in Court to be due to
the ſd Sam: Overton & hereof thou art not to faile given
under my hand & ſeale the 29th day of the ii month being
the 36 yeare of the kings Raigne & the 4th of the propria
=torys govrmt 1684

To the Sherrife of the Said
County or his deputy Theſe
A writ granted for A Jury

                              (7)

            The 29th day of the $\frac{ii}{mo}$ 1684

Willm Biles of the County of Bucks plt agt Ralph =
Sidwell of the ſd County deft in an acction of trover
& Converſion for with holding of goods he hath found
of the ſd plts to the value of fifty Shillings, & refuſes to
deliver them upon demand

            The declaration of Willm Biles
                the 29th $\frac{ii}{mo}$ 1684

Willm Biles plt   }
      agt   } Willm Biles plt makes Complt agt Ralph
Ralph Sidwell deft} Sidwell how that the Said Ralph

Sidwell hath found of his goods to the value of fifty
Shillings & refuſes to deliver them to the ſd plt tho
the Said plt demanded them upon the i9th Inſtant & there
fore the Said plt prays Judgment of Court agt the Said
deft for his goods & damages & Coſt of Suite

A Summonce granted for the ſd Ralph Sidwell
Cou : Bucks

To the Sherif Theſe　　By vertue of the kings
Authority in
the name of the propriatory & govrnr Theſe are to
Require thee
to Summonc Ralph Sidwell, Carpenter if wthin thy
Balywick
to appeare att the next Court to be holden for this County
the
iith day of the i2th month att the falls to Anſwer Such
things as
Shall then & there be objected agt him & there have this
Summonce given undr my hand & ſeale the 26th ii month
1684
being the 36 yeare of the kings Raigne & the 4th of the propriatorys govrmt

A writ grantd for A Jury　　The Sherrifs Return

The 29th $\dfrac{ii}{mo}$ 84　　This Summonce was executed

　　the 26th $\dfrac{ii}{mo}$ 1684

8　　County of Bucks in the provinc of Pennſilvania
At A monthly Seſſions held by the kings Authority in the
name of Willm penn propriatory & govrnr of the Said
provinc & Territorys thereunto belonging att the
Court houſe of the ſaid County the iith day of the i2 mo
i684 in the 37 yeare of the kings Raigne & the 4th of
the propriatorys govrmt

The Juſtices then prſent
James Harriſon Prſident
Tho Janney　Willm Biles
willm Beakes　wm yardley
John otter
John Brock Sherrife
Luke Brindley his deputy
Phinehas pemberton Clarke

This day was acknowlit
in open Court one mortgage
from Jon Acker
man to willm Beakes
This day willm Beakes
Signed and ſealed one
letter of Attorney to A man
in London
wch was Certifyed under my
hand & County
ſeale

Willm Biles Appears to A rt of Trover & Converſion
    Ralph Sidwell Call'd appeareth not
declaration read & proved
The Courts Anſwer to Rich Hedleys pettition is that
Inas much the ſd Hedley has done his worke
well; & that he has not had A valuable Conciceration
for his worke he the ſd Hedley Shall have 5 £ more
then mentioned in his Contract, he the ſd Hedley doing
Some Smal matter of worke as the Revieuers ſhall
appoint; & remitting that worke wch he has done all
=ready above what is mentioned in the Contract & that
the ſd 5 £ is Intended to be payd in or before ioth month
    next
Juſtice otter Informes the Court that Derick Clawſon
is Atteſted Conſtable & that ffrancis walker is not
capable of serveing therefore the Court ordrs Claws
Jonſon Conſtable & that Jon otter, & Edmund Bennet
see that the Conſtable be Atteſted & make Returne there
of the next Court
the Collectors hath this day brought in theire accts of what
monys they have Collected, & pd in the ſd monys to the
    Treaſurors
according to ordr
It is ordered that in as much the Ptyes formerly ordered
    to Lay out the
Road to phinehas pembertons plantation have not done it
the Court doth ordr that Willm: Biles Lyonel Brittan

(9)

& Samuel Darke along wth Robt Lucas Lay out the
Said Road before the next Court & that it be layd
out to A landing below the Lower line of george Herrote
    Land
It is alſo ordered that the Road about the falls that is not
allready pfected be done afore next Court, & that Willm
    Beakes
along wth the ptyes for merly ordered to pfected it take
    Care
it be done
        The Court adjorns for one houre
Inas much as Ralph Sidwell hath not appeared to the
Suite the Court gives Judgmt that the ſd Sidwell ſhall
pay to the plt willm Biles fifty Shillings & Coſt of suite
Edward Smith haveing been cald into Court & aſked

for for the monys due to the wid milcome pleads
    difapointments
by water and wether & prays one months time more w^{ch}
    was
given him by Ann milcome daughter
walter pomferet hath defired the Court to ftay proceedings
agt: him for i0 days that in the meane time he
may make up his accts wth gilbert wheeler & willm
Biles wch the court grants him
The Court doth ordr that gilbert wheeler & Samuel
Dark do take Care to provide A place for na: Weft
that he may in al refpects Satisfye the Judgmt
of Court, & that phinehas pemberton returne
in to theire hands an acct of all the Courts ———
Sentenc upon him
Daniel Brinfon craves that he may have Na Weft to worke
for him, io days or untill the ptyes above can pvide
A place for him, & he will Engage for his Apperance
at the io days End or before if he be Calld for
It is ordered that willm Biles willm Beakes
Shall take care to buy io or i2 Ackers of Land to be Laid
    to the
prifon for y^e: publique ufe of the County & that they do itt
if the Can before the next Court

The Court Adjorns till the 2nd 4th day of the
                next month

    Daniel Brinfon haveing been Calld into Court about
            the prefentmt
of John Ackerman for keeping unlawfull Cattle and none
appearing agt him to pfecute the Court difcharges him
        paying
his fees

10
        The i8th day of the i2th month i684
Thomas Janney of the County of Bucks Truftee for John
    neild his Servant plt agt
Jofeph Milner of the fd County deft in an acct of Cafe for
with holding, of Six pounds five Shillings due to the Said
    Jon
neild Since the 5th month i683

    The i8th day of the i2th month i684

Thomas Janney Truftee
to Jon neild plt
agt.
Jofeph Milner deft

} Thomas Janney makes Complt agt the
Said Jofeph milner how that the Said
deft in the 5th month i683 borrowed
of him of the monys of Jon neild his —

Servant To whom he the Said Thomas

Janney is Truftee; The Sum of 6 £ 5 s & he the Said deft when he Borrowed the Said

monys promifed to give Suffitiont Security for the payment there

of with Lawfull Intreft for the Same dureing the

time he had it; but never Since wold the Said deft either pay

the monys Intreft or give Security for they payment thereof where

fore the Said plt prays Judgment of Court agt the Said deft for

damages & Coft of Suite

A Summonc granted for the Said Jofeph milner
County of Bucks in the Provinc of Pennfilvania

Thefe are by the kings Authority in the name of the propriatory &

govrnr to require thee to Summonce Jofeph milnor of the Said County & Provinc that he be & appeare att the next Quartr

Seffions to be held for this County on the ii^th day of the $\frac{i}{mo}$

next then & there to Anfwer the Complt of Thomas Janney

Truftee to Jon neild, for wth holding of Six pounds five fhillings

wch is Said will be made to appeare in Court to be due to the Said Jon

Neild & hereof thou art not to faile given undr my hand & feale

The i9th day of i2 month i684 being the 37 yeare of the kings Raign

& the 4th of the propriatorys govrmt

To the Sherrife of the Said County
or his deputy thefe

(11)

The i8th $\frac{i2}{mo}$ 1684

John Brock of the County of Bucks plt agt
Jofeph Englifh of the fd County deft in an acct
of Cafe for wth holding of ten fhillings due
to the Said plt

The declaration of John Brock agt Jofeph Englifh
The i8th day of the i2 month i684

John Brock plt	John Brock makes Complt agt Jofeph
agt	Englifh how that the Said deft laft Summer Came & defired to have his
Jofeph Englifh deft	

horfes wch were then plowing to drive Cattell wth all (as
farr
as gilbert wheelers) wch Cattell he an Indian had brought
out of the woods So wild they Cold not get them any
further without
affiftanc & the deft promifed ten Shillings reward for the
ufe of the
Said horfes wch fd horfes according to the fd plt he the fd
deft had but hath ever Since unjuftly
detained the fd monys from the fd plt wherefore the fd
plt prays Judgmt
of Court agt the fd deft for his fd monys & Coft of fuite
A Summonc granted for Jofeph Englifh
County of Bucks in the Province of Pennfilvania
Thefe are by the kings Authority in the name of the
Propriatory
& govrnr to Require thee to Summonc Jofeph Englifh of
the fd County & Province that he be & appeare att the
next Quartr

Seffions to be held for this County on the iith day $\frac{i}{mo}$
next then
& there to anfwer the Complt of John Brock Sherrife of
this County for wth holding of ten Shillings wch is Said
will be
made appeare in Court to be due to the fd John

Brock & hereof thou art not to faile given undr my
hand & feale the i9th day of the i2 month i684 being the
37 yeare of the kings Raigne & the 4th of the Propriato
rys govrmt

To the deputy Sherrife
of the fd County Thefe

The 2ist of $\dfrac{i2}{mo}$ 1684

(12)

Willm Sanford of
the County of Bucks plt agt David Davis of the Said
County Deft in an acct of Cafe for with holding of
nine pounds Elleven Shillings Eight penc wch was due
to be pd

to the Said plt the 30th $\dfrac{9}{mo}$ laft paft

The declaration of the fd plt

The 2ist $\dfrac{i2}{mo}$ i684

willm Sanford plt ⎫ willm Sanford makes Complt agt the
                ⎪ fd David
     agt   ⎬ Davis how that the Said deft is
                ⎪ Indebted
David Davis deft ⎭ to him the Sum of nine pounds
                  Elleven —
                  Shillings Eight pence wch Said Debt
                  the
Said Deft hath promifed to pay either by acceptable bills
    or monys
by the 30th of the 9th month laft paft as will be made to
    appeare
by bill under the hand of the Said deft bearing date the
    24th
of the Said ninth month laft paft but never Since hath the
    fd deft ever paid
him any monys nor given nor ordered him the fd plt
    any Bills except one
of two pounds five Shillings but unjuftly detaines his
    Said Debt

wherefore the Said plt brings his acction for his Said Debt
& prays Judgment of Court agt the fd Deft for Damages &
Coſt of Suite
                    A Summonce granted for the Said David Davis
        County of Bucks in the Provinc of Pennſilvania
Theſe are by the kings authority in the name of the
        propyatory
& govrnr to Require thee to Summonc David Davis of
        the Said County
& provinc that he be and appeare att the next Quarter
        feſſions
to be held for this County on the ii[th] day of the firſt month
next then & there to anſwer the Complt of Willm Sanford
for with holding of nine pounds Elleven Shillings Eight
        pence w[ch]
is Said will be made to appeare in Court to be due to the
Said Willm Sanford & hereof thou art not to faile given

under my hand & Seale the 2i day $\dfrac{i2}{mo}$ being the xxxvii

yeare of the kings Raigne & the 4th of the propriatorys
govrmt 1684
To the Sherrife of the Said County
    or his deputy Theſe

                                                (13)
            County of Bucks in the Province of Pennſilvania
At A Quarter Seſſions held by the kings Authority in the
        name
of willm Penn propriatory & govrnr
of the fd provinc & territorys thereunto belonging att the

Court houſe the ii[th] day of the $\dfrac{1}{mo}$ 1684

            The Juſtices th prſent
                James Harriſon prſident
        Tho Janney   John otter   willm Biles
        Edmund Bennett   willm yardley   willm Beakes
        John Brock Sherrif
        Luck Brindley deputy
        Phinehas Pemberton Clark
    Inas much as Rich Noble not knowing of the
day of the orphants Court came this day to treat about
the orphants of Clarkes this Court upon A full debate of
        the
matter do ordr that Rich Noble Shall have twenty pounds

pd him out of the lands of the orphants of the fd Clarkes
    & that at
the next orphants Court an ordr Shall be Isued out to y^t
Intent & that he hath accepted of the Same
Samuel Dark & gilbert wheeler hath not given in an acct
to this Court of what they have done about Nathaniel
    Weſt
therefore the Court doth ordr that the bring in an acct to
    y^e
next Court
In as much as walter pomferet hath not according to
    requeſt
made up his accts wth willm Biles & gilbert wheeler nor.
    any
way made them Satiſfaction therefore this Court doth ordr
that the Sherrif do take Care to Sell thoſe goods allready
attached by him & make returne thereof to the next Court
in order to Satisfye the Judgment of Court paſſed upon
    them
Jane Lyon hath this day appeared in Court and deſired
    to have
James Harriſon admitted guardian, & She being att
    Lawfull
age to make Choyce, this Court haveing knowledg of the
fd James Harriſons Suffitioncy hath Commiſſionated the
    fd James
Harriſon to act as guardian for her*

      The Court adjorns untill the 2nd 4th day of the
         next month

(14)

The i8th day of the $\frac{i}{mo}$ 1684

Thomas wright of weſt new Jarſey plt agt Daniel Brinſon
of the County of Bucks in the provinc of pennſilvania
    planter
deft in an acct of Covenant for wth holding of —— horſes

---

*The above entry crossed out in the minute book was evidently
intended for the records of the Orphan's Court.

to the value of 15 £ wch he the fd deft was obliged by
A bond of twenty pound to deliver upon demand

$$\text{The i8}^{\text{th}} \text{ day of the } \frac{i}{mo} \text{ i684}$$

Thomas wright plt agt Daniel Brinſon deft	Thomas wright makes Complt agt Dan: Brinſon how that the fd deft entered into A bond of twenty pounds to the fd plt (bearing date the i9th day of the ioth month i682)

To deliver To the ſaid plt upon demand one
mare 2 horſes & 2 colts; & the fd deft contrary to
    Covenant keeps back & unjuſtly detaines
pte of the ſd beaſts══════ to the value of fiveteen pounds
& refuſes to deliver them to the fd plt tho he hath
Severall times demanded them Therefore the ſaid
plt brings his acction agt the fd deft & prays Judgmt
of Court agt: him for Damages & Coſt of Suite
        The Summonce granted agt Daniel Brinſon
        County of Bucks in the provinc of penſilyvania
Theſe are by the kings Authority in the name of the
    proprya
=tory and govrnr to require thee to Summonce
Daniel Brinſon of the ſd County and provinc that he be &
appeare at the next Court to be held for this County on the
8th day of the 2nd month next then & there to anſwer the
    Complt
of Thomas wright for withholding of goods or Cattles to
    the value of
fiveteen pounds which is ſd will be made appeare in Court
    ought to have beene delivered
upon demand to the ſd Tho: wright & hereof thou
art not to faile given under my hand & ſeale the i8^th
day of the firſt month being the xxxvii yeare of the kings
Raigne & the 5th of the propriatorys govrmt i684
To the Sherrife of the ſd County
    or his deputy Theſe
        The ſherrifs Return
A writ granted for A Jury
        Thomas wright prayd this action might
        be with drawn

(15)

The 25th day of the $\dfrac{3}{mo}$ $\underline{1684}$

Entry of ⎫   Ann milcome of the County of Bucks in the
       ⎬   provinc of penfil
the Action ⎭   vania wid plt agt gilbert wheeler & martha
       his wife of the fd County &
province deft in an action of Cafe for
       flanderous words
Spoken by the fd martha wheeler, agt the
       fd plt to
the defameination & difcredit of the fd plt
       thereby
damnifying her to the value 200 £

The 25th 3 month <u>1685</u>

The   Ann milcome makes Complt agt
                             martha the
Declaration ⸺   wife of gilbert wheeler how that
                             the
of   fd martha wheeler malitioufly &
                             Slandrou
Ann milcome plt ⸺   =fly ; doth what in her lyes
                             endeavor to ⸺
agt   render the fd plt unjuft & odious
                             in the minds of
gilbert wheeler &   people, by making great
                             exclamations
martha his wife deft   agt her wth out any caufe given
                             her
by the fd plt at any time &
often Calld her Cheat
but pticulerly upon 3 day of the

$\dfrac{i}{mo}$ & upon

the 29th of the Said month She
       the fd martha
Cald the fd Ann milcome Cheat &
       faid fhe
had Cheated her of 25^s thereby
       wholely
deftroying the Credit & reputation of the fd plt who is
       A wid

& hath beene of good Credit amongst the
    neighbourhood &
the ſd plt hath uſed many endeavors to have re=
=claimed the ſd martha from thoſe Slanderous expreſſions
but Shee wold not be reclaymed but hath uſed them in her
publique diſcours above A yeare whereby the ſd plt is
disabled in her Credit & dampnifyed to the value of 200 £
wherefore the ſd plt brings her action agt the ſd defts & —
prays Judgment of Court agt them for damages & Coſt of
Suite

25th 3 mo : i685

A Summonce granted agt the ſd gilbert wheeler & martha
    his wife
for theire Appearance at the next Court to be held for

this County the ioth of the $\frac{4}{mo}$ next to anſwer the Complt
    of

the ſd Ann milcome

The ſherrifs return

25   3   i685
mo

A writ granted⎱
for A Jury — ⎰
    A 25 3mo 85

Subpeane for wittneſſ: Jane greaves John Ackerman &
    Jon purslone

———

(16)   County of Bucks in the provinc of Pennſilvania
At A Quarter Seſſions held att the Court houſe for the
County of Bucks by the kings Authority in the name of
    Willm
Penn propriatory & govrnr of the ſd provinc & Terri
thereunto belonging the ioth day of the 4th month i685

The Juſtices then prſent

willm yardley   willm Biles
Willm Beakes   John otter   Edmund Bennet
John Swift
Phinehas Pemberton Clark
Luke Brindley deputy   The grand Inqueſt Calld
Sherrife   over & Atteſted

foreman
Hen: Baker
wm: Dark
Joſu: Boare
Rich: Ridgway
Law: Bannor
Hen: Marjorum
Joſep: milner
Lyonel Brittan
Jam: paxſon
wm paxſon
Jo: Engliſh ſr
Tho: Stakehous ſr
Tho: Adkinſon
Jam: Boyden
Hen Bircham
Tho: Dungan
wm: Dungan
Tho: Rowland
Ed: Lovet
Tho: Woolfe
Rand: Blackſhaw
wm Hycock

ffrancis Walker Atteſted doth Say
    that Joſeph Luinn
upon the 3i day of the 3 month laſt
    paſt Swore
Several oathes 3 times att leaſt
John Hill Atteſted doth Say that the
    aboveſd
Joſeph Luinn the day aboveſd ſwear
many oathes
the Court ordrs the ſd Joſeph Luinn
    Shall pay
for the three oaths i5^s or Suffer i5
    days
Impriſonment in the houſe of
    Correction att
hard labour & be fed with bread &
water
Derrick Clawſon for ſtriking his
    ſervant Joſeph
Luinn unreaſonablely the Court ordrs
    him to be bound to his good
behavior & to appeare att the next
    Court
ffrancis walker & Claws Jonſon
    Stand ob=
lidged in 20 £ to the propriatory &
    govrnr
for the appearanc of the ſd Derrick
    Clawſon
at the next Court & to be of good
    abearing
in the meane time
        The Court adjorns for one houre
Derrick Clawſon has engaged to pay
    the fine
    of Joſeph Luinn and his fees &
    Joſeph has
engaged to ſerve the ſd Derrick for
    ten
days after the Expiration of his
    Servitued
for his ſo doing & what the fees
    Comes to
grand Inqueſt prſentments brought
    in & read

(17) Katherin knight being examined concering A bafterd
     Child born upon her body who the father of it is & fhe
     Says the father of it is Charles Thomas

     Charles Thomas being afked whether he own him
     Self to be the father of the fd Child & he Says he be=
     lieves it is his Child

     The Court orders that Charles Thomas Shall
     tomorrow morning be brought to this place
     and whipt 20 lafhes upon his bare back well layd on
     & is enjoyned to marry the fd katherine
     & After he Shall make good the damage his mr
     has fuftained by this thing at the expiration of his
     time

     The Court ordrs that katherin knight Shall be
     brought to this place & whiped to morrow ——
     morning wth io Lafhes on her back
     Whereas the fd Charles Thomas after Sentenc of the
     Court did Sweare by the name of god & ftampt
     & behave him felf rudely in the prfenc & hearing
     of the Court for wch the Court ordrs he fhall
     pay 5^s or fuffer 5 days Imprifonmt
     Ann milcome plt & gilbert wheeler & martha his wife
         defts have
     Joyntly defired theire tryall may be deferred untill the
     next Court day to fee if it Cann in the meane time
     be Ended & have both declared in Court that neither
     of them will take advantage by the fd demurr but
     if the diferenc be not Ended betwixt them before
     the next Court that then they will joyne Ifue
         The diferenc being Ented the plt defired to have the
             action
     with drawn

         The Sherrif makes return that the goods of walter
         pomferet by him formerly attached were apprized by
         the apprizors as followeth

                    The i4th ii 1684 one mare 2 Colts att
                            mo
                    9 £ : 10^s. 00^d

and further reports that the ſd   Henry Baker
wm Biles & g: wheeler wold   Henry margerum
accept them for theire debt   Lyonel Brittan
    Adjourned untill the 2nd 4th day of the 7th mo: next

The 3 day of the 6th mo: <u>i685</u>

(18) James Boyden of the County of Bucks in the
Provinc of Pennſilvania makes Complt agt
Jon: Collins of the ſd province in an action of
Debt for wth holding of 19 s 2 d wch was due
to be pd to the ſd plt i0 month ago

declaration

James Boyden plt	The 3 day of the <u>6 i865</u>
agt	mo
John Collins deft	James Boyden makes Complt agt the
	ſd John

Collins how that he the ſd deft is
    Indebted
    to him the Sum of 19 s 2d
& the ſd deft unjuſtly detaines his ſd monys
tho due above i0 month ago & the ſd deft is about to
depart out of the provinc wherefore the ſd plt prays
Judgment of Court agt the ſd deft for damages & Coſt of
Suite

    Attachment granted agt the goods of
    the ſd Collins

Theſe are   wth drawn at the Same time Entered

The i5th day of the 6th month i685
    Joſeph Blowers of Burlington in weſt new Jarſey
    makes

The	Complt agt gilbert wheeler of the County of Bucks
Action	in the
entered	Province of Pennſilvania in an acction of Debt for
	with

holding of i8 £ 06 s 03 d Silver monys wch Sum was
awarded to be payd to the ſd plt At or before the
i9th
of the 3 month laſt paſt by Thomas mathews &
    martin Holt
Arbitrators Indiferently Choſen by the ſd deft to
    heare & determin all
difirences & accounts depending betwixt them —

Declaration   The i5th day of the 6th month i685

Joseph Blowers plt

agt

gilbert wheeler deft

Joſeph Blowers makes Complt agt
    gilbert wheeler
how that the Said deft is Indebted to
    him the
Summ of i8 £ 06 ˢ 03 ᵈ Silver monys
    wch Sum
was awarded (to be pd to the ſd plt

in 10 days;) by martin Holt & Thomas mathews
    Arbitrators
Indiferently Choſen by the ſd plt and deft to heare
    & determin
all diferences & accounts depending betwixt them
    & yett
not with ſtanding the ſd deft Entered in to A bond
    of 20 £
to Stand to the award of the ſd Arbitrators So
    Indiferently
Choſen he refuſes to pay the ſd debt & Unjuſtly
    detaines his ſd
monys wherefore the ſd plt brings his action & prays
Judgment of Court agt the ſd deft for his ſaid
debt damages & Coſt of ſuite

Summonce granted the i5th 6 mo i685

for gil: wheeler to appeare At the next
Quarter ſeſſions to be held the 9th 7mo next
to anſwer the Complt of of ſd Blowers

The Sherrifs Return
A writt granted for Jury on tryall of Blowers plt agt wheeler
    deft

(20)   At A Quarter Seſſions held for the County of Bucks
    by the kings Authority
in the name of Willm Penn propriatory and
Governor of the Province of Pennſilvania and
Territorys thereunto belonging the 9th day of the
7th month 1685

The Juſtices then prſent
Thomas Janney   willm Biles
John otter   willm yardley
    Luke Brindley deputy Sherrife
    Phinehas Pemberton Clarke

The petty Jury Joseph Blowers plt in an action
of debt agt gilbert Wheeler deft the fum
i8 £ : 06ˢ 03ᵈ Silver monys wᶜʰ fum was awarded upon
the 8ᵗʰ $\frac{3}{mo}$ laft paft by Thomas mathews &
martin Holt arbitrators Indiferently Chofen
The Jury Attefted
Joseph Blowers hath defired the action to be wᵗʰ drawn
gilbert Wheeler hath declared that he will pay the Charge
of Court
John Otter hath declared that upon the 3 day of the 6ᵗʰ
    mo 85
James Boyden Complained that Joⁿ Collins
was Indebted to him the Sum of 19ˢ; 2ᵈ where
upon the fd Collins was brought before the fd Jon otter &
Edmund Bennet Juftices & yᵉ fd Collins acknowledged yᵉ
fd debt to be due to yᵉ: fd Boyden whereupon the fd
Juftices gave theire Judgment the fd Collins
Shold pay the debt wᵗʰ Coft of fuit wᶜʰ Judgment the fd
    Juftices have
reported to this Court wᶜʰ Judgment by this Court is
    allowed
of, &
The fd Justic otter hath declared in Court the fd Jon
Collins did Sweare in his presenc wherefore this
Court ordr the fd Collins to pay 5ˢ wᶜʰ fd five fhillings
the fd Collins hath defired to have time to pay it till
the next Court
    Derrick Clawfon has this day according bond appeared
    nothing appearing agt him the Court
    difcharges him paying his fees
    A prfentmt from Philadelphia County referred to the
        Court of this County Concerning a Child that was
        put to nurf to one Robt marfh of Southamton was
            this day read
        ordrd that the fd march, be fent for and examined
        before
    Some Juftice of Peace

(21)

Gilbert Wheeler being laft Court prfented for turning
of the high Road where it was layd out & fencing it
up hath this day beene Calld before this Court
& being examined about the fd prfentmt to wᶜʰ he

Submitted therefore this Court taking in to Con=
cideration the ſaid treſpaſſe of the ſd gilbert wheeler
hath ordered Thomas Janney & willm Beakes together
wᵗʰ the overseers of the high way to veiue wher
the ſd Road Shall Lye & make it out & that gilbert
wheeler take down his fence that it may Run according
    to
theire directions in 18 months time
This Court doth ordr that Henry marjorum do ſerve
as Conſtable for the falls for the Succeeding year
& that willm Hycock do ſerve Conſtable for the
middle Lotts for the ſucceeding yeare
for the further ſide of Neſhaminah & there about
    Samuel Allen
& John purslone
This Court doth ordr that Joſuah Hoops Henry paxſon
& Jonathan Scaife to ſerve as peace makers
for this County the Succeeding yeare
This Court doth ordr that Henry Baker John Rowland
& Thomas Stake houſe & Edmund Cuttler do ſerve
    over ſeers of the high ways
for this county for the ſucceeding yeare
    The Court adjorns for one houre
The over ſeers of the high ways for the prſedent yeare
    have brought in
an accᵗ of the ſeverall psons that are in arreare in
doing theire duty according to ſummonce therefore
this Court doth ordr that the ſd overſeers Shall
Collect the ſd arrears
This day was dd & acknowledged in open Court A deed
of 200 Ackers of Land adjoyning to Rich Noble Land
    in
this County by phinehas pemberton Conſtituted
    attorney
on the behalf of Abraham man & Eliabeth his wife of
    the County of Newcastell
unto Jacob pellexon of philadelphia _____

This day was deliv & acknowledged in open Court A
deed of 200 Ackers of Land Lying neare yᵉ: Cold
    Spring
by Rich Lundy to willm Biles both of this County
for the uſe of Jacob Tellnor

The Court adjorns untill the 2ⁿᵈ 4ᵗʰ day of the
$$\frac{io}{mo}$$ next

(22)   23 $\frac{9}{mo}$ 85

the ⎧ Sam overton of the County of Bucks in the provinc

action ⎬ of Pennſilvania plt agt Jacob Hall of the ſd County

entered ⎩ an pvinc in an act of Caſe for with holding of

    4 £ i3 s due to the ſd plt

The Dlarat

The 23 9 85   County of Bucks in the province of
     mo   Pennſilvania

Sam Overton plt ⎫   Samuel overton makes Complt agt

agt ⎬   Jacob Hall how that the ſd Deft is

Jacob Hall deft ⎭   Indebted to the ſd plt the Sum of

in an act
of
Caſe

foure pounds thirteen Shillings due
for dyet & other ſervices &
things wᶜʰ
ſd Sum the ſd deft unjuſtly detaines
and refuſes to pay
wherefore the ſd plt brings his
action of Caſe prays Judgmt
of Court agt yᵉ: ſd deft for the ſd
Sum of 4 £ : 13 ˢ damages & Coſt of
Suite

23    $\frac{9}{mo}$ 85

Sumonce ⎧ Summonc granted agt Jacob Hall to Anſwer the
⎨ Compt of Sam overton at the next Quarter ſeſſions
⎩ to be held for this County the 9ᵗʰ of the io mo next

Return   The ſherrifs Return The above mentioned Summonc
was executed the 24ᵗʰ $\frac{9}{mo}$ p   Luke Brindley
                                deputy Sherrif

Subpene   A ſubpene for Jon Brock to give his evidence
in A Caſe depending betwixt Sam overton plt
agt Jacob Hall deft

the evidenc Summonced the 24th of 9th mo p
Luke Brindley
deputy Sherrif

A writ for } to trye the Caufe depending betwixt fd
the Jury { overton plt agt Ja Hall deft
the 9th day of the io'th mo 1685 Samuel overton
defired to have the above action agt Jacob Hall
withdrawn

County of Bucks in the Province of Pennfilvania   (23)

The 23 day of the 9th mo 1685

the ⎫
action ⎬ Nicholas moore Efqre of the County of Philadelphia
Entered ⎭ and
Province aforefd plt agt gilbert wheeler of ye:
County of Bucks & province aforefd in an action of
Debt for wth holding of forty foure pounds Sixteen
fhillings
and io d & Intreft for thirteen months

The   ⎫ County of Bucks in the Province
Declaration of   ⎪   of Pennfilva
Nicholas moore Efqre plt   ⎬ nia the 23 day of the 9th month 1685
agt   ⎪ Nicholas moore Efquire of the
gilbert wheeler deft   ⎭   County
of Philadelphia & provinc aforefd
in an action of   makes Complt agt gilbert whee
ler of the County of Bucks &
Debt — —   provinc aforefd how that the
fd deft is Indebted
the Sum of 44 £ : 16 s: io d
due to be payed to ye: fd plt upon
demand as will
appeare by A bill under the hand
of the fd deft bearing date the 29th
of october 1684 & altho the fd plt
hath divers times made demand of his Said monys yet the
fd deft unjuftly detaines the Same wherefore the fd
plt brings his action of debt and prays Judgmt of Court
agt the fd deft for the fd fum of forty four pounds Six

teen Shillings & ten penc wth Intreſt for the ſame for i3
months damages & Coſt of ſuite

Summonc 23 9 85
        ‾‾‾‾‾‾
           mo

Summonc granted agt gilbert
Wheeler to anſwer the Compt of N moore
att the next Quarter feſſions to be held
for this County the 9th of the io mo: next

Sherrifs ⎫ The above written Summonc was executed the
Return ⎰ 24th of the 9th moth i685 p Luke Brindley deputy
                                                        Sherrif

A Writ   ⎫ — to try the Cauſe depending betwixt N moore
for A Jury ⎰ plt & gilbert Wheeler deft —

action wth drawn ⎰ The 9th of the ioth mo i685 A note came to my
         ⎱ Hand from Nicholas more deſireing me to
         ⎰ with draw the action abovemention agt
         ⎱ gilbert wheeler if the ſd wheeler wold
         ⎱ pay the fees wheeler being demaned
in open Court whether he wold pay the
fees or no promiſed to pay them
wherefore the action was
accordingly with drawne

(24)   24 9 85
                       ‾‾‾‾‾‾
                         mo

The action ⎫ Jacob Hall of the County of Bucks in the Provinc
Entered   ⎰ of Penn ſilvania plt agt Samuel overton of the ſd
            County and
provinc in an action of Caſe for with holding of
3 £ 6 ^s: 00 ^d due to be pd to the ſd plt

The   24th 9 1685
                         ‾‾‾‾‾‾
                           mo
Declaration of   County of Bucks in the Province of
Jacob Hall plt   ⎫ Pennſilvania
    agt   ⎰
Samuel overton deft ⎰ Jacob Hall makes Complt agt

Samuel overton both of the County, & provinc aforefd how
that yᵉ:

Sd deft is Indebted to him fd plt the fum of three pounds Six
Shillings wᶜʰ fd Sum the deft unjuftly detaines and
refufes to pay wherefore the fd pltf brings his action of
Cafe & prays Judgmt of Court agt the fd deft for the fd fum
of 3 £ 6ˢ for damages & Coft of fuite

$$24^{th} \quad 9 \quad 1685$$
$$\overline{\quad mo \quad}$$

Summonc

    ⎧Summonc granted agt Sam Overton to
    ⎪anfwer the Complt of Jacob Hall att the
    ⎨next Quarter Seffions to be held for this County
    ⎩the 9ᵗʰ of the io mo next

              the above mentioned Summonc was executed
Return   the 25ᵗʰ of the 9ᵗʰ mo: 1685

                  p   Luke Brindley Deputy fherrif

The 9ᵗʰ of the ioᵗʰ month 1685 Jacob Hall defired to have
the above action agt Samuel Overton
with drawn

                                        (25)

$$25 \quad 9 \quad 1685$$
$$\overline{\quad mo \quad}$$

The action ⎰ ffrancis Hough of the County of Bucks in the
entered ⎱ province of Pennfilvania plt agt Elenor
        pownall of the fd County & provinc in an action
        of Cafe for wᵗʰ holding of 5 £ : 13ˢ: 06ᵈ wᶜʰ is
        due to be paid to the fd plt for work done

The— — — — —⎫   25ᵗʰ   9   1685

Declaration of   ⎪   mo

ffrancis Hough plt ⎬County of Bucks in the Provinc of

    agt   ⎪Pennfilvania

Ellenor pownal deft ⎭ ffrancis Hough plt makes Complt
                          agt Ellenor Pownal of the County &
                          Province aforefd how that the fd deft is
                          Indebted to the fd plt the Sum of

5 £ : 13ˢ: 06ᵈ for worke done for the ſd deft wᶜʰ ſd ſum
the ſd deft unjuſtly detaines & refuſes to pay wherefore the ſd
plt brings his action of Caſe and prays Judgment of Court
agt the ſd deft for the ſd ſum of 5 £ : 13ˢ: 06ᵈ damages
and Coſt of Suite

$$25^{th} \quad \frac{9}{mo} \quad 1685$$

Summonce ⎰ Summonce granted agt Ellenor Pownall to
⎱ anſwer the Complt of ffrancis Hough att yᵉ:
next Quarter ſeſſions to be held for this County
the 9ᵗʰ of the io moᵗʰ next

Return ⎰ The above mentioned Summonc was executed
the 25ᵗʰ
of the 9ᵗʰ moᵗʰ 1685   p Luke Brindley Deputy
Sherrif

A
writ for A Jury granted to ſerve in the ſeveral action
tryable the Quarter ſeſſions to be held the 9ᵗʰ
of the io ᵗʰ month next

A
Supeane granted for John Brock John Brearley &
willm morton to give in their Evidenc in A
Caſe depending betwixt ffrancis Hough &
Ellenor Pownal

Return   The above Subpene for wittneſſes was executed
the 25ᵗʰ of the 9ᵗʰ moᵗʰ 1685
p Luke Brindley Deputy ſherrif
The 9ᵗʰ of the io ᵗʰ mo: 1685 ffrancis Hough deſired
to have the above action agt Ellenor Pownall
with drawn

(26)   2 day of the $\frac{io}{mo}$ 1685

The action ⎰ Samuel Burges of the county of Bucks in
Entered ⎱ the provinc of penſilvania plt agt Jon Wright
late of this County in an act of
Debt for wᵗʰ holding of 4 £ : 3ˢ: 00ᵈ
due to be pd to the ſd plt

2 io mo 1685

Attachment } an attachment granted agt the goods of Jon
granted } wright non Refident for his appearanc att y^e:
next Quarter feffions to be held for this County
the 9th of this Inftant io^th mo:

County of Bucks in the Province of
Pennfilvania the 2nd of io^th mo 85

Declaration of } Samuel Burges of the County & provinc
Sam Burges plt } afforefd makes Compt agt Jon wright late
agt } of this County how that the fd deffendent
John wright deft } in Aprill laft bought of the fd plt one psell of
goods Come to foure pounds three fhillings
for wch fd fum y^e: fd deft gave A bill under his hand
but the fd deft unjuftly detaines the fd monys & never as
yet payd any pte thereof wherefore the fd plt brings his action
of
Debt & prays Judgmt agt y^e: fd deft for y^e: fd Sum of 4£: 3^s: 0:
damages & Coft of fuite

the 9th of the io^th mo: 1685

Samuel Burges defired to have the
above action agt wright with drawn

(27)

At A Quarter Seffions held by the kings authority in
the name of willm Penn Propryatory & govrnr of the
Provinc of Pennfilvania & territorys thereunto
belonging for the County of Bucks att the Court houfe
the 9th day of the io month being the firft yeare of the
king James the 2nd his Raigne & the 5th of the propry
atorys govrmt 1685

The Juftices then Prefent

James Harrifon Thomas Janney willm Biles wm yardley

Jon Otter Edmund Bennet The petty Jury returned by

Nicholas walnn Sherrif   the Sherrif the day abovefd

Luke Brindley deputy   Robt Cartor   John White

Phinehas Pemberton Clark   James Boyden   george
                                               Brown
                            Lyonel Brittan   willm
                                        Sanford
                            Henry Burcham Jonathan
                                             Scaife

Edmund Lovet Thomas Adkinſon Daniel Brinſon Jon Clows

   * Joſeph Hollinghed being Calld into Court there
       Comeing none
to proſecute him the Court diſcharges him paying his
       ffees

Edmund Bennet Complanig to this Court that Joſeph
growden hath ffenced up the kings Road wherefore yᵉ
Court orders yᵗ Na: Allen Conſtable do take Care to
Speake to ſd Growden to open yᵉ: ſd Road or ſett
gates ells furter courſe will be taken about it

   Complt being made by willm Biles how that he had
       Rd Abuſe by Philip Conway
the ſd=Philip Conway being Calld into Court acknowl-
       edged his fault
& promiſed to be of better behavior
       for time to come the ofence being paſſed by the ſd
       W B where
fore the Court diſcharges him paying his fees
Complt being made agt Jacob Hall for Selling Rum to
       the Indians
the ſd Jacob Hall was Calld into Court & the wittneſs
       examined
Andrew Heath aged about twenty years being Atteſted
       & examined
Saith that about 3 weeks afore micheal maſs laſt Saith
       he ſaw
Jacob Hall Sell 2 Single pints of Rum to an Indian wᶜʰ he
taſted and att another time neare the time afforeſd he
       ſaw an
Indian Carry away 3 bottles of Rum wᶜʰ Contained i
       gallon &
1 pt: out of the ſaid Jacob Halls Houſe

---

*Scratched out in the original record.

Samuel Hough Aged about twenty being Attefted &
   examined
Saith that the íd Jacob Hall Sold An Indian i ga: i pt
   of Rum
being the day before philadelphia yearly meeting laft
   & that he
was the Interpreter betwixt the íd Indian & the íd Jacob
   Hall
   the íd Jacob Hall being examined about it doth
      acknowledg
that he fold the above mentioned Rum to the Indians
wherefore the Court fines him the Said Jacob Hall in five
pounds

Jofeph Hollinfhead having been Comitted to goale
   becaufe of
Several abufes done to Ellenor ffenbank of this County
   & for

(28) for not giveing Suertys for his good behavior the íd
   Hollinfhed
being calld & after proclamation made none appearing agt
the íd Hollins head the Court difcharges him

   This day was deld & acknowledged in open Court by
      Jon
& Thomas Rowland unto Samuel Burges one deede of
A Certaine tract of Land being about 200 ackers lying
betwixt Randulph Black fhaw & the great timber Swamp

   This day was deld & acknowledged in open Court by
      gilbert
wheeler Conftitute Attorney for morgan Druet one bill of
Sale of ioo Ackers of land adjoyning unto the fferre houfe
land over agt Burlington unto Thomas Holm
   for the ufe of Hannah Salter

   This day was deld and acknowledged in open Court one
bill of Sale of 500 ackers of Land lying neare the
lands of Ar: Cook of this County by David powell
   Conftitute
attorney by grifith Jones unto Thomas Holme
for the ufe of Thomas LLoyd

The Court adjorns till to morrow morning att 8 th Clock
   ioth Inftant the Court being Calld

Robt Lucas & Robt Cartor were Ellected & Attefted high Conftables for this County

The Court adjorns till the ioth of the i month next

4th i2 85 County of Bucks & Province of Pennfilvania
  mo

The action } Phinehas Pemberton Clark of the fd County plt
       agt Daniel
entered— } Brinfon of the fd County planter deft in an action
     of Cafe for wth holding 7 ^s 6 ^d due
     to the fd plt for fees
      4th i2th mo 85

the Declaration———— } Phinehas Pemberton makes Complt
       agt
  of   }Daniel Brinfon of the County of
       Bucks and
Phinehas Pemberton plt } Province of Pennfilvania Planter
       how that
  agt   the fd deft is Indebted to him the
       fd plt the
Daniel Brinfon deft Sum of Seven Shillings Six pence due

to the sd plt for fees wch the fd deft unjuftly detaines tho the
fd plt hath fent two feverall times on purpofe for
his pay wherefore the fd plt brings his action of Cafe agt the
fd deft & prays Judgmt of Court agt the fd deft for the fd fum
of Seven Shillings Six pence damages & Coft of fuite

This action is with drawn the plt being Satiffyed

   The 5th day of the i2th month 1685   (29)

The action } John Brock of the County of Bucks in the
     Province of
entered } Pennfilvania yeoman plt agt Charles pickring late of the
     County of new Caftle in the fd Province yeoman deft in an

action of Cafe for wth holding of 5 £ : 12^{s}: 6^{d}
due to the
fd plt

The 5th day of the i2th month i685

the Declaration of ⎫ John Brock of the County of Bucks &
                    ⎪   Province of Penn
John Brock plt   ⎪ Silvania makes Complt agt: Charles
    agt   ⎬   Pickring late of
                    ⎪ Crifteena Creeke in the County of new
Charles Pickring   ⎪   Caftel and Provinc
    deft —   ⎭ afforefd how that the fd deft is Indebted
                      to the fd plt
the Summ of five pounds twelve Shillings
    Six pence
wch fd Sum he hath divers times promifed
    to pay to the
fd plt but doth not pay it; but hath
    unjuftly detained the fame
above three yeares & never as yett payd
    any pte thereof
wherefore the fd plt brings his action of
    Cafe &
prays Judgment of Court agt the fd deft
    for the fd fum
of five pounds twelve Shillings & Six
    penc damages &
Coft of fuite

Summonce   5th i2th mo 85

A Summonce granted agt: Charles Pickring
    to anfwer the
Complt of John Brock att the next Quarter
    feffions to
be held for this County att the Court houfe
    the ioth
of the firft month

Return   this Summonc was executed according to
            direction the i8th $\frac{i2}{mo}$
            1685 by Luke Brindley Deputy Sherrif

Wittneffes*   A Summonce for Epharm Jackfon to give
in evidence in yᵉ:
afforefd action

A Summonce for Joseph millner to give
in evidenc in the aforefd
action

executed 4ᵗʰ $\frac{i}{mo}$ 85

pr Luke Brindley

5ᵗʰ day of the i2ᵗʰ month i685

The Declaration of ⎫ John Brock of the County of Bucks &
                     Province
John Brock plt   ⎪ of Pennfilvania plt makes Complt agt
                     Charles
    agt   ⎬ Pickring late of Criftina Creeke in the
                     County
Charles Pickring ⎪ of newcaftell & Province afforefd how
                     that the
    deft   ⎭ fd plt agreed with the fd deft in
                     liverpoole in
                     old England in the yeare i682 to bring
                     him

A paffenger for this provinc & pd him for the fame in Englifh
    monys
to the value 5 £: 12ˢ 6ᵈ in this Cuntry pay but the fd plt
was difpointed of the fd paffenger as he was not brought
as above wherefore the fd plt demanded back his —
monys but the fd deft refufed to pay the fame whereupon
whereupon the diferenc betwixt them depending was
Referred to willm yardley & Thomas Philips arbitrators In
diferently Chofen by the fd ptyes wᶜʰ fd arbitrators awarded
upon the ioᵗʰ 3 mo i683
that if the fd Charles went for England & returned back
the yeare following that then the fd deft fhold bring over
a paffenger att his owne charge if the fd plts Correfpon
dent in England put A paffenger Aboare wᵗʰ the fd deft
to wᶜʰ the fd deft agreed but he did not go
for England nor bring the fd paffengr according to the fd
    award

---

* Crossed out in original record.

wherefore the íd plt demanded his monys wch the íd deft promiſed
to pay but doth not pay it but hath unjuſtly detained the Same
above three yeares & never as yet pay any pte thereof
    wherefore
the íd plt brings his act of Caſe and prays
Jugmt of Court agt the íd deft for the íd
Sum of 5 £ : 12 ˢ: 6 ᵈ damages & Coſt of ſuite

(30) the 22 day of the i2th mo: i685 an Execution was granted
        agt
    Jacob Hall for the levying of A fine of five pounds
        Impoſed
    upon him the 9th of the io mo laſt paſt (att A Quarter
        ſeſſions
    then held) for ſelling Rum to the Indians Conterary to the
    laws of this Province
    Jacob Hall gave Security for the above 5 £ to be pd to
        the
    govrnr on demand wch íd bond is in P Pembertons
        hands

            The 22 day of the   i2   i685
                                ───────────
                                   mo

The Action ⎤ gilbert wheeler of the County of Bucks and
Entered   ⎦   Province
            of Pennſilvania plt agt Daniel Brinſon of the íd
            County and Province in an acction of Aſſault &
                Battery
            to the damage of 5 £

    The   County of Bucks in the Province of
Declaration of ⎤   Pennſilvania
gilbert wheeler plt ⎬ the 22 day of the i2th mo 85
    agt: ⎭ gilbert wheeler of the County and
Daniel Brinſon deft   Provinc aforeſd
            makes Compt agt Daniel Brinſon of the
                íd County
            and Province how that the íd deft upon
        the 9th
    day of this Inſtant the i2 month Came into the houſe of the
        íd plt

& did then and there aſſault beate and with his hands
   violently Strike martha the wife of the ſd
plt & in A moſt outrageous manner as he hath heretofore
   done did then greatly abuſe
the ſd martha wife of the ſd plt
by Calling her beast repeating the Same with proteſtations
   that She was whore & often the Duch=
=man's whore which together wth the violence of to the great
   affrighting hurting & terrefying of the ſd martha thereby
   & Damnifying the ſd plt to y^e: value of 5 £
he the ſd plt being then not att home who had left the Con=
=cerns and management both of his publique & private
   affaires
with his ſd wife and who through the violence of the ſd
   deft was
made Incapable of managing the affaires and hath ever
   sinc been in great pains through the violence of his
   blows therefore
that the ſd deft may be brought to
an acknowlegment of the great wrong done & that the ſd
plt may not be Ruined in his family & Eſtate by such wicked
outrages in his abſence the ſd plt brings his action & prays
Judgment of Court agt the ſd deft for damages & Coſt of ſuit

Summonc   A Summonc granted agt Daniel Brinſon to
                Anſwer
             the Compt of gilbert wheeler at the next Quarter
             Seſſions to be held for this County at the Court
                houſe
             the ioth day i mo next

Return   this was Executed the 23 day of the   i2   1685
                                                  ----
                                                   mo

ioth   i   p Luke Brindley Deputy Sherrif
-----   witneſſes A Summonc granted for mary
  mo   Ackerman
85   Ellizabeth Ridgway & Ellizabeth Lucas to
gilbert wheeler   give in theire evidence in the action
 prayed this   depending betwixt gilbert wheeler plt
 action to be   and Daniel Brinſon deft
 with drawn

              this was execu   ⎤
              ted the 2   1   85 ⎬
                    -----   ⎪
                      mo   ⎪
                p L Brindley   ⎦

(31)

The Action ⎱   The 24th day of i2 moth 1685
Entered   ⎰   Roger Hawkins of the County of Bucks &
         Province of
Pennſilvania plt agt gilbert wheeler of the ſd
         County
& Province in action of Caſe for with holding of
three pounds fiveteen Shillings due to the ſd plt

The Declaration of ⎱   County of Bucks in the Province of
                   Pennſilvania
Rogr Hawkins plt   ⎰ the 24th day of the i2th mo i685
      agt   ⎱ Rogr Hawkins of the County and
                   Province
gilbert wheeler deft ⎰ afforeſd makes Complt agt gilbert
         wheeler
of the ſd County and Province how that
         the ſd deft
is Indebted to the ſd plt the Sum of
         five pounds
wch is due & owing for A pſell of goods Sold to John wright
late of the County afforeſd in the 2nd month laſt paſt w^{ch}
ſd ſum of five
pounds the ſd gilbert wheeler promiſed to pay or Cauſe
to be pd to the ſd deft on acct of the ſd wright att or before
         the latter end of the third month enſueing but
the ſd plt hath only pd in pte
of the ſd Sum 1 £ 5^s 0^d and the remameing pte being
three pounds fiveteen Shillings the ſd deft unjuſtly detaines
to the great damage of the ſd plt wherefore the ſd plt brings
         his action of Caſe
& prays Judgmt of Court agt the ſd deft for
the ſd Sum of three pounds fiveteen ſhillings damages &
         Coſt
of ſuite

24th   i2   84

mo

Summonce   A Summonce granted agt gilbert wheeler to
         Anſwer
the Complt of Rogr Hawkins att the next Quarter
Seſſions to be held for this County att the Court
houſe the ioth day of the i month next

Return   This was executed the 25th day of the i2th month
1685 p   Luke Brindley Deputy Sherrif

wittneffes   A fumm granted for Jofuah Boare to give in
evidenc in the action depending betwixt Rogr
Hawkins plt & g wheeler deft
this was executed the 2nd i 85 p L Brindley
mo

ioth   i   1685 Rogr Hawkins declared that
mo
he wold
have the above action with drawn &
accordingly
it is with drawn

The i2 day of the iith month i685
willm Hague appeared before James Harrifon one of
the Juftices
for this County & then oblidged him Self in the fum of
20 £
to the propryatory & govrnr for his appearance att the
next
Court to be held for this County the ioth i next & to
be of good   mo
behavior in the meane time as allfo Robt Lucas & Jon
wood
have as fuertyes for the fd willm Hague in like manner
oblidged
them felves in 20 £ Apeice for the appearance of the fd
will and
for his good behavior in the meane time

(32)
At A Quarter feffions held by the kings authority in the name
of wm Penn Propryatory and govrnr of Pennfilvania and the
territorys thereunto belonging for the County of Bucks
att the Court houfe the ioth day of the i^{ft} month 168 6
                                                            5

being the 6th yeare of the propryatorys govrmt

The Juftices then prfent

James Harrifon   Thomas Janney   Edmund Bennet
william yardley   willm Biles   Jon Otter
willm Beakes

Nicholas walm Sherrif
Luke Brindley his deputy
Phinehas Pemberton Clark

the Court being Called the Court adjorns untill
the ellection of the reprſentatives to serve in
Counſell and Aſſembly for this County
be Ended

poſt meridian

i deed of 100 Ackers of Land Conveyed by Jeffry
Hawkins to his brother Rogr was this day deld
& acknowledged in open Court by phinehas =
pemberton Conſtitute attorney by the ſd Jeffery
unto the ſd Rogr Hawkins

i deed of 130 Ackers of Land Conveyed
by Tho woolf unto Elizabeth gibbs was
this day dld & acknowledged in open Court
unto Edmund Lovet Conſtitute Attorney by the
ſd: Tho woolf

willm Hague having this day appeared in Court
the Court diſcharges him & his baile none
Coming to pſecute him.

Jon Brock plt appeares to the action agt
Charles pickring,

      Charles pickring appeares not

In as much as y^e: ſd Charles pickring hath not this day
appeared according to Summonce this Court gives Jugmt
agt him by default & it is adjudged the ſd
Charles Shall pay the ſd ſum of 5 £: 12^s: 6^d
& the Coſt of ſuite

      The Court adjorns for 2 houres

(33)

In as much as Complt hath beene made this day to this
Court that the new road is not Layd out ſo well as
it may be this Court orders that Robt Lucas Henry
Baker Sam Dark Rich Hough Thomas Stackhouſe
& Jon Brock with the Aſſiſtance of John Swift &
Henry marjorum Henry pointer Robt Hall Nich
waln & Iſreal Taylor do lay out the ſd Road
to the ut moſt of Extent of the ſd County

In as much as the Conftables of this County hath
this day prfented the want of men in the
Several divifions of this County to veiue the
Sufitienty of al fences this Court doth ordr
that Rich Ridgway & Sam Dark ferve in y^e:
office for that pte of the river below the falls
as far as the govrnrs plantation
Henry marjerum & Andrew Ellot above the falls
Jon palmer & Jonathan Scaife for the middle
p pte Nefhaminah Robt Heaton Ezra Crofdale
Lower pte of Nefhamina James Boyden & Robt Hall
that pte the river below the govrnrs

David Davis hath this day appeared in Court & hath
defired that his appearance may be Recorded
wch is accordingly Recorded in as much as he
Reports that he was bound by the laft affizes
here to appeare here

David Davis haveing been Cald into Court this day
to give Security for the Eftate of H Comley orphan Son of
    H. C. deceased according to A former ordr of the
laft orphants Court & to give in his accts & he
hath promifed to give Sufitiont Secury for the
fd Eftate in one months time or for fo much of
the Eftate as is realy in his hands & will furrendr
up all the Specialtys that he hath taken on the
fd Eftate and the accountf of what is due
by the feveral pfons Concerned in the fd
Eftate

The Court adjorns untill the 9th 4th mon^th next

(34)
        At a private Seffions held by the kings
    Authority in the name of willm Penn proprya
    tory & govrnr of this Provinc and Territorys
    there unto belonging this i3 day of the 2 86
                                            ─────
                                             mo
            The Juftices then prfent
        James Harrifon   willm yardley
        willm Biles   willm Beakes
                P P Cl:
Inas much as David Davis laft Court of Quarter

Seffions promifed to give fecurity for the Eftate
of Henry Comeley orphan to Henry Comeley
& that the fd David Davis is Since dead
therefore the Juftices Saw there was A neceffity
to meete together this day to Concider of Away
how to fecure the Eftate of the fd orphan where
==fore it being ppofed wch way it Shall be fecured
David powel on the behalf of the fd David Davis
hath offered that if this Court will ordr any pfons
to Rc what goods there is in David Davis Cuftody
or on the plantation he did occupy he will
deliver them or So much of them
as Can be fpared & will give fecurity for
the remaneing pte of what is due So that
he may be Sufitiontly difcharged for what he
pays on the orphans acct: wherefore
this Court orders that willm Biles and
willm Paxfon do go on 5th
day next & then Rc fuch goods & specialtys as fhall be
delivered by David powell for the ufe of the
fd orpant, & give him difcharges for fo much
as they Rc from him either in fpecialtys
or goods at the prices as they fhall be valued
by 2 Juditious pfons or more as may be
Chofen by the fd wm Biles willm paxfon &
David powel

   This Court adjorns

                (35)

Ejectione ffirme Bucks in Pennfilvania The 22 day of the
         3 month 1686

The action Abraham Cocks of the fd County plt agt
Entered   micheal Huff
     of the fd County Deft in an action Ejectione
     firme
     for with holding the fferry houfe over gainst
     Burlington & lands wth the appurtenances
      thereunto belonging

The Declaration ⎫   Bucks in Pennſilvania the 22 day of the
of   ⎪
Abraham Cocks plt ⎬   3 month i686
agt   ⎪
micheal Huff deft ⎭   Abraham Cocks of the County & provinc
                afforeſd

planter makes Complt how that he had Confirmed
to him by leaſe (bearing date the eight
day of the   3
                   mo

1686 & to be Expired the 30 day of the 2 month
next enſuing from Joſeph Engliſh Junior of the ſd
County planter) one houſe Called the fferry houſe over
agt Burlington & 32 Ackers of land with the appur –
=tenances thereunto belonging late in the poſſeſſion of
Samuel Clif of the afforeſd County deceaſed and
father in law to the ſd Joſeph and that after poſſeſſion
of the ſd houſe & lands was delivered
to the ſd Abraham Cocks micheal Huff of the ſd County
ordinary keep entered the ſd houſe and —
forceably keeps poſſeſſion thereof & of the lands
thereunto appertaining to the damage of
the ſd Abraham Cocks and Conterary to the kings
peace wherefore that the ſd plt may have the ſd
houſe and lands with the appurtenances thereunto
belonging according to Contract he the ſd plt brings
his action Ejectione ffirme and prays Judment
of Court that the ſd micheal Huff may be removed

The ⎫
Endorsmt ⎭   24th 3 mo 1686

micheal Huff thou may pceive that Abraham
Cocks hath brought his action agt thee for the houſeing
and lands in thy poſſeſſion tryable at the next
Court to be held for this County the 9th   4
next Theſe are therefore   mo

to defire thee to defend thy tittle or they undr whom
thou Claims to appeare to this declaration and make him or them felves defts there unto
and by rule of Court Confefs the leafe Entry & Ejectmt & Infift only upon the tittle Ells Judgt will be Entered by default & poffeffion will be delivered accordingly to the plt.

Phinehas Pemberton

22   3   86   Cl   p   Bucks
     mo

Summonc   granted agt micheal Huff to anfwer the Complt of Abra:
     Cocks att the next Court to be held for this County att ye:
     Court houfe the 9th of the 4th month next

Return   this was Executed the 25th of the 3 month 1686
     p   Luke Brindley deputy fherrif

(36)

County of Bucks in Pennfil: the 22 day of
The action Entered   the 3 mo i686

Nicholas moore Efquire of the County of Philadelphia plt agt gilbert wheeler of the County of Bucks deft in an action of debt for with holding of i2 £ : 04 s: io d due to be pd upon demand

The declaration of
Nicholas moore plt   Bucks in pennfilvania the 22   3   86
                                            mo
agt   Nicholas moore Efquire of the County of
gilbert wheeler deft   Philadelphia and province afforefd makes
Complt agt gilbert Wheeler of the County of Bucks afforefd
how that the fd deft is Indebted the Sum of
34:£: 16 s: 10 d Currant monys of Pennfilvania due to be

payd upon demand as will appeare by A

bill undr the hand of the ſd deft bearing date

the 27ᵗʰ of 8ᵇᵉʳ 1684 and all tho the ſd plt

hath divers times made demand of his ſd monys yet

the ſd deft unjuſtly detaines the ſum of 12 £ 04 ˢ : 10 ᵈ being pte of the ſd Debt

wherefore the ſd plt brings his action of Debt

and prays Judgmt of Court agt the ſd deft for

the ſd Sum of twelve pounds Sixteen ſhillings

and tenpence damages & Coſt of ſuite

Summonce   granted 22 3 mo 1686 agt gilbert Wheeler to anſwer the

Complt of Nicholas moore att the next Court

to be held for this County att the Court houſe the 9ᵗᵇ of the 4ᵗʰ mo next

Return   this was Executed the 23 day of the 3 month

1686 p Luke Brindley Deputy Sherrif

with drawing   The 9ᵗᵇ of the 4ᵗʰ month 1686

Nicholas moore deſired to have the action with drawn

(37)

At A Court of Quarter Seſſions held by the kings Authority in the name of Wm penn propryatory and govrnr of Pennſilvania and the territorys thereunto belonging for the County of Bucks at : the Court houſe the 9ᵗʰ day of the 4 mo 1686 being the 6ᵗʰ yeare of the propryatorys govrmt

The Juſtices then prſent

Thomas Janney   Willm Biles
willm yardley   John otter

Sherrif
Nicholas waln
Luke Brindley deputy
phinehas pemberton Clark

Abraham Cocks plt being called to profecute his fuite agt micheal
Huff deft appeared
  micheal Huff being calld appeared
The Jury Attefted John Clows foreman John Brock Rich Hough
Lyonel Brittan Jon wood Tho: Tunneclif H: Baker
Samuel overton Tho: woolfe Robt Heaton wm: Paxfon Tho: Stakehouf fenᵉ
    the declaration of Abraham Cocks being
Read & proved by the teste mony of ffrancis Roffell & phinehas pemberton who fay the faw the leafe fealed & delivered on
the premises & after faw the fd micheal Huff to Enter the fd houfe
& Land
after micheal Huff being Calld to Anfwer fd he had no tittle to the fd houfe or Land & therefore Shold yeild it up
the Jury returned & Calld over do fay they find for the plt
Therefore the Court gives Judgment & it is adjudged that
the fd Abraham Cocks Shall have poffeffion accordingly delivered to him
this day was delivered and acknowledged in open Court one deed of 50 ackers of land fold by Jon Bainbridge of this County to James Clay poole of Philadelphia by Rich Hough Conftitute attorney to Thomas Woolfe
    Conftitute attorney to the fd James Clay poole of Philadelphia bearing
date 7ᵗʰ 3 month 1686
this day was returned and acknowledged in open Court by Shadrach walley Conftitute attorney by Robt Holgat one deed of 250 ackers of Land bearing date 19ᵗʰ of the 3 month 1686 unto Robt Heaton of this County
this day was delivered and acknowledged in open Court by phinehas pemberton Conftitute attorney
to Thomas Holmes of Philadelphia one deed of one hundred and i8 ackers of land bearing

date the i8 day of the 3 moth 86 unto Nicholas
Waln of this County

(38)   whereas there was Judgment of Court formerly paſt
agt Charles pickring by default in an action depending
betwixt the ſd Charles deft & John Brock plt and
the the ſd Charles hath this day appeared in Court
and there alledged that he Cold not poſſible appeare
att the Court when the ſd Judgment was obtained
being farr diſtant wherefore he the ſd Charles offered
that if the ſd Jon Brock wold be pleased to lett fall
the ſd Judgmnt & take no advantage thereof he
the ſd Charles wold referr the ſd matter w^{ch}
was the grownd of the ſd action to Such pſons
as ſhould be by them Indiferently Choſen where
upon the ſd John Brock hath deſired the ſd Judgment
of Court may be made voyd & they have both this
day in open Court declared that they have wholey
referred the ſd matter to James Harriſon
Nicholas Waln Thomas Janney & william yardley
pſons Indeferently Choſen by them to whom they
leave the Same and all matters relateing there to to
be wholey deſided & determined by the ſd partyes
& for theire true pformance and obſervance
of the ſd award the ſd partyes Shall make the ſd
Charles pickring & John Brock have obliadged themſelves
theire heires Executors & adminiſtrators Each to other
        in
in the penal Sum of ten pounds for Confirmation
whereof the ſd Charles pickring & Jon Brock the ſd
day have put here to theire hands

Charles pickring
John Brock

the Court adjorns for one houre

Robt Doue & Ellizabeth Andrews hath this day
        appeared
in Court and there acknowledged A bond bearing date
the 3 day of the i2th month 1685 wherein they are
obliadged to Richard Bagnel of Burlington in Sixty
pounds to Confeſs or Cauſe to be Confeſſed Judgment in
the County of Bucks of all & ſingular there reſpective
Shares of all theire lands good cattles & Chattles that
they are then poſſeſſed of or with in the space of 4

yeares Shall be poffeft of & they the faid Robt
Doue & ffrancis Andrews have this day appeared
in this Court & have accordingly Confeft Judgmt
of all theire eftate they have or fhall have as above
fd

whereas there was A diferenc depending betwixt   (39)
      Ellenor
pownall and ffrancis Hough wch diference so depending
was heard and determined by willm yardley & Thomas
Janney wch Judgmt was this day Read & by this
Court approved of
where as Severall pfons upon Ne fhaminah
creeke have complained of the want of A road to
the ferry houfe over agt Burlington this Court doth
therefore ordr that Edmund Bennet Nicholas waln
Robt Heaton Jon otter Ifrael Taylor & Robt
Hall & Shadrach walley do lay out A Road from
wrights town to the fd fferry houf being a convenient
      Landing and give an
acct thereof to the next Court
whereas there was formerly ordered fome pfons
to lay out A road to the Extent of this County
from the ferry houfe att the falls & thereupon
the fd Road was accordingly layd out but Richard
Thacher makes Complt that the fd road runs through
his land to his great damage wherefore this Court
ordrs N waln and Henry paxton to veiue the
fd road in that place & endeavor to regulate
it as well as may be for the Eafe of the fd
thacher
this day was delivered and acknowledged in open Court
      by
Nicholas Waln of this County one deed of 200 ackers of
lands bearing date 6th 4 month
1686 to James Dilworth* Conftitute attorney to Edmund
      Cuttler
of this County
This day was delivered and acknowledged in open Court
by the fd Nicholas Waln one deed of 50 ackers of land
      bearing

---

* Name crossed out in record book.

date the 5ᵗʰ 4ᵗʰ month i686 unto Thomas Stackhoufe
Junior of this County.
This day was delivered and acknowledged in open Court
   by
Richard Ridgway of this County one deed of A Small
piece of land being in Eftimation about 4 ackers of
Land bearing date the firft 4 mo: i686 unto philip
Conway of the fd County
This day was delivered and acknowledged in open Court
by philip Conway abovefd one deed of 2 peices or
parfells of land the one being the above mentioned
of about 4 ackers and the other of 50 ackers
bearing date the 6ᵗʰ 4 month 1686 unto
Thomas Dickenfon of this County
* This day was delivered and acknowledged in open
Court by phinehas pemberton Conftitute
attroney to James Harrifon of this County one deed of
   iio ackers
of land bearing date the firft of the 4ᵗʰ month 1686
unto Edward Stanton of the Said County

(40)   This day was deld and acknowledged in open Court
one deed of four hundred Eighty ackers of Land
bearing date the 5ᵗʰ 4 mo: i686 by James Dillworth
of this County to, Jon Hornor of weft new Jarfey
This day was delivered and acknowledged in open Court
by Jeffery Hawkins of this County one deed of iio
   ackers of land
bearing date the i 10ᵗʰ mo i685 to Jon Collins of
the fd County
This day was delivered and acknowledged in open
Court by Phinehas Pemberton Conftitute attorney
by James Harrifon of this County one Conveyance
of iio ackers of land bearing date the firft of
this Inftant the 4ᵗʰ month unto Edward ftanton
of this County
The Court adjourns to the 8ᵗʰ of 7ᵗʰ month next
                     Willm Beakes plt agt: Lawrenc Bannor
                     deft:
       The   The 28ᵗʰ day of the   5   i686
                                             ─────
                                              mo

---

* This paragraph has four scratch marks in ink over it in the original
record.

action Entered

28   5   86
      ─────
      mo

Summonce

the Declaration of ⎫
Willm Beakes plt   ⎬
       agt   ⎪
Lawrenc Bannor   ⎭
       deft

Willm Beakes of the County of Bucks and
Provinc of Pennfilvania plt agt: Lawrenc
Bannor of the fd County
& provinc deft.
in an action of debt for with holding
of 4 £ 10 ˢ 00 ᵈ

granted agt Lawrence Bannor to anfwer
    the Complt
of Willm Beakes at the next Court to be
    held the 8 day
of the   7   next
       ─────
        mo

Return this was executed the 28: 5 86
                                  ─────
                                   mo
by me Luke Brindley Deputy Sherrif
Bucks in Pennfilvania the
    25ᵗʰ day of the   5   1686
                    ─────
                     mo

Willm Beakes of the County afforefd
yeoman makes Compt agt Laurence
    Bannor
of the fd County Hufbandman how that
    the fd deft
is Indebted the Sum of foure pounds ten
    fhillings
Currant Silver monys of Pennfilvania
    due to be
payd to the fd Willm Beakes the 29ᵗʰ
    day of the
7ᵗʰ month laft paft as will appeare by A
    bill
under the hand & feale of the fd
    Lawrenc Bannor
bearing date the 20ᵗʰ day of the 2 month
    1685 & altho
the fd plt hath divers times made
    demand of the

ſd debt yet the ſd deft unjuſtly detaines the

Same wherefore the ſd plt brings his action

& prays Judgmt of Court agt the ſd deft for

the ſd Sum of 4 £ : 10 ˢ 00 ᵈ damages & Coſt of

Suite

County Court	The 28 __5__ i686 (41)
of	mo
Bucks — —	Willm Beakes plt agt Lawrenc Bannor
action entered	deft in An action upon A Replevin for 2 oxen Impounded by ſd Deft

The 28ᵗʰ __5__ 86

mo

County Court of
Bucks

A Replevin granted
for the twoo oxen of Will Beakes Impounded by
Laurenc Bannor

The Sherrifs Return

This was executed the 28ᵗʰ __5__

mo

i686 by mᵉ Luke Brindley
deputy Sherrife

The	willm : Beakes of the County
Declaration of	of Bucks & Provinc of
Willm Beakes plt	Pennſilvania Complaines of
agt	Lawrence Bannor of the
Lawrenc Bannor deft	ſd County in A plea for that

. . 6   where as the afforeſd Lawrence Bannor did
= 18 . mo   on the
28 day of the __5__ Laſt paſt take of the

mo

goods of the ſd plt that is to Say 2 oxen
of the price of 12 £ : and tha Same did un=
=juſtly detaine againſt the ſuertyes & Safe pledges

of the Said Willm Beakes whereupon the ſd
Willm Beakes Saith he is worſe & hath damage
to the value of forty Shillings & therefore he
hath brought this Suite & Craves Judgmt of
this Court agt. the afforeſd Lawrenc Bannor
for the Said damage & Coſt of Suite

23   6   86
    ―――
    mo

Summonce granted agt Laurence Bannor to anſwer
the Complt of W: Beakes (in A plea for takeing
of 2 oxen of the ſd Wm: Beakes & unjuſtly
detaineing the ſame) att the next Court to be held
for this County the 8ᵗʰ day of the 7ᵗʰ month next

Return The 24ᵗʰ   6   i686 the within Summonce was
              ―――
              mo

executed according to direction by Luke Brindley
                              deputy ſherrif

(42)   Pennſilvania   i6ᵗʰ   6   86
                                            ―――
                                            mo

County Court ⎤
     of   ⎬ Joſeph knight plt
   Bucks   ⎦   agt

           Ralph milner deft in A plea of Debt
           for with holding of twenty pounds ____

Declaration
County Court of ⎱ Joſeph knight plantife ⎱ i6ᵗʰ   6   86
    Bucks   ⎰   agt   ⎰   ―――
                  Ralph milner deft   ⎰   mo

Joſeph knight of the towne & County of
    Philadelphia
Cuttler Complaines agt Ralph milner of the
    County of Bucks
wheelwright in A plea of Debt for that
    whereasthe
Said deft by his penal bond under his hand &
    Seale dated
the i7ᵗʰ day of the ioᵗʰ month i685 bound and
    oblidged
him ſelf to have pd to the ſd plt his heires or
    aſſigneſs therein

mentioned the fum of twenty pounds Currant Silver

monys of the Said provinc Conditioned for the Saveing harmles

from al action or Caufes of action or charges that may come or accrew for or by reason of a bond of tenn pounds ====

bearing date the i9ᵗʰ day of the 10ᵗʰ month i685 ====

wᶜʰ the fd plt: at the requeft of fd deft Entered into

& Stands bound thereby wᵗʰ the fd deft to

Jon Crapp of Philadelphia Senior for the pformance

of the Condition therein expreffed as the fd obligation of

twenty pounds herewᵗʰ in Court to be produced will

teftefye all wᶜʰ the fd plt doth averr, and altho

the fd plt hath divers times requefted & defired the

fd deft to pforme his Covenats & Contracts wᵗʰ the fd

Crapp that he the fd plt might not be any ways Indemnifyd

by the fd penal bond of io £ yet never the lefs the fd

deft hath hitherto neglected & not pformed the Same

where fore the fd John Crapp hath brought his action

of debt agt the fd Jofeph knight herein plantife and

at A Court held at philadelphia the 7ᵗʰ of the 5 month

laft paft the Said John Crapp obtained Judgmt agt the

Said Jofeph knight herein plantif for the fd Sum of

ten pounds & the Cofts of Suite whereupon Execution was

accordingly granted as will be made appeare in Court

by the records of the ſd Court of Philadelphia whereby
the ſd plt Joſeph knight is there by demnifyed to
the value of ten pounds wᵗʰ the Coſt of ſuite allowed &
adjudged by the ſd Court where upon the plt brings his
Suite & craves Judgmt of this Court agt the ſd deft for
the ſd Sum of twenty pounds Currant ſilver monys as
afforeſd wᵗʰ Coſt of ſuite

$$\frac{i6^{th} \quad 6 \quad 86}{mo}$$

Summonce   A Summonce was granted agt Ralph milner
to anſwer the above Complt of of Joſeph
knight att the next Court of Quarter
Seſſions to be held for this County att
the Court houſe the 8ᵗʰ day of the 7ᵗʰ
month

Return   This was executed the 25 of the 6ᵗʰ month
1686 by me   Luke Brindley deputy Sherrif
Jon pidcock plt agt g wheeler deft in plea
of debt for wᵗʰ holding 25 £
iſt $\frac{7}{mo}$ 86 Joſeph knight prayed the ſd
action agt
Ralph milner might be wth drawn
wᶜʰ is accordingly   (43)

(44)

John gray agt gilbert wheeler of A plea
of debt:
gilbert wheeler plt agt Jon pidcock in a plea of
covenant

gilbert wheeler plt agt Jon pidcock deft
in A plea of treſpaſs on the Caſe

45

(46)

Att A Court of Quarter Seffions held by the
 kings authority
in the name of Willm Penn Propryatory and
 govrnr
of the Province of Pennfilvania and the
 Territorys there
unto belonging for the County of Bucks att the
Court houfe of the fd County the 8th day of the
 7th month
being the 2nd yeare of the raigne of James the
 2nd
over England &c king & the 6th of the
 Propryatorys
govrmt 1686

  The Juftices then prfent
 Arthur Cooke Thomas Janney Willm Biles
 and Willm yardley
  Sherrif Abraham Whearley
   deputy Sherrif Luke Brindley

   Phinehas Pemberton Cl:
John gray agt gilbert Wheeler in A plea
 of Cafe
Jon gray appears gilbert wheeler appears
Jury attefted the dec
The declaration being read the deft
acknowledged the Complt: & Confeffed the
debt & promifed to pay the Same in Rye
att 3 s the bufhell & wheat att 4 s the
bufhell the one half thereof in twoo days
time and the other half in ten weeks time
to be pd in Rye two thrds & wheat one
thrd & delivered att the prices above att
the houfe of the fd Jon gray
This day was delivered and acknowledged in
 open
Court one patten of 500 ackers of land wth
an affignment on the back thereof from
Willm Cartr to Robt Cartor bearing date
the 23 5 mo 86 by Ifral Taylor Conftitute
attorney to fd Wm Cartor
whereupon the Court ordrs that if the
Said gilbert wheeler faile in payment according

to promiſe that then Execution be granted
for Leying the ſd debt on the eſtate of the
ſd g wheeler upon requeſt of the ſd Jon gray

(47)

John pidcock plt agt g wheeler deft in an
action of debt for 25 £
John pidcock appeares: gilbert wheeler deft apprs
the declaration being read & the bill of debt for 25 £
being
produced the ſd deft Confeſſed the bill
willm yardley Conſtitute attorney to Jon Alſop
delivered i Conveyance of 1000 ackers of
- land date the i9ᵗʰ day of the 5ᵗʰ month 1684
unto Tho: Tunneclif
Jeffery Hawkins acknowledged & delivered one
deed of iio ackers of land to Jon Collins
bearing date the firſt day 7 mo
gilbert wheeler agt Jon pidcock in A
plea of Covenant
The declaration being read
the deft craves A hours time to put in his plea

The Court adjorns for one houre

The Anſwer Read defends the force & puts him
Self on the Cuntry
grand Jury Atteſted Jon Brock Charles Biles Rich
Ridgway Richard Lundy micheal Huff Iſrael Taylor
Robt Heaton Joſeph Engliſh ſr John
Coates John Cuff ffrancis Hough Tho Stackhouſe Ser
Jon Collins
Jeffery Hawkins Joſhua Boare Joſeph wood
bill found   RandulphSmalwood
being Convicted of abuſeing and endeavoring
to force Ellizabeth Wilſon by the teſtemony
of the ſd Ellizabeth & by the teſtemony of Iſaac
partington & Willm ffowler puts him ſelf on god &
the Cuntry
his Cuntry hath found him guilty
The Court adjorns till 7 tomorrow morning

petty J:
Atteſted   John Clows one of the Jury for not attending
the

Wm Beakes
Jo milner
Jo: Brock
Sa overton
Tho Tunneclif
La: Bannor
Lio: Brittan
Jo: purſlone
wm Dungan
wm paxſon
wm Dark }
Jon Hough }
atteſted

Court according to the houre appointed the
Court fines him in ten ſhillings
    This fine was remitted by ordr of Court

(48)

John Pidcock being Indicted & arraignd for
makeing an aſſault on his maſter g wheeler
hath pleaded gilty to the ſd Indictmt
and the Court awards Judgmt on his ſd
    Confeſſion
Randulph Smalwood being Indicted &
    arraigned
for Scandelizeing & defameing Rachel milner

Wm Beakes
J: milner
J Brock
S overton
T Tuneclif
L Bannor
L Brittan
J purſlone
W Dungan
w paxſon
w: Dark
J Hough
atteſted

wife of Ralph milner & ſd Smalwood hath
pleaded not gilty & for his tryal hath put him
Self on god and the Cuntry
wch Cuntry hath found him gilty

whereupon the Court awards Judgmt
george glave being Indicted & arraigned for
    aſſaulting
Edmund Bennet hath pleaded gilty & refers
him ſelf to the mercy of king propryatory
& the bench
whereupon the Court awards Judgmt
The Court give Judgmt & it is adjudged
that george gleave Shall for his offence pay
to the govrnr A fine of 10ˢ & his fees &
that he be bound to the good behavior & to
appeare att the next Court

The Court gives Judgmt that Jon pidcock
for his offence Shall pay to the govrnr A
fine of 3 £ & be bound to his good behavior
& to appeare at next Court
The Court adjudges that Randulph
    Smalwood

for his firſt offence be whipped on his bare
back 20 Laſhes & pay fees
The Court adjudges that the ſd Randulph
   for
his defameing Rachel milner Shall pay A
fine of 10 £ to the governr & 10 £ damages
   to to Ralph
milner & fees & be bound to his good
   behavior and
to appeare att the next Court
The Court ordrs the ſd priſoners to be taken
   into
Cuſtody and Secured untill the ſd fines &
   fees be
pd or ſecured to be payd.

(49)

the Court nominates & appoints Conſtables
for the falls Jon wood
James Dilworth for the uper pte of neſhaminah
for the lower pte of neſhaminah
John Bowen
for the midle lotts Rogr Hawkins atteſted
wᶜʰ Conſtables Shall Serve for the Succeding
yeare
willm Dungeon for the lower pte of the river
The Court appoints Henry Baker Jon Rowland
Thomas Stakehouſe & Edmund Cuttler do ſerve
overſeers of the high ways for the succeeding
yeare
The Court appoints the ſame peace makers yᵗ:
were the laſt yeare
This day was delivered and acknowledged
by one conveyance of 102½ ackers of land
bearing date the firſt day 3 moᵗʰ 86 by
Rich Ridgway Conſtitute attorney to Daniel
Brinſon to Jon Nicholls & Ellias Nicholls
This Court ordrs that Phinehas Pemberton & Jo Nicholls
Shall heare & examine the County Treaſurers
accounts & bring them into the next Court
& that in the meane time the Collectors bring
in theire arreares of the monys due & theire
accounts forthwith

   The Court adjorns for one houre

This day was deld & Acknowledged one deed
of i50 ackers dated the i day of 7 mo: 86
by Henry pawlin to willm paxſon
grand Jury prſented gilbert wheeler upon the
Information of Jon pidcock for ſelling Rum
Contrary to the law
to wᶜʰ prſentmt he has pleaded not gilty & traverſes
the ſd prſentmt
A petition dated the 8ᵗʰ day 7 mo: 1686 from Tho Cartor
of
Philadelphia Concering A boy of ſd Cartors then in
Cuſtody of
wm Beakes was read in Court to wᶜʰ the Court answered
haveing
heard the alegations on both ſides that the boy mentioned
in the ſd
petition Shold be delivered by the ſd wm Beakes to the
Said
tho Cartor the ſd Cartor firſt paying ſd Beakes 4 ga: Rum
and

(50) wm Beakes to pay charges of Court
wee Jon pidcock and gilbert wheeler both of
the County of Bucks do acknowledge our ſelves
to be bound to the propryatory and govrnr
in the ſum of Six pounds for
the true payment of A fine of three pounds
to the propryatory & govrnr Impoſed on the
ſd pidcock by this Court & for fees to be paid
upon the ſaid Conviction to be levyed on the
lands goods & Chattles of the Said pidcock & wheeler
theire heires Executors & adminiſtrators
wee george glave & Jon: Hough both of this
County do acknowledge our ſelves to be bound
to the propryatory and govrnr in the ſum of
three pounds for payment of A fine of io ˢ
& fees upon the ſd Conviction to be levyed as above
george glave in like mannor ſtands obliged to
the govrnr in 40 £ to be of good behavior &
appeare at the next Court
John pidcock in like mannor ſtands oblidge to the
govr in 40 £ to be of good behavior to ward
all people & to appeare at the next Court
              The Court adjourns untill the 20ᵗʰ 8   next
                                                  ───
                                                  mo

This day Rich Noble hath appeared in Court & defired to
have the monys that hath been made appeare formerly
to the orphans Court to be due wch was 20 £ owing
to him out of the Eftate of willm Clark pte thereof being
        Con-
= tracted by the fd Clark & his wife in theire life time
& for the fuftenance of the orphans of the fd
Clark Sinc there parents deceafe therefore this Court
doth ordr that i00 Ackers being pte of the tract of
land belonging to the fd orphans Shall be layd out to the
                fd R Noble in full
Satiffaction for his debt; if it appeare that
the whole tract of the fd orphans Land do amount to
300 Ackers or upwards

                adjourned 5th   8 ·   next
                                ————
                                 mo
                                        ————

        County of Bucks in the Province of Pennfilvania
        At an orphans Court held by the kings Authority in
            the name
        of Willm Penn propryatory and govrnr of the fd
            Province
        and Territorys thereunto belonging att the Court
            houfe
        the 2 day of i month being the firft third day of the
        weeke in the fd month i685
                The Juftices then prfent
        James Harrifon   Willm Biles   Willm Beakes
        Jo'n otter   Edmund Bennet Willm yardley
            The Sherrif N waln
                his   Deputy L Brindley
                    phinehas pemberton Clark
        John Otter & Edmund Bennet have brought in an
            acct of the
        Age of James Spencer
        the age of Samuel Spencer
        & the death of theire father as will apeare upon
            record
        before
        and the acct of the Eftate they Say they have not
            as yett
        brought in therefore this Court orders that A true &
        pfect acct of the fd Eftate of the fd Spencer be
            brought
        in to the next Court

the Indentures of Peter Hall were drawn & ſealed
before 2 Juſtices according to order _____

according to order Lawrenc Bannor hath brought
    in an
acct of the orpans of Willm Venables & it doth
    appeare
by the ſd accts that of Heycocks & venables
Eſtate there remains 400 ackers of Land wth the Im
provements thereon to the ſd orphans of venables
Except two pounds Nineteen Shillings five pence
    w^{ch}
ſd ſum is Chargeable upon the ſd Eſtate of Land w^{ch}
ſd acct is by this Court allowed & accepted
David Davis hath pleaded that he was not Legally
    Summonced
to this Court & therefore had not time to Anſwer the
Said Summonce
this Court orders that David Davis Shall bring in
    his acct.
in twelve days time to willm Biles & wm Beakes in
    wch ſd time
the ſd Davis has promiſed to bring in his accts.
this Court orders that there be no monys
or debts that are pte of the Eſtate of H Comley
    orphan drawn out of any Suffitient pſons hands
    by the ſd Da Davis untill Such
time as the ſd Da Davis has brought in his accts &
    Sattiſfy
the ptyes ordered to take the accts & that the ſd
    Eſtate is

(51)   Secured for the uſe of the ſd orphan by the ſd David

This Court doth ordr that the Indtures for peter
    Hall be
drawn & ſigned before Some 2 Juſtices of peace
willm Biles being aſked about the placeing of the
    2 orphants
of James Hall unplaced do Say they made Enquiry
    for A place but
before they heare of A place the mother of the Said
Childrn removed them out of this County
Lawrence Bannor hath brought in an Impfect acct
    of the
Eſtate of the orphants of willm venables therefore
    this
Court doth ordr that Lawrence Bannor bring in A

true & pfect acct unto phinehas pemberton
before the firſt day of the ii[th] mo
next
this day was deld A deed of 5000 Ackers of Land
fold by Tho Rudyard unto Andrew Robinſon by
　　Robt
Lucas & Luke Brindley Conſtitute attorney by
　　Thomas
Rudyard unto Lyonel Brittan Conſtitute attorney by
Andrew Robinſon
this day was deld & acknowledged in open Court A
　　deed of 200 Ackers of Land fold by
Ann milcome to willm Biles
this day was deld & acknowledged in open Court A
　　deed of 50 Ackers of Land Sold
by Ann milcome to philip Conway
　　this Court adjorns untill the firſt third of the
firſt month next
A Summonce for David Davis to appeare att the
　　orphants
Court to be held the 2 　i　 next then & there to give
　　　　　　　　　　mo
an acct of the Eſtate of Henry Comley orphant &
to give Secury for the ſd Eſtate

Whereas Complt hath beene made to me by Joane the
　　wife of Joſeph
Englifh Senior of the County of Bucks & Province of
　　Pennſilvania how that David Davis
of this County was nominated Executor to the laſt will
　　& teſtament of Henry Comley late
of this County deceaſed & former Husband to the ſd Joan
　　& that the ſd
David hath adminiſtered on the ſd Eſtate & taken
the Same into his poſſeſſion
& that Shee is afraid that if Some Speedy Courſe be not
taken for the ſecuring of the ſd Eſtate now in the hands
　　of the ſd
David, that Henry Comley orphant & Son to Henry
　　Comley
aforeſd will Suſtain loſſe in his Eſtate by the ſd David
Theſe are thereforc by the kings Authority in the name
　　of the
Propryatory & govrnr to require thee to Summonce the ſd
David Davis that he be & appeare att the next orphants
　　Court
to be held for this County the 2nd day of the firſt month

next then & there to give A true acct of the ſd Eſtate as
    allſo to give
Suffitient Securty for the ſame to the ſd Court & hereof
    faile not given undr
my hand & Seale the 8ᵗʰ day of the   <u>12</u>   being the 5th
    yeare of   mo
the propryatorys govrmt   1685   (52)

him the Art miſtery & faculty of Skinner & glover
for the placeing of 2 more more of the Childrn the Court
    doth ordr yᵗ:
willm Biles & willm Dark take Care to Enquire of places
    that
may be Convenient for them & that they do it wᵗʰ what
Expedition may be
Lawrenc Bannor haveing beene Calld into Court to give
   - an
acct of the Eſtate of the orphants of willm venables &
    he ſaith
he hath them not ready therefore the Court doth ordr that
he make Ready his accts before the next orphants Court
& bring them to the Clarke

    The Court adjorns untill the firſt 3 day of the
weeke in the 8ᵗʰ month next

        County of Bucks in the Province of Pennſilvania
At an Orphants Court held by the kings authority in the
name of willm Penn propryatory & govrnr of the
provinc & territorys thereunto belonging: for this
County att the Court houſe the 7ᵗʰ day of the   8   1685
                                  mo

        The Juſtices then prſent

     Thomas Janney   willm yardley   willm Biles
       Edmund Bennet   Willm Beakes
Edmund Bennet &c being Cald to an acct about the
    Eſtate
of the Childrn of John Spencer & do ſay that there is
as yett matters depending that the aCount Cannot as yet
be brought in therefore this Court ordrs that they bring
in theire accounts to the next Court & the time of
the Childrs freedome & of theire fathers death
    (53)

County of Bucks in the
Province of Pennſilvania
The 3d day of the   i

1684   mo

At an orphants Court held for this County the day above
    ſaid
att the Court houſe by the kings authority in the name of
willm Penn Propriatory & govrnr of the Said
Province & Territory
      The Juſtices then preſent
      James Harriſon   prident
      Willm Biles   willm Beakes   (54)
      John Otter   Edmund Bennet
         willm yardley
Jon Oter & Edmund Bennet do Say that they have not
    as yet
pfected the accts relateing to Jon Spencers orphants
    therefore
the Court ordrs that they be pfected & brought in to
    next Court
James Harriſon doth Say that he hath Spoke wth the
    orphants Con=
=cering theire willingneſs to be bound to the ſd
    Executors &
they have declared theire willingneſs to be bound untill
    the
age of 21 yeares & they are bound James Spencer to
to Jon Otter for 7 yeares & Samuel Spencer to Edmund
    Bennet
for 9 yeares but the days of theire freedome they know
    not
therefore they are ordered to give an acct thereof att or be
fore the next Court
Hannah the widow of James Hall hath this day prſented
    to the
Court her Neceſſity of releiuf her Huſband being dead
haveing left 4 Smal childrn the Eldeſt peter Hall 5
yeares of Age the 7th of the 2nd month next w[ch] Child the
    Court
together wth the Conſent of the Said wid hath placed him
    w[th]
willm Dark as an apprentice until the age of 2i yeares
& the ſd willm hath promiſed to find him meat drink
    waſhing
Lodging & Apparell during the Said terme, & to teach
    him

20th $\dfrac{8}{mo}$ 86   (55)

At A Court of Quarter Seffions held by adjornmt
    The Juftices then prfent
    James Harrifon   Thomas Janney
    willm yardley   willm Biles
        Jon Otter
    Abraham Whorley Sherrif
      P P Cl Com
This day was deld and acknowledged in
open Court one Conveyance of the moyety of
of land bearing date i4th 7 mo 1686 ———— by Abr
whorley attorney Conftitute to Antony Tomkins unto
    willm yardley
by ordr of Cha: pickring attorney conftitute by george
    martin
  This day was deld and acknowledged in open
Court one Conveyance of 230 ackers bearing
date the i8th day of 8 month 85 by N waln
to Robt Heaton attorney Conftitute by
Jedidiah Allen
  This day was deld and acknowledged in open
Court one deed of Sale & mortgage
of 500 ackers of land bearing date the 8th day of 7th mo
1686 by Abraham whearley Attorney Conftitute to Dan=
=iel Jones unto Rogr Hawkins attorney Conftitute to
Andrew Robefon
      The Court adjorned to the 8th ioth month
      next

(56) At A Court of Quarter Seffions held by the kings
authority in the name of wm Pen Propryatory
and govrnr of the Provinc of Pennfilvania
& Territory thereunto belonging at the
Court houfe for the County of Bucks the 8th
day of the ioth month being the 2nd yeare of
the Raigne of James the 2nd ovr England &c
King & the 6th of the Propryatorys govrmt
i686
      The Juftices then Prefent
      James Harrifon   Arthur Cook   Thomas Janney
      wm yardley
        Abraham whearley Sherrif
        Phinehas Pemberton Clark

Simon Roufe plt ⎤   Simon Roufe appears by
       agt   ⎬   his attorney wm Looker
wm Biles   ⎦   wm Biles deft appears

Robt Dow Summonced to be on
the Jury the Court fines him in 5 ^{s} for
his non appearance he after appearing the Court
tooke of the above fine
The Jury being attefted for tryal of the
Caufe betwixt Roufe and biles wch Jury is
as followeth
Jon: Cuff: Richard Thacher James paxfon
Samuel Burges Richard Ridgway Ed: Stanton Jr
Lawrenc Bannor Jon Cuttler Steven Sands
Richard Lundy Jon Croffdale Thomas Stakehoufe
The Declaration Read
   wm Biles anfwer read
the atteftation of Joseph frezey taken before
Samuel Dennis Juftice in Eaft Jarsey read
Jofuah Bradley attefted doth Say about the time
of the laft orphans Court here Roufe was here & wm
Biles Said that he had bought of Simon Roufe
one Negro; & was to give him for him 30 £
and that he paid him in hand 4 £ & that he had

pd more in pte i2 £ but the fd Roufe had Cheated   (57)
him & that he wold
give him 20 Skins or 20 Shillings but whether he doth not
well know & fd he wold give no more & further fth not
the plt attorney acknowledged to have Re in pte 17 £ as
   allfo 30 ^{s}

A lettr from wm biles to fd Roufe dated the 6th 2   85
   read   —————
                                                        mo
plt being Calld appeares   deft Calld appears
            after adjornmt
verdict the Jury being Calld over do Say thet they are
   agreed
& find for the plt that the declaration is true according
according to Evidence
Tho: Holme on behalf of the govrnr ⎤   plt appeares
            agt   ⎬
   Ifrael Taylor deft ═══════   ⎦   deft appeares
george glave being bound to appeare at this Court &
to be of good behavior in the meane time hath

been this day Calld & none appearing agt: him the Court
difcharges him paying his fees
John Smith being bound to appeare at this Court
    according
to recognizance appeared & the Court difcharges him
    paying
his fees.
      adjourned for one houre
i deed dated the 22 iith mo: 1685 of one moyety of A tract
    of Land
formerly
in poffeffion of Daniel Brinfon was
deld and acknowledged in open Court by Rich
Ridgway attorney Conftituted by Daniel Brinfon
unto jon wood of fd County
John Pidcock being bound to appeare at this Court
& to be of good behavior in the meane time has
been this day Calld & none appeareing agt him the
Court difcharges him paying his fees

(58) James grayham plt being Calld Henry waddy appeares
    on his behalf
gilbert wheeler deft being Calld appeares
John Cuff one of the Jury for abfenting him felf
with out the Courts leave & afore bufinefs was
ended the Court fines him in io ^{s}
The Jury attefted Edward Stanton Robt Doue Rich
    Thatcher
James paxfon Samuel Burges Rich Ridgway Lawrenc
    Bannor
Jon Cuttler Steven Sands Rich Lundy Jon Croffdale
Thomas Stakehoufe
declaration read
Anfwer read
& g w after acknowledged the debt & that he wold pay
    the monys
in any goods he had
verdict   The Jury returned & Calld over bring in theire
    verdict & fines for the plt wth 15 ^{s} damages
    & Coft of fuite
      the Court adjorns till 9 tomorrow morning
Tho Holmes plt   apeares
    agt
Ifrael Taylor   apeares

The Jury Attefted & Calld over
Declaration Read
Anfwer Read
\# Ifrael Taylor promifes to pfect al his Surveys
& make returns thereof in three months time
& that he will make Returns of wrights towne
in twoo weeks time: & that he will give an account
in ten days time of all the lands that he has furveyed or
    begun
to Survey Since he Came into office & the time when
it was furveyed

Tho Holme plt   apeares   (59)
    agt
Ifrael Taylor deft   apeares
The Jury attefted
Declarat read
Anfwer read
Tho Holmes Commiffion read dated i8th 2 mo: 1682
proved the right of Survey mony to him
Ifrael Taylors Commiffion read dated the ioth $\dfrac{7}{mo}$ 1683

proved he ought to be accountable to y^e: plt for his
    furveys
\# looke back
       The Court adjorned for one houre
Jon: Brock having made Complt: to this Court
that he is out of purfs Conciderably on the
Countys account & therefore defires to know
wch way he Shall have his monys pd him
& this Court ordrs that y^e: tax be collected wth
Expedition & he pd out of it
verdict   the Jury Calld we find that the deft hath
Surveyed land & received mony for the fame w^{ch}
doth belong to the plt:
      in the Cafe Roufe plt
        biles deft
Judgmt *it is adjudged that the debt be pd that wch
  remains unpd with 20^s damages & Coft of fuit
      *James graham plt
       wheeler deft
Judgmt—*it is adjudged that the deft pay
  the debt wth 15^s damages & Coft of fuite

*Tho: Holme plt
Iʃrael Taylor deft

(60) A petition read from Randulph Smalwood
It is ordrd by this Court That Randulph Smalwood
be releaʃed from Impriʃonmt & that he firʃt make
Satisfaction for the time he has been abʃent from from
his mr & that he Imediately give
bond to ʃatis ʃye the fine damage & Coʃt of ʃuit by
Servitude after the Expiration of his time wᵗʰ Jacob
Hall and that he give Such Security in 3 days time
& it is further ordrd that he give bond to ʃerve the govern
6 months after he hath ʃerved out his time wᵗʰ ʃatiʃfaction
of his fine with Jacob Hall & to Serve 6 months after
that wᵗʰ Ralph milner & to give his own bond
for the fee

The Court fines gilbert wheeler for his diʃturbing the
Court & Stoping the Juʃtices in the pformance of there
duty in 15ˢ

Jugmt The Court gave Judgmt yᵗ: Iʃrael Taylor Shold bring
in his accounts & yᵗ:
the monys due from the ʃd I: Taylor to ʃd Tho Holme
Shold be repayd him
by the ʃd Iʃrael Taylor

Judgmt The Court gave Judgmt that wm Biles Shold pay
Simon Rouʃe ii £ : ioˢ: 0 &
20ˢ damages as alʃo Coʃt of ʃuite

Judgmt The Court gave Judgmt that gilbert wheeler Shold
pay 5 £ : 16ˢ: 0ᵈ to James grayham
and 15ˢ damages as allʃo Coʃt of ʃuite

The Court adjorns till the 2ⁿᵈ 4ᵗʰ day of the
firʃt month next

Henry paxʃon plt ——— ——— ——— ———
 agt
Robt Cartor & Jon Cartor ʃon of the ʃd Robt Defts
in an action of treʃʃpaʃs
The Complt Entered the 23 ii mo.: 1686
Summonc granted for ʃd Robt & Jon Cartor yᵉ: 9ᵗʰ 1 86
                                                                    ‾‾‾‾
                                                                    mo

* Crossed out in original record.

(61)

At A Court of Quarter Seffions held by the kings
    authority
in the name of wm Penn Propryatory and govrnr
of the Provinc of Pennfilvania and Territorys there
unto belonging at the Court houfe for the County of
Bucks the 9ᵗʰ day of the firft month being the 3ᵈ yeare
of King James the 2ⁿᵈ his Raigne & the 7ᵗʰ of the
Propryatorys govrmt i686

      The Juftices then prefent
      James Harrifon
      Thomas Janney   Willm: yardley
      Arthur Cooke   Willm: Biles
      A whearley Sherrif
       P P Cl: Com c:
    ffrancis Hough plt appeares
    Henry paxfon plt — —   appeares
        agt
    Rob Cartor & Jon Cartor defts appeares
      The deft Craves time for want of his
          wittneffes
      wᶜʰ is allowed untill afternoone
i deed of i25 acker of Land deld in Court bearing date the
    4ᵗʰ day of the
i mo: 1686 by Robt prefmall unto Jon Baldwin
    adjorned for one hour
Henry paxfon appeares
Robt Cartor   appeares
    The Jury Attefted
The declaration Read
The anfwer Read
    wm plumley attefted doth Say Seeing the fmoak &
      fmelling
the fire went to the meadow & there found the
hay rick on fire there was Robt Cartor & his fon
Jon & Henry paxfon fd Robt What had thou done
to wᶜʰ he Sayd I have done foolifhly & Sayd
his Son had fired it

(62) Henry pawlin & wm peas attefted
H p doth Say that he was prfent when the land was
    layd out for Henry paxfon & the meadow was pte of the
      land layd
    out to Henry paxfon

w peas doth Say that he was one that was At Laying
out of Henry paxſons land & that the pt of yᵉ:
meadow owned by Henry paxſon to be his was
layd out to Henry paxſon at the firſt ſurveying
of the ſd land

Iſrael Taylor atteſted doth Say that when the ſd land
was firſt layed out the meadow
was wthin the ſd Survey

James plumley atteſted doth Say when Iſrael Taylor
had ſhewed the breadth of the land to Henry
paxſon that Henry paxſon was not willing
that Iſrael Shold make any further
Survey but Iſrael Said he wold do it to
full fill his vmore (sic) and Henry paxſon was pſwaded
to go along wᵗʰ them Some way but at laſt
the Said Henry bid him be gone & Said he diſcharged
them of his land

wm plumley Says he Cannot well tell what quantity of loads
the
hay was

Henry pawlin Said he thought it was about 5 or 6
tun & ſd he heare Robt Cartor ſay
he thought it was about as much

Rich Lundry atteſted doth Say he thinks it was about
4 tun of hay

Samuel Burges atteſted doth Say that he heard Henry
paxſon Say that Robt Cartor had offered him
Such Satiſfaction for the burning of his hay that he
thought he Shold not
put him in Suit

the Jury Returnd

verdict we find for the plt damages 5 £ wᵗʰ
Coſt of Suite

Judgmt the Court gave Judgmt & it was adjudged
the ſd Robt Cartor Shold pay the ſd Sum
of 5 £ wth Coſt of ſuite

(63)

Joſeph Hall being calld into Court for Slandering &
abuſeing
arthur Cook, Juſtice of peace Confeſſed the Same &
ſubmitted
to the benc
wherefore the Court fines him in 40ˢ

The Court adjourns thill tomorrow morning at 9 A
   Clock
deld and acknowledged in open Court one Conveyance of
160 = ackers of land dated the 27ᵗʰ day of 5 mo i686 by
wm Biles attorney Confitute by Hannah Salter to P
   Pem:
attorney Confitute by Tho LLoyd
Abra: wearley Requeft to this Court that his owne
Bond for 20 £ orpanage monys belonging to Spencers
Childrn & now in the hands of Jon Otter might be
   accepted
To wᶜʰ the Court Anfwers they will accept it and
ordrs the Clark to take the fd Bond from the fd
A whearley
Thomas Holm pap agt Ifrael Taylor read
The Court there upon ordrs that Ifrael Taylor
Shall pforme the Judgmt of the laft Court
The Court adjourns till after the Ellection
   Joseph Hall being Calld & the fine demanded he refufed
   to pay the Same or Secure it to be payd
   therefore this Court ordrs that he
   remaine A prifoner till the Said fine & fees be
   payd
      the fine & fees difcharged by wm Biles
one releafe of 150 ackers of land dated the ioᵗʰ day 1 mo
   1686
this day was Sealed and delivered by nicholas waln
unto the Juftices of this Court for the ufe of Henry
   walmsley
orphan of Tho: walmfley deceafed
in like mannor he Sealed & deld A releafe of the fame
date of 100 ackers for the ufe of Tho walmfley brother
to the fd Henry
The Court ordrs that thefe releafes be kept by
Ezra Croffdale for the ufe of the fd orphans till
further ordr from this Court

   The Court adjourns untill the 27 of the   2   nth
                                            ────
                                            mo

[Here begins a half page insert between pages 62 & 63 of the original
records]

deld and acknowledged in open Court by wm
Biles unto Charles Biles brother of wm one Indenture of
   ptition for one moiety

of A Certaine pſell of land Layd out for
472 ackers granted to the ſd wm Biles
& Charles Biles wm: bearing
date the i4ᵗʰ day of the 8 mo i686
in like mannor deld & acknowledged one Indenture
of partition for the other moiety of the ſd land
dated as above by Charles Biles unto wm
Biles Brother of the ſaid Charles
one Conveyance of yᵉ ſd wm Biles moiety of the
before mentioned tract of land bearing date
the i8th day of the 8 month i686 was by the
ſd wm Biles deld & acknowledged in open Court
to Jon Cuſſ of the ſd County

(64) At A Court held at the Court houſe
 by adjournmt the 27ᵗʰ   2   i687
                        ‾‾‾‾‾‾‾
                          mo

The Juſtices present
 A Cook   Ja: Harriſon
 wm yardley   N waln
 A whearley Sherrif
   P   P   Cl:
Commiſſion Read
  Acknowledged and delivered in open Court one
conveyance of 60 ackers of land bearing date
the 27ᵗʰ of the 2 mo: 87 by Nicholas waln
unto Jon Auſtin

The Court adjourned untill the
8ᵗʰ day of the 4ᵗʰ month next

County ſſ: Bucks
Richard Thather plt
    agt:
Samuel Abbot deft:

County ſſ: Bucks   65
At A Court of Quarter Seſſions held by the
kings authority in the name of wm Penn
Propryatory and govrnr of the Said Provinc
and Territorys thereunto belonging held
at the Court houſe the 8ᵗʰ day of the
4ᵗʰ month 1687.

The Juſtices present
A Cook   J Harriſon   wm yardley
Tho Langhorn   Jo: growdon   Nich Waln
A whearley Sherrif
P   P   Cl:

The Juſtices Commiſion Read
& the declaration by them ſubſcribed
Rich Thather plt⎫   appears
          agt   ⎬
Sam Abbot   ⎭   apears
Henry paxſon Summonced to appeare on the grand
Jury who appeared not wherefore the Court
fines him in 5ˢ This againe taken of
The grand Jury atteſted
John Rowland Robt: Heaton Jacob Hall
John white Jonathan Scaiſe Tho: adkinſon
Tho: Stakehouſe Senr: Jon: Nicholls Henry Pointr
Jon: Cuff Shadrach walley Seemercy Adams
Sam: Allen Jon: Purſley Tho: green

The Complt of Jane Coverdale agt Philip Conway
Jane Coverdall atteſted doth Say that Philip
Conway about 3 months ago: came to her bed ſide & did
    Say he had ſworn
he wold fuck her either by night or by day
& about A month after that he Came to the houſe
& ſd he had Sworn about 4 yeares he wold fuck
her & ſhe Said ſhe was ſo afraid leſt hee Shold lay

(66) violent hands on her that Shee was forced
to Calld back A youth that was newly gone out of the
houſe to Stay untill ſaid Conway was gone
Elliza Hickman Atteſted doth say that about
the going away of the laſt froſt philip Conway
Came in to the houſe of Rich Ridgway
drunk & was very abuſive & threw Severall things
into the fire & Swore ſeverall oaths 4 at
leaſt by the name of god & once Curſed the Quakers
    Elliza: Ridgway atteſted doth Say to the Same
effect

        Court adjourns for one houre

one Conveyance of one hundred ackers of land in fee
    dated
the 8ᵗʰ day i2 moᵗʰ i684 was delivered and acknowledged

in open Court by Jon: Swift unto : Henry pointer
for the tryall of Cafe between Rich Thather plt agt
    Abott deft

    The Jury Attefted John Brock Tho Rowland
walter Bridgman Jacob Janney wm Dark
Ed Lovet wm Buckman Tho woolf
Abra Cox Samuel Overton James Moone
Tho: Tunneclif

The declaration read

The Anfwer read

prfentmts brought in by the grand Jury

    The plt declareing for 16 £ & upon the
    examination of the accounts the debt appearing
    undr: 5 £ the fd thatcher not having his accts
      ready the deft Craved Anon fuite
    according to the law in that Cafe wch was
    accordingly granted by the Court
one conveyance of three hundred ackers of land in fee
dated the firft day of the 4th month i687 was delivered &
acknowledged in open Court by
John Rowland & Tho: Rowland unto gilbert wheeler
               2
one Conveyance of twoo hundered ackers of land in
fee dated the 7th day of the 4th month i687 was dld
& acknowledged in open Court by Jon green to his fon
    Tho green
Jon Rowland acknowledged in Court that on the ift day
    of the 7 month
laft paft he Rd of g wheeler 5 £ being in full of A bill
    he had
under the hand of fd wheeler & one Jon wright for the
    payment of fo much dated
the 8th of the 2 mo 1685

      The Court adjourns till tomorrow moring at 6
      A Clock

                                               67

philip Conway for his oaths & Curfe in the houfe of
    Rich Ridgway the
Court fines him in 25 ^{s}
the fd Conway behaved him felf contemptuoufly toward
    y^e: Court

& for his Contempt the Court
fines him in five pounds
for his attempting to lye wth Cloverdales
wife the Court ordrs him to give fecurity
for his good behavior & appearanc at next Court
& that he Shall pay fees of Court in all the fd
Cafes
whereupon he was commited to the Sherrifs Cuftody
untill the Said fines & fees be pd or Secured to be
payd & Security given for his Good behavior
gilbert wheeler being Calld upon his Recognizance for his
appearance this day in Court accordingly apeared
gilbert wheeler being Indicted for felling
Rum to the Indians & upon his Indictemt
he was arraigned there upon
he pleaded not gilty & for his tryall put
him felf upon the Cuntry
The Jury Attefted John Brock Tho: Rowland
walter Bridgman Jacob Janney wm Dark Edmund
Lovet wm Buckman Tho woolf Abra: Cox Samuel
overton James moone Tho Tunneclif

firft Indict   The Jury returned bring in theire verdict do fay
that gilbert wheeler is guilty of felling
Rum to the Indians on the iith day of the
2 month laft paft & fo they fay all
whereupon the Court awards Judgmt

'2nd   The bill agt g: wheeler for felling Rum to ye.
Indians the 2nd day of 2 mo returd by y^e
Jury that they find for g wheeler & fo they Say all

(68)   Philip Conway being Indicted for felling Rum to
the Indians upon his Indictemnt was arraynged
& upon his arraignent pleaded not guilty &
for his tryal put him Self upon the Cuntry
the Jury Attefted John Brock Tho: Rowland walter
Bridgman Jacob Janney wm Dark Edmund Lovet
wm Buckman Tho woolf Abraham Cox Sam overton
James moone Tho Tunneclif
returned do find for p: Conway & fo they fay all upon w^{ch}
fd Indictmt the Court difcharges paying his fees:
martha the wife of g wheeler being prsented
for fchoulding & Currying Shee being Calld g wheeler
her hufband appeared on her behalf & fubmitted to the
Court for wch the Court fines her in 5^s

Joseph Hollinſhead being prſented for Common
Swearer being calld he Submitted to the Court for wᶜʰ the
Court fines him 5ˢ

upon the prſentmt of the upper and Lower Road of
this County from the falls towards philadelphia the
Court ordrs the Said Roads be repaired before
the latter End of the 7ᵗʰ month next

Judgmt

The Court gave Judgmt & it was adjudged that
gilbert wheeler Shold pay 5 £ to the govrnr
according to the law in that Caſe made and
provided agt the Sale of ſtrong liquors to yᵉ: Indians
Be it Remembered that Philip Conway doth here in open
Court acknowledg him ſelf to ſtand indebted to the govrnrs
uſe in 40 £ to be Levyed on his lands goods & Chattells
Conditioned that the ſd Philip Conway Shall appeare at the
next Court of Quarter Seſſions to be held for the County
of Bucks & to ſtand to and abide the Judgmt of the ſd Court
& thence not to depart without Lycenc & in the meane
time to be of his good behavior towards all the kings
Subjects

The Court adjourns untill the 29ᵗʰ day of this month

County ſſ Bucks.   (69)

At A Court of Quarter Seſſions held by the kings
authority in the name of wm Penn Propryatory and
govrnr of the Province of Pennſilvania and Territorys
thereunto belonging (at the Court houſe) for the afforeſd
County the 14ᵗʰ day of the 7ᵗʰ month being the 3d yeare
of king James the SecOnd his Raigne over England &
the 7ᵗʰ of the Propryatoryatorys govrmt i687

The Juſtices then prſent

Arthur Cooke   william yardley
Thomas Langhorn   Nicholas waln

A: whearley Sherrif

Da LLoyd the kings attorney
P P Cl.

Jon Auſtin plt appears ⎫
agt   ⎬ —
Jon Clawſon appears not ⎭

The Jury Atteſted between
Jon Auſtin plt ⎫
& ⎬
Jon Clawſon deft ⎭

wm Beakes Junr plt appears ⎫
agt   ⎬ —
Tho: wood deft appears not ⎭

Jon Brearley plt appeares ⎫
agt   ⎬ —
Tho wood deft appears not ⎭

Auſtin agt Clawſon — —

Joſuah Hoops   Jon: White
Henry marjorum   Joſ: milnor
Henry Pawlin   ffrancis Roſſel
John Palmer   Sam Dark
wm Dark   Tho: Stakhouſe
Jeffery Hawkins   Rich Ridgway

witttneſeſs   Samuel wilton atteſted doth Say that Jon Clawſon
his servant & Son did enter upon the land of his
mr Jon Auſtin & did mow & Carry away graſs from
thenc about 3 weeks after corn harveſt
James Spencer atteſted doth Say that he being the
Servant of the Said Jon Clawſon was ordrd by his
ſd maſter to Cut graſs & when they had Cut it
& weare making of his Son Derrick Clawſon Came
to them in that time & Shewed them the tree
Jon Auſtin ſd was his marked tree & that they Cut ſd hay
within the ſame & ſays that
ſd hay was cut about 3 weekes after they had
* * * * *

(70)   Jon Auſtin plt appeares
vèrdict   The 14th of the 7th mo i687 we of the Jury do find for
the plt 40 ˢ wth Coſt of Suite

Jury   The Jury Between wm Beakes Junior plt & Tho wood deft
Joſuah Hoops   Jon white   Henry Margerum   Joſeph milner
Henry Pawlin
ffrancis Roſſill   Jon palmer   Sam Dark   wm: Dark   Tho
Stakehouſe Jnr
Jeffery Hawkins   Richard Ridgway
Beakes agt wood   Jury atteſted
A whearley Atteſted doth Say that upon the 4th day
of this month Tho wood acknowledged
to him he owed the ſd Beakes 9 £
Jo: Hull Atteſted doth Say that upon the 3 day
of this month Tho: wood ſd if he Cold get 6 £ wm
Beakes wold take it inſtead of 9 £
wm Morton Atteſted doth Say that laſt weeke
he ſpoke wth Tho: wood & ſd he heard he denyed
to pay wm Beakes the 9 £ he owed him wood ſd no

I never denyed it but intend to pay it but if he fue me he
  fhall get
nothing by it

verdict
Jury

The Jury Say they find for the plt wth Coft of Suit
The Jury attefted Betweene Jon Brearely plt & Tho: wood
Jofuah Hoops Jon white Henry Marjorum Jofeph milner
Henry pawlin ffrancis Roffill Jon palmer Sam Dark
wm Dark Thomas ftackhoufe Junr Jeffery Hawkins Rich:
  Ridgway
Brearley agt wood
The bill being produced in Court wm: yardley
one of the Juftices doth Say that he drew the fd bill
& is A wittnefs to it

verdict
Judgment
by default

the Jury Say they find for the plt wth Coft of fuite
in the Cafe Between J: Auftin plt & Jon: Clawfon deft
   The Court gave Judgmt that Jon Clawfon Shall pay 40 ^s
damages & Coft of Suite to Jon Auftin

Judgment

in the Cafe Between wm Beakes Junr plt & Tho: wood Deft
the Court gave Judgmt that Tho wood Shall pay 9 £ to fd
  Beakes
Junr & coft of Suite

(71)

whereas Hannah overton attefted before wm yardley that
  Tho: Tunneclif was abufive to her that fhe
was afraid of her Life & of her Childrns lifes whereupon
fd Tunneclif was ordered to appeare at this Court to give
  Security for his good behavior
Be it Remembered that Thomas Tunneclif doth
here in open Court acknowledg him felf to ftand
Indebted to the govrnrs ufe in 20 £ to be leviyed on
his lands goods & Chattles
Condition   Jofeph miller Likewife in io £
              & ffrancis Roffill Likewife io
Conditioned that the fd Tho: Tunneclif Shall
appeare att the next Court of Quarter feffions
to be held for the County of Bucks
& to be in the mean time of good behavior towards all the
  kings
Subjects
Tho: Tunneclif Imediately as he was bond abufed
the bench & Said I Care not A pin for none of
you you have abufed me & wronged me

& bid them do theire worſt
wherefore the Court adjudges that yᵉ aboveſd ſum
be pticulerly levyed on the lands goods & Chattels
of the pticular pſons & Charge of Court
The overſeers of the high way laſt yeare are
ſtill Continued becauſe they have not appeared
this day in Court

Execution   The Several plantives before memtioned Craved the Court
that they might have Execution granted them upon
the Severall Judgmts by them obtained wᶜʰ was
accordingly ordered by the Court that Execution ſhould
be granted them when they pleaſed to take it out
Philip Conway being bound laſt Court in 40 £ for his
appearance at this Court & for his good behavior in the
meane time the ſd Conway being in Cuſtody for other
miſdemeanors & being in the priſon below the Court
was very unruly in words & actions to the great diſturba=
=nce of the kings peace & to the Court in the Exerciſe
of theire dutys Curſing the Juſtices & other officers
kicking his legs againſt the door & Endeavoring to make
a disturbance

(72)   wherefore the Court ordrs that the Said 40 £ So forfeited
by him be Levyed according to his Said
Recognizance on his Lands goods & Chattles

The Court adjourns untill the ı4ᵗʰ day of the ıoᵗʰ
month next

(73)   County ſſ. Bucks At A Court of Quartr Seſſions held
by the kings authority in the name of
wm Penn Propryatory & govrnr of
the Said Provinc and Territorys thereunto belonging
held the ı4ᵗʰ day of the ıoᵗʰ month ı687 att the Court
houſe of the ſd County being the 3 yeare of King
James the 2ⁿᵈ his raigne & 7ᵗʰ yeare of the propryatorys govrmt
The Juſtices then prſent
Arthur Cook   Thomas Janney   Joſeph growden
wm: yardley & nicholas waln
A: Whearley Sherrif
P. Pemberton Cl. Com:
one conveyance of 500 ackers of land in fee
acknowledged and delivered in open Court by
Abra: whearley Conſtitute attorney to Anthony

Thompkins unto Rich Ridgway attorney to grifith
Jones dated the 22 day ⟨6 87⟩
                              mo

wm Smith ⎞   appeares   ⎞
   agt   ⎬   ⎬ The Jury attefted
Tho millard ⎠ appeares not — ⎠

Anthony Burges ⎤ this with ⎤ declaration read & the bills
      agt   ⎬   ⎬ therein mentioned and one
Luke Brindley ⎦ drawn — ⎦ letter & pettition from T millard

Richard Thatcher ⎤ appeares ⎤   declaration read referred as
       agt   ⎬   ⎬   on the other fide
Sam: Abott   ⎦ appeares ⎦

Joseph Chorley ⎤
      agt   ⎬ with drawn
mathew pugsley ⎦

Henry grub ⎤
    agt   ⎬ with drawn —— ⎫
David Lilly ⎦ Charge 5ˢ: 9ᵈ — ⎭

one conveyance of 500 ackers of land in fee acknowledged
and delivered in open Court by Robt Doue attorney
to Tho: Adkinfon, unto Jofeph kirkbride dated the
i2 day 8 mo 87

(74)

delivered and acknowledged one releafe of lands
by Richard Lundy to his father in law Thomas williams
of 200 ackers of land dated i2ᵗʰ day of 9 mo 1685
Richard Thatcher and Samuel Abbot have refted
theire action to be Ended and arbitrated by Jofeph
growdon & nicholas Waln provided they give in
theire award within twenty days after
this day for pformance whereof the fd Rich Thatcher
& Samuel Abbot do oblidge themfelves
theire Executors adminiftrators & affignefs Each
to other in the Sum of 20 £ to be pd upon defa
to yᵗ: part pforming
        adjourned for one houre
The Court gives Judgmt by default and it is adjudged that
Thomas millard Shall pay to willm Smith 3 £ : 14ˢ: 0ᵈ and iˢ
damage wᵗʰ Coft of Suite
A petition of wm black Read
ordered that J growdon to Speake wᵗʰ the magiftrates of
philadelphia to know what they have done about fd black
& what they Expected

one Conveyance of A Small tract of land from Jeffery
Hawkins in fee delivered & acknowledged by ſd Jeffery
Hawkins unto his ſon Daniel Hawkins dated the
firſt day of this Inſtant yᵉ: io^th month
   ordered that Abraham wherley & Phinehas Pemberton
do examin the accounts of wm Biles as they ſtand
between him and the County

adjourned untill the i4^th   i   next
mo

County ſſ: Bucks   75
At A Court of Quarter Seſſions held by
   the kings authority in the name of wm
   Penn Propryatory and govrnr of the Provinc of
   Pennſilvania and territorys thereunto belonging
   (at the Court houſe) for the afforeſd County the i4^th
   day of the i month being the 4th yeare of king James
   the 2nd over England &c and 7th of the propryatorys
govrmt 16\frac{87}{8}

The Juſtices then Preſent

Arthur Cook wm yardley Joſ: growdon N: waln
Abraham wharley Sherrif

P: P Cl: Com:

The grand Jury Atteſted ⎫
Iſrael Taylor bound in io £ ⎪
to the propryatory for   ⎬ appeares
his appearance here this   ⎪
day for abuſe done to   ⎪
nicho: walln Juſtice of peace ⎭
mary ſckeane bound   ⎫
to appeare at this Court ⎬ appeares
on the penalty of 20 £   ⎭
& Examined

76   Richard Thatcher plt appears ⎤ the Jury Atteſted between
               agt   ⎦
          Sam Abbot deft appeares
          Joan Huff   ⎫
              agt   ⎬ this action
          James Sutton deft ⎭ withdrawn

Jacob Hall plt ⎫ appeares not ⎫
    agt   ⎬   ⎬ this action withdrawne
Tho Tunneclif deft ⎭ appeares not ⎭

Joan Huff plt —— ⎫ this action ⎫
    agt   ⎬ defired to ⎬
Jofeph growdon deft ⎭ be forborn ⎬
                by both plt & ⎬
                deft —— ⎭

gilbert wheeler plt ⎫ appeares ⎫
    agt   ⎬   ⎬ this action withdrawn
Jofeph Chorley deft ⎭ appeares ⎭

Jofuah Ely plt ⎫ this to be ⎫
    agt   ⎬ Entered ⎬
John Brock deft ⎭ for the ⎬ at the requeft of the plt
            next ⎬
            Court ⎭

Declarat—Thatchers Declaration red ⎱ one Conveyance of 200
Anfwer—Abbots Anfwer Read   ⎰ ackers of land in fee from
                                wm Pickring to Jon penqu
                               =oit was delivered and
                               acknowledged in open
                               Court

The grand Jury Return brought in no prfentmts   (77)

The Court adjourns for on houre

Abraham Wharley Complaines to this Court agt:
Randulph Smalwood for that there is due to him for fees
2£ : io^s : 06^d upon wch the Court ordrs Execution fo be granted
agt: fd Randulph Smalwood for the fd Sum
wm: Looker petition read for requefting the monys obtained
in Roufe Cafe agt wm Biles
mary Beakes acknowledged one letter of Attorney to her
brother in law Edmund Beakes of Porif head in the County of
Summerfte in England date the i4th day of the i mo i688
Randulph Blackfhaw Complaines that he wants mony due
to him for repaireing the high ways to wch the Court anfwers
they will return anfwer next Court
mary fckeane examined and Attefted hath declared
as written on A loofe pap
Ann oxley the midwife Examined and attefted doth fay
as declared on A loofe pap

verdict   the Jurys verdict in Thatchers Cafe agt Abott
the find for the plt 5£ : i3ˢ: 0ᵈ: and io⁸ damage wᵗʰ Coft
of fuite to be payd in goods Equivalent to filver mony
or in filver
this day was deld and acknowledged in open Court one
Conveyance of 50 ackers of land in fee dated the i3
day of the   i   1688
         mo
the Sherrif Returns the Execution the goods diftraining
are overprized and therefore Cannot fell for want of buyers
In as much as the apprizers formerly Chofen have overprized
the goods taken on Execution therefore this Court appoints
and Chooes John Brock wm Paxfon & Robt Heaton to
be apprizers until further ordr Attefted
        wm Beakes acknowledged one letter of attorney
made to Thomas Cotterill of Almfberry in
the County of glofter dated i4ᵗʰ   ift   being this day
                   mo
        fteeven Beakes acknowledged one
letter of Attorney Edmund Beakes
of portif head in the County of Sum=
=merfet dated i4ᵗʰ   iˢᵗ being this day
           mo

78   ordered that whereas the Sherrif has Returned the laft
Execution in Roufes Cafe this Court ordrs that
another Execution be granted to the Sherrif for
the Anfwering the debt to fimon Roufe
The Court gave Judgmt: and it is adjudged that Samuel
Abbot Shall pay to Rich Thatcher the Sum of 5£ : 13ˢ: 00ᵈ
and io⁸ damage wᵗʰ Coft of fuit
ordered that an Execution be granted
for the Levying the abovefd
Sum
ordered that Richard Thather allow
Samuel Abbot 10ˢ for damages on the non fuite
formerly granted
        adjourned to the 13 day of the 4ᵗʰ mo next
acctt of all fines and forfeituers from the
firft holding Courts in this County untill the
i2ᵗʰ day of the 4ᵗʰ month i688 given in to
wm markham Secratary

County ſſ: Bucks   79
At A Court of Quarter Seſſions held by the kings authority
in the Name of wm Penn Propryatory and govrnr
of the afforeſd Province and Territorys thereunto
belonging at the Court houſe of the ſd County the
i3ᵗʰ day of the 4ᵗʰ month being the 4ᵗʰ yeare of
the kings Reigne & 8ᵗʰ of the Propryatorys govmt
    The Juſtices then prſent
    Arthur Cook wm yardley
    Nicholas Waln Henry Baker
    Abraham Wharley Sherrif
    wm: Croſſdale his deputy
    Phinehas Pemberton Cl: Com:

Actions Entered

Joſuah Ely ⎫
    agt ⎬ in A plea of Caſe   { both —— }
Jon Brock ⎭   { Appeared }

            declaration filed   The Jury Atteſted
            plea Read   John Swift   Henry Marjerum

Evidences ⎧ mahlon Stacy ⎫   walter Bridgman Tho: Stakehouſe, ſr.
          ⎪ John Redman ⎬ Atteſted
          ⎪ mary Staniland ⎭   Robt Heaton   Henry paxſton
          ⎨
          ⎪ Proved the declaration Tho: Stakehouſe Jr: Joſ: Clows
          ⎪
          ⎪ Joſeph milner Atteſted James paxſtone   Rich: Lundy
          ⎩ for the deft   wm Dark   James moon

adjournmt   The Court adjourned for one houre

verdict   we find for the plt Seven pounds Eleven Shillings to be
           pd by the deft with Coſt of ſuite the plt firſt makes
           the deft an aſſurance of the boy

Judgmt   The Court awards Judgmt according to verdict
           and that Execution Iſſue accordingly

deed   of three ackers of Land in fee dated the ioᵗʰ day
           of the 9ᵗʰ month i688 deld & ackd
           by Joſeph Engliſh grantor to ffrancis Roſſell

(80) Action David Evan plt ⎫   { appeares ⎫
            agt ⎬ A plea { } The Jury atteſted
        Joſeph wood deft⎭   { appeares ⎭

declaration plea Read Anſwer Read

Evidences | John Brearley, wm Beakes— attefted proved the mare when dead had Shot in her flank & green

Corn in her mouth &: the marks

of ſd mare

Ellias Nicholls attefted that Jon Wood father of ſd Joſ: Said a mare lay on his Corn & he muſt

or wold ſhoote her.

attefted | Jon Owen proved the marks of the bell about the mare that was killed

Hugh Williams proved the marks of the mare

Joſuah Elly & mary Eire attefted proved that Joſeph

wood ſhot at the flank of A horſe or mare

in the beginning of the 2nd month

Joſuah Elly Senr proved y^t: at after the report of the gun he faw he faw Joſeph with the gun on his neck

mary wood—, Sarah wood attefted proved y^t: Joſ: wood ſhot

Salt at A horſe about 9 days afore the killing of the ſd mare

verdict | the Jury return find for the plt 5 £ for the mare and 40 s damages wth Coſts of ſuite

Judgmt | the Court thereupon awards Judgmt according to law

Execution | Joſeph wood being required by the Court to ſatiſſy^e: the ſd Judgmt he refuſed the Same whereupon ye: Court Comitts him in Execution to the Sherrifs Cuſtody untill the ſd Judgmt be ſatiſſyed

Indictmt | Iſrael Taylor being Indicted laſt Court for defameing ffrancis the wife of John Swift upon his Indictment

Arainemt pleading | he was arraigned upon his arraignment pleaded not gilty and for his tryal put him ſelf on the Cuntry

The Jury attefted   (81)

Richard Ridgway   Henry Marjerum   Walter Bridgman
Tho Stakehoufe fenr   Robert Heaton fAndrew Ellet
Tho Stakehoufe Junr   Jofeph Clows   wm Dark
James Paxftone   Rich Lundy   James moone

Evidentes

John naylor Attefted doth Say that Ifrael Taylor Said he
veryly believed that nich meaning the man of John
Swift did lye wth John Swift wife and that he believed in
his Contience he did god good fervice in telling of it
John Towne attefted teftefyes as above the laft Claws
   Excepted
Andrew Dunk Attefted doth Say that he heard Ifrael Taylor
tell micheal Bucher that gabriel Shallow fd nicholas
Randulph wold lay his head upon his mrs lap until
i2 a Clock at night and then they wold go together into
the barn
mark Betrice teftifys the fame
Benjemame Jons Attefted doth Say that gabriel
Shallow Said nicholas Randulph wold fleepe with his
head in his mrs lap & Shee fleep wth her head in his lap &
that he Called John Swift Cuckoldy Rogue & that
his muftard pot wold work when he was from
home and that they wold go into the barn together
in the night

deed   of 250 ackers of land in fee dated the ift day 4th month
             1684 delivered and acknowledged by Rich Hough grantor
             to Henry marjorum grantee
             Jury Returned do Say they find him guilty
                  in mannor and form as he ftands Indicted

Judgmt   The Court awards Judgmt that Ifrael Taylor
             Shall give Security for his appearance at next
             Court and to keepe the peace in the meanetime
             and to pay al charge of Court and y^t Execution

Execution   Iffue accordingly

Recognizance memorand that Ifrael Taylor oblidges him felf in io
             and Benjemame Jons in 5 £ to the propryatory and govrnr
             to be levyed on theire lands goods and Chattles
             * * * * *

82   The accts of wm Biles the Receiver of the County tax was
     examined according to An ordr of A former Court
     by Phinehas Pemberton & Abraham wharley and were
     againe this day examined and made up in open Court
     and it appeares by the books of affeffmt ⟩   £   s   d

that the whole Tax amounted to — — ⌠ i28: 04: 05½
of wch the ſd wm Biles   ⎱   £   ˢ   ᵈ
acknowledged he had Red —⌡ 56: i9: 09
out of wch he has diſburſt
as it made appeare in
open Court by the Courts
order and otherwiſe w^ch   ⎬ 59. 06: 07
the Court allowed of
the ſum of — —

So that this Court doth
allow of the aboveſd acctt
and acknowledg that the   ⎬ 02: 06: 10
County is debtr to ſd wm
Biles the Sum of — — —

and further that it doth appeare by the
acctt now brought in by the ſd wm Biles
As may be ſeene in pticulars on
the file that there remains unpayd   ⎬ 07i: 04: 08½
of the ſd aſſeſſmt — the ſum of — — —

and whereas it doth appeare that the County is ſtill debtr
to John Brock Randulph Blackſhaw gilbert wheeler
and others this Court doth ordr y^t: the ſd wm Biles do
take the moſt expeditious way for getting of the arrears
of the ſd aſſeſſmt and paymt of the ſd debts or that if
the ptyes to whom the County is debtr will take upon them
to Collect So much as is due to them that then the ſd
wm Biles do give A Cattalogue of the names of ſo
many as are in arreare as may anſwer the ſd debt
and that A warrant be
Iſſued out from anyone Juſtice of Peace or more
to Impower the ſd pty to levy the Same by
diſtreſs and ſale on the pſons goods refuſeing to pay theire
aſſeſſmt unpd
and further the Court ordrs Henry pointer Samuel Allen
Collect the arreares of the tax betweene Neſhaminah
* * * * *

83   i3^th   4   88
          ———
          mo
A deed of 1000 ackers of land in ffee dated the i2^th day 2 mo 1688
acknowledged and delivered

by P. Pemberton attorney to Jacob Tellner grantor unto
Rich Lundy grantee

A deed of 50 ackers in fee dated the 6th day $\underline{\quad 1 \quad}$ 88 ack &
$\qquad\qquad\qquad\qquad\qquad\qquad\qquad$ mo

deld by Joſ: Engliſh grantor to arthur Cook attorney to Rich
willſon grantee

upon David LLoyd the Attorney generalls motion in relation to levying
the fines and forfeitures the Court thinks fitt to take time to deliberate
upon it and to Speake with the Commiſſioners of propryety afore
they return anſwer what Courſe muſt be taken for levying of the ſame
and do ordr that in the meane time the ſd Eſtreats above writ be
taken out of the Records of the ſd County may be Certeſyed under the
$\qquad$ Clarks
hand

This was done at the Same Inſtant

$\qquad$ The Court adjourned to the ı2th $\underline{\quad 7 \quad}$ next
$\qquad\qquad\qquad\qquad\qquad\qquad$ mo

$\qquad\qquad\qquad\qquad$ County Court ſſ Bucks $\qquad\qquad\qquad\qquad$ 84

At A Court of Quartr Seſſions held by the kings authority
in the name of wm Penn Propryatory and govrnr
of the afforeſd Province and Territorys thereunto be=
longing at the Court houſe of ſd County the ı2th day of
the 7th month being the 4th yeare of the kings reigne
and 8th of the Propryatorys govrmt ı688

$\qquad$ The Juſtices then Preſent
$\qquad$ wm yardley $\qquad$ Joſeph growdon
$\qquad$ Nicho: Waln $\qquad$ Henry Baker
$\qquad\qquad$ A wharley $\quad$ Sherrif
$\qquad\qquad\qquad$ wm Croſſdale $\quad$ deputy Sherrif
$\qquad\qquad\qquad$ P. P $\quad$ Clark

ffrancis Hough ⎫
$\qquad$ agt $\qquad$ ⎬ debt
Iſrael Taylor ⎭

deed $\qquad$ ⎧ 1 deed in fee from wm Biles
$\qquad\qquad\quad$ | grantor delivered by Rich
$\qquad\qquad\quad$ | Ridgway his attorney to
$\qquad\qquad\quad$ ⎨ Jo: Engliſh grantee for
$\qquad\qquad\quad$ | 200 ackers dated the 5th $\underline{\quad 5 \quad}$
$\qquad\qquad\qquad\qquad\qquad\qquad\qquad\quad$ mo
$\qquad\qquad\quad$ ⎩ Ellected and appointed

Conſtables for the upper pte of the river

Conſtable {
wm Beakes atteſted
for the lower Tho wms
for the midle Lotts Je: Hawkins
for yᵉ: upper pte of neſhaminah Tho ſtakehouſe Atteſted
for the other pte of Neſhaminah & thereaway
    neamiah Allen
}

overſeers
of the
highway {
over ſeers of high way Ellected for the upper pte
of neſhaminah
Robt Heaton Henry Poynter
for yᵉ: lower pte thereof Samuel Allen Junʳ
for the lower pte of the rivere wm Dungan
for the middle lotts Joſeph Kirkbride
for the upper pte of the river Joſeph milner
}

(85)

Recognizance Iſrael Taylor being bound by Recognizance none appearing
agt: him the Court diſcharges him paying his fees

ſfra Hough }
agt }
Iſrael Taylor } Att: Jon Brock app another attorney being
Appeares Joyned wᵗʰ Jon Brock and not appearing

non ſuit   Iſrael Taylor Craved A non ſuite wᶜʰ was granted
and the Court ordrd the plt to pay the Coſts

deed — {
A deed in fee of one acker of land dated ioᵗʰ $\frac{7}{mo}$ 88
from ſfra: Roſſill grantor acknowledged & delivered
to Tho Brock attorney to Joan Huff grantee
}

Corronors } { A return of the ſudden death of Rogr Scott was this
return — } { day made to this Court under the Jurys hands

Recognizance Daniel Hawkins & Robt Benſon appeared according
to Recognizance Court diſcharges them paying fees

Eſtreat.   {John oldſeild appeared not but forfeted his
{Recognizance being 5 £

Eſtreat.   {John Ruſh being Calld according to Recognizance
{appeared not therefore forfeited the ſame
being 20 £

petition { Jacob Hall not being well defired the Court to allow
          to the next adjournmt for bringing in his Complt
          agt Jon Rufh fd Rufh being Calld and not appearing

anfwer   the Court allowed of it
            The Sherrif Returned his execution levyed on the
            goods of Jon Brock i gray mare & i7 grofs buttons
Execution   at 7 £ 11 ˢ wᶜʰ the Court declared was not
            Suitable & over priced & therefore yᵉ: Court orderd that
               another
            Execution be granted & layd on such goods as
            will anfwer mony
adjournmt   adjourned to the 2 8   88
                                ─────
                                 mo

     Pennfilvania   County Court ff Bucks   (86)
          At A Court of Quarter Seffions held by adjourn mt by
          the kings Authority in the name of wm Penn propryatory
          and govrnr of the afforefd Province and territorys
          thereunto belonging at the Court houfe of the faid
          County the 2ⁿᵈ day of the 8ᵗʰ month being the 4ᵗʰ
          yeare of James the 2ⁿᵈ his Reigne over England &c—king
          and the 8ᵗʰ of the propryatorys govrmt i688
                     The Juftices then prfent
                         willm yardley   Henry Baker
                         wm Crofdale   deputy Sherrif
                         P P   Clark
          i deed of 50 ackers in fee dated the ift 8   88
                                                   ─────
                                                    mo
          delivered and acknowledged in Court by Jon
          Naylor grantor to Jon Smith grantee
          whereas John oldfeild was Calld laft Court being bound
          to appeare there and appeared not Came this day
          and appeared & alleadged that he was Sick and unable
          to Come Sooner
          * Whereas there Shold have been A tryall this day
          between Jon Swift plt & Tho millard deft & yᵉ:
          Court Cold not be held for want of Juftices they
          Submitted the Same to Reference & oblidged them
          felves in prfence of the Juftices then prfent
          Jon Swift & Tho millard for them theire heires Executrs
          & adminiftrators do oblidg them felves Each to other in yᵉ:
          penall fum of fifty pounds to Stand to & abide the award

─────────────────────────────
*[This paragraph is crossed out in the original records.]

& Judgmt of Jon: Jones Nicholas Waln wm gabitas &
& Thomas marle Indiferently Chofen between them
provided they give in theire award before the 20ᵗʰ day of yᵉ:
9ᵗʰ month next In witnefs whereof they have openly declared
the Same & hereto put theire hands   John fwift
                                             Tho: millard

adjourned to the i2ᵗʰ   io   next
                       ———
                        mo

              Pennfilvania County Court ii: Bucks   (87)
(1) At A Court of Quarter Seffions held by the kings authority
     in the name of Wm Penn Propryatory and govrnr
     of the afforefaid Province and Territorys thereunto be=
     =longing att the Court houfe of the Said County the
     i2ᵗʰ day of the ioᵗʰ month being the 4ᵗʰ yeare of yᵉ:
     Reigne of James the 2ⁿᵈ of England &c king and 8ᵗʰ
     of the propryatorys govrmt i688

                  The Juftices prfent
           wm: yardley Jofeph growdon   Henry Baker
              Jon: Brock   Nicholas Waln
                 Abraham Wharley Sherrif
                  wm Corfdale deputy Sherrif
                 Phinehas Pemberton   Cl: Com:

Comiffion: The Commiffion of Peace Read

Laws: The laws laft made Read

             The grand Jury

           ⎧ Richard Ridgway fforeman
           ⎪ Henry Paxton Jofeph miller John wood Andrew Ellet
grand Jury ⎨ Jon: Palmer Samuel Dark Jon Crofdale Henry Bircham
           ⎪ Jofeph Englifh Jon: Hough Shadrach walley wm: Buckman
           ⎩ ffrancis Roffill attefted

adjournmt   adjourned for one houre

adjournmt: ⎧The Court Calld and adjourned untill 8 in the
             ⎨morning

             ⎧ i deed in fee of 2 ackers of land dated the 6ᵗʰ day
  deed —   ⎨ of the 7ᵗʰ month 1688 delivered and acknowledged by wm
acknowledged ⎬ Crofdale (attorney to James Swafer grantor) unto
             ⎩ James Croffley for the ufe and upon the requeft made
     of Richard willfon grantee

88

deed ack :   ⎫ one deed in fee of 125 ackers dated the i3 : $\frac{io}{mo}$ i688 acknow

:nowledged ⎰ ledged and delivered by James Hill grantor to James
Moone for the ufe of him Self and his fon James moone
grantees

Inditmt   Bucks ff :   i2ᵗʰ $\frac{io}{mo}$ i688

(1) The Jurrors for the propryatory and govrnr by yᵉ :
kings authority do prfent A Run away negro who Says he
Coms from verginia and Calls him Self by the name of
george for that he upon the i7ᵗʰ day of the 9ᵗʰ month laft
paft did Steale and fraudelently take and Carry away twoo
turkeys worth 6 ˢ being the goods of Tho : Janney Senʳ
Conterary to the kings peace and agt the law in that
Cafe made and provided

profecutr   peter worral pfecutr

witneffes   ⎰ Tho Janney Junior ⎱
                           ⎱ Jofeph Hollinfhead ⎰   wittneffes Attefted

A true bill   This bill found by the grand Jury

arrignmt   upon wᶜʰ Bill the fd negro was Arraigned

pleading   And he pleaded guilty

Inditmt   Bucks ff :   i2ᵗʰ $\frac{io}{mo}$ i688

The Jurrors for the propryatory and govrnr

(2) by the kings Authority do prfent A Run away negro who
Says he Come from verginia and Calls him Self by the name of
george for that he about the
beginning of the 8ᵗʰ month laft paft did fteale and fraudulent
=ly take and Carry away 1 ax 1 Skellet Corn peafe —
Stockings and other goods to the value of twenty five
Shillings being the goods of Thomas Rogers Conterery to yᵉ :
kings peace and agt the law in yᵗ : Cafe made & provided

profecutr   Tho Rowland profecutr

witneffes   ⎰ Tho Rogers — ⎱
                      ⎱ Samuel Hough ⎰   wittneffes Attefted

A true bill   This bill found by the grand Jury

arrinmtt　　　upon wch Bill the íd negro was arraigned

pleading　　　{and upon his arraignemt pleaded guilty of takeing
　　　　　　　{all the afforeíd goods Save half A buíhell of peaíe

89

Bucks íí　　　The i2th　io　i688
　　　　　　　　　　　　　　mo

Indictmt　　　The Jurrors for the propryatory and govrnr by the kings
　　　　　　　authority príent A Runn a way negro who says he Comes from
　　　　　　　virginia and Calls him íelf by y^e: name of George for y^t he
　　(3)　　　upon or about y^e: beginning of the 8th month laít paít did
　　　　　　　Steale and fraudelently take and Carry away one Cloath Coate
　　　　　　　one leather Coate twoe Shirts; one íuítian waít Coate
　　　　　　　one hat one Silk neckcloth to the value of five pounds
　　　　　　　being the goods of Rogr Hawkins Conterary to the
　　　　　　　Publique Peace & agt the law in y^t: Caíe made & Provided

Proíecutr　　　　　　　Roger Hawkins　Proíecutor

witneííes　　　　　　{ Joíeph Hollinshead }
　　　　　　　　　　{　Samuel Hough　}　wittnesses atteíted

A true bill　　This bill found by the grand Jury
arrignemt　　upon wch Bill the Said negro was arraigned
pleading　　　And upon his Arraignemt pleaded guilty

Indictmt　　　Bucks íí: The Jurors for ye Propryatory & governor by y^e
　　　　　　　Kings authority doe present y^t John Collins of the County
　　(4)　　　affore Said Huíbandman on the twenty Seventh day of the
　　　　　　　eighth month laít paít did by Violent aííault & fforce
　　　　　　　Robb and take away from the períon of gilbert wheeler
　　　　　　　upon the Kings high way & Road within the íd County
　　　　　　　one mare and other goods to the value of tenn pounds
　　　　　　　being the prop goods of gilbert Wheeler afforeíd Conterary
　　　　　　　to the publique peace and agt the law in Such Caíe
　　　　　　　made and Provided

Proíecutr　　　　　　　Joíeph Wood Proíecutor

　　　　　　　　　　gilbert wheeler
　　　　　　　　　(John martin 　)
　　　　　　　　　| Jacob Hall 　　|
witneííes　　　　{ Edward Cartor }　witneííes atteíted
　　　　　　　　　| Joan Huff 　　　|
　　　　　　　　　| Daniel Beakes 　|
　　　　　　　　　(Ellenor Beakes)

A true Bill   this bill return found
arrainemt   upon wch Bill the Said Collins was arrained
pleading   and upon his arrainemt pleaded not guilty
requeſt   but craved A few houres time of the Court to give in what he had
Anſwer   further to Say in anſwer wch was granted by the Court

90

grand Jurys }   The i2^th io^th mo: i688
  prſentmt }   we the grand Jury do Preſent it needfull that A Suffitiont
            Cart Roade Shall be layd out from the upper plantations
            above the falls unto the fferry houſe where the Common
            landing is over agt Burlington
                       Richard Ridgway fforeman

Action }   gilbert Wheeler agt Luk Brindley in A plea of debt
wheeler
  agt
Brindley }   gilbert Wheeler appeared

non appearance   Luke Brindley appeared not

Sherrifs } { wm Croſſdale deputy Sherrif made Return that he had given
                 him lawfull
Return } { Summonce
Declarat   Pennſilvania County Court ſſ: Bucks

         gilbert wheeler }
              agt   }   &c: Read
         Luk Brindley }

Bond   and the bond therein mentioned proved by the Evidence
Evidences   of wm Biles atteſted the other wittneſs to the ſd bond being
            Robt Jeffs deceaſed proved by the writeing
            The penal Sum of the bond and the Sum declared for

           { being 31 £ & the real debt being but i5 £ i2^s the Juſtices
Queſtion { on the bench aſked of ſd gilbert wheeler whether
           { he Expected Judgment for any more y^n: the reale debt

           { To wch ſd g wheeler made Anſwer he Expected Judgmt
Anſwer { for no more then i5 £ i2^s with Coſt of ſuite

Judgmt }   Whereupon the Court gave Judgment by default &
by default }   it was adjudged that Luke Brindley Shold pay to
           gilbert wheeler the Sum of i5 £ : i2^s with Coſt of ſuite and that

Execution	Execution Shold Iſſue accordingly

Compt about ye tax	wm Biles Receiver of the County tax made Complt to this Court that there was A greate deale of the County tax yet unpd & in Arreare and yᵗ: he Cold not levy the Same without a warrant

Courts ordr	Chattles of the party refuſeing to pay his Share of ſd tax unpd to the afforeſd wm Biles by twoo Juſtices of Peace for Levying the ſd tax in Arreare & unpd on the goods & Whereupon this Court ordrs that A warrant be granted

91

(2)	County Court ſi Bucks

A pattent & Aſſignmt thereon acknowld & delivered	A pattent of 296 ackers of land to Edward Luff dated the 30ᵗʰ 3 1688 with an aſſignment of the ſd pattent & mo grant of the ſd Land therein mentioned on the back ſide of the ſd patent in fee dated the 4ᵗʰ day of the 4ᵗʰ month 1688 was delivered and acknowledged by Tho: Lambert Attorney to Edward Luff grantor unto Henry marjorum granted

deed acknowledged	A deed in ffee dated the tenth day of the 10ᵗʰ month 1688 delivered & acknowledged by Joſeph Engliſh grantor to wm Biles grantee being for 162 acres of land

action	Edward Hancock agt Tho Revel in A plea of debt both upon Call appeared and the deft declaring yᵗ: he was but yᵗ day arreſted to appeare to the ſd action wᶜʰ appeared to be true by the Sherrifs return yᵉ: action was deferred by Conſent of both partyes untill the next Court the ſd Tho Revel giveing bond

deffered to next Court uppon baile	with Suffitiont Suertyes to appeare at the next Court

Action	Tho: millard agt S: Burdon in A plea of Debt
appearance	both calld appeared
Declaration	Tho millard agt Samuel Burdon read

Aníwer   The deft Saith he hath pformed the award & ows
              nothing and of this he puts him Self upon the
              {Cuntry for A tryal
Iſſue Joyned {& the ſd plt in like mannor

              {Therefore the Sherrif is Commanded to return A Jury
Jury return   {of twelve more &c:

The Jury   The Jury Atteſted
                        Tho Rowland fforeman
              Ezra Croſdale   Henry marjorum   James Paxſtone
              Steephen Sands   Peter Worral   Wm Clows
              James moone   John Towne   John Penquoit
              Richard Lundy   wm Dark

92

declarat
articles   The articles Read & acknowledged by the deft

bond   The bond Read & acknowledged by the deft

award   The award Read & acknowledged by the deft

Jon ffleckney {The Atteſtation of John ffleckney of Burlington
   evidenc   {taken before James marſhall Juſtice for yᵉ ſd place read

              ⌐Anthony Burton Atteſted Saith he was with John ffleckney
              | on Burdons Iſland when he went to veiue the work
Ant: Burtoɩ { and yᵗ: he Saw Tho millard had not ſtuff to work on for
              | the firſt mill being the mill Contracted for and mentioned
              ⌐in the afforeſd articles and award & further faith not

              ⌐Thomas Terry Atteſted Saith he wrought at the mill and
Tho: Terry   { to his knowledge Thomas millard wanted plank to work
              ⌐on and further Saith not

              ⌐ffrancis Roſſill Atteſted Saith that he veiued the work
ffra: Roſſil { when ffleckney and Burton aforeſd did & he Saw no
              ⌐timber to work upon for the firſt mill as aforeſaid

              ⌐John ffurnas Atteſted for the defet Saith that he
              | wrought for Samuel Burdon att the ſame time and
              | Some time before and he never heard Tho millard
Jon ffurnas { aſk for or Complaine for want of ſtuff to work on and
              | ffurther Saith that ffrancis Roſſill when he Came to
              | veiue the work was Drunk So that he reeled too
              ⌐and fro in the path and fell down to the grownd

Edward
Lancaſter

Edward Lancaſter atteſted for the deft Saith he
wrought with Samuel Burdon from the 4th month
laſt paſt and was often in work with Thomas millard
and that he knew not that Tho millard did want
Stuff to work on but for the moſt part found him ſelf
work about the mill agreed on according to the articles
Except it was at the latter End of the work

The Jury went forth

adjournment

The Court adjourned for one houre

93

deed
acknowled

one deed in ffee of two hundered and three ackers of land dated
the ioth day of the 8th month 1688 was acknowledged and
delivered by Samuel Dark attorney of Lyonel Brittan
grantor unto Stephen Beakes grantee

Judmt
on the
(1)
Indictmt

The Court gave Judgmt upon the firſt Indict agt george
the negro for Stealeing the turkes they not being
reſtored it was adjudged that he Shold pay by Servitude
as the Court hereafter Shold order unto Thomas —
Janney ſenr aforeſd to the value of i8ˢ and Charge
of Court and be whipt for the Said offence Elleven
Stripes on his bare back

on
Indictmt
(2)

The Court gave Judgmt upon the Second Indictmt agt george
the negro for Stealing og goods from Thomas Rogrs
pte of the goods being reſtored it was adjudged that
he Shold pay by Servitude as the Court hereafter —
Shold order unto Thomas Rogers afforeſd to the value
of 48ˢ and Charge of Court and be whipt ii Stripes
on his bare back

on
Indictmt
(3)

The Court gave Judgmt upon the third Indictmt agt
george the Negro for Stealing the goods of Roger Hawkins
the goods being reſtored it was adjudged that he
Shold pay by Servitude as the Court hereafter Shold
order unto Roger Hawkins afforeſd to the value
of 50ˢ and Charge of Court the ſd Hawkins deſiring
from the Court no further Satiſfaction Save that he be whipt
on his bare back i9 Stripes

ordr
Commitmt:

ordered that he be once whipt in the Sight of the Court
untill A Conveniant place of ſervitude be found for
him the Court Committs him to the Sherrifs Cuſtody

Recognizance discharge	paterick kelly being Called according to recognizance none appearing agt him the Court difcharged him paying his fees

Commitmt	Richard Thatcher Junior for abufeing the Juftices on the bench the Court Committed into Cuftody untill the next morning

adjournmt	The Court adjourned untill 8 A Clock next morning

(94)

Attion	Tho millard agt Sa Burden
Jury	The Jury Returned
verdict	we find for the plantif according to evidence
requeft	The deft Samuel Burden Craved an appeale to the provincial Court in Equity
Judgmt	The Court gave Judgmt and it was adjudged that Samuel Burden Shold pay to Thomas millard the Sum of twoo hundered pounds
requeft for an appeale Bond offered	The deft Samuel Burden Craved an apeale to ye: next provin==cial Court in Equity and tendered his own bond for 400 £ to pay all Cofts of the fd Court & of this Court occationed by the afforefd action and to pfecute the fd — appeale with effort
bond accepted appeale granted	wch fd bond was accepted by the Court & Liberty of an appeale granted to the fd Sa: Burden deft to the next provincial Court in Equity
Indictmt (4) requeft	John Collins upon the Indictmt affrefd returned into Court and Confeft he had affaulted gilbert wheeler on the high Road but not with any Intent to Robb him gilbert Wheeler Craved the Court to forbeare any further proceedure agft: the Sd Jon Collins for that the Said Collins had made him full Satiffaction for any wrong or Injury he had done to him
fees promifed	and fd Wheeler promifed to pay all fees due on the fd Indictmt:
order on the prfentmt of the want of A Road	upon the grand Jurys prfentmt of the Want of A Roade from the upper plantations above the falls of Delaware to the landing agt Burlington the Court orders —— Henry Baker John Brock wm yardley Jof: miller Richard Hough John Rowland Jofeph Englifh and

Abraham Cocks to lay out the Said Road and give an
acctt there of to the next Court:

Richard Thatcher Junior afforeſaid for Inſulting the Juſtices
fine   upon the bench and giving them abuſive words the Court
Commitmt   fines him 50ˢ and Committs him to the Sherrifs Cuſtody
untill he Shall find Suertyes for his good behavior & his
appearance at the next Court
adjournmt   adjourned untill the 3 day of the firſt month next

95

County ſſ: Bucks
At a Court of Quarter Seſſions held the
i3 day 4ᵗʰ mo 88
               ―――
                9   Juſtices   Wm Biles
Commiſſion Read   Henry Baker   Jon Brock
Conſtables ellected
Joſeph Chorley for below the falls to the govrnrs
peter worrall for above the falls
adjourned untill the 27ᵗʰ Inſtant

Pennſilvania   96
County Court Bucks ſſ:

At A Court of Quarter Seſſions held by the kings autho=
=rity in the name of Wm Penn Propryatory &
govrnr of the afforeſd Province & territorys
thereunto belonging held by adjournmt the
27 day of the firſt month being the 5ᵗʰ yeare
of the kings Reigne & 9ᵗʰ of the proprya=
=torys govrmt 1689
The Juſtices prſent
Joſeph growdon   Wm Biles   Henry Baker
Nicholas Waln   John Brock
Wm: Beakes ˙ Sherrif
Phinehas Pembeton Cl:

Commiſſion   Read
engagemt   Signed Wm Biles Henry Baker John Brock the reſt haveing
                   Signed it   formerly

action   Randulph Blackſhaw agt Charles Pickring in a plea of Caſe
            Blackſhaw deſired the Court that the action might at
            prſent be ſtayed untill another Court becauſe he had

not his Wittneſſes in Readineſs one of them being gone out of the province

A deed   in fee from Jo: growdon grantor to ſte newel grantee of 202 acres
             dated the i2th day i2th mo 1688

A deed   in fee dated the i2th $\frac{i2}{mo}$ 1688 for 102 ackers
             acknowledged & delivered by Jo: growdon grantor to Abel Hinkſton grantee

A deed   in fee for 102 acres dated the i2th $\frac{i2}{mo}$ 1688 ack by
             Jo: growdon grantor to Abel Hinkſonte attorney to Wm Reale grantee

A deed   in fee for 102 acres dated ioth $\frac{i2}{mo}$ 1688 ack & dld
             by Jo: growdon grantor to Stephen newel Attorney wm Reale grantee

A deed   in fee for 40 acres dated ioth $\frac{i2}{mo}$ 1688 ack & dld
             by Joſeph growdon grantor to Abel Hinkſtone attorney to Tho ffox & Joſeph willſford grantees

(97)

A deed   of 100 acres of land in fee dated the 23 day $\frac{i2}{mo}$ 1688
             de & ack by Wm Hayhurſt grantr to Henry Hudleſton grantee

Recognizanc Richard Thatcher being Calld appeared the Court diſcharged him paying his fees

ye negro   george being brought into this Court to anſwer the Several Judgmts of the laſt Court that was then adjudged to be payd by Servitude

Recognizance Richard Ridgway engaging by bond for the appearance of george the negro hath accordingly
diſcharge   brought him into this Court
Commitmt   Whereupon this Court Commits the ſd george negro in execution
             to the Sherriſs Cuſtody untill further order

non ſuite   Action Randulph Blackſhaw agt: Charles Pickring
pickring deſt appeared according to Summonce
& Craved a non ſuite the ſd Blackſhaw haveing
declared that he was not in readines to pſecute
his action the Court granted him A non ſuite on
the ſd action

Recognizance Hugh march being bond in 20 £ for the appeara
nce of Job Houle the ſd Houle being Calld appeard
Jon Swift & philip Conway being Calld declared they
had no thing at prſent to object wherefore the Court
diſcharge   diſcharged the ſd Houle

Recognizance Tho millard being bound in 30 £ & ffarncis Roſſill
in 15 £ for the appearance of Tho: millard at this
Court the ſd millard being Calld appeared & Samuel
Burden declared he had nothing at this time to object
diſcharge   Wherefore the Court diſcharged him

Recognizance Charles Brigham being bound as by the
Information of Joſ: growdon & Arthur Cook Juſtices
being Calld appeared & more Complaints Coming
agt: him the Court ordered him to give Security to

Commitmt   appeare at the next Court Wᶜʰ he the ſd Charles —
refuſed whereupon this Court Commits him to yᵉ:
Sherriſs Cuſtody untill he give Security as above

                                                 (98)

     of Sale & mortgage of of 2 Iſlands in this County agt
         Burlington
A deed   Called kips Iſland & A little Iſland northward of the ſame
dated the 6ᵗʰ day i mo: $\frac{1688}{9}$ acknowledged &

ded by nicholas Waln attorney to Samuel
Burdon grantor to Arthur Cooke Subſtitute attorney of Sam:
         Carpentr to Joſe
Burden grantee

A deed   of 100 acres of land in fee dated the ioᵗʰ
day of the i mo: 1688 ack & ded by Tho: Rowland
grantor to philip conway grantee

A deed   of 100 acres of land in fee dated the iſt $\frac{4}{mo}$ 88 ack &
ded by wm Dungan grantor to Arthur Cook grantee

Recognizance Edward Cartor & Tho: Brock oblidged themſelves
in 40 £ to the propryatory for the appearance of
John Allen at this Court who appeared accordingly
& nothing objected agt: him whereupon the Court
disſcharge   diſcharges him

ordered by this Court that george the negro be deliverd
from his Impriſonmt to Stephen Newel wᶜʰ
Said negro is by this Court adjudged to ſerve
the ſd Stephen Newel or his aſſignes fiveteen yeares and at
the end of fiveteen yeares to be returned
to the maſter of the ſd negro or aſſignes if he the ſd
maſter or aſſignes make demand of him in Concd
eration whereof the Said Stephen
Newel is to pay il £ 4ˢ to anſwer
the ſeveral Judgmts of Court

Stephen Newel & Joſeph growdon both
declared & promiſed that they wold pay the Said ii £ : 4ˢ
to anſwer the Judgements of Court in Cuntry
produce at Currant price the pay
to be delivered at philadelphia at or
before the latter end of the third month

99

next to Such perſon or perſons as Shall be appointed
by this Court to Receive the Same for payment of
wᶜʰ Said mony the Said Stephen Newel & Joſeph
growdon in open Court oblidged them ſelves theirè
executors & adminiſtrators

arbitration ⎫
not   ⎬
Concluded ⎭

Thomas millard & Sam Burden appeared in
Court declared that they had agreed to put yᵉ:
matters of difference between them to arbitration
but the ſd partyes not agreeing on the pſons to
arbitrate it Entered into no engagemt before
this Court

adjourned   to the i2ᵗʰ day of the 4   i689
                                        ——
                                         mo

100

Penſilvania
County Court Bucks ſs:

At A Court of Quarter Seſſions held by the kings authority

in the name of Wm: Penn Propryatory
& govrnr of the afforeſd province & territorys
thereunto belonging the ii[th] day of the 7th
month i689 being the 9th yeare of the
propryatorys govrmt

The Juſtices prſent

wm: Biles   Henry Baker
John Brock   Nicholas Waln
Wm Beakes Sherrif
Phinehas Pemberton   Cl: Com:

Actions

		Recognizances
Mary Beakes — agt: Tho: Coverdale	in a plea of debt——— with drawn by ordr of wm Beakes	Philip Conway Come forth & Save thee & thy baile elſe thou forf thiy recognizance
John Swift agt: Philip Conway	in a plea of Caſe —	wm Roles bring forth p: C: Ells thou for feiteſt thy recognizance
Tho: Revel agt: Junr Richard Thatcher & Iſrael Taylor —	in a plea of aſſault & treſpaſs —	H: march bring forth p C: John Swift Come forth & pſecute the peace agt: p: C: or ells he Shall be diſcharged
Richard Ridgway agt: John Heeſem —	in a plea of Caſe with drawn by ordr of Richard Ridgway	Jon: Swift Come forth & Save thee wm Roles bring forth J: S:

101

A deed   of 125 acres in fee dated the io[th] day of the i2[th] mo
i688 was acknowledged & delivered by Henry
paxſon grantor to wm plumley grantee

A deed   of ioo acres of land in fee dated the io[th] day of
the i2[th] month i688 was acknowledged & deld
by wm plumley grantor to Henry paxſon grantee

A deed   of 310 acres of land in fee dated the 8 day
of the 7th month i689 was acknowledged
& delivered by Richard Noble grantor
to moſes maſley grantee

A deed   of mortgage for 310 acres in fee dated the
9th day of the 7th month i689 was acknowledged
& delivered by moſes maſley grantor to
Richard Noble grantee

A deed   of a tract of land about one hundred acres
in fee dated the tenth day of the 7th month
i689 was acknowledged & deld by Tho:
Coverdale grantor to Henry Siddall grantee

             Conſtables appointed for the Succeeding yeare

Conſtables   for the upper part of the River peter worrall
for the Lower part near the falls of the River Joſeph Chorley
     atteſted
for the Lower part of the river Tho: greene
for the middle Lotts John Rowland atteſted
for the upper pte of Neſhaminah James Paxſson atteſted
for the Lower pte of Neſhaminah John white

action   The action between Jon Swift plt & philip
Conway deft declaration & anſwer read the
plt was pleaſed to deſire the Court that ye: ſd
Conway might purg him ſelf by his atteſtation
wch was Condecended to the deft

philip Conway atteſted declared that he had
Said he knew who killed the Colt of John Swift
but upon his atteſtation declared that he knew
nothing neither directly nor Indirectly of of the

kiling of the ſd Colt neither did he ever
of his owne knowledge know that Jon
Swift had any Colt killd

102

action   Jon Swift   plt appeared
philip Conway   deft appeared
Jury   atteſted

       declaration read

     Anſwer Read

Edmund more attefted doth Say that about Chrismas laft paft
ph: Conway Said

evidence

to Jon Swift that he wold have the man y^t the killd his Colt to
come & work out the price of the Colt with him but if he
pleafe to accept of 50^s in recompence for the Colt
the fd Conway wold give him a bill undr his
hand for the paymt of fo much if there was a
pen & ink in his houfe & further Saith that he

the fd Conway Said he was prent at the killing of the fd Colt

evidence

Job Houle attefted doth Say that that philip Conway told
him he was prfent by when the Colt was Shot & y^t:
when Jon Swift was at his houfe he had offered
40 or 50^s for the fd Colt if he y^e: fd Jon Swift wold Say no
more
of it & that young mark Betrice killd the fd Colt

evidence

philip parker attefted doth Say that philip Conway fd he
was prfent when young mark Betrice killed Jon fwift
Colt & y^t: the fd Colt gave 2 or 3 Jumps & then
feldown dead

Tho Coverdale defire an witnes Concering a will
made by Daniel Hawkins to be examined it haveing
Relation to a trect of land left to fd Coverdale by fd
Hawkins & the fd land by fd Coverdale this day
conveyed to Henry Siddall to wch the Court heard the fd
evidence being Jon Clement Attefted doth Say that
Saw the fd will bearing dated the 30th of the

103

io^th month 1688

Sealed & delivered by fd Hawkins & further Saith that the
fd Hawkins did give his land to fd Coverdale
& his heires forever

The Court adjourns forone houre

negro

The Court ordrs that Richard Rigway or
his affignefs do Re the money due from
Jos: growdon & Stephen Ncwel upon y^e:
acctt of the negro & that y^e: fd Richard Ridg
have an ordr Signed by Some one Juftice
for to Impower him to rece the Same Richard Ridgway
haveing this
day in open Court promifed to Anfwer all

the Charges that has beene out upon him the negro
& allowed by the Court

ordered   that a requeſt be drawn to the govrnr
that Regiſter may be appointed in this
County for the probat of wills that people
be not put to yᵉ: Extrordinary Charge
of going to philadelphia

A deed   of 50 acres of land in fee dated the firſt
day of the 7ᵗʰ mo: i689 by Rich
Willſon grantor to Jon gibbs grantee

A deed   of about 90 acres in fee dated the 8ᵗʰ day
of the 4ᵗʰ month 1688 by Luke Brindley
grantor to peter worral grantee
    Iſaac Burges being Calld & none appeareing agt: him yᵉ:
Court diſcharges him paying his fees

Jury   returned Calld over do Say they are not agreed
were returned back againe

104

        The grand Jury atteſted
petit Jury   return againe not agreed
        whereupon the Court return them back

Recognizance   John Swift being Calld upon his recognizance
appeared & the Court diſcharged him none appeare
ing agt him

Recognizance philip Conway being bound to good behavior
& appearance at this Court accordingly & none
appeareing agt him the Court diſcharged him
paying his fees

        Jon Swift agt: Philip Conway

        Jury Returned to find for the deft & so they Say all

        The Court adjourns untill 8 a Clock
        to morrow morning

action   Tho: Revel
           agt   plt appeared &
    Rich Thatcher junir }treſpaſs & aſſault
        &   Iſrael Taylor appd
    Iſrael Taylor

declarat read

Aníwer read

Iííue Joyned

Jury return

Jury   Calld over &
            declaration & ⎱
            Aníwer againe read ⎰

evidenc   ⎰ grace Langhorn
         ⎱ Thomas preiítcorin ⎤
          Richard Thatcher Senior ⎬ atteíted
          Benjemaine Jons ⎦
          Ezra Croaídell —— ——

     105

grand Jury return brought in the bill agt Rich Thatcher
Ignoramus
& at Same time priented íd Thatcher for bringing a
dead hogg to the houíe of Iírael Taylor on the firít
day of the weeke

,overíees   ⎰ over íeeres of the high ways for the íucceding yeare
             for the upper pte of Neíhaminah Henry paxíon
of ye: and
             for the Lower pte of Neíhaminah Henry Bircham
high ways   for the other íide of Neíhaminah Tho: Hardin
             for the Lower pte of the river John Cooke
             middle Lotts Randulph Black íhaw
             for the upper pte of the River
             wm: Clows

action   Jon Swift agt philip Conway

Judgmt   The Court gave Judgment and it was adjudged that
             John Swift Shall pay Coít of Court

Judgmt   the Court gives Judgmt & it is adjudged yᵗ:
             philip Conway for the lye he told in Jon Swifts
             Caíe whereoí he was Convicted by his owne
             Confeííion before this Court that he Shall pay
Eítreat   2ˢ 6ᵈ

grand Jury againe brought in príentmts about the roads in
     this County

ordered   that the overſeeres of the high Roads do take Care
to repair the ways & bridges by the grand Jury
prſented

106

action   Tho: Revel ——— ———
                agt:
        Richard Thacher Junr
        & Iſrael Talor ———

Jury   return & Calld over
verdict   =find for the plt 30 ˢ damages with Coſt of ſuit
Iſrael Taylor abuſed the Jury but
upon his Submiſſion & acknowledgmt of
his fault the Jury deſired the Court to paſſe it by

Recognizance Richard Thatcher Junior being Calld appeared according
             Recognizance
             Richard Thatcher Junior for his Contempt to yᵉ: Court
             and abuſes done to yᵉ Tho: Revel. & for ſuſpition
             of takeing a hogg that was none of his owne
             the Court Commits him into the Sherriffs Cuſtody untill
             he find Suffitient Suertyes for his appearance at the next
             Court & for his good behavior in the meane
             time

Commitmt   Charles Brigham being Calld & none appeareing agt him
the Court diſcharges him paying fees

A deed   of fifty acres of land in fee dated the io day of yᵉ:.
7ᵗʰ month 1689 acknowledged & delivered by
Nicholas Waln grantor to wm Hayhurſt grantee

             The Court gave Judgmt in Revells Caſe agt
Judgmt   {Rich Thatcher Junr & Iſrael Taylor & it is adjudged
           {that the ſd Thatcher & Taylor Shall pay 30 ˢ —
             damage wᵗʰ Coſt of Suite according to verdict &
             that execution Iſſue accordingly
               adjourned to the iiᵗʰ io   89 next
                         mo

Bucks ſs: 107

             At a Court of Quarter Seſsions held by
             the authority of king William & Queen mary
             in the name of William Penn propryatory &

govrnr of the afforefaid Province and —
Territorys thereunto belonging At the
Court houfe for the Said County the ii[th] day
of the io[th] month being the 9th yeare of
the propryatorys govrmt i689

The Juftices then prfent
Jofeph Growdon
William Biles   Henry Baker
John Brock   Nicholas Walln
William Beakes Sherrif
Phinehas Pemberton Cl: Com:

The Juftices being met for Several reafons thought
it not Convenient to Sit there being no actions to
try therefore the Court was not opened

Bucks ff: 108

At a Court of Quarter Seffions held by the
kings and Queens authority in the name of
Willm Penn propryatory & govrnr of the
afforefaid province & territorys thereunto
belonging at the Court houfe for the faid
County the i2 day of the firft month being
the io[th] yeare of the propryatorys govrmt
i689

Juftices prfent
Jofeph growdon   wm Biles
wm yardley   Henry Baker
Nicholas Waln   John Brock
wm Beakes Sherrif

John Shippey ⎫
    agt   ⎬ plea of Cafe
Ifrael Taylor ⎭

P Pemberton Cl: Com:
grand Jury Attefted

Jofeph growdon ⎫
    agt   ⎬ plea of Cafe ⎫
Tho Hutchins— ⎭ demurred   ⎭

Tho: Coverdale for Comeing
in Court before the bench
drunk the Court fines him in
five Shillings

Tho: Revel ⎫
    agt: ⎬ plea of debt
Ifrcal Taylor ⎭

Arthur Cooke ⎫
    agt   ⎬ plea of Cafe ⎫
Jofeph Crofs ⎭ with drawn— ⎭

paterick Conway & philip Conway
being Calld into Court & fecurity
being required of them to anfwer

gilbert wheeler ⎫
     agt ⎬ plea of Cafe ⎫
Luke Brindley ⎭ with drawn ⎬

the feveral Compts objected agt:
them & wch they refufeing the
Court Commits them into the fherrifs
    Cuftody till
further order

gilbert wheeler ⎫
     agt ⎬ plea of Cafe ⎫
John pidcock ⎭ demurred ⎬

A deed of 200 acres of land in fee dated the 24 day of the $\frac{3}{mo}$ 89

was acknowledged & deld by Sam Burges & Rud: Black fhaw
    grantors to Rich
Lundy grantee

A deed of ioo acres of land in fee dated the io day of the
12 mo: 1688 ack & dld by Jofeph growdon grantor to
Claws Jonfon grantee

109

Complt made by Derick Clawfon that formerly he delivered to
    Arthur Cook & James Harrifon 3 wolves two of them
    bitches & one dog & that he hath but Red in part of
    the fame 7ˢ the Court being Satiffyed of the truth
    thereof by Arthur Cooke orders that He be pd
    what remaines due to him out of the firft mony
    that Comes to the receivors of the publique ftock

notice from John Blackwell not to pay Quit rents to any but
    Robt Turner or his fubftitutes Read

adjourned for one houre

A deed of Some land for a mill pond in fee dated the 20 day
    of the 9th mo 89 ack & dd by Wm Beakes attorney
    to Jon otter grantor to ffra Roffill grantee

Conftables nominated & appointed for the lower pte of the
    fettlemts between nefhaminah & poquefin Samuel
    Allen Junior for the upper pte John purflone attefted

Eftreat wm Clows & Tho kirl being fummonced to appeare
    on the Jury & not appearing the Sherrif being attefted
    they had lawfull Summonc the Court fines them in
    three fhillings apeice

prſentmts brought in by the grand Jury
the death of Ann Hawkins prſent to the Court to be
Caſual by
faling from a mare

adjourned to 8 a Clock tomorrow morning

1 Inditmt philip Conway & patrick Conway for breaking
open the houſe of wm: ffisher read
pleaded not giuilty for
tryal put them ſelves on the Cuntry

2 Inditmt philip Conway for ſealing amare read
pleaded not giuilty for
tryal put him ſelf on the Cuntry & deſired time till the next
Court for tryal

3 Indictmt paterick Conway for ſtealing half a hide of
leather read
pleaded not guilty & for tryal put him Self on the Cuntry

110

4 Indictmt agt paterick Conway & philip Conway for
Robing of wm ffiſher of one Colt read
plead not guilty for
tryal put them ſelves on the Cuntry
motion being made by wm Biles the Rec^or of the publique
Stock of the County that there was Several neceſſary
Charges of the County to be defrayed as the fees
of the Councel & aſſembley men killing of woolfs &c
& that he had
no effects in his hands
whereupon the grand Jury prſented the the neceſity of haveing
a new tax raiſed

paterick & philip Conway brought to y^e: barr

Jury Called over & atteſted
no Chalenges made agt them

wm ffiſher Atteſted aged about 35 years Saith that about y^e:
latter end of January being at the houſe of philip Conway
in order to Seeke a mare of his that was loſt
after he had found her he returned
home againe

at wᶜʰ time he found his houſe broken op & his Cheſt unlocked
the key ſtuck in his Cheſt wᶜʰ key at his going away
he hid under his beds tead & none knew of the having
of it there Save paterick Conway was prſent when
the key was hid that upon Serch of his goods he found
pte of his goods in philip Conways houſe viz: an Inke
horn

Sam: roſe aged about 19 yeares Atteſted Saith that on the 6ᵗʰ
of the weeke at night being laſt day of January
being to haul the hay of wm ffiſher went there for
Some hay where they found al well on the next
morning went againe where they found a man

111

& horſe had been and tracked the ſd man & horſe in the
Snow between 3 & 4 miles & as they
did apprehend the track did lead towards the houſe of
philip Conway & further Saith not

Janes paxſon aged about 40 years atteſted Saith that he being Conſtable
Serced the houſe of philip Conway where was found an
Inkhorn wᶜʰ wm ffiſher owned to be his & not any
thing Ells & further Saith not

prſentmts brought in by the grand Jury

3 Indictmt agt: paterick Conway for ſtealing ½ hide of leather
read

adjourned the Court for one houre

grand Jury prſent the neceſſity of a Tax to defray the
requiſit Charge of the Councill & aſſembleymen
wᶜʰ the County is in arreare to them

petit Jury Return on the firſt Indictmt of brakeing wm ffiſhers houſe
do Say yᵗ: paterick
Conway & philip Conway are not guilty

3 Indictmt agt pa: Conway
Charles Thomas aged about 41 yeares atteſted doth
Say in Dec laſt pat yᵗ he Came to w: fforſt mill with
lether at wᶜʰ time he ſold ſd pa 1 ſide of lether
where his lether lay out of doore 2 or 3 days & he
then telling over his lether he miſt i ſide there of and after
Some time wm ffiſher; told him he ſaw 2 ſides of lether

in pt: Conway houſe & yᵗ: paterick Conway told ſd ffiſher
    yᵗ: Charles Thomas ſold him one & gave him —
    another

wm ffiſher atteſted doth Say Seeing 2 ps of ſides of lether in
    phi: Conways houſe pa: Conway told him he
    bought one of Charles Tho: & yᵗ: he gave him yᵉ
    other

- Jury returned Say Pa Conway is guilty of ſtealing the ſide of lether
    from Charles Thomas

112

Jon Shippey   ⎫   Jury Atteſted
   agt   ⎬   decl Read
Iſrael Taylor⎭   Anſwer Read

    wm: Biles atteſted doth Say that Iſrael Taylor laſt fall was i2 months did
        Come to him & promiſe to pay him on John Shippeys
        acctt: two ponds ten Shillings

    Joſeph Croſs atteſted doth Say that Iſrael Taylor about
        the beforementioned time told him he had Anſwered
        to wm Biles two pounds ten Shillings for worke
        done for ſd Iſrael Taylor

    Rich: Thather Junr atteſted doth Say that he heard Jon
        Shippey Say to Iſrael Taylor if he wold pay to
        wm Biles 50ˢ he wold ſaw him 1500 foot of Sawing

    Jon purſlone atteſted doth Say yᵉ day Andrew Jenks dyed
        he heard Iſrael Taylor Say have been at
        wm Biles to paſs my word to him for 50ˢ for
        work: thou haſt done & will thou now leave
        my work

    adjourned this Court to morrow morning at 7 a Clock
        & the orphans Court tomorrow

*Judgmt given agt: paterick Conway for ſtealing of Charles
        Thomas Thomas & it is adjudged that the ſd paterick
        Shall make 3 fold

grand Jury Returnd bring in three prſentmts

---

*This paragraph is crossed out in the record.

Iſrael Taylor being Calld into Court upon the prſentmt for the
  abuſe done to Thomas Tunneclif he Confeſt the fact
  whereupon the Court orders he give bond for his
  peace & appearance at the next Court

Recognizance Iſrael Taylor oblidges him ſelf in 8 £
  to be pd to the propry
  & govrnr his heirs & succeſſors to be levied on his
  lands tenemts goods & Chattles Conditionaly for the
  appearance of Iſrael Taylor at the next Court of
  Quarter ſeſſions & to keep the peace in the meane time to all

113

James Shippey ⎱   Jury returned & Calld over
          agt ⎰   do ſay they find for the plt wth 4 ^d
Iſrael Taylor ⎰   damages & Coſt of ſuite

A deed for 150 acres of land in fee
  Dated the ioth day of february i689 by Robt
                                    ——
                                     90
  Heaton Attorney to Henry ſflower
  grantor to Tho: Harding grantee

Henry marjorum Calld for ſelling Liquors upon the
  grand Jurys prſent mt he deſired to have what
  was done paſt by & he wold for the future he wold forbear

Henry marjorum upon the prſentmt of his ſwearing by
  god ſubmitted to the Court for wch the Court fines
Eſtreat him 5^s

philip Conway Indicted for ſtealing i mare
          Indictm read
          pleaded not guilty for tryal puts him ſelf
          upon the Cuntry

    Chaleng agt g wheeler

        Jury atteſted

    Indictmt read

    John Swift aged about 43 yeares ſaith that he tooke up a
    mare Supposed to be about 3 yeares of age un marked of Colours
        bl mealy mouthed about
    4 yeares paſt in the 2nd month next of wch mare he gave

notice to the raingers but they refufed to take her & yᵗ:
he fpoke to James Harrifon to buy her to wᶜʰ
J Harrifon gave way but put no price upon her
upon wᶜʰ he Eare marked her
wᵗʰ a half peny Cut on the
under fide of the nearror eare & wᶜʰ mare he
Saw feveral times Since in philip Conways Cuftody but more
      pticulry
about 3 weeks ago / & about the i3 day of the 1   1688
                                              ⎯⎯⎯⎯⎯⎯⎯
                                              mo   9
& that Since then he Saw the mare with her eare mark Changed

                                                    114

Nicholas Randle aged about 23 yeares attefted doth Say that
about the latter end of the 2 next will be 4 yeares paft John
                           ⎯⎯⎯⎯
                            mo
Swift & others took up a mare about 3 yeares of
age un Eare marked of Colour bl mealy mouthed a —
broad forehead a wid noftrill whereupon notice was given
to Luke Brindley & Robt Heaton yᵉ: Rangers to take
her away for the govrnr but they refufed & about
6 weeks after yᵉ: fd mare broke away but afore fhee
broke away Shee was Eare marked by Jon Swift
with a half penny Cut on the under fide of the nearror
Eare about a yeare after (She broke loofe) philip Conway
told him he wold have the fd mare & feveral times
after that he faw the fd mare in fd Conways Cuftody
& pticulerly about 2 or 3 weekes ago in harnes at p: C: houfe being
      about yᵉ:
latter end of the i2ᵗʰ month laft paft
& farther Said yᵗ: when he fpoke with Conway
about the fd mare he told him he beleived yᵗ: Jon Swift
had bought the mare of James Harrifon to wᶜʰ Conway
Said that the govrnr was not here to fell the mare
& that James Cold not & y yᵗ he the fd Conway wold have her
      attefted the i3 day of ift month 1689 in open Court
                                          ⎯⎯⎯⎯
                                           90
for the County of Bucks p Nicholas Randal

micheal Bucher aged about 23 years attefted doth Say yᵗ:
      he was prfent when the mare above mentioned was
      taken up of the aforefd marks & Colour & that
      he Saw the fd mare Severall times in the

Cuſtody of philip Conway & that he ſaw him ſeveral
times Rid on her about 2 yeares ago he Chalenged
the mare under him & he thereupon Rid away from
him / that he knew of a half penny Cut on the under
ſide of the nearror Eare put there by Jon Swift

Atteſted the i3 day of 1 month 1689 in open Court
                                    90
for the County of Bucks   p   the marke of
                                  X
                        micheal Bucher

4th Indictmt

    wm ffiſher atteſted doth Say he had ordr to take up a Colt by
        Capt markham belonging to yᵉ: govrnr wᶜʰ according
        ly he did & when he had yᵉ: Colt in his yard
        the 2nd day of this Inſtant pat & ph. Conway
        came to his houſe demanded the Colt the ſd ffiſher
        refuſeing to deliver it pa: Conway knockt him over
        & philip Con: in the meane time tooke away the ſd
        Colt

3 Indtmt   Jury Cald over to the ſd Indict ſay Philip Conway
        is guilty of ſtealing the mare whereof he ſtands Indᵗ

4 Ind   Jury ſay paterick Conway & philip Conway are
        guilty of forceably takeing a Colt from wm ffiſher
        whereof he ſtands Indictd

5 Indt   Jury atteſted

Witneſ atteſted John purſlone aged about 60 years faith yᵗ: he
        loſt a hog of Colour neare white about
        2 yeares ago with a ſlit in the further eare & yᵗ
        he doth ſuſpect Ric Thather the younger ſtole the
        ſd hogg & about the ſame time he loſt the ſd hog
        another hogg of his Came home cut Croſs the noſe

    Tho Revel aged about 35 yeares of age atteſted doth
        Say that about the beginning of harveſt laſt Richard
        Thather Jnr brought a hogg to the houſe of Iſreal
        Taylor a hog of Colour neare white Some what red
        on the Sholders but whether it was Sanded or blood he
        knows not & one of the eares had a ſlit in it but
        whether he knew not wᶜʰ hog ſd Rich Thather told him was

2 yeares old or upwards
attested

116

Ifrael Taylor aged 30 doth Say that Rich Thather
Junr did bring to his houfe a Hog of red Colour
with one or both Sholders Sanded about 80ᵗᵇ weight when he
was killd as he Suppofed wᶜʰ hog was brought to
his houfe Some time afore harveft & yᵗ: he told fd
Thather he wifht he had not brought the fd Hog for
he doubted it was his fathers hog

A deed   of 250 acres of land in fee dated the i3 day of the
firft month 89 ack & ded by Ifral Taylor grantor to
wm Biles for the ufe of Jon Coates grantee

Jury   Calld over
do Say they find Rich Thather guilty of ftealing
a Hogg

Tho Revel   ⎫   Jury Attefted
   agt   ⎬
Ifrael Taylor ⎭

dect Read: Anfwer Read:
Jof growdon attefted to the bill
Ezra Croafdel / fd he heard Ifrael Taylor deney he owed him
any
thing
ffra: Roffill attefted Saith he knows nothing of the bill
Jury Returned do fay they find for the plt with 6ᵈ
damages & Coft of fuite

117*

paterick Conway	paterick Conway
philip Conway	for ftealing One halfe
Rich Thather	hide of lether the prop
	goods of Charles Thomas
	Shall make three fold
	Satiffaction being 30ˢ
	to be levied on his
	goods & Chattles or for

*Pages 117 and 118 are on the sides of a small sheet about one quarter the size of the
other pages.

want of goods & Chattles
to be & to remaine bond
man to Charles Thomas
untill he be ſatiſfyed
& to be whipt on his
bare back 15 stripes
in the fight of the Court & people

paterick Conway & philip
Conway ——— for takeing
away by force & violent
aſſault from the pſon of
wm ffiſher one Colt the prop goods
of wm pen propryatory
& govrnr Shall make
4 fould Satiffaction
being 4 £ : to be levyed
on your goods & Chattles
Lands & tenements or
for want of
Lands
&
whipt on your bare back each
in the fight of the
people

paterick 15 & philip one
ſtripe

118

philip Conway for fraudelently
takeing & ſtealeing being the 3 ofences
one
being the prop goods of
wm pen propryatory &
govrnr Shall make 3 fould
Satiffaction being 12 £ to be
levyed on his lands & tenemts
& be whipt on his bare back 39 stripes
goods & Chattles & Baniſhed
out of the govrmt never to
return againe upon the
penalty of one hundered pounds
Richard Thather Junr for
fraudelently takeing & ſtealing
one hogg ſhall make
3 fould Satiffaction to yᵉ :

owner & be whipt on his
bare back twenty one ſtripes

119

At a Court held by adjournmt the
26ᵗʰ day of the 1 mo: 1690

prſent

Arthur Cook

wm Biles   wm yardley

nicholas waln   John Brock

Henery Baker

wm Beakes Sherrif

Steven Beakes deputy Sherrif

P P Clark

Severall accts & requeſts this day brought in from
them yᵗ: have Served In Councill & aſſembly that
they may be Satiſfyed what the law alows
them for theire attendance
this Court with the approbation of the grand Jury
have thought good to order that a tax be raiſed
for defraying the neceſſary Charge of the
County & it is therefore ordered that a tax be
forth with raiſed of 300 £ ——— on the
males & land according as the law directs
& that the Collectors after named do Collect the ſame
with in theire ſeveral diviſſions as may be rated
on them for theire Shares
& give an acctt of the lands and males with in the Several
    diviſions
viz: for above the falls to Jon wood &
Joſeph milner
from thence to the govrnrs
plantation Steven Beakes from thence to
neſhaminah Creeke & up the Creeke to Robt Hall plantation
    James Boyden Junior
thence up the Creek to the uppermoſt
land taken up on Neſhaminah Tho Rowland
for the midle lotts wm Dark for between
Neſhaminah & poqueſſing to the upper moſt part of
Jo: growdons land Samuel Allen the younger
from thence to the upper moſt lands taken up

Henry pointer & that acctt of the lands & males be
returned to the Juftices the 23 day of the 2nd mo
next At the Court houfe
    adjourned to the 23 day of the 2 mo next

     * * *   adjournment   * * *

*Henry pointer attefted doth Say that about the time aforefd

120

he was prfent at the takeing up of an unmarked mare of
the Colours & property aforefd wch he Saw in the
Cuftody of philip Conway about a yeare ago w^{ch}
he doth believe was the fame mare taken up by
Jon Swift but Cannot fay poffitively its the mare

Jury returned Calld over fay they find
Philip Conway guilty of ftealing a mare of
the govrnrs

adjourned for one houre

Court Calld

    adjourned till tomorrow morning at 8 a Clock

    adjourned the orphans Court till tomorrow

Judgmt paffed upon the 4 feveral Inditms

Judgmt awarded by the Court in the Cafe of J Shippey agt I
    Taylor that fd Taylor Shall pay Shippey 2 £ 10 ^s wth
    4^d damages & Coft of fuite & that execution Iffue
    accordingly

Tho Revell declared Ifrael Taylor had Satiffyed him what was
    awarded by the verdict & defired Judgmt to be fufpended

ordered that execution Iffue agt the goods of Rich Thatcher
    for fees due to the feveral officers if he does not
    take Speedy Courfe to Satiffye the Same

---

*Crossed out in the record.

Recognizance Rich Thather Junior obliges him felf in 20 £
    to be pd to the propryatory & govrnr his heires
    & fucceffors Conditional for His appearanc at y^e:
    next Court of Quarter feffions & to be of good
    abearing in the meane time

adjourned to y^e: 26 Inftant

  orphans Court to ye fame time

      County Bucks fs:

        At a Court of Quarter Seffions held by the king
        & Queens authority in the name of willm Penn
        propryatory & govrnr of fd province & territorys
            annexted at the Court houfe
      for the fd County the iith day of the 4th month
      i690

                                    121

      Juftices prfent
        willm Biles   Nicholas waln
        Henry Baker   Jon Brock
          wm yardley Sherrif
          P P Clark

Ifrael Taylor calld appeared nothing appearing agt him the Court
    difcharges him

A deed of 6 acers of land in fee dated the 4th day of the 4th month
    i690 acknowledged by wm yardley attorney to Sa: Burges
    grantor to wm Biles & Jofuah Hoops grantees for the ufe of
      them felves &
    Tho: Janney & Rich Hough

a deed in fee dated the i8th i2 89
                 mo
    ack & dld by wm Beakes grantor to Tho: Tunneclife
    attorney to Jon worrilow & walter worrilow in truft for
    the ufes therein expreffed

meffage from the affembley delivered by Edmund Bennet that
    there is due from this County to the Clarks of the affembley
    1 £: 7^s: 0^d & defired that Care be taken to anfwer the fame

ordered thereupon that the fame be payd out of the
the County Stock when it
Comes in

Tax   whereas Tho Rowland, laft Court was ordered to bring
an acct of all the lands & males between 16 & 60
from Robt Halls to the uppermoft lands taken up in order
to be Taxed for the ufes then expreffed & yᵗ Tho Rowland
Since is dead & yᵗ: divifion is now thought too large for
one man therefore its

ordered   that wm Hayhurft from fd Robt Halls pltation & new
Town & yᵗ: Shadrach walley from thence to the uppermoft
land taken up give an acctt of all the lands & males between
i6 & 60

agreed   with Ifrael Taylor to bring in an acctt of
all lands Surveyed & Seated or unfeated with in the

122   limits of this County for wᶜʰ the fd Ifrael is to have
20ˢ difcounte out of the County tax to be raifed & if fd Ifrael
gives
a juft & true acct faire drawn out at or
before the next Court

whereas   it appeares that there is occafion for a Corroner a
boy being lately drowned & none being Commiffionated
it is

ordered   that wm: Biles & Arthur Cook & wm yardley take Care
to Endeavor that a Cornor & Regifter be appointed
in this County

ordered   that the fd perfons requeft the Council that the
upper Road for the upper moft plantations in
this County be layd through Philadelphia County

Complt   being made by John Cartor that his brother
Edward Cartor doth not allow him meate and
apparrel

ordered   that A: Cook & wm Biles forth with take Care
about it & see for what time time yᵉ: fd Jon
was placed to him by the orphans Court & to
Endeavor to redrefs the Complt

adjourned to the ioth day of the 7th mo next

30th 4 1690 execution granted agt: Philip Conway
<u>mo</u>

for Damages and Coſt in Jon Swifts Caſe i6 £ : 3^s : 3^d

return executed the Same day p wm yardley

Sherrife

in the hands of mark Bettrice by a bond
taken of ſd mark for payment of ſaid mony

i8th 4 1690 execution granted agt Paterick Conway
<u>mo</u>

& Philip Conway in wm: ffiſhers Caſe for
damages & Coſts is 6 £ i6^s 1^d

- returnd executed the 30th 3 1690 p wm yardley
<u>mo</u>   Sherrife

in the hands of mark Bettrice by a bond taken of
ſd mark for paymt of ſd mony

Action Entered } Peter Jenings }
the 16th 7 1690 }   agt: } plea of Caſe   123
<u>mo</u>   Thomas ffox }

Summonce granted the   day of the   month i690

Return made by wm: yardley Sherrife that the ſd ſummonc
was executed the   day of the   month i690

Action Entered } John Teſt }
the 20th 7 1690 }   agt   } plea of Caſe
<u>mo</u>   Thomas ffox }

Summonce granted the   day of the   month i690

Return made by wm yardley Sherrif that the ſd
Summonce was executed the   day of the   mo: 90

Action Entered } Joſeph ffarington }
the 20th 9 i690 }   agt   } plea of debt
<u>mo</u>   John Tatham }

Summonce granted the 27 day of the 9 month 1690

Return made by wm yardley Sherrif that the ſd ſum
was executed the   day of the   month 1690

Action Entered ⎱ John Brock ⎱
the 27ᵗʰ 9 1690 ⎰   agt   ⎱ in a plea of debt
    mo   gilbert wheeler ⎰

Summonce granted the   day of the   month 1690

return made by wm yardley Sherrif that the ſd Sum
    was executed the   day of the   month i690

Action Entered ⎱ Tho Tunneclif ⎫
the 27ᵗʰ 9 1690 ⎰   agt   ⎬ plea of Caſe
    mo   John Lee ——— ⎭

Summonce granted the   day of the   month 1690

return made by wm yardley Sherrif that the ſd Sum
    was executed the   day of the   month 1690

Penſylvania

County Court Bucks ſſ: 124

At A Court of Quarter Seſſions held by the king & Queens
authority in the name of william Penn Propryatory
& govrnr of the afforeſaid Province & territorys
thereunto belonging at the Court houſe for the
Said County the ioᵗʰ day of the ioᵗʰ month being
the 2ⁿᵈ yeare of the king & Queens reigne & ioᵗʰ
yeare of the propryatorys govrmt i690

The Juſtices then prſent

Tho Janney   Willm Biles

Nicholas waln   Henry Baker   Jon Brock

John Cook Corronor

willm yardley Sherrif

P Pemberton Cl:

grand Jury   atteſted

Action   peter Jenings ⎱
            agt   ⎬ Calld but neither partie appeared
        Tho ffox ——— ⎰

Action   John Teft ⎱
            agt   ⎬ Calld neither partie appeared
        Tho: ffox ⎰

Action   Joſeph ffarington ⎫
                 agt   ⎬   ffarrington appeared
         John Tatham   ⎭   Jon Tatham appeared not

Requeſt   being made by Jon Tatham to reſpite the action
makeing it appeare that he was ſick & Indiſpoſed
& not able to Come, Edward Hunlock & Richard
Bagnet Engaged for his appearance at the next Court
to anſwer to the action with out further
Summonce or proceſs

accidental death of John ſtolon returned & read
adjourned the Court for one houre

Action   Tho: Tunneclif ⎫' both appeared
               agt   ⎬
   125   John Lee —— ⎭ The action with drawn
& Tho Tunneclif agreed to pay half the
Charge

Iſrael Taylor Calld appeared pleaded not guilty & for
tryal puts him ſelf on the Cuntry

Jury atteſted

Indictmt Read

Richard Thather atteſted doth Say that being at work at Iſrael
       Taylors in the fall
la laſt was i2ᵗʰ month he ſaw Iſrael Taylor give the
heifer of John Naylor bread ſeveral times &
he the ſd Taylor ſd to ſd Thather come let us kill
the heifer, but at that time
he left the ſd Taylors houſe for want of proviſions
& in a few days after Iſrael aſked the ſd Thather to
Come againe for he had proviſions enough & he
came there & ſaw in the ſeller of ſd Taylor in
a brrl Several pieces of ſmall meate & he
then ſaw the hinder part of a hide of
Colour red & the end of the taile white & he
Saw the ſd Taylor bury the ſd piece of hide
& that about io or i2 weeks ago the ſd Thatcher
went to the houſe of Iſrael Taylor the ſd Thather then
underſtanding that he was under ſuſpition of
being guilty of aſſiſting in the killing of the ſd heifer
he aſked the ſd Taylor's wife what heifer it was
that was killed & who killd it & ſhee ſaid Ben Jons

& Iſrael kill her & that ſhee beleived it was
naylors heifer

Bartholemew Thather atteſted doth Say laſt fall was 12 months
ago he was at Iſrael Taylors where he ſtayed alnight
& ſaw Iſrael Taylors wife dreſs ſome meate w^{ch}
he thought was young heifer beefe & before that
time the heifer of John naylor was wanting #

The will of Richard Thather being delivered into
Court it was ordered that Phinehas Pemberton
Clark ſhold keep it untill further order

126

adjourned for one houre

verdict   jury returned do ſay Iſrael Taylor is not
guilty of the felony whereof he ſtands Indicted

A deed in fee of 200 acres dated the 3 day of the 9th
month i690 acknowledged by Joſuah Hoops attorney
to Joſ Engliſh grantor to Sa Dark grantee

The executions before mentioned both returned Satiſfyed

wm Biles acknowledged in open Court that
he had Red full satiſfaction from Derick Jonſon 1 bl mare
with a long taile & dule back with Some white haires
in her fore head & a half peny Cut on the further eare
wch ſd mare the ſd Derrick is allowed to take up when
he can find her & her encreaſe that Shall lawfully
appeare to belong to her & that he the ſd wm Biles
will warrnt the ſd mare & her Increaſe to the ſd Jonſon &
defend
from all perſons

Reported to this Court by John Brock that Richard
Thatcher did confeſs he owed to Derrick Jonſon the
Sum of one pound eight Shillings & that
it was to be payd in good wheate

Judgmt given & its adjudged by the ſd Jon Brock that
the ſd Sum Shall be accordingly payd wth Coſts wch Judgmt
is aproved of by this Court & thereupon

ordered that execution Iſſue accordingly

Judgmt given & its adjudged that John naylor Shall pay
Coſts of ſuite & that execution Iſſue accordingly

Iſrael Taylor promiſed to pay the fees in both actions wherein
    Revel was Concerned agt him _____ to the officers

adjourned the Court to the 20ᵗʰ day of this month to the houſe
    of Tho Janney

        8ᵗʰ io i690 ececution granted agt Rich Thatcher for 3 £ : 9ˢ : 4ᵈ
        mo   for fees

        returnd i3 io i690 executed p wm yardley Sherrife
                mo

        i2 io i690 execution dated agt Rich Thatcher & Iſrael Taylor
          for 4 £ 14ˢ 6ᵈ in Revels Caſe

        i6 io i690 returnd executed on the effects Iſrael Taylor in Tho
        mo   Brocks
        hands 2 £ 7ˢ 0ᵈ & of the good of Rich Thatcher i hors
          apprized at 5 £

        i2 io 1690 execution agt ſd Thatcher in Derick Jonſons Caſe
        mo   was dated 1 : 16 : 0

      127

        Att a Court held by adjournmt the 20ᵗʰ day
        of the ioᵗʰ month i690 at the houſe of Tho:
        Janney
            Tho Janney   wm Biles
              Nicholas waln   John Brock
              wm yardley Sherrif
               P: P: Cl:

Richard Thather being bound in 20 £ : to appeare at
this Court none appearing agt: him the Court
diſcharges him _____

Action
decl read   } Jᵒhn Brock
bill read — }   agt   } action debt gilbert wheeler appeared not
         gilbert wheeler   John Brock appeared

    wm: Biles appeared on ſd wheelers acctt & ſd
    that g: wheeler was before him this day
    & Confeſt the bill mentioned in the declaraᵗ

John Brock Confeſt he had Red in pte of the ſd
bill the ſum of 1 £ : 10ˢ 09ᵈ

Judgmt given by default that in as much
as the ſd gilbert wheeler did not appeare here
according to ſummonce but Confeſt the bill
before wm : Biles one of the Juſtices of peace
it is adjudged that gilbert wheeler ſhall
pay to John Brock 4 £ : 05ˢ : 03ᵈ & 5ˢ dama
=ges with Coſts of Suite / & that execution Iſſue
accordingly

*Ordered that in as much as yᵉ Severalˡ orders of
Court about the Collecting of the arrears of
the firſt Tax is not observed that wm :
yardley the Sherrife do Collect the arrears
of the Tax & that a warrant be Iſſued
accordingly to Impower him

whereas it is the Sherrife hath made return of
the executions out agt : the goods & Chattles of Joſeph
Holden for the ſeveral Sums obtained by

128

John Duplovis philip Richards & Cornelius empſon
that there is no goods nor Chattles to Satiſfye the ſd debts
& that the ſd pſons have requeſted to have execution
agt the ſd Holdens land it is ordered by this Court
that execution Iſſue agt the lands of the
ſd Holden to Satiſfye the Severall Judgmts
obtained by the aforeſd perſons

whereas the grand Jury did preſent the neceſſity
of haveing the County devided into townſhips it is ordered
that Henry Baker Thomas Janney wm Biles
Phinehas Pemberton Arthur Cook Edmund
Bennet James Boyden Nicholas waln
Joſuah Hoops Jon Rowland
Joſeph growdon Saml Allen & that they
meete together the day before the next
Court at the Court houſe & then
& there devide this County into Townſhips that
the Same may be prented to the next Court

---

* Crossed out in the record.

to have the approbation thereof
whereas the grand Inquefts prfented the
neceffity of having weights & meafures equall
according to law its referred to be further
confidered of

adjourned to the ii day of the firft month
next

The 3 Executions aforefd granted agt the land of Jofeph Holden
in Duplovie Richards & Empfons Cafe dated the 20th day
of the iith month i690

i3 1   1690 execut in Is: Taylors Cafe for i7^s 6^d
mo   1

returned agt Rich Thather ————————

Bucks fs

129

County Court y^e: iith 1 90
mo 1

(1)

Action Entered }   Jofeph ffarington agt John Tatham plea Debt
the 20th 9 i690 }   ffor tryal at the ioth Court but the —
mo   tryal Refpited to this Court becaufe of
the fd Jon Tathams Sicknef or Indifpofednefs

(2)

Action Entered }   John Smith plt agt Thomas peirce deft in a plea
the i i2 i690 }   of
mo

(3)

Action Entered }   Zachariah whitpaine plt agt gilbert wheeler
the 16th i2 i690 }   deft in a plea of Debt
mo

Summonce   granted the i6th i2th month i690 for fd wheelers appearanc
the iith of the firft month next Enfueing

rcturn made executed the i6th of the i2th mo: i690 on fd wheeler
by willm yardley Sherrif

withdrawn by wm Biles order

(4)

Action Entered   ⎫ Thomas Revel plt agt Iſrael Taylor deft in a
the 23 day of i2ᵗʰ 1690 ⎰ plea of Caſe
       mo

Summonce granted for ſd Taylor in ſd Revells Caſe dated the 23 i2 i690
                                            mo

Return —

Summonce granted for Thomas Brock & John Jones wittneſes in the ſd
        Caſe Revel agt Taylor

Return

     (5)

Action Entered ⎫
24ᵗʰ i2 i690 — ⎰   Andrew Heath agt wm Beakes in a plea of treſpaſs
  mo

Summonce granted for ſd Beakes appearance in ſd Heaths Caſe the 24ᵗʰ
    i2 90
    mo

  return

Summonce granted for James Sutton & John Richard ſon witneſſes in ſaid
        Caſe Heath agt Beakes the 4ᵗʰ of the iſt month i690
                                           1

return — &

                                    130

     (6)

Action Entered ⎫ willm: yardley plt agt Hugh marſh & Robt marſh
the 25ᵗʰ i2 i690 ⎰   in an action of Debt
  mo

Summonce   granted the 25ᵗʰ of the i2ᵗʰ mo i690 for ſd marſhes
    appearance in ſd Caſe

Return

     (7)

Action Entered ⎫ Thomas Janney by his attorney John Neild plt
the 25ᵗʰ i2 i690 ⎰ agt
  mo   John Lees & Joſeph milner defts in plea of debt

Summonce   granted for ſd Lees & milners appearance date the
    25th i2 1690

        mo

Return

   with drawn by order of Thomas Janney

    (8)

Action Entered ⎱ Thomas peirce plt agt: John pidcock in a plea of
the 25th i2 i690 ⎰ Caſe

    mo

Attachment granted agt ſd pidcocks goods & Chattles for his appearance
   in ſd peirces Caſe dated the 22 day of the iith mo i690 ——

Return   the 23 of the iith mo i690 by vertue of this warrant attached
    of the goods of John pidcock i buck ſkin 3 doe ſkins
    2 guns a parcel of Red Lead about 30 lb weight ——

   Bucks ſſ

131

    At a Court of Quarter Seſſions held by the
    king & queens authority in the name of
    willm Penn propryatory & govrnr of
    the ſd province & territorys thereunto
    belonging at the Court houſe the iith day of
    the i i690 being the iith yeare of the

     mo 1

    propryatorys govrmt

          The Juſtices then prſent
    Arthur Cook   Joſeph growdon
    Henry Baker   Nicho waln &
       wm yardley Sherrif
        P P Clark

action Jos farrington ⎫
         agt ⎬ both appeared & deſired one
    Jon Tatham ⎭ hours time before the
              matter was brought
              to tryal wch was allowed

action Tho Revel ⎫
        agt ⎬ neither appeared
    Iſrael Taylor ⎭

action   Andrew Heath ⎱
                    agt ⎰ both appeared
         wm Beakes

         declarat read

         Anſwer

         Iſſue Joyned

action   wm yardley   ⎱ plt appeared the
                    agt   ⎰
         Hugh marſh & Rob marſh   deft appeared not
         whereupon the Court Suspended the action
         untill tomorrow

      Jury atteſted

Andrew Heath ⎱ Declra & anſwer read ———   132
          agt ⎰
   wm Beakes

wittneſſes   wm Thomas James Sutton Joſeph Henry atteſted
             Tho kirl atteſted george Cockram Joſeph ſteward
             atteſted
             Tho Tunneclif atteſted Ann Ellot Sarah biles
             atteſted John wood Andrew Ellot atteſted

             Adjourned for one houre
             adjourned untill tomorrow morning at 9 a Clock

      Jury returnd Say they find for the plt wᵗʰ 3ˢ
      damages & Coſts of Suit

   Joſeph ffarington ⎱
                  agt ⎰ both Calld appeared
   John Tatham

             declarat read
                Anſwer read
             obligation Read & Confeſt to by yᵉ: deft
             award read — & Confest

      *Upon Complt of Daniel garner how that he was
      abuſed beaten & aſſaulted by Richard Thatcher
      Tho Coleman & Tho Coverdale: the ſd Thather
      being Calld in Court for the ſd abuſe & other

———
* Crossed out in the records.

           misdemeanors & Suerties demaned of him
for his appearance at next Court & keeping
the peace in the meane time but for want
thereof the Court Commits him Into Cuſtody untill
he Shall find ſuerties and appeare at ſd Court

and as for the abuſe done by ſd Coverdale
& Coleman its referred to wm Biles to Inſpect &
take Care of

Jury returnd do Say they find for the plt wth
Coſts

John Thatham deſired the Court to allow him
           an appeale

- adjourned the Court for one houre

A deed of morgage of 400 acres of land by John pidcock
           grantor to Edward Hunlock grantee dated the i2th of
           io mo: 1690 with a ſcedule thereunto annexed was
           tendered by Ed: Hunlock to ſd pidcock to b ack
           nowledged

     133   acknowledged according to law wch ſd pidcock refuſed to
           do with ſheweing
           any Cauſe for his ſo refuſeing

John Smith agt⎱   appeared —⎱
   Tho peirce —⎰   appeared   ⎰
                declaration read & both partes
                referd the matter to the bench

   Tho peirce agt ⎱   both appeared
    Jon pidcock agt⎰   declarat read
                Anſwer read
                Jury atteſted
                declarat proved by the atteſtation
                of Tho peirce gilbert wheeler &
                policarpus roſe

        Jury returned find for the plt 20^s
           with coſt of Suite
           the

     Adjourned the Court to 9 tomorrow morning

Adjourned the orphans Court untill 2 a Clock
tomorrow

wm yardley
      agt   } both appeared read
Hugh marſh & Robt marſh

declaration being read
bill obligate read
deſt Anſwer he owned the bill to be his
act & deed
Tho peirce produced a diſcharge undr John
Smiths hand in full & the ſd peirce pro=
=miſed in open Court to pay & diſcharge all
Coſts & fees

adjudged by the Court that the action agt peirce be with drawn

Judgmt Entered in thathr Caſe agt Beakes According
to verdict & that execution Iſſue accordingly

134

Judgment given & it is adjudged that John Tatham
pay to Joſeph ffarington 50 £ with Coſt of Suite

Diference
after Judgment given both parties referred to yᵉ:
Juſtices on the bench what Shall be abated
of the penalty

Judgment
given that John pidcock Shall pay to Tho peirce
20ˢ with Coſt of ſuite & that execution Shall Iſſue
accordingly

Tho Revel agt }
Iſrael Taylor } both Calld & neither of the appeared

adjourned for one houre

i3ᵗʰ i   whereas Joſeph ffarrington & John Tatham
  mo   referred to the Juſtices on the bench what
 1690 they Juge in equity the ſd John Tatham
  1   Shall pay to the ſd ffarrington in full Satiſfaction of the
      afforeſd Judgement whereupon the
     ſd Juſtices do Judg award & determine that

the íd John Tatham Shall pay to íd —
ffarrington, 28 £ in Silver mony or in
good merchantable wheate at Silver mony
price in one months time after the day of the date hereof
    & further that the íd John Tatham
Shall pay to the reípective officers the fees due
to them by reaíon of the afforeíd Judgmt & —
upon paymt of the Said mony that the íd parties
Shall íeale Each other general releaíes & that
if the íd John Tatham Shall faile payment
of the íd mony as above expreííed that then
execution Iííue according to the Judgment
firít obtained & further it is expreííed that
the íd John Tatham Shall make payment to the
íd Joíeph ffarrington or his attorney at the
ferry houíe over agt Burlington

135   george Brown being Calld upon his recognizance
        being bound for aííaulting & abuíeing wm.
        Biles one of the Juítices of the peace of this
        County; & upon his examination Confeít that he
        twice he pusht him with his hand whereupon
        the Court gave Judgmt & it was adjudged
        that the íd george Browne, Shall give his own
        bond for his appearance at th next Court & be of
        good abeareing in the meane time & Shall pay
        a fine of 20^s to be diípoí of as the Juítices here
        after Shall think fit
        geo: Brown acknowledged him íelf Indebted to y^e:
        propryatory & govrnr in io £ to be levyed on his
        lands & tenements goods & Chattles
        conditioned for his appearance at the next
        Court & to be of good abearing in the meane time

          adjourned till tomorrow morning
             at 9 a Clock
          adjourned the orpans Court to 10

whereas the píons appointed to devide the County have
not done it is ordered that the íd píons meete
to gether on the 20 day of the 2 month next to
devide it into towníhips
adjourned the Court unto the 20 day of the 2 month next

County Court Bucks ſſ $\overline{136}$

At a Court of Quarter Seſſions held by the
king & Queens authority in the name of
wm Penn propryatory & govrnr
of the province of Penſilvania & territorys
thereunto belonging at the Court houſe of the
aforeſd County the io[th] day of the 7th month $\overline{1690}$

Juſtices prſent

Joſe: growdon   wm Biles Tho: Janney
Nicholas Waln   Henry Baker
John Brock
wm yardley Sherrif
P P Cl: Com:

Commitmt   wm Evans for Suſpition of Confederacy of fellony
with Joſeph Trevithan is Commited to Cuſtody*
untill further order

adjourned untill 9 a Clock
tomorrow moring

Action   Jon Jones & attorneys ⎫ a
                    agt   ⎬ plea of debt
          Joſeph Holden deft ⎭
          patterick Robinſon Jon Swift his attorneys appeared
          Joſe: Holden appeared not

declara Read

A Coppy of the letter of attorney & Certificate on the back
  bond   read & proved

  bill   read & proved by the atteſtation of Jon: Swift &
         Henry pointer

Judgmt given & it is adjudged that Joſeph Holden Shall pay
        to Jon Jones, or attorneys the Sum of thirty
        pounds Silver mony as allſo the Sum of Six
        pounds eight Shillings & Six pence with Intereſt for
        the thirty pounds from the firſt day of the 3 month
        $\overline{1690}$ with Coſt of Suite to w[ch] marſh the ſd Holdens
        attorney aſſented

ordered by the Court that Paterick Robinſon becom bound
        upon record in Court in 100 £ that John Jones Shall
        ratefye what he & other attorneys has done in relati
        -on to the afforeſd action

137 Paterick Robinſon oblidges him Self his heires executrs
& adminiſtrators to the Juſtices
now prſent on the bench being Joſeph growdon
wm: Biles Thomas Janney nicholas waln Henry
Baker & John Brock theire executrs & adminiſtr
the Sum of one hundered pounds to be levyed
on his goods & Chattles Lands & tenements —
Conditioned for the procureing of an authentick
power from John Jones or that ſd Jon Jones or heires executrs
adminiſtrators in 12 month time do Ratefye
what ſd paterick Robinſon & the rest of the attorneys
of John Jones has done or Shall do in relation
to an action of debt for 36 £ 8ˢ 6ᵈ now
brought agt Joſeph Holden
                                        Pat: Robinson

Action   John Duplovies ⎫
                agt   ⎬ plea of debt
         Joſe Holden   ⎭

paterick Robinſon appeared

letter of attorney to Impower him produced &
Hugh marſh attorney appears

letter of attorney to prove the Same was produced
debt acknowledged by the attorney

Judgmt given & it is adjudged that Joſeph Holden Shall
pay to John Duplovie the Sum of 13 £ : 18ˢ 7½ᵈ
The ſd plt attorney haveing promiſed to allow what
Shall be further made appeare upon acctt if any
be

Action   philip Richards plt ⎫
                agt   ⎬ in a plea of debt
         Joſeph Holden deft ⎭

paterick Robinſon attorney appeares

letter of attorney produced to prove the ſame

Hugh march attorney appeares   138

Declaration read

Anſwer he ownes the debt

Judgmt given & it is adjudged that Joſeph Holden Shall
pay to philip Richards the ſum of 10 £ : 2ˢ 3ᵈ
The ſd plts attorney haveing promiſed to allow what Shall
be further made appeare to pd on acctt

action   Jon wood plt ⎫
         agt   ⎬ in a plea of Caſe
   John Swift deft ⎭

     plt appeares

     deft appeares

decl   read

Anſwer he doth owne the takeing up the negroes

   The matter referred to the bench

Judgment given that John Swift Shall pay to John wood
25ˢ & yᵗ: John Swift Shall pay Coſt of ſuite

Action   Samuel Beakes plt ⎫
         agt   ⎬ in a plea of debt both appeared
   Jonathan Eldridge deft ⎭

declaration read — — —

Anſwer he Confeſſes the debt

   Judgmt given & it is adjudged that Jonathan Eldridg
Shall pay to the plt the Sum of two
pounds three ſhillings Seven pence with Coſt
of Siute wᶜʰ Sum of 2 £ : 3ˢ 7ᵈ willm Embley
in open Court declared he wold pay to the plt or
attorney in 3 months time
& willm Biles likewiſe in Court promiſed to pay
the fees

Deed   of 72 Square Rods of land in fee dated the 4 day
of 7ᵗʰ mo 1690 by Tho Janney grantor Joſuah Hoops
& wm yardley for the uſe of themſelves & the reſt of the
grantees

139   adjourned for one hour

A deed in fee of 200 acres of land dated the ioᵗʰ day
of the i2ᵗʰ month i689 by P Pemberton grantr
to mary Radclif the widow of the grantee

A deed   in fee of 250 acres of land dated the 8th day of
the 7[tb] month i690 by wm Clows & margery clows grantors to
Joſeph Clows grantee

A deed   in fee of 250 acres of land dated the 8th of the
7th month i690 by Joſeph Clows grantor to
wm Clows grantee

grand Jury atteſted

Indictmt agt Tho Brock for extortion in his ferriage
pleaded guilty

A deed   of 500 acres of land in fee dated the 9th day of the
7th month i690 by John Rowland grantor to
gilbert wheeler grantee

A deed   of 236 acres in fee dated the i5[th] of the 9th
mo: firſt yeare of the reigne of wm & mary
by wm Biles attorney to Jon Cuſt grantor
to Sam Beakes grantee

A deed   of 60 acres of land in fee dated the 20th of the
6th mo: i690 by Joſeph growdon grantor to
Tho: ſcot grantee

Action   Iſrael Taylor
                     agt
Tho Brock Jo ſtedon Ra Boome ffra Roſill &
mathew miller deft plea of Caſe
Iſrael Taylor appeared
Tho Brock ffra Roſſill & John ſtedon appeare
on the behalf of them ſelves & the reſt

declarat Read

Anſwer they Confeſt to the declaration & Sayd that
they wold pay Iſrael Taylor 5 £ : 10[s] & Coſt of
Suite

reply   Iſrael Taylor, that he was Content with it
& Craved Judgmt for the ſame

Judgmt given & it is adjudged that the ſd defts Shall pay to ſd
plt 5 £ : 15[s] with Coſt of ſuite & that execution Iſſue
accordingly

Penſylvania   (140)

(1)   County Court Bucks ſs:

action = Entered | John Jones by his attorney Samll Carpenter——

the 2i 6

$\overline{mo}$

1690   } Paterick Robinson John ſſuller & John Swift plt

agt

£

Joſeph Holden deft in an act of Debt 66: 8^s::6^d
granted the i9th day of the 6 month i690 p A Cook

Attachmt —   made by the Sherrif executed the 2i 6 90

Return $\overline{mo}$

wm yardley ſherrif

---

(2)

Action Entered   John Duplovie plt

the 23 day of

6 1690   agt   £ s d
mo   in action of Debt 15: 16: 7

Joſeph Holden deft

Attachmt for ſd Holdens appearance agt his goods granted
the 2i day of the 6th month i690 p A Cook
Return made the 30th of the 6th month 1690 Executed p
wm yardley Sherrife ————

---

(3)

action Entered   Philip Richards plt

the 23 day $\frac{6}{mo}$

              agt   in an action of debt

i690   Joſeph Holden deft

Attachment for the ſd Holdens appearance agt his goods granted

	the 2i day of the 6th month i690 p A Cook

Return   made the 30th 6 1690 executed p wm yardley Sherrif

mo

(141)

(4)

Action Entered the 24th of the 6th month — i690 ———

Ifrael Taylor plt

agt:

Thomas Brock

Ralph Boome

John ftedon

ffrancis Roffill

mathew miller

plea of Cafe Sum: 8 L — —

Summonce   granted the 26th 6 1690 p Jon Brock

mo

Returne   made executed the 30th day of the 6th month 1690 p wm .
yardley
Sherrif

---

(5)

Action Entered the 26th 6th
mo
1690

Pilocarpus Rofe plt
agt
John Pidcock deft

plea of trefpafs & affault

Summonc   granted the 26th 6 90 p Jon Brock

mo

Return   made the 29th day of the 6 month i690 Executed
p wm yardley fherrif

Summonce   for wittneffes in fd Cafe granted the 26 day of 6th mo: 90
for Jon Lee & his wife Rachel Lee martha Lee & Robt
Benfon

Return   made the 28th & 29th of the 6 . 1690 executed p wm
yardley   mo
Sherrif

(6)

Action Entered the 26th $\dfrac{6^{th}}{mo}$	$\left.\begin{array}{c} \text{gilbert Wheeler plt} \\ \text{agt} \\ \text{John Pidcock deft} \end{array}\right\}$ in a plea of Cafe

Summonce   granted the 26th $\dfrac{6}{mo}$ i690 p Jon Brock

Return   made the 29 day of the 6th month 1690 Executed
p wm yardley ſherrif

(7)

Action Entered the 26th $\dfrac{6}{mo}$ 1690	$\left.\begin{array}{c} \text{Iſrael Taylor plt} \\ \text{agt} \\ \text{John Shippey deft} \end{array}\right\}$ in a plea of Cafe	(142)

Summonce   granted the 26th day of the $\dfrac{6^{th}}{mo}$ i690 p Jon Brock

Returne   made the 29 day of the 6th month i690 p w $\underline{yard}$
Sherrif

Summonce   granted for appeareranc of witneſs wm Roles the 26th
6 mo 90

Return made   the 29th $\dfrac{6}{mo}$ 90 executed p wm yardley Sherrif

---

(8)

Action Entered the 28th $\dfrac{6}{mo}$ 1690	$\left.\begin{array}{c} \text{John wood plt} \\ \text{agt} \\ \text{John Buttler deft} \end{array}\right\}$ in a plea of Cafe

Attachmt   granted the 28th day of the 6 month $\underline{1690}$ p Jon Brock

Return,—   made the 29th & 30 days of the 6th month i690 p wm
yardley Sherrif

---

(9)

Action Entered the 28th $\frac{6}{mo}$ 1690	John wood plt agt John Swift deft	in a plea of Cafe

Summonce — granted the 28 day of the $\frac{6}{mo}$ i690 p Jon: Brock

return — made the 29th day of the 6th month i690 executed
p wm yardley Sherrif

Action Entered the 28th $\frac{6}{mo}$ 1690 — mary Beakes adminiftratrix to her late hufband willm Beakes by her attorney Samuel Beakes plt

agt

Jonathan Eldridg def —————————

Arreft granted — the iith 4th mo i690 p wm Biles

return made — the iith $\frac{4}{mo}$ 90 taken into Cuftody

143

Cornelius Empfon Craved in open Court that wm Embley
might be his attorney to profecute an action of
debt agt Jofeph Holden for 8 £ filver mony
wch was allowed by the Court

wm Evans being examined about a horfe found in the Cuftody
of Jofeph Trevitham Said that he lent the fd Trevithan
the horfe

adjourned the Court untill 8 a Clock tomorrow
morning

£   s   d

Execution Signed for Jon Jones for the Levying of 36: 8.: 6
& 2 £ : 3^s 1^d, Cofts on the goods of Jofeph Holden

Action Cornelius Empfon plt agt Jofeph Holden ———	Cafe of debt

appeares by his attorney willm Embley

Jo Holden appeares by his attorney Hugh marſh

decla: read

Anſwer   Confeſt the debt

Judgmt given & it is adjudged that Joſeph Holden Shall
pay to Cornelius Empſon the Sum of 8 £ : Silver —
mony with Coſts of ſuite & that execution Iſſue
accordingly

> Iſrael Taylor
>   agt } plea of Caſe
> Action John Shippey

    plt appeares

    deft appeares

  decla read

    Anſwer that he owes the plt 33^s & will pay Coſts
      of ſuite

      the plt: declared that the Same pd to him
      will Satiſfye him

Judgmt given & it is adjudged that John Shippey Shall
    pay thirty three ſhillings with Coſt of Suite & that
    Execution Iſſue accordingly

                        144

Joſeph Trivithan to his Indictm pleaded not guilty
for tryal puts him Self on the Cuntry

Tho ffox atteſted Saith that upon the 8th day of this
Inſtant he came to the houſe of Jos: growdon & ſaid
Jos: growdon had ſent him for Cloths for he & his wife had
fallen in the river & wanted them & thereby obtaned
from the negro woman i Cloth Coate i p pluſh breeſhes
i womans cloak

John Hawkins atteſted Saith that upon munday laſt
being the 8th Inſtant he ſaw the ſaid Trevithan at
the houſe of J gro: where he ſaid he Saw the
ſd Trevithan have upon his horſe i Cloth Coate one

paire plu{sh breaches & womans Cloake wch under —
pretenc of Jo{seph growdons being wet in the
river he had obtained from the negro —
woman

Action withdrawn ro{se agt pidcock

Con{stables for above the falls Jo{suah Hoops
  for below to pen{sberry Jo{seph Chorley
  for the middle lotts — wm Duncan
  for the upper part of Ne{shaminah John White
  for the other {side of the upper pt of Ne{shaminah Jon pur{slone
  for the lower pt on the other {side Sam Allen Junr:
  for the lower pte of the river Tho green

Jury · returned do {say they find Jo{se Trevithan as he is
  Charged in the Indictment

Tho king to his Indict pleaded not guilty
puts him {self on y^e: Cuntry for tryal
Hugh mar{sh atte{sted Says in or about the 3 month la{st pa{st
  Says that Tho King {sd
there was a witch neare
by being asked who it was {sd he Su{spected ffra: Searls wife
for Shee was an ugly Ile favored woman & he did
believe her to be one

Robt mar{sh atte{sted Says he heard Tho king Say that there
  was
a witch hard by

Action Jon wood ⎤ plea of debt
   agt ⎬
145 Jon Butler ⎦

 plt appeares

 de{st appeares not

declarat read

 Ric Ridgway atte{sted Saith that he knows that Jon
 wood did deliver a conciderable quantyty
 of wheat & that he beleives Buttler owed Jon wood
 at his going away above 20 £ to be the be{st of knowledg
 21 or 22 £ as he heard Jon Butler {say & further
 Saith that Jon Butler promi{sed Cattle for the {sd Corn

Joſeph wood atteſted proves Every article of the acctt

Judgmt given by default & it is adjudged that John Buttler
Shall pay to John wood the ſum of 5 £ ii^s wth
3 £ damages & coſt of ſuite that execution Iſſue
accordingly

Jury returned finds Tho king guilty of defameing Joan
the wife of ffrancis Searle in Saying he believed She was
witch

gilbert wheeler promiſed to pay the fees of polls act

Action g wheeler⎞
         agt ⎠ Caſe

J pidcock

plt appeare

deft appeares

decl read

Anſwer read

acctt brought in & read & atteſted

Jo Hollinſhed atteſted proves pt of the debt

verdict find for the plt wth Coſts of ſuite

adjudged that John pidcock Shall pay 2 £ : 14^s : 00^d wth
Coſts of ſuite & that execution Iſſue accordingly

A deed in fee of 296 of land dated the i2th day of the firſt mo:
$\frac{1689}{90}$ ack & dd by Hen: marg: grantor
to John Clark grantee

146

Judgmt given & it is adjudged that Tho king Shall
pay Coſt of ſuite & be bound to keep the peace
& appeare at next Court of Quarter ſeſſions

regcognizance Tho king acknowledgs
him ſelf Indebted to the pro prya & govrnr
in the ſum of 10 £ to be levyed on his
lands & tenemts goods & Chattles upon

Condition that he Shall appeare at the
next Court of Quarter Seffions & to keep
the king & queens peace in the meane
time

Adjourned to 8 in the morning

Judgmt given & it is adjudged that wm Evans none appearing
agt him Shall be difcharged paying fees & Cofts

Judgmts given & it is adjudged that Jofeph Trevithan upon
his Indictm Shall make double Satiffaction wch is he fhall
pay to Jofeph growdon ten pounds & that Jofeph
growdon Shall pay the Cofts & fees the goalers fees excepted
& whereas
the fd Trevithan hath not eftate to anfwer the fd
Satisfaction it is adjudged that the fd Trevithan
for the Same Shall Serve the fd Jofeph growdon
one yeare & a Quarter except he doth ferve
very well & fathfully one yeare then to be free at the
yeares End to wch Judgment both Jofeph growdon &
Trevithan declared theire Satiffaction

Jon: pidcock being Calld appeared & declared polcarpus Rofe
had made him Satiffaction

polcarpus Rofe appeared & nothing appearing agt him the Court
difcharges him paying his fees

overfeeres of the high way

* 148   for above the falls Ruben pownal
for below to y^e: govrnrs Jofeph Chorley
for y^e: lower pte of the river Rich wilfon
for y^e: lower pte of Nefha minah Derick Clawfon
for the upper pte of Nefha minah wm Hayhurft
the middle lotts John webfter
for the lower End of Nefhaminah on the further
fide walter fforeft & Sam Allen
for a bove Tho: Harding

Ajourned to the 7th of the 8th mo next

execution agt the goods & Chattles of Jofeph
Holden in Jon Duplovies Cafe in Philip —

Richards Cafe & in Cornelius Empfons Cafe
were dated the 19th $\frac{7}{mo}$ 1690 & returned by

the fherrife the 29 $\frac{7}{mo}$ 1690 no Goods or

Chattles to be found   wm yardley

County Court Bucks fs
$\overline{149}$

Entered the 20 day 1 month
$\frac{1691}{2}$

(1)

{ Daniel Cox by   his attorney John Tatham
   agt   plea of Debt

Gilbert wheeler }   Sum dated 26th $\frac{3}{mo}$ $\frac{90}{1}$

Entered   Gilbert wheeler

the 21 day   agt   } in a plea of Slander
                  Sum granted the 26 day of 3 mo $\frac{90}{1}$
i month   John Tatham —

(2)

14th $\frac{3}{mo}$ i69i an arref granted agt Henry Boucher to anfwer the Complt
                        of Jofeph knight 29 $\frac{3}{mo}$ 1691 return made

                   by wm yardley fherrif not to be found

Zacharia whitpaine

     agt   } in a plea of Debt }

gilbert wheeler —   not carryed on —

Entered
23 $\frac{3}{mo}$ Jofeph England
                        agt   } in a plea of Debt——— } with drawn
1691
      Lawrence Parker   Arreft dated 25th $\frac{3}{mo}$ 9i } by ordr of
(3)

                                     philip England

John Bud

agt   } plea of debt not pſecuted

Daniel gardner

(4)

Entered } Tho Hudſon agt Jacob Hall action of debt } with drawn

25th   3   ſum dated 26 3 9i } by ordr of

mo   mo   Wm Biles

(5)

Entered } John otter agt: ffrancis Roſſill

25th 3   Sum dated 26 3 91

mo   mo

1691

(6)

Entered

25: 3 9i Joſeph Chorley }

mo   agt } in a plea of

margery Clows }   Caſe   Sum dated 26 3 i69i

mo

with drawn by ordr of ſd Chorley

(7)

Entered   John Tatham

the 25 3   agt } plea of Caſe

mo Joſeph Growdon }   ſum dated 25th 3 169i

169i   mo

John Tatham not appearing a non ſuite

granted thereupon

Entered   Tho Revel ———

the 25 3   agt } action

mo   of debt   ſum dated 25th 3 i69i

(8)   ffrancis Roſſill }   mo

The 26th 3 1691

mo

150

Thomas Brock ⎫
     agt   ⎬ of a plea of Cafe ím dated 26th $\frac{3}{mo}$ 9i
ffrancis Roffill ⎭

$\frac{9^{th}\;\;\;3}{mo}$ i69i execution granted agt Jon Pidcocks

goods for 3 £ : ii^s 7^d in Tho peirce Cafe

debt 1: 0:0   iith $\frac{3}{mo}$ 9i returnd taken in execution i raw

Cl:—1: 2:1½   buck fkin 3 raw doefkinf i8 boards

Jury—0: 8:0   about 350 foot 2 smal guns with one Lock 31 lb red lead

Sherrif 0: 9:6   18th $\frac{6}{mo}$ 9i apprifed by the apprizors

witnes 0:12:0   wm Paxfon Robt Heaton the boards 6^s pc

    3:11:7½   the Skins 4^s 6^d the guns io^s the lead i5^s 6^d

the guns Lead & Skins were ordr to me by Tho peirce
for mony he owed me

about the latter end of the firft month Jon pidcock defired
me to let him have the goods as apprized & he wold pay
what they were valued at & gave me a Cannoe in pte
at 20^s & the reft promifed to pay on demand if fd peirce
did not

County Court Bucks fs   151

At a Court of Quarter Seffions held by the
authority of william & mary king & Queen
of England &c: & in the name of william
Penn propryatory & govrnr the ioth day
of the 4th month being the 3 yeare of the king
& Queens Reigne & iith yeare of the propry
atorys govrmt 169i

The Juftices then prfent
Arthur Cook   Jofeph Growdon   wm Biles
Nicholas waln   Henry Baker   John Brock
John Cook   Corronor
   wm yardley   Sherrif
Phinehas Pemberton Clark

george Brown continued on recognizance untill next Court

Judgment given by willm Biles in Cafe for thirty apple trees &
three fhillings & nine pence between Ifrael Taylor
plt & Rich Thatcher defend whereupon it was adjudged
that Rich Thatcher Shold pay Ifrael Taylor 3ˢ: 9ᵈ & thirty
apple trees or for want of the apple trees the fd Thacher to pay
ten Shillings Inftead thereof wᶜʰ Judgment is by this Court
allowed and adjudged that execution Iffue accordingly

John otter
      agt   } acᵗ debt both appeared
ffrancis Rofill

Declara read

bond Red read

Anfwer   deft owned the bond

plant   declared that he defired nothing but ten pounds with the
Intreft fince it was due

A proclamation agt vice from the govrnr read

Tho Revel agt: ffrancis Rofill in an action of debt
both appeared declarat read bill read

Anfwer   ffrancis Roffill owned the debt but not the damages

reply   Tho Revell declared that the debt without damages
wold Satiffye him

152   Tho: Brock agt: ffrancis Roffill in a plea of Cafe

both appeared

declara read

Anfwer   ffrancis Roffill owned the debt & the plant declared he

reply   defired not the damages

Judgment   given & it is adjudged that ffrancis Roffill pay to
John otter ten pounds with Intreft fince it was due
& coft of fuite & that execution Iffue accordingly

Judgmt   it is adjudged that ffrancis Roffill pay to Tho
Revell 7 £: 01ˢ: 3ᵈ with Coft of fuit & that execution
Iffue accordingly

Judgmt   it is adjudged that ffrancis Roffill pay to
                Tho Brock 10 £: 19ˢ 5ᵈ with Coſts of ſuite & that execution
                    Iffue accordingly

*Action   Daniel Cox ⎤ gilbert wheeler appeared
                        agt   ⎬
                    gilbert wheeler ⎦ Daniel Cox appeared by attorney

                Edward Hunlock & george Hutchinſon & Thomas Revel
                Edward Hunlock & Thomas Revel both of Burlington
                in weſt Jarſey do acknowledg them ſelves to ſtand
                Indebted to gilbert wheeler in the ſum of two
                hundered pounds Currant mony of this province
                to be levied on theire goods & Chattles lands and
                tenements Conditioned for that whereas an
                action being brought this Court by Daniel Cox
                agt Gilbert wheeler on a bond of 100 £ dated
                the 3 day of Aprill i690 & that they appearing on
                behalf as attorneys to the ſaid Cox & theire power
                not appearing to be Sufitiont from the ſd Cox to pſecute
                the ſd action if therefore the ſd Hunlock & Revell
                Shall hereafter
                upon demand from ſd Wheeler procure a legal authority from
                ſd Cox, to Ratefye what Shall be done by the ſd
                Hunlock & Revell in Relation to the ſaid tryal &
                make good al damages that Shall be adjudged to be payd
                by ſd Cox then the above Recognizance
                to be voyd Ells to remaine in force

Cox   letter of Attorney read

agt   declara read   ⎤
                          ⎥   153
wheeler Anſwer read   ⎥ geo: Hutchinſon
                          ⎬
         Iſſue Joyned   ⎥ James Hill
                          ⎥
         Jury atteſted   ⎥ Barnard Devoniſh
                          ⎦
         bond read

James Hill ſays that Gilbert wheeler was arreſted by him over night & that
        geo Hutchinſon engaged to bring him forth next morning
        & accordingly next morning he thinks

---

* This paragraph crossed out in record.

geo: Hutchinſon ſent for him where he found ſd wheeler in ſd
   Hutchinſon houſe & the bond was ſealed & delivered
before the ſd wheeler was acquited from the arreſt he was
under

Bernard Devoniſh Saith that he arreſted ſd wheeler late over night
   & geo: Hutchinſon engaged that ſd wheeler ſhold be forth Coming
next morning & next morning he tooke Charge of him &
delivered him to the high Sherrif

geo: Hutchinſon Saith what is before expreſſed & further ſaith yᵗ:
   next morning the Sherrife tooke Charge of him

action John Tatham ⎱
            agt ⎰
      Joſ: Growdon⎭
in an action of Caſe

John Tatham appeared by his attorneys aforeſd who
Say they are not Informed anything concerning the
ſd action & therefore deſired a continuation untill
⎰ next Court
⎱ Jos: Growdon appeares
& Craves a non ſuite with Coſts

non ſuits ⎰ whereupon it is adjudged that John Tatham not appearing
        ⎱ he ſhall ſuffer a non ſuite, & pay the Coſts

Jury return

action Jon Tatham ⎱
             agt ⎰
      gilbert wheeler⎭
Jury fines for the deft with Coſts of ſuite

Judgmt it is adjudged that Daniel Cox pay Coſts of ſuite
action gilbert wheeler ⎱
             agt ⎰
      John Tatham—⎭

ordered that the ſherrif ſum the witneſ in the aforeſd Caſe
wheeler agt Tatham

adjourned for 1 houre

gilbert wheeler & John Tatham, by his attorneys deſired the action
to be Continued untill next Court whereupon it is
continued

adjourned to the i6ᵗʰ of the 7ᵗʰ mo next

(1)   Bucks ſs: Actions Entered for the Quarter Seſſions
Action   to be held the 16ᵗʰ 7 1691
                                           mo

154 Gilbert Wheeler ⎫
              agt ⎬ in an action of Slander
      John Tatham ⎭

              Entered for Tryal laſt Court but —
              the tryal of its ſuſpended by Conſent to this

with drawn

2 Action   Stephen Beakes ⎫
  Entered   agt: ⎬ in an action of Caſe
  the 29 6 George Brown ⎭
         mo
      i691

3) Action   Stephen Beakes ⎫
   Entered   agt: ⎬ in an action of Cafe
   29ᵗʰ 6   Joſeph Steward ⎭
          mo

   169i   Summonce dated the i 7 91
                                    mo

4 Action   John Tatham ⎫
  Entered   agt⎬ in an action of Cafe
  3i 6 169i Gilbert wheeler⎭
     mo
                Summonce dated the i 7 9i
                                      mo
5 Action   John Tatham ⎫
  Entered   agt ⎬ in an action of Cafe
  the 3i 6 Joſeph Growdon ⎭
         mo
  169i   Summonce dated the 1 7 9i
                                    mo

155

7 Action ⎫ James Bleake by his Attorney ⎫
  Entered ⎪   Christopher Snodon   ⎪
  3i 6   ⎬   agt ⎬ in a plea of Cafe
    mo   ⎪ John Clawſon ——————————   ⎭
  1691   ⎭

      Summonce dated the i 7 9i
                            mo

Bucks ff:

> At a Court of Quarter Seffions held by the king
> & Queens authority in the name of William
> Pen propryatory & govrnr at the Court
> houfe for the afforefd County the i6th day of the
> 7th month being the 3 yeare of the king & Queens
> reigne & iith yeare of the propryatory govrmt

   169i   The Juftices then prfent

     Arthur Cook   Jofeph Growdon Thomas Janney
     Henry Baker
        wm yardley Sherrif
       P P Clark

A deed of a peice of meadow land about 5 ackers in fee
    dated i4th day of the 7th month i69i delivered and
    acknowledged by James moone fenior & James moone
    Junior grantors to Sam Dark grantee

grand Jury attefted

Action gilbert wheeler⎤ both appeared
          agt   ⎬
     John Tatham ⎦ & defired the action to be fufpended

for one houre wch was granted by the Court

Action Stephen Beakes ⎤ plt appeared the deft appeared not
         agt   ⎬ but it was alledged by R Hough
    Jofeph Steward ⎦ that there was Caufe for his

abfenc by reafon of a referrence difcourfed between
the parties therefore it is by Confent referred to an
other Court

      Stephen Beakes⎤ attorney to Jon Jonfon
156   agt ⎬   both appeared
      Geo Brown ⎦

    The declaration read

    Anfwer read

Judgmt, given and it is adjudged that Stephen Beakes
    Shall fuffer a non fuite & pay Coft of Court

george Brown acknowledged what was due to Jonſon
& promiſed to pay the ſame to Stephen Beakes before
the next Court of Quarter ſeſſions wᶜʰ he acknow
=ledges to be due 26 buſhels of wheate with Intreſt

*but Stephen Beakes refuſed to Rec it ſo & diſcharges the ſd
geo: Brown from his promiſe

Adjourned for one houre

grand Jurys prſentmts brought in

overſeeres of the High ways

for above the falls Reuben pownal
from thence to the govrnrs Edward Lucas
from thence below to neſhaminah Richard wilſon
for the Lower part of neſhaminah James paxſon
for newtown
for middle Lots James moone
for the lower part between neſhamina & poqueſin
John Gilbert & Sam Allen Junior
for ſouthhampton Tho Hardin

Tho Brock atteſted ſaith that Christopher Snodon deſired
the action agt John Clawſon to be ſtayed this Court

Aprizers appointed untill furter ordr
Sam Dark Joſeph kirkbride & John Rowland

george Brown being bound to appeare laſt Court
was continued & therefore deſired this
Court to diſcharge him who as accordingly diſcharged

157

action   gilbert wheeler agt John Tatham againe Calld

withdrawn   gilbert wheeler deſired the action to be with drawn

Daniel Cox by his attorneys

Action   John Tatham agt G Wheeler

withdrawn   by ordr of John Tatham in open Court

———

*Crossed out in record.

The Conſtables for this County already Choſen are ſtill
Continued till further ordr

Action John Tatham ⎫ both appeared & Joſeph Growdon
           agt ⎬ made Claim of the benefit of
Joſeph Growdon ⎭ the law for magiſtrates &
Councill men becauſe the time was but Short &
therefore was not prepared for tryal & therefore
the Court, gave him time untill the next Court

adjourned untill 8 a Clock tomorrow morning

        Juſtices prſent   A Cook Joſeph Growdon
          Tho Janney   Henry Baker   Jo: Brock
          wm yardley   ſherrife
          P P Cl

ordered   whereas the grand Jury prſented at a Court
               held the 12th i 89 the

by the Court   mo
              neceſſity of haveing a tax raiſed to pay the Councell
that a   & ſſembley men
              for theire attendance already & other publique Charges of
tax of   the County
              it was accordingly ordered by a Court held the 26th 1 90 that
300 £ ſhall   mo
              a Tax of 300 £ be raiſed according to on the lands & males
be raiſed   of this
              County for the uſes aforeſd & that returns be pſected
for the ſd   according
              to former ordr of lands & males & now ordered that &
              duplicates made thereof to every
uſes   Collector for raiſeing the ſd mony

158   george philips being taken up for a runaway by
        Thomas Brock & brought before this Court being
        ſearſhed was found in his pocket 1 purs in
        which was foure pounds 9^{d} ſilver mony & one braſs
        9^{d} bit who upon his examination Confeſt that he
        had taken the Said monys in the night time out
        of the Cloſet of Denis Linſtone with whom he had
        lived about 3 months as alsoe one paire of gloves
        wch ſaid gloves he the ſd philips Confeſt he tooke out of
        the ſaid Cloſet

Judgment given and it is adjudged that the faid George
philips Shall make fatiffaction to the partie greived
as the law requires by fervitude & that he the fd
george philips have 15 ftripes on his bare back
well Layd on now in the fight of the Court
& that he be Confined in the Sherrifs Cuftody (untill
his mafter have notice hereof) & that he be not ——
delivered to his faid mafter witout order
from Jofeph Growdon to whom this Court
referrs the fd Denis Linftone to treate about the
fd george philips freedome or fervitude being obte
ined as is fd Conterary to law

ordered yᵗ: the Said monys be kept by Phinehas
Pemberton as allfo the Gloves
& that after alcharges fees & Cofts are deducted
that the remameing part be delivered to the
owner thereof

adjourned to the ioᵗʰ month next

County Court Bucks ff 9ᵗʰ io i69i   159
                        mo

Action Sufpended laft Court untill this Court —		
John Tatham a agt Jofeph growdon	in a plea of Cafe	

Action Entered the 23 9ᵗʰ mo: i69i	Jofeph Growdon agt John Gray als Tatham	in a plea for trefpafs done	Sum Granted the 23 9 i69i mo

Action Entered the 23 9ᵗʰ mo: i69i	Jofeph Growdon agt John White	in a plea of trefpafs ——	Sum Granted the 23 9 169i mo

Action Entered the 23 9 mo i69i	Jofeph Growdon agt Edward Cartor	in a plea of trefpafs	Sum Granted the 23 9 169i mo

Action Entered ⎱ Joſeph Growdon ⎱ in a plea of ⎱
the 23 9ᵗʰ mo i69i ⎰   agt   ⎰   ⎰ Sum Granted
            Henry Hudleſtone ⎰ treſpaſs ⎰ the 23 9 1691

                                                         mo

Action Entered ⎱ Joſeph Growdon ⎱ in a plea of ⎱
the 23 9   mo i69i ⎰   agt   ⎰   ⎰ Sum Granted
            Tho : Stakehouſe Junr ⎰ treſpaſs ⎰ the 23 9 1691

                                                         mo

160   County Court Bucks ſs:

At

A Court of Quarter Seſſions held by the authority of Willm
& mary king & Queen of England &c: & in the name of
Willm Penn propryatory & govrnr of the province
of Penſylvania & Territorys annexed att the Court
houſe for the aforeſd County of Bucks the 9ᵗʰ day of the
ioᵗʰ month being the 3 yeare of the king & Queens
reigne & iiᵗʰ yeare of the propryatorys govrmt 1691

     The Juſtices then prſent

        Tho Janney willm Biles Henry Baker John Brock
        wm yardley Sherrife
        P P Cl: Com

the mony found upon Geo: philips viz 2 £ : 10ˢ: 9ᵈ & one bad
     9ᵈ bitt wᶜʰ was delivered to phinehas pemberton to
     be kept, for the owner thereof untill the owner was
     known being what remained Charges
     being deducted out of the whole for takeing of him
     up & other fees then Contracted, was delivered
     to Arthur Cook; by the ſd phinehas pemberton wᶜʰ
     this Court doth allow of & diſcharges the ſd phinehas
     Pemberton of the ſd mony the remaneing part
     thereof wᶜʰ was kept back for fees & Charges was 30ˢ
     the whole being 4 £ & 9ᵈ & one 9ᵈ bitt

     whereas there has none Comen to Complaine agt Geo
     philips for any miſdemeanor Committed by him
     the Court by Conſent of the boy has put him to
     H Baker for 6ᵗʰ months to ſee what may in the
     meane time be alledged agt him

        adjourned to the 9ᵗʰ 1 mo next

28 day of the ii^th i69i Joſeph Holdens Land was taken in
execution by willm yardley Sherrife to ſatiſſye the debt
and Coſt of Jon Duplovies Philip Richards & Cornelius
Empſon

Bucks ſs: (161)

At A Court of Quarter Seſſions held by the king & Queens
authority in the name of wm Penn propryatory & govrnr
A the Court houſe for the afforeſd County the 9th day
of the firſt month 169i
$$\frac{2}{}$$

Juſtices prſent
Joſeph Growdon   wm Biles
    Nicholas waln   Henry Baker
    willm yardley   Sherrif
    P Pemberton   Clark

Atteſtation Samuel overton atteſted doth Say that he lent two Chaines to John
Clows
that he never Rd the ſd Chaines either from ſd Clows or
any other pſon directly or indirectly Since that time

Dunckin Williams & his ſon william williams, being bound over to this
Court upon Complaint of Joſeph Growdon & his baile deſireing
to be diſcharged declareing they will not ſtand bound any longer
& the ſd Dunckin
williams Craveing untill an other Court to prepare him ſelf

Comitmt for tryal, wch is allowed & the Court Commits them into Cuſtody
untill they Shall give
Suffitient Security for his appearance at next Court & keeping the
peace in the meane time
*& Hannah williams the ſd Dunckin williams daughter being
Committed
upon the ſd Complt: She is likewiſe Committed untill the next Court
or untill ſecurity be given for her appearance at next Court
But at the requeſt of Joſeph Growden Shee is ſet at liberty upon
her promiſe to appear at next Court

John Bowen & Ralph Boome being Calld upon Complaint of Geo:
Philips

*Crossed out in original record.

It appearing that the ſd Geo Philips was Ilegaly ſold by John Bowen
& Ralph Boome unto Denis Linck who lives out of the province
it is ordered that John Bowen Shall Diſcharge Ralph Boome
& Reimburſe what Denis Linck has payd towards the price he
was to give for him & that Ralph Boome Diſcharge the
ſaid Linck: & that the ſaid Geo Philips Shall ſerve the
Said John Bowen in Conſideration of the damage done to him by ſd
    Philips 2 yeares from this day & that he the ſd John
Bowen Shall pay to Henry Baker for what Cloths he hath bought for
him what they may be Judged to be reaſonably worth & yᵗ: all parties
declared theire Satiſſaction herein

adjourned the 4ᵗʰ month 8ᵗʰ day

162

The Second day of the _3_ i692 the Land of Joſeph
                       mo
Holden formerly taken in execution was
appriſed to eighty pounds
    by Joſuah Hoops James Dilworth Robt Heaton
        Tho: Stakehouse Jon Purſlone Peter Chamberlaine
        Iſrael Taylor Hugh marſh Robt marſh
        Jonathan ſcaife Henry Hudleſtone Joſias Hill

163 At a Court of Quarter Seſſions held by the king &
    Queens authority in the name of wm Penn propry
    atory and govrnr at the Court houſe of the ſd County
    the 8ᵗʰ of the 4ᵗʰ month 1692

            Juſtices prſent

            Joſeph Growdon   wm Biles
            Nich waln   Henry Baker
            John Cook   Corronor
            P: P: Cl Com:

—A deed of 27 acres of land in fee dated 6ᵗʰ _2_ 92 from Joſeph Engliſh
                                            mo
    grantor to Tho Brock Grantee was dld & ack by P. P. attorney
    to yᵉ: ſd grantor
—A deed of 500 acres of land in fee 8ᵗʰ io mo 169i acknowledged and
    delivered by John Rowland Grantor to Henry Baker
    grantee
—A deed of 200 acres of land in fee 4ᵗʰ 4 mo 92 acknow

ledged & delivered by John Cooke attorney to Sam Allen Grantor to John
Baldwin Grantee

—A deed in fee of 500 acres of land in fee dated 16th day $\frac{7}{mo}$ 169i
    acknowledged
    and delivered by Joſeph Chorley attorney to Jacob
    Hall grantor unto wm Biles attorney to Thomas
    Hudſon grantee

—A deed in fee of 200 acres of land acknowledged and
    delivered by Samuel Allen grantor to Samuel
    allen his ſon grantee dated the 8th day of the
    4th month 1692

—A deed in fee for 200 acres of land acknowledged and
    delivered unto Jon Baldwin by
    Sam Allen grantor for the uſe of his grand
    daughter Elizabeth Pegg dated the 7th day of the
    4th mo: i692

Complaint being made agt Boome for Some extavigant
        ſpeeches he Submitting to the Court it was ordered
        that Ralph Boome ſhold pay to the wittneſſ 4^{s} &
        other Coſts of Court

wm Duncan wm being bound to this Court to appeare to anſwer
        the Complt of Joſeph Growdon deſired the ſd Court to
        ſuſpend the tryal untill another Court for that his
        wittneſes were not in readyneſs

        2 Rods through the Land added in breath to the breath mentioned
164   A deed of one hundered & 20 acres in fee dated the 8th $\frac{4}{mo}$ 169i
                acknowledged and dd by R: Ridgway grantor to
                Sam Beakes grantee

Corronors   Inqueſt Concerning the death of Ellizabeth Chappel
            taken before John Cooke Corronor the i5th of the
            3 month i692 was this day returned into this
            Court that the death was Caſual by falling of
            her horſe into the water

Corronors Inqueſt Concerning the death of an unknown pſon
found neare the mouth of Neſhaminah Creeke
the 8ᵗʰ day of the 3 month i692 taken before
John Cooke Corronor the i2ᵗʰ day of the ſd 3
month was this day returned into this Court
that he was wilfully murthered

upon due examination of things it appeared that a Conſiderable
Quantyty of blood on the wall and on the bed of one
Derick Jonſon or Clawſon about the ſuppoſed time
that the above murthered pſon loſt his life
was diſcovered & the ſd Derick
refuſed to give any acctt how the
ſd blood Come there whereupon this Court Commits
him the ſaid Derick claws ali Jonſon into
Safe Cuſtody of the Sherrif untill he ſhall be delivered by due
Courſe
of Law

ordered that the ſaid Dearricks houſe be ſearched forthwith
for ſuſpitious goods or other things that may make
any further diſcovery by John Purſlone James
Paxſon & Tho Stakehouſe with what further aſſiſtance
they may ſee Cauſe for the doing thereof

adjourned to the 7ᵗʰ mo next

Entered   Seſſions held the 14ᵗʰ 7. 92
                                        mo

29ᵗʰ   wm Biles
  6   agt: in a plea of Caſe
 mo
1692   gilbert wheeler

29ᵗʰ   Stephen Beakes
6ᵗʰ mo   agt   in a plea of Caſe
1692   gilbert wheeler

30th ⎫ John whitpaine ⎫
6 mo   ⎬   by his attorney   ⎬
92   ⎬   willm Nichols   ⎬ in a plea Ejectione firme
—   ⎬   agt   ⎬
      ⎭   John Teft   ⎭

Examina^t of Derrick Jonſon Saith he Showed the blood on the   165
    wall to Edward Lane & his Brother Claws Jonſon & to mary
    Boyden
    he also Saith there was no blood on the bed but whas by a
    man that Came to thraſh for him 3 yeares ago & that he had
    Spoke of the blood fully as much as it was

Corronor Saith that when he went to veiue the blood on the wall he
    perceived that it had run in Several ſtreames down the
    boords on the wall wch ſtreames Continued untill they
    went behind the planks that lay on the grown floore

Examina^t of Brighta the wife of ſd Derrick Saith that the blood ſeene
    on the wall was diſcovered between day & ſun riſeing
    & that there was a Sheet hanged on the out ſide
    of the bed in ſtead or manner of a Curtaine & that there was no
        blood
    on the bed
    being aſked when they put freſh Straw in the bed ſhee
    Said Shee was not Certaine but ſhee thought about the
    latter end of march or beginning of Aprill

        adjourned the Court to the i4th of the 7th mo next

Penſylvania
        Bucks County Court

    166   At a Court of Quarter Seſſions held
                by the king & Queens authority in the
                name of willm Penn propryatory & govrnr of the
                afore Said Province & Territorys thereunto
                    belonging
                at the Court houſe for the Said County the i4th day
                    of
                the 7th month being the 4th yeare of the reigne of
                willm & mary king & Queen of England &c: & i2th
                yeare of the propryatorys govrmt Anno dm: 1692

The Juſtices prſent

Arthur Cook Joſeph Growdon willm Biles
Nicholas Waln   Henry Baker
John Cook   Corronor
Samuel Beakes Sherrif
Phinehas Pemberton Cl: Com:

Entered the 29th 6 92
mo

Willm Biles plt————⎱
  agt   ⎰ action of the Caſe
Gilbert wheeler deft ⎰

Summonce dated the 3i 6   this action withdrawn by
mo   order of willm Biles

declaration & Summonce ſerved —
by Sa Beakes Sherrife the 2nd 7 92
mo

entered 29th 6mo 92

Stephen Beakes plt
  agt   action of the Caſe
Gilbert wheeler deft   this action withdrawn by ordr

declaration & Summonce ſerved   of the plt
by Sa Beakes Sherrife the 2nd 7 92
mo

Entered the 30th 6 92 wm Nichols letter of attorney from Ed Antil Leaſor
mo

John whitpaine plt: proved
by his attorney wm Nichols
  agt: in action of Ejectmt It appearing to this Court
                  that this action was not
John Teft deft   brought according to —
declaration with the notice endorſed   former method the Court
Served & read upon the premiſes the 2nd 7th mo92 was not willing to admit
                  the tryal but Gilbert —
    wheeler then poſſeſſt of the premiſes prayed that
    he might be admitted defent & that the action might be —
    brought on notwithſtanding they had varyed from the former
    method & So did the plant attorney whereupon the Court
    gave way & ordered the tryal accordingly Shold be pmitted to paſs
    and thereupon Iſſue was Joyned

deft   pleaded not Guilty as to terme with force & armes
Aníwer

but as to the treípaís defends the force for that the íd Ed Antill
   Leaíor did enter upon the premíses as a diíeizor   (167)

reply   And the Sd Edward Antil by his íd attorney replyes that he did
   not enter as a diíſeizor & this he deſires may be enquired of by
   the Cuntry & So doth the deft in like mannor wherefore

venire   the Sherrife is Commanded to return a Jury

Jury returned {
Richard Hough
Robt Heaton
James paxſon
John Rowland
Edmund Lovet
Joſeph kirkbride
John white
Samuel Dark
Stephen Beakes
Joſeph milner
Job Bunting
Thomas Brock
} atteíted

declara read

Aníwer read

deed from gilbert wheeler unto Ed Antill of the premíses read &
   owned by Gilbert wheeler

two letters read Said to be from Gilbert wheeler to Ed Antill owing
   mony due to be pd to Ed Antill but the íd letters were not owned
   nor diſowned by, íd wheeler the one dated December the i8th i686
   the other dated auguít the ioth i689

A deed in fee for 200 acres of land dated the 20th of the 9th month i690
   acknowledged & delivered
   by Hugh marſh & Anthony morgan grantors
   unto Joſias Hill grantee

A mortgage dated the 20th of the 9th month i690 for 200 acres of Land
   acknowledged
   & delivered by Josias Hill grantor to Anthony morgan grantee

Adjourned the Court untill tomorrow morning at 8 a Clock

petition of Evan Prothera read Concerning george Philips Servitude

petitioner referred to treat with John Bowen for the ſaid Philips time of ſervi =tude & if done to Content of all parties the Juſtices will ratefye the agreem

ordered   that it be aſſented to that if the Said Evan prothera do make reaſonable

Satisfaction to John Bowen his prſent maſter & that the ſd Jon Bowen

and geo: Philips be agreeing to the ſame that then the ſd Evan Prothera

the remainder of the time he is to ſerve the ſd John Bowen by order of Court for what loſſ time the ſd geo Philips & Evan Prothera Can agree for

Thomas Bowman atteſted doth Say that to his knowledg after that Ed Antill

---

168   had attached the goods of gilbert wheeler to his knowledg Gilbert wheeler Stood in So much feare of Ed Antill that he durſt not Come to York for a time except privately untill that he had given him a mortgage of his land

Conſtables & overſeerers of the High way — appointed —

Conſtables

over Seers of the High way for the ſd places

Conſtables	over Seers of the High way for the ſd places
above the falls Ruben Pownal—	Peter Worral
thenc to the govrnrs Ed Lucas—	Stephen Beakes
thence below to neſhaminah Ricd Wilſon ————	willm Dungan
Neſhaminah — Tho: Stakehouſe ſr ————	Henry Pawlin
middle lotts—Edmund Lovet—	Abraham Cox
the other ſide of Neſhaminah Jon: Gilbert ————	Samˡ Allen

Jury returned Brought in theire verdict for the plt ————

An Appeale preſently thereupon Requeſted by the defent to the next provincial

Court in Equity wᶜʰ was then by the Court allowed of & adjudged that he the ſd deft

giveing Security to proſecute the ſd appeale & pay Coſts ought to

have an appeale

By Confent

& on

requeſt to the Court

⎫
⎬
⎭
of both plt & deſt that the ſd appeale might be
deferred to the
provincial Court in Equity wᶜʰ Shold happen in
Spring next
wᶜʰ was allowed of by the Court & ordered that
ſecurity be taken accordingly

Recognizance morand that Gilbert wheeler and Robt Cole both of the affreſd
County
Came before this Court & acknowledged them ſelves to be
Indebted to
Edward Antill of new York Gente: in the Sum of fifty pounds
Currant
mony of this Province to be pd to the ſd Ed Antill for true
paymt
whereof they grant for them ſelves theire heires executors &
adminiſtrators
that the Said Sum be levied & recovered from their lands and
tenemts goods Chattles & heriditaments of them the ſd Gilbert
Wheeler
& Robt Cole theire heires executors & adminiſtrators & aſſigns
where
ever they be found

Condition — And this upon Condition that the ſd Gilbert Wheeler Shall
appeare
at the provintial Court which Shall be held for this County in
the Spring next and then & there Shall proſecute his appeale
wᶜʰ is taken in Equity with effect and if he be Caſt in the ſd
Court Shall not only
pay all the Coſts and damages he ſhall be Caſt in al
the ſaid Court but alſo all the Coſts & damages of this prſent
Court

A deed in fee of 248 acres of land dated the 8ᵗʰ day of the 4ᵗʰ month i692
was acknowledged & delivered by Henry Baker grantor to
Job Bunting grantee

A deed in fee of 60 acres of land dated the 7ᵗʰ day of the 4ᵗʰ month i692
was acknowledged & delivered by Robt Heaton attorney to
John Auſtin grantor unto Nicholas waln grantee

169

road — whereas the order formerly for laying out the road from the
upper plantations upon Delaware to the Landing at the ferry
houſe agt: Burlington was not obſerved & that Some of the pſons

ordered are removed its therefore now

ordered that Henry Baker Ruben Pownal Joſeph milner Enoch yardley
Jacob Janney Richard Hough Abraham Cox & Edmund Lovet
or any 6 of them do lay out the Said Road & give an acctt
thereof to the next Court

townſhips whereas there was Encouragemt formerly for the deviding
of this County into Town ſhips from the Council & that there
upon there was an ordr from the Court to pticulers for the
deviding the Same & that it was not pformed accordingly
its therefore now

ordered That Arthur Cook Joſeph Growdon John Cook Tho: Janney
Richard Hough Henry Baker Phinehas Pemberton Joſuah Hoops
wm Biles Nicholas waln Edmund Lovet & Abraham Cox James
Boyden or the greater number of them meet together at
the meeting houſe at neſhaminah the 27th of this Inſtant & devide
this County
in to Town ſhips

adjourned this Court to the meeting houſe at Neſhaminah to the 27 day
of this Inſtant month

At a Court held by adjournmt the 27th day of the
7 mo: 1692

The Juſtices then prſent

Arthur Cook   Joſeph Growdon

Tho: Janney   Nicholas waln   Henry Baker

Sam Beakes   Sherrif

P Pemberton   Cl: Com:

whereas there
was a tax
formerly
ordered it is now ordered that the Same be forthwith raiſed
that warrants be iſſued to the
　　　　　Conſtables of every deviſion for the doing thereof yt when
　　　　　　　　　　　　Rd it be pd to Joſeph growdon
Arthur Cook, Nicholas waln & Sam Beakes
that the publique Charges of the County
may be defrayed

ordered that the receivers be accountable to every Court of Quarter
ſeſſions from time

to time as they receive any of the
íd mony
adjourned to next third day at Court houſe

i4 __8__ 1692 the lands of Joſeph Holden taken in Execution
mo
to ſatiſfye the debts & Coſt of Duplovies Richards & Empſon
were Sold to Joſeph Growdon at ſeventy ſeven
pounds by Sam.ˡˡ Beakes Sherrife

170

Entered the 23 9 mo 1692

John Nichols   by his attorneys Phinehas Pemberton & Henry Baker,

witneſſes   agt
    Bartholomew Joſeph & Amos Thatcher
Joſeph Henbery   Executors of   plea of debt
    John Brearley
            Richard Thatcher

Summonce dated the 26 __9__ 92
                                mo

Entered the 23 __9__ 1692   Sum for witneſes date 29 __9__ 92
            mo   mo

Tho: Brock

            agt
Roger Litgraine
Anthony Banks   plea of debt
    Rich Thatcher Bartholomew Thatcher
        & Joſeph Thatcher

Sum dat: 26 __9__   92
                mo

Entered the 23 9 month i692   Sum for witneſes dated 29.ᵗʰ __9__
                                                            mo

wm Biles

wm Yardley   agt
P Pemberton   } plea of Debt

    Ralph Boome   Sum dat 28 9   92
                                mo

with drawn by order of wm Biles

Entered 26 9 mo i692   Sum for witnefes dat 29 9   92
                                           mo

Jofeph Chorley
      agt   } plea of Cafe
Edward Lucas   Sum dat 28 9   92
                         mo

John Nichols
      agt   } plea of Cafe
John Smith   withdrawn

John Nichols
      agt: } plea of debt
Thomas Stakehoufe Junr   withdrawn

Ric Thatcher
      agt   } plea of Cafe
Henry Greenland

Arreft granted dated 4th day 9   92
                             mo
return executed 4 day 9   92 & baile
                      mo
Taken for him

Bucks ff   (171)

At a Court of Quarter Seffions held by the king &
Queens authority in the name of wm: Penn propry
ator & govrnr of the Province & Territorys there
unto belonging at the Court houfe for the afore
faid County the i4th day of the io 1692
                                  mo

Juſtices preſent

wm: Biles   Nicholas waln   Henry Baker
Sam: Beakes Sherriſe
P Pemberton Cl: <u>Com</u>

adjourned to Joſeph Chorleys houſe

The preſentments of the over ſeeres of the high way for
Buckingham brought in

A deed in fee for 340 acres of land dated the 2ⁿᵈ day of the
ninth month 1692 acknowledged and deliv by wm Biles
attorney to Elliz Bennet grantor to n waln grantee

action Jos Chorley ⎫
          agt ⎬ both appeared
    Ed Lucas ⎭

declar read

Anſwer not guilty put them ſelves upon tryal

Jury Atteſted

witneſſes examined

adjourned for one houre

verdict   find for the deft

A deed in fee of 500 acres of land dated the 12ᵗʰ day of the
7 mo 92 was ack & dd by Rich Lundy grantor to
ffrancis Roſſill grantee

An Appeale requeſted by Joſeph Chorley
but the pretended damages not being 10 £ Sterling & the Jury
declareing they had reviued the ox & that he was So little harmed
by the Shot that the ſd Chorley needed not to have loſt 2 days
work for any harme the ox had Rd by the Same
as alſo the deft: Craveing the benefit of the
law that where the debt or damages is pretended to be above
5 £ & it prove under that in ſuch Caſe the plt Shall loſe his
action whereupon the Court ſaw no Cauſe to grant him an

appeale ——

Judgment Granted and it is adjudged that Joſeph Chorley pay Coſts
& that Execution Iſſue accordingly

Richard Thatcher ⎫ both Called but   ⎫
        agt   ⎬   ⎬
Henry Greenland ⎭ neither appeared ⎭ adjourned to the
                                         8th of the firſt month

J: Whitpaine a ⎫
172   agt   ⎬ ejectione firme   Execution agt Thatcher & Taylor
J   Teſt ─────── ⎭   ˢ   ᵈ   in revell Caſe ── 4 : 19 : 6

filing dec. & Coppy ₋₋ 2 : 3	agt Thatcher in ──⎱ 1 : 16 : 0
Sum: & return ───── 2 : 6	Derrick Jonſons Caſe⎰
Sum: for the Jury ─ 1 : 0	fees ───────── 3 : 09 : 4
entering the action ─ 0 : 7½	Taylors Caſe ───── 0 : 17½: 6
Anſwer & Coppy ──── 2 : 0	pd grace Langhorn 1 : 05½: 0
Judgmt & Coppy ──── 2 : 7½	apprizers ──── 0 : 01 : 5
verdict .1 : 3	Sherrifs fees ───── 1 : 16 : 0
recording letter attor 3 : 0	
Juſtices fees ───── 3 : 6	13 : 19 9
appeale ──── ──── 7 : 0	
recognizance ───── 1 : 0	
amo & coppy ───── 1 : 0	taken in execution ⎫
	to ſatiſfye the above ⎬
1 : 7 : 9	in Tho Brocks hand ⎬ 2 : 07 : 6
	for Iſrael Taylor ſhare ⎭
3 evidences 3 : 0	

Holdens good apprized at

but Sold att   i red Cow ─────── 3 : 10 : 0

                                     i horſe ──────── 5 : 0 : 0

                                   Rich Thatcher pd him⎫
                                   ſelf in Iron ware to ⎬i : 8 : 2
                                   wm Beakes ───────⎭

Ste Newel—ferving the warrant iˢ : 0 — 0 : 0
rideing Charges ——— 0 : 6
Summmonce — 0 : 7½
order of Court — 0 : 7½
Coppy thereof ——— 0 : 7½
= 3 : 4½

pd in Tho ſtackhous }
to Derrick ——— }   1 : 8 : 0
.
Holden Caſe ═══13 : i3 : 8

Jon Jones execut   38 : 11   7

Sherrifs fees
  Jon Duplovie ——— i5 : 08 : 06

  Sherrifs fees — —
  Philip Richards— ii : 10 : 03

  Sherrifs fees
  Cornelius Empſon 8 : 15 : 04

Jon Swift for the pp.ᵗʳ

agt Philip Conway Execution is 16£ 3ˢ : 3ᵈ
  pat & Philip Conway is   6 : 16 : 1

      22 : 19 : 4

* [173]

Pennſylvania

Bucks ſs: At a Court of Quarter Seſſions held by the
authority in the name of wm Penn Propryatory of
the aforeſaid Province & Territorys thereunto belonging
at the houſe of Samˡ : Beakes the 8ᵗʰ day of the 1ˢᵗ month 1693

Juſtices prſent
Joſeph Growdon   wm Biles
Nicholas Waln   Henry Baker
John Cook —— Corronor
Sam Beakes Sherrife
P P Cl Com:

Adjourned the Court for one houre

*Number lost with the portion of page torn off and missing.

Recogniz: wm Duncan being Calld on his recognizance none appearing agt
him the Court
diſcharges him paying his fees

Recognz: Derick Clawſon als Jonſon being bound by recognizance in 100 £
& Claws J
& Peter Rambo in 50 £ apeice for the appearance of ſd Derick
Clawson
als Jonſon at this Court & for his good abearing in the meane
time
were all them Calld but none of them appeared

Recogniz: Robt Benſon being Calld on his Recognizance appeared none
appearing agt
him the Court diſcharges him paying his ffees

Sum: Stephen Newel being Summonced to Court for Selling a Servant
out of
yᵉ: Province he alleadged htat he had not ſold him but lent him
for Some time & that he wold bring him back in 3 months time

A deed of 5 acres of land in ffee dated the 8ᵗʰ day of march
acknowledged & delivered in open Court by Thomas * * *
his wife grantors to Tho: Brock Grantee

A deed in fee of 5½ acres of land was acknow * * *
by Tho green & Rachel his wife grantors * * *
Burton grantee
Richard Thatcher being bound Commited into * * *

requeſt — of ffellony being Calld requeſted his Tryal might be deferred
time & that in the meane time he might * * *
until his Tryal wᶜʰ is left to the diſcretion * * *
the ſd Thatcher Shall apply him Self * * *

Recogn: Job Houle being bound to this Court * * *
Complaint Coming agt him by Tho Brock * * *

174

* * * n als Jonſon & Jon Clawſon & Peter Rambo againe
* * * appeared not
reas Prudence the negro of An fforeſt was oblidged * * *
appeare at this Court & hath departed the ſame without
examination
ordered that warrant do Iſſue to apprehend the Said Negro for
the apprehending & for the Safe keeping of the Said negro, that She may

Anſwer
all ſuch Complaints as Shall be layd agt her at the time this
Court Shall be adjourned unto & that Wm Biles Take Care about it

Adjourned this Court untill the day the aſſizes Shall be
the i4ᵗʰ day of 2ⁿᵈ month next

At a Court of Quarter Seſſions held by adjournmt at
the Court
houſe for the afforeſd County the i4ᵗʰ day of the 2
month i693

The Juſtices prſent

Joſeph Growdon   wm Biles

Nicholas waln   Henry Baker

Saml Beakes   Sherrife

P: P: Cl: Com

Addington plt ⎫
              ⎬ in a plea of Caſe this action with drawn by order
    agt   ⎪ of yᵉ: plt:
Hewit deft — ⎭

* * * & Rich Burges, atteſted to Dericks Indictm Iſrael
Taylor
Atteſted
* * * for 250 acres of land dated this day acknowledged & dd
* * * Taylor grantor to James yates grantee

Tho Lacy being bound by recognizance to appeare here
being
* * * to get mary Roles with Child appeared accordingly
* * * being examined about the Same declared that Tho: Lacy
had
* * * with child & Sayd he lay with her Several times one
* * * time was the firſt
day afore Isaac page dyed wᶜʰ is Said to be
about the
the 9ᵗʰ month & lay with her but once afterwards & that
was about 13 or 14
* * * from this time

Tho Lacy give bond to anſwer the ſd Complt at the next Court

* * * Tho: Lacy acknowledged him felf Indevted to
the propryetor

* * * Ifrael Taylor in 5£ to be levyed on their lands &
Tenemts

* * * les & this is upon Condition for the appearance of
the fd

* * * next Court to the aforefd Compt of mary
Roles

* * * el Taylor had arrefted him & that he defired
* * * granted him he being about to depart the * * *

the goods mentioned in the acct owned by the deft but not
were delivered upon the acctt of the finifhing of a barn

wm Plumley attefted for the plt   175

Robt marfh attefted for the deft

A Contract for Hugh Marfh his finifhing Ifrael Taylors barn read &
parties

Job Houle appeared according to recognizance & none appearing agt him.
difcharges him paying the fees

adjourned for one houre

ᵗ Robt Benfon Jon Clark Jon Crofdell Jon penquoit Jof Chorley Witneffes
agt: R Thather for ftealing amare attefted

grand Jury Impaneled & attefted

Richard Thather being Calld appeared according to recognizance
ordered that he be taken into the Sherrifs Cuftody untill further order

adjourned for one houre

one deed of 300 acres of land in fee dated the i4ᵗʰ $\frac{2}{mo}$ ack &

H marfh & Sa: marfh grantors to Jo Eaftbourn grantee

Jury returned to find for Hugh Marfh deft with Cofts

defᵗ came into Court & acquainted that Ifrael Taylor had Satiffyed h
to be fufpended

Rich Thatcher Calld & arraigned upon his Indictmt.
pleaded not guilty put him felf for tryal puts him felf on the Cuntry
x x x el Taylor had arrefted him & that he deʰired
x x x granted him he being about to depart the

Robt Benſon Atteſted doth Say that he never Saw the mare but Said
he bought the mare & Colt of John Clark

Joſeph Chorley atteſted doth Say that on a firſt day John Clarke * * *
on a black mare wᶜʰ ſd Ric Thatcher ſd was his mare * * *
in her foreh head wᶜʰ Thather now Confeſes was the mare that
Croſdells paſture

Robt Cole atteſted doth Say that he ſaw Rich Thather when he brought
mare over the river wᵗʰ a mare Colt with her of a bla * * *
with a large Star in her face & a Snip on her noſe & a Croſs on
one Ear
& he aſked ſd Thather where he had the ſd mare he ſd b * * *
an eaſt Jarſey man & that he bought her on the road be * * *
Brinſon, & doctor greenlands & that Jon Richards * * *
Houghtons was prſent when he bought her wᶜʰ mare
Thather Confeſſes that it was the ſame wᶜʰ he ſold to Jon * * *

Jon Croſdell atteſted doth Say that Thater Came to ſee the mare   ;
brothers paſture & that ſd Thather Confeſt it was the mare he
Clark & that he knows that ffrancis white or his mother * * *
the Same mare of Tho ſtakehouse Junior

jon penquoit Saith as above

Derick Clawſon appearing this Court according to recognizance
the Court diſcharged him of the ſd recognizance & his * * *
Jon Gilbert being accused with begeting a bastard Child on a
negro on the window fforeſt.   & it appeare on * * *

Judgmt given & it is adjudged that Rich Thatcher Shall pay to ffrancis
white 40ˢ & Coſt it being all that ffra white deſired to have
awarded him & that he be whipt i5 Laſhes on his bare back
adjourned to the 4ᵗʰ month next

176

Pennſylvania

Bucks ſs: 177   (176)*

At a provincial Cercular Court held by the king & Queens
authority
in the name of William Penn propryeter & govrnr of the
Said province & territorys thereunto belonging at the
Court
houſe for the Said County the i4ᵗʰ day of the 2ⁿᵈ month 1693
being the 4ᵗʰ yeare of the king & Queens reigne

* This page is numbered as above.

The Judges prſent

Samuel Jenings   Joſeph Growdon

Samuel Beakes Sherrife

P P: Cl: Com

Commiſſion Read

grand Jury atteſted

Edward Lane Jon: purley & Tho: ſtakehouſe ſenr atteſted

Court adjourned for 2 houres

Adjourned untill tomorrow moring at io a Clock

grand Jury returned do prſent Derick Clawſon als Jonſon for murthering an unknown perſon found neare the mouth of Neſhaminah Creek the 8ᵗʰ of the 3 month 1692 being Suppoſed to be murthered about the beginning month i692

Derrick Jonſon als Clawſon being brought into Court & the grand Jurys prſentmt
read to him he pleaded not guilty & he Craved to have further time for his Tryal he not being
prepared for it wᶜʰ was allowed him by the Court untill the next provincial Circular Court to be held for this County being the kings not So full as hereafter is expected & yᵗ: the kings attorney here to proſecute

Recognizance Edward Lane John Purſley Thomas Stakehouſe Senr
& Richard Burges acknowledges them Selfs to be Indebted to the govrnr: each of them in the Sum of forty - pounds
to be levied on theire lands & tenements goods & Chattles
Condition that the appeare at the next Circular provincial
this County to give in Evidence the truth of theire
the prſentmᵗ agt Derick Clawſon als Jonſon for the muther of an unknown peron found nere the mouth of neſhaminah

adjourned for 2 houres

grand Jury returned do prſnt Brighta the wife of Derick Jonſon Elliza: Jonſon ſiſter of the ſd Derrick for aideing & aſſiſting the to murther the aforeſd the aforeſd unknow pſon

preſented alſ a young man his name Suppoſed to be John He * * * Derrick Clawſons ſiſter

ordered that Brighta the wife of Derick Jonſon & Elliza
* * * ſd Derick Clawſon als Jonſon be Committed into the
* * * ther order * * * ta Jonſon & Elliza; Jonſon be

adjourned for 2 houres

* * * they were Charged with * * *
* * * pleaded not guilty * * *
* * * that Derick Jonſon * * *

178   grand Jury i4th   2   1693
                  mo

Provincial Court	Jon Swift	Tho Hardin	Joſuah Hoops
for Bucks	geo Brown	Jos milner	Jo: Bunting
i4th day 2 month	Abra Cox	Samll Dark	Henry paxſon
i693	Jona: ſcaife	Jos: kirkbride	ffra Roſſill
	Janes Paxſon	wm Beakes	Jon palmer

*178a

* * * held by the kings
* * * wm Penn Propry-
* * * Said province &
* * * nging att the Court
* * * County the i4th day
* * * ——i693 being the 4th
* * * gs Reigne & 8th of the
* * * vrmt

* * *   Arthur Cooke

* * *   Joſeph Growdon

* * *   rley Sherif

* * *   Pemberton   C1:

grand } The grand   atteſted
Jury }

Recognizance Iſrael Taylor being bound in io £ to the propryatory
        for his appearance here this day for abuſe done to Nicholas
appearanc waln Juſtice of peace appeared accordingly & was
diſcharged

---

*This page is not numbered in the Record Book

Recognizance Mary Skeane being bound to appeare att this
Court to the propryatory in 20 £

appeared accordingly

Examinat ſd mary Skeane being Examined Concerning a baſtard
Child brought forth by her Said She was fforced by
one walter pomſeret who is father of it the Said
pomſeret liveing in weſt Jarſey being according to her
atteſtation & Examination formerly taken before A Cook

midwife An oxley atteſted & Examined Said Shee Confeſt yᵉ:
Same to her about 24 hours after the ſd Child was
born

A deed of 200 acres of land in fee dated the i3 day of $\frac{i}{mo}$ i688
was acknowledged & delivered in open Court by
Wm Pickring grantor to Jon penquoit grantee

*178b

action whereas * * *
　　　plt & * * *
　　　to Joſeph * * *
　　　willing * * *
　　　not being * * *
　　　Joyntly * * *
　　　Court * * *
decl Declaration * * *
plea Anſer aſo * * *

　Jury——Called over and
　atteſted

Evidences { Rich Th　 * * *
　　　　　{ & Barthol　 * * *

adjourned the Co * * *

complaint was made * * *　　　　　　　　　　　　that
　　　Randulph * * *　　　　　　　　　　for fees thc
　　　Sum of 2 £ 10ˢ: 0 * * *　　　　and before the
　　　ioth month laſt paſt * * *
　　　　thereupon was a * * *　　　agt the ſd Randulph

*This page not numbered in the Record Book.

Smalwood for the ſd Sum & that Execution
Iſſue accordingly

petition   of Wm L   Read Requeſting the Court for the
monys obtained by Judgmt in Rouſe Caſe agt
Wm Biles

A letter of   attorney acknowledged by mary Beakes to her
brother in law Edmund Beakes of portishead in
the County of Summerſet in England dated the
i4th i i688 & Certeſyed undr the County ſeale
      mo

Complt   was made by Randulph Black ſhaw that he wants
mony due to him for repaireing the highway
to wch the Court Says they will give him an
anſwer next Court

verdict   the Jury return & Calld over do Say they find for y^e:
plt five pounds thirteen Shillings & io^s damages
with Coſt of ſuite to be pd in goods Equivalent to ſilver
mony or in Silver

179

A deed of fivety achers of land in fee dated the i3 day of
the firſt month i688 Was acknowledged & delivered
in open Court by Henry pawlin grantor to John Taylor
grantee

Return made by the Sherriſ that the goods taken in Execution
in Rouſe Caſe agt Biles are overprized & Cannot
Sel for want of buyers

apprizers In as much as the former apprizers overprized
goods taken in Execution this Court nominates
& appoints Jon Brock Wm paxſon & Robt Heaton
to be apprizers untill further ordr & were atteſted
accordingly

ordered   that whereas the Execution granted Simon
Rouſe agt the goods of wm Biles was returned
not Satiſfyed for want of buyers that another
Execution be granted the Sherriſ to Satiſfye
the ſd Rouſe the Judgmt of Court formerly
obtained

A lettr   of attorney dated the i4ᵗʰ iᶠᵗ 1688 was acknowledged
$$\frac{}{mo}$$
by wm Beakes of this County to the ufe of Thomas
Cotterill of Amfberry in the County of glofter England
& Certefyed in Court undr the County feale

A letter   of attorney dated the i4 day of the iᶠᵗ month
1688 was acknowledged by Stephen Beakes
of this County to the ufe of Edmund Beakes
aforefd & Certefyed in open Court under the
County Seale

Judgmt given & it is adjudged by this Court that Sam
Abbott pay to Richard Thatcher the Sum of five
pounds thirteen Shillings & Coft of Suit & that Execution Iffue
accordingly & that the ioˢ damages be allowed to
Sam — Abbott on the non Suit formerly obtained

prfentmts   brought in by the grand Jury

ordered by the Court that the overfeeres of the high way
do take Care to repaire the high ways prfented

prfentmt   agt Ifrael Taylor deferred for Tryal at the next Quarter Seffions

adjourned this Court untill the 13 day of the 4ᵗʰ month
next Enfueing

Bucks ís: Penfylvania
180   At a Court of Quarter Seffions held by the
Kings authority in the name of William Penn
Propryetory and Govrnr of the affore Said Provinc
and Territorys thereunto belonging at the
Court houfe for the afforefaid County the i3 day
of the 4ᵗʰ month being the 4ᵗʰ yeare of the
kings Reigne & 8ᵗʰ yeare of the proproprya
torys Govrmt i688

The Juftices Prefent
Arthur Cook William yardley
Nicholas Waln   Henry Baker
Abraham Wharley   Sherrife
wm Crofdel   Deputy Sherrife
Phinehas Pemberton   Cl: Com:

Action   Jofuah Ely plt
     agt   } in a plea of Cafe both appeared
   John Brock deft

declarc   read

Anfwer   that the deft owed not the mony & for Tryal put him Self
        upon

Iffue Joyned the Cuntry & fo did the plt whereupon the Sherrife was —
venire   Commanded to return the Jury

Jury   returned & attefted

       John Swift Henry Marjerum walter Bridgman
       Thomas Stakehoufe Robt Heaton Henry paxfon
       Tho: Stakehoufe Junr Jofeph Clows James paxfon
       Richard Lundy willm Dark James Moone

witnefes   mahlon Stacy John Redman mary Staniland all Attefted
Proved the declarc:
wittneffes Jofeph milner attefted for the deft
adjourned the Court for one houre

verdict   we find for the plt Seven pounds Elleven Shillings to be
      payd by the deft with Coft of fuite the plt firft makeing
      the deft: an affurance of the boy

Judgmt   The Court awards Judgmt according to verdict & that
Execution Iffue accordingly

A deed   of Three hundred acres of land in fee dated the i0th day of
      the 9th month i683 delivered and acknowledged by Jofeph —
      Englifh Grantor to ffrancis Roffill grantee

Action David Evans plt   181
     agt   } in a plea both appeared
  Jofeph wood deft

declarcon: read
Anfwer deneys } the fact & for Tryal puts him Self upon the Cuntry
Iffue Joyned —

venire wherefore the Sherrife is Commanded to return the Jury
Jury returned & Attefted being the Same Jury before mentioned
witneffes John Brearley william Beakes Ellias Nichols John owen
    Hugh williams Jofuah Ely mary Eire Jofuah Ely Junior
    all atted proved the declar:

witneffes for the deft mary wood Sarah wood attefted proved y^t:
  Jofeph wood Shot Salt at a horfe about 9 days afore the
  killing of the Said mare

verdict   we find for the plt 5 £ for the mare & 40^s damages with
  Cofts of Suite

Judgmt   The Court thereupon awards Judgmt according to law

execution   ⎧ Jofeph wood being required by the Court to Satiffye the
             ⎪ Said Judgement he refufed the Same whereupon
             ⎨ the Court Commits him in Execution to the Sherrifs Cuftody
Comitment   ⎩ untill the fd Judgmt be Satiffyed

  action   mary Jeffs plt ⎫
                agt   ⎬ with drawn
         Jofeph Chorley ⎭

  action   John Nichols plt ⎫
                agt   ⎬ with drawn
         Jofeph Chorley deft ⎭

  action   Stephen Beakes plt ⎫
                agt   ⎬ with drawn
         John Pidcock deft ⎭

⎧ Indictmt ⎫ of Ifrael Taylor being defferred for Tryal untill this
⎨   or   ⎬
⎩   ⎭ Court for defameing ffrancis the wife of John Swift
  prfentmt—

  Bucks fs: The Jurrors for the propryetory & govrnr by the kings authority
    do prfent that Ifrael Taylor of the County of Bucks aforefaid
    Chyrurgeon about the i4th day of the iith month laft paft did
    Scandeloufly and malitioufly defame ffrancis the wife of
    John Swift of the aforefaid County yeoman agt the ——
    Kings peace and agt the Statute law in Such Cafe made
    & provided   The i4th i 1688
                                        mo
verdict of the grand Jury   we of the grand Inqueft do find this

bill

pleaded to the Said Indictmt not guilty & for Tryal put him Self upon
  183*   the Cunty

---

*There is no page numbered 182 in the Record.

venire   whereupon the Sherrife was Commanded to Cauſe to Come before the
         Juſtices i2 honeſt & Lawfull men

Jury returned and Atteſted

     Richard Ridgway Henry Marjorum walter Bridgman
     Tho: Stakehouſe Senr: Robt Heaton Andrew Allott
     Tho: Stakehouſe Junr Joſeph Clows wm: Dark
     James Paxſon Richard Lundy James Moone

witneſſes John naylor Atteſted doth Say that Iſrael Taylor Sayd he
         veryly beleived that nick meaneing Nicholas Randolph the
         Servant of John Swift did lye with John Swifts Wife
         and that he believed in his Conſcience he did god good ſervice
         in Telling of it

    John Town Atteſted doth Say that ſd Taylor Sayd he verily
    beleived nick meaning the ſd Nicholas Randle did lyewith
    John Swifts wife

Evidences

    Andrew Dunk atteſted doth Say that he heard Iſrael Taylor
    tell micheal Butcher that Gabriel Shallow Sayd nicholas –
    Randel wold lay his head upon his Mrs lap until i2 a Clock
    at night & then they wold go together into the barn

    mark Betrice atteſted Teſteſyes in like manner

    Benjemame Jones Atteſted doth Say that Gabriel Shallow
    Said nicholas Randel wold Sleep with his head in his Mrs
    lap & Shee Sleep with her head in his lapp & that he Calld
    John Swift Cucoldy Rogue & that his muſtard pot wold
    work when he was from home & that they wold go into
deed   the barn together in the night

deed   of 250 acres of land in fee dated the iſt day of the
    4th month i684 delivered and acknowledged by Richard
    Hough grantor to Henry margerum grantee

 verdict   in Swifts Caſe Jury Say they find Taylor guilty in —
    manner & form as he Stands Indicted

 Judgment The Court award Judgment that Iſrael Taylor Shall
    Shall give Security for his appearance at the next Court &
    to keepe the peace in the meane time & pay all Charge

 Execut: of Court & that execution Iſſue accordingly

 Recognizance memorand That Iſrael Taylor oblidges him Self in

15 £ & Benjemame Jones in 5 £ to be pd to the proprietor
to be levied on theire lands & Tenemts goods & Chattles & upon
this
Condition that Iſrael Taylor appeare at the next Court of
Quarter Seſſions & to keepe the kings peace in the meane
time

184

The accts of William Biles the Receivor of the County Tax
were examined according to an ordr of a former Court
by Phinehas Pemberton & Abraham Wharley & were
againe This day examined & made up in open Court & it

	£	s	d
appears by the books of Aſſeſſment that the whole Tax amounted to———	i28:	04:	05½
of which the Said William Biles acknowled -ged that he had Red———	056:	i9:	09
& he hath disburſt as is made appeare in open Court By the Courts order & otherwiſe which this Court allows of———	059:	06:	07
So that this Court doth allow of this aboveſd acctt & acknowledges that the County is debtor to Said willm Biles the Sum of———	02:	06:	i0
And further that it doth appeare by the acctt now brought in by the ſd william Biles —- That there remaines unpayd of the ſd aſſeſſ ment the Sum of———	7i:	04:	08½

And whereas it doth appeare that the County is Still
debtor to John Brock Randle Black ſhaw gilbert
wheeler & others this Court doth order that the Said
william Biles do take the moſt expeditious way for
getting of the arreares of the ſd aſſeſſment & payment
of the ſd debts or that if the parties to whom the
county is debtor will take upon them to Collect ſo
much as is due to them that then the ſd willm Biles
do give a Catalogue of the names of So many as are in –
arreare as may anſwer the ſaid debt & that a warrant
be Iſſued out from any one Juſtice of peace or more
to Impower the ſaid partie to levy the Same by diſtreſs &
& Sale on the parties goods refuſeing to pay theire aſſeſſ
– ment unpaid

And further the Court orders Henry pointer & Samuel
Allen to Collect the arreares of the Tax between neſha
-mina & poqueſſin with what expedition may be & that
Nicholas waln be aſſistant to them therein

A deed of 1000 acres of land in fee dated the i3 day of the i2ᵗʰ
month i688 acknowledged & delivered by Phinehas
Pemberton attorney to Jacob Telner grantor unto —
Richard Lundy grantee

A deed of 50 acres of land in fee dated the 6ᵗʰ day of the iſt month
i688 acknowledged & delivered by Joſeph Engliſh grantor
to Arthur Cook attorney to Richard Wilſon grantee

185

motion being made by David Lloyd the Attorney Generall
in relation to Levying the fines and forfetures the
Court thinks fit to take time to adviſe upon it & to -
Speake with the Commiſſioners of propryety afore they
return anſwer what Courſe muſt be Taken for levying

ordered that in the meane time the Said Eſtreats above writen
be taken out of the records & be Certefyed under the Clarks
hand

wᶜʰ Said Eſtreats were Imediately extracted out of the
records according to ordr

Adjourned this Court to the i2ᵗʰ 7 next
mo

Bucks ſs: Penſylvania

At a Court of Quarter Seſſions held by the kings
authority in the name of william Penn Propryetor
and govrnr of the afore Said Province & Terri
- torys thereunto belonging at the Court houſe
for the Said County the i2ᵗʰ day of the 7ᵗʰ month
being the 4ᵗʰ yeare of the kings Reigne & ——
8ᵗʰ yeare of the propryatorys govrmt 1688

The Juſtices prſent

Joſeph Growdon	william yardley
Nicholas Waln	Henry Baker
Abraham wharley	Sherrife
willm Crosdel	Deputy Sherrife
Phinehas Pemberton Cl: Com:	

A deed of 200 acres of land in fee dated the 5th day of the 5th month
1688 acknowledged & delivered in open Court by william
Biles grantor unto Richard Ridgway attorney to attorney
to Joſeph Engliſh Grantee

Conſtables Ellected & appointed for the upper part of River wm: Beakes Att:
for the Lower pte _____ Tho williams
for y^e middle lotts _____ Jeffery Hawkins
for the upper pte of Neſhaminah Tho: Stakehouſe Atteſt
for the other ſide of Neſhaminah Neamiah Allen

overſeers of the High way appointed for the upper pte of Neſhaminah
Robt Heaton Henry Pointer
for the Lower pte thereof Samuel Allen Junior
for the Lower pte of the river willm Dungan

186

over Seers of the High way for the middle lotts Joſeph kirkbride
for the upper pte of the River Joſeph Milner

Recognizance   Iſrael Taylor being bound by Recognizance for his
appearance at this Court & none appearing agt him this Court
diſcharges him paying his fees

Action   ffrancis Hough by his attorneys

John Brock & Tho: wood plt ———— ⎤ in a plea of debt
                agt   ⎬
    Iſrael Taylor deft   ⎦

appearance John Brock ⎤
                  &   ⎬ appeared but wood & Brock being
       Iſrael Taylor ⎦ Joynt attorneys & wood not appearing

Taylor Craved a non Suite wch was granted him & the Court
non ſuite awarded the plt to pay the Coſts

A deed   of one acre of land in fee dated the ioth 7 i688 was acknow
                                                               mo
ledged & delivered by ffrancis Roſſill Grantor to Thomas
Brock attorney to Joane Huff grantee

action   wm Brian agt Jon Pidcock withdrawn

Inqueſt ⎱ of the Suden death of Roger Scot was that it was accidentall
return ⎰ Through is owne Carleſnes

Recognizance Daniel Hawkins & Robt Benſon appeared according to
    to Recognizance & none appearing agt them the Court diſcharges them
    paying theire fees

Eſtreat John oldfield not appearing according to Recognizance forfeited
    the Same being 5 £

Eſtreat John Ruſh being bound by Recognizance appeared not —
    accordingly but forfeited the Same being 20 £ :

requeſt being made by Jacob Hall he not being well deſired that in as
    much as the ſd Ruſh appeared not that the Court wold give
    him time to the next adjournmt for bringing in of his complt
    agt the Said Ruſh

Anſwer the Court allowed of

return of an execution made by wm Croſdel deputy Sherrife for
    the Satiſfying of Judgmt obteined in Joſuah Elys Caſe of the
    goods of John Brock i gray mare and i7 groſs of buttons
    att 7 £ : iiˢ wᶜʰ goods being brought to this Court & the ſd
    Ely Complt of the wrong done by the Sherrife in that caſe
    the Court Juding them to be unſuitable goods to raiſe the
    mony & over prized awarded that another execution be
    granted & layd on Such goods as will anſwer the Judgmt
    obtained

Adjourned to the 2ⁿᵈ $\frac{8}{mo}$ 1688

187

Bucks ſs: Penſylvania

          At a Court of Quarter Seſſions held by adjournment
          by the kings authority in the name of william Penn Propry
          atory & govrnr of the afforeſaid Province & ——
          Territorys thereunto belonging at the Court houſe of
          the Said County the 2ⁿᵈ day of the 8ᵗʰ month
          being the 4ᵗʰ yeare of the kings reigne over
          England &c: & 8ᵗʰ of the propryetors govrmt i688

              The Juſtices prſent

           william yardley   Henry Baker

           wm Croſdel   Deputy Sherrife

           Phinehas Pemberton Cl: Com:

a deed of 50 acres of land in fee dated the i^{ft} of the 8th month i688
acknowledged & Delivered in open Court by John Taylor
grantor to John Smith grantee

whereas John oldfeild was called laft Court according to his
recognizance & appeared not he Came this day and
appeared before the Juftices & alleadged that he was
Sick & unable to Come Sooner

adjourned to the i2th ioth month next

Jon Swift & Tho: millard Submitted theire action to arbitra
- tion & with drew the Same

Bucks fs: Penfylvania

At a Court of Quarter Seffions held by the
kings authority in the name of william Penn
Propryetor & govrnr of the afforefaid Province
& Territorys thereunto belonging at the Court
houfe for the Said County the i2th day of the
ioth month i688

The Juftices prfent

William yardley Jofeph Growdon   Henry Baker
Nicholas Waln John Brock
Abraham wharley Sherrife
wm Crofdel   deputy Sherrife
Phinehas Pemberton Cl: Com:

Commiffion of Peace read

Laws read

grand Jury Impaneled & attefted Richard Ridgway foreman
Henry Paxfon Jofeph Milner John wood Andrew Ellot Jon Palmer
Sam Dark Jon Crofdel Henry Bircham Jofeph Englifh Jon Hough

188

Shadrach walley wm: Buckman ffrancis Roffill

adjourned the Court for one houre

adjourned the Court untill 8 a Clock in the morning

a deed in fee of 2 acres of land dated the 6th day of the 7th month
i688 acknowledged and delivered (william Crofdel attorney
to James Swafer grantor) unto James Crofdel attorney
upon the requeft made of Richard Wilfon grantee

a deed of i25 acres of land in fee dated the i3 day of the ioth month
     i688 acknowledged & delivered & open Court by James
     Hill grantor to James Moone for the ufe of him felf and
     his Son James Moone grantees

Indictmt

       Bucks ís: i2th   io   1688
                               mo

             The Jurrors for the propryeter & Govrnr by the
      kings authority do prfent a run away negro who Says he
(1)   Coms from virginia and Calls him Self by the name of george
      for that he upon the i7th day of the 9th month laft paft did
      Steale & fraudulently take and Carry away 2 Turkeys being
      the goods of Tho: Janney Senior Conterary to the
      kings peace and agt the law in that Cafe made & provided

                  peter worral Pfecuter

wittneffes   Thomas Janney Junior⎫
             Jofeph Hollinshead — ⎭   Attefted in Court

bill found ———

arraigmt   pleaded guilty

Indictmt Bucks ís

            The Jurrors for the propryetor & govrnr by
      the kings authority do prfent a runaway negro who Says
(2)   he Coms from verginia and Calls him Self by the name of george
      george for that he about the beginning of the 8th month
      laft paft did Steale & fraudulently Take & Carry away 1 ax
      1 Skellet Corn peafe Stockings & other goods to the value of
      Twenty five Shillings being the goods of Thomas Rogers —
      Conterary to the kings peace and agt the law in that Cafe made
      & provided

Profecuter   Thomas Rowland

  witneffes   Thomas Rogers ⎫
              Samuel Hough ⎭ attefted in Court

  bill found

arrainemt pleaded guilty of Takeing all the aforefaid goods
             Save ½ bufhel of peafe

189

Bucks ís   The i2ᵗʰ ioᵗʰ moth i688

                 The Jurrors for the propryetory & govrnr by the
Indictmt   kings authority prſent a run away who Says he Coms
(3)   from virginia & Calls him ſelf by the name of george
         for that he upon or about the beginning of the 8ᵗʰ month
laſt paſt did Steale and fraudulently take and Carry away one
cloth Coate one lether Coate Two Shirts one fuſtian waſt
Coate one hat one Silke neck cloth to the value of five
pounds being the goods of Roger Hawkins Conterary to
the kings peace and agt the law in that Caſe made and
Provided

Proſecutor ·   Roger Hawkins

witneſſes   Joſeph Hollinshead ⎫
            Samuel Hough ——⎭   atteſted in Court

bill found

arrainemt   he pleaded guilty

Bucks ís: The Jurrors for the propryetor & governr by the kings
         authority do prſent that John Collins of the County aforeſd
Indictmt   Huſbandman on the 27 day of the 8ᵗʰ month last did by
(4)   violent aſſault Robb & Take away from the perſon of gilbert
wheeler upon the kings high way & Roade within the Said
County one mare and other goods to the value of Ten pounds
being the proper goods of Gilbert wheeler afforeſaid Contera
-ry to the kings peace and agt the law in Such Caſe made &
Provided

Proſecutor   Joſeph wood

            ⎧ Gilbert wheeler ⎫
            ⎪ John Martin   ⎪
            ⎪ Jacob Hall   ⎪
witneſſes   ⎨ Edward Cartor   ⎬ atteſted in Court
            ⎪ Joan Huff   ⎪
            ⎪ Daniel Beakes   ⎪
            ⎩ Ellenor Beakes ⎭

the bill found

arrigmt   pleaded not guilty but Craved a few houres time of
requeſt the Court to give in what he had further to Say wᶜʰ was granted
Anſwer   the Court

Roades grand Jurys prſentmt   i2ᵗʰ io 1688
                                            mo

> we the grand Jury do prſent it need full that a Suffitiont Cart
> Roade Shall be layd out from the upper plantations about the
> falls unto the fferry houſe where the Common landing is over
> agt Burlington   Richard Ridgway foreman

190

action   Gilbert Wheeler plt ⎫ plt appeared   ⎫
              agt   ⎬   ⎬ a plea of debt
         Luke Brindley deft ⎭ deft appeared not ⎭

non appearance

Sherrifs return   willm Croſdel deputy Sherrife made Returne upon his ‚—
        atteſtation that he had given him lawfull Summonce

Declarat read

Bond therein mentioned proved by the Evidence of william Biles
        atteſted the other witnes being Robt Jeffs deceaſed proved by
        the writeing

Queſtion ⎧ The penal Sum of the bond & the Sum declared for being 3i £
         ⎨ and the real debt being but i5 £ : 12ˢ the Juſtices on the
         ⎪ bench asked of Said gilbert wheeler whether he expected
         ⎩ Judgmt for any more then the real debt

anſwer   ⎧ To which Said wheeler made anſwer he expected Judgmt for
         ⎨ no more then 15 £ i2ˢ with Coſts of Suite

Judgmt   ⎧ whereupon the Court gave Judgmt by default & it was adjud
by   ⎨ ged that Luke Brindley Shold pay to Gilbert wheeler the
default ⎪ Sum of i5 £ : i2ˢ with Coſt of Suite & that Execution shold
         ⎩ Iſſue accordingly

Complt   ⎧ William Biles Receivor of the County Tax made Complt to
about   ⎪ this Court that there was a great deale of the County Tax
ye   ⎪ yet unpaid and in arreare & that he Cold not levy the
Tax   ⎨ Same without a warrant
         ⎪ whereupon this Court orders that a warrant be granted to
order   ⎪ the aforeſaid william Biles by Two Juſtices of peace for
         ⎪ Levying the Said Tax in arreare & unpayd on the goods and
         ⎩ Chattles of Such refuſeing to pay his Share of the Said Tax

A patent   and affignemt thereon of 269 acres of land in fee dated the
            30th day of the 3 month 1688 and the affignemt thereupon dated
            the 4th day of the 4th month of the Said yeare was delivered
            and acknowledged by Thomas Lambert Attorney to Edward
            Luff grantor to Henry Marjerum grantee

A deed   of i62 acres of land in fee delivered and acknowledged
          by Jofeph Englifh Grantor to william Biles Grantee

. action Edward Hancock agt Thomas Revel in a plea of debt both
          upon Call appeared and the deft: declareing that he was but
          that day arrefted to appeare to the Said action which appeared
          to be True by the Sherrifs return the action was deferred
          by Confent of both parties untill the next Court the Said —
          Revel giveing bond with Suffitient fuerties to appeare at
          the next Court

action   Thomas Millard agt Sam Burden in a plea of debt

appearance   both upon Calld appeared

                191
            declarat Read

Anfwer   the defendt Saith he hath performed the award & owes nothing

Iffue ⎱ and of this he put him Self upon the Cuntry for Tryal
Joyned ⎰ & the plt in like manner   Sam Burden

         ⎧ wherefore the Sherrife is Commanded to Caufe to Come i2 honeft
venire ⎨
         ⎩ & lawfull men &c:

Jury Attefted   Tho: Rowland Ezra Crofdel Henry Marjerum James
                   Paxfon Stephen Sands Peter worrall willm Clowes
                   James Moone John Towne John Penquoit — —
                   Richard Lundy willm Dark

articles read & acknowledged

award read and acknowledged

bond read and acknowledged

wittneffes ⎱   ⎧ John ffleckney
for the plt ⎰   ⎪ Anthony Burton
                ⎨   ⎱ all attefted
                ⎪ Thomas Tery —   ⎰
                ⎩ ffrancis Roffill

witneſſes ⎱ ⎰ John ffurnas ⎱
    for the ⎰ ⎱ Edward Lancaſter ⎰ atteſted
deſt ⎰

adjourned the Court for one houre

one deed in ffee of Two hundered acres of land in ffee dated the ioth
    day of the 8th month i688 acknowledged and delivered in
    open Court by Samuel Dark Attorney to Lyonel Brittan
    grantor unto Stephen Beakes grantee

Judgmt on the firſt Indictmt agt George the negro for Stealing
    the Turkeys they not being restored it was adjudged that he
    Shold pay by Servitude as the Court hereafter Shold ordr
    unto Thomas Janney i8ˢ & Charge of Court and be
    whipt for his Said offence Elleven Stripes
    on his bare back

Judgmt on the 2nd Indictmt agt George the negro for Stealing of
    goods from Thomas Rogers parte of the goods being reſtored
    it was adjudged that he Shold pay by Servitude as the Court
    hereafter Shold order unto Thomas Rogers afforeſaid to the
    value of 48ˢ & Charge of Court & be whipt eleven Stripes
    on his bare back

Judgmt on the 3 Indictment agt George the negro for Stealing
    the goods of Roger Hawkins the Goods being reſtored it was
    adjudged that he Shold pay by Servitude as the Court here
    after Shold order unto Roger Hawkins aforeſaid to the
    value of 50ˢ and Charge of Court the ſd Hawkins deſire
   =ing from the Court no further Satisfaction Save that he
    be whipt on his bare back i9 ſtripes

ordered   that he be once whipt in the Sight of the Court

192

Commitment   untill a Convenient place of Servitude be found for him the
    Court Committs him the ſd George negro into the Sherrifs Cuſtody

Recognizance   Paterick kelly being Called according to recognizance
    none appearing agt him the Court diſcharges him paying his
diſcharge ffees

Commitment   Richard Thatcher Junior for abuſeing the Juſtices on the
    bench the Court Commits him into Cuſtody untill the next morning

adjourned the Court untill 8 a Clock tomorrow morning

action Tho: millard agt Sa: Burden

verdict we find for the plt according to evidence

*requeſt the deft Samuel Burden Craved an appeale to the provincial
Court in Equity

Judgmt the Court Gave Judgmt & it was adjudged that Samuel Burden
Shold pay to Thomas Millard the Sum of Two hundered pounds

requeſt ⎤ the deft Sam: Burden Craved an appeale to the next provin-
for an ⎬ cial Court in Equity & tendered his owne bond for 400 £ to pay
appeale ⎦ all Coſt of the ſd Court and of this Court occationed by the aforeſd
action & to proſecute the ſd appeale with Effert
wch ſd bond was accepted by the Court & liberty of an
appeale granted to the Said Samuel Burden deft to the next
Provincial Court in Equity

Indictmt   Jon: Collins returned into Court & Confeſt he had aſſaulted
4ᵗʰ Gilbert wheeler on the high road but not with any intent to Rob
him

requeſt made by Gilbert wheeler & Craved the Court to forbeare any
further proceedure agt the Said Collins for that the Said Collins
had made him full Satisfaction for any wrong or Injury he
had done to him & Said wheeler promiſed to pay all fees due on
the said Indictment

order on the   upon the grand Jurys prſentmts of the want of a
⎤ roade from
prſentmt of the   ⎬ the upper plantations above the falls of Delaware
⎫ to the
want of a Road ⎦ landing agt Burlington the Court ordrs Henry
Baker
John Brock wm yardley Jos: milner Richard —
Hough John Rowland Joſeph Engliſh and Abraham Cox to lay
out the Said Road & give an Acctt thereof to the next Court

Eſtreat Richard Thatcher Junior aforeſd for his abuſe done to the
Juſtices on
Juſtices on the bench the Court fines him in 50ˢ & Commits —
him to the Sherrifs Cuſtody untill he Shall find Suertyes for
his good behavior & his appearance at next Court

adjourned the Court untill the i3 day of the firſt month next

_____
*Crossed out in Record Book.

193

Bucks ſs: Penſylvania

At a Court of Quarter Seſſions held by the kings
authority in the name of william Penn propryetory
& govrnr of the aforeſaid Province & Territorys
thereunto belonging at the Court houſe for the ſd
County the i3 day of the firſt month i688

Juſtices Preſent
William Biles   Henry Baker   John Brock

Phinehas Pemberton Cl: Com: ⎫ action
                                               ⎪
Commiſſion Read   ⎬ Edward Hancock
                                               ⎪   agt:
Conſtable Ellected Joſeph Chorley for the falls ⎪
                                               ⎭ Tho Revell
         peter worrall for above the falls

adjourned the Court untill the 27ᵗʰ Inſtant   with drawn

                                                     by the plt ordr

Bucks ſs: Penſylvania

At a Court of Quarter Seſſions held by the kings
authority in the name of william Penn propry
-etor & govrnr of the afforeſd Province & Terri
torys thereunto belonging held by adjournmt
at the Court houſe for the afforeſaid County
the 27ᵗʰ day of the firſt month i689

The Juſtices Present
Joſeph Growdon   william Biles Henry Baker
Nicholas Waln   John Brock
william Beakes Sherrife
Phinehas Pemberton Cl: Com:

Commiſſion of Peace Read

action Randle Black Shaw plt ⎫
              agt   ⎬ in a plea of Caſe
        Charles Pickring deft ⎭

requeſt was made by Said Black ſhaw & declared that he was
not in readiness to bring his action on to Tryal & deſired
to have it deferred untill another Court

A deed of 202 acres of land in ffee dated the i2ᵗʰ day of the i2ᵗʰ month
i688 acknowledged & delivered by Jof: Growdon grantr
unto Stephen Newel Grantee

A deed of i02 acres of land in fee dated the i2ᵗʰ day of the i2ᵗʰ month
1688 was acknowledged & delivered by Jofeph Growdon Grantr
to Abel Hinkstone Grantee

A deed of 102 acres of land in fee dated the i2ᵗʰ day of the i2ᵗʰ month
1688 was acknowledged & delivered by Jofeph Growdon
grantor to Abel Hinkstone attorney to william Reale grantee

194

A deed of i02 acres of land in fee dated the ioᵗʰ day of the i2ᵗʰ month i688
was acknowledged & delivered by Jofeph Growdon Grantor to
Stephen Newel Attorney to william Beal Grantee

A deed of 40 acres of land in fee dated the ioᵗʰ day of the i2ᵗʰ month
i688

A deed was acknowledged & delivered by Jofeph Growdon
grantor to Abel Hinkftone Attorney to Thomas ffox and —
Jofeph wilsford grantees

A deed of 100 acresof land in fee dated the 23ᵈ day of the 12ᵗʰ month
1688 acknowledged & delivered by william Hearft Grantor
to Henry Hudlefton Grantee

Recognizance   Richard Thatcher being Calld according to recognizance
appeared the Court difcharges him paying his ffees

negro George being Calld for into this Court to anfwer the several
Judgmts of laft Court that was then adjudged to be payd by
Servitude

Recognizance Richard Ridgway according to recognizance —
brought the fd Negro into Court whereupon the Court difcharged
the fd Ridgway from the fd Recognizance

Commitment whereupon this Court Commits the fd George the negro in
Execution into the Sherrifs Cuftody until further order

non Suite   Charles Pickring deft in Randle Blackshaws Cafe
appeared according to Summonce & Craved a non fuite
agt fd Blackshaw the Said Blackfhaw haveing declared

he was not in readynes for Tryal a non ſuite thereupon
was granted

recognizance Hugh Marſh being bound in 20 £ for appearance
of Job Hole the ſaid Hole being Calld appeared John Swift
& Philip Conway being Calld appeared & declared they had
nothing agt Hole whereupon the Court diſcharged him

recognizance Charles Brigham being bound as by the Information
of Joſeph Growdon & Arthur Cook Juſtices being Calld appeared
& more Complts Comeing agt him the Court ordered him to
give Security to appeare at the next Court which he the
Said Charles refuſed whereupon the Court Commits him
in to the Sherriſts Cuſtody untill he give Security

recognizance Tho: millard being to appeare at this Court according
-ly appeared none appeareing agt him the Court diſcharged
him

A deed of Sale & mortgage of 2 Iſlands in fee lying in this
County the one Calld kips Iſland & the other a little Iſland
northward of the other & both lying agt Burlington
dated the Sixth day of the firſt month 168 8 was —

$$\frac{}{9}$$

acknowledged & delivered by by Nicholas waln attorney to
Samuel Burden grantor to Arthur Cooke Subſtitute —
attorney to Samuel Carpenter attorney to Joſeph Burden grantee

195

a deed of 1oo acres of land in fee dated the Tenth day of the
first month 1688 was acknowledged and delivered in
open Court by Thomas Rowland grantor to
Philip Conway grantee.

a deed of 100 acres of land in fee dated the firſt day of the
fourth month 1688 was acknowledged and delivered
by william Dungan grantor Arthur Cooke Grantee

Recognizance Edward Cartor & Tho: Brock being bound in 40 £ for
the appearance of John Allen at this Court who appeared
accordingly & nothing being objected agt him the Court
discharged him

ordered by this Court that George the Negro be delivered
from his Impriſonment to Stephen Newel wᶜʰ Said
negro is by this Court adjudged to ſerve the Said Stephen

Newel or his affigns fiveteen yeares and at the
End of fiveteen yeares to be returned to the mafter
of the fd negro or affignes if he the fd mafter or affignes
make demand of him in Confideration whereof the faid
Stephen Newel is to pay Elleven pounds foure Shillings to
anfwer the Several Judgments of Court formerly Impofed upon him

Stephen Newell and Jofeph Growdon both oblidged them
Selves theire Executors and adminiftrators to
pay the Said Sum of Elleven pounds foure Shillings to
anfwer the Sevearl Judgments of Court aforementioned
in Cuntry produce at Currat price & to deliver the
Said pay at Philadelphia at or before the latter End
of the third month next enfueing to Such perfon or perfons
as Shall be appointed by the Court to receive the fame

action John Brock plt ⎤   withdrew his action by the plts ordr
             agt   ⎥
       Job Houle John Butler ⎬ withdrew his action by the plts ordr
             &   ⎥
       Ellizabeth venables ⎦

action   Stephen Beakes plt ⎤
                agt   ⎬ withdrawn by the plts ordr —
           John Pidcock deft ⎦

adjourned to the i2ᵗʰ day of the 4ᵗʰ month next

no bufnes prfenting in the 4ᵗʰ month no Court was held

Penfylvania

County Court Bucks fs: 196

At a Court of Quarter Seffions held by the kings author
-ity in the name of william Penn Proprietory & govrnr
of the aforesaid Province & Counties annexed the
iiᵗʰ day of the Seventh month i689 at the Court
houfe for the fd County being the 9ᵗʰ yeare of the
propryetorys govrmt

The Juftices Present

William Biles Henry Baker
Nicholas waln, John Brock
wm: Beakes Sherrife
Phinehas Pemberton Cl: Com:

actions

mary Beakes plt
    agt   } by the plts ordr withdrawn
Thomas Coverdale deft

Richard Ridgway plt
    agt   } withdrawn by the plts ordr
John Heesome deft

a deed of i25 acres of land in fee dated the io^th day of the i2^th month i688 was acknowledged and Delivered by Henry Paxſon grantr to William Plumley grantee

a deed of 100 acres of land in fee dated the io^th day of the i2^th month i688 was acknowledged and delivered by William Plumley grantor to Henry Paxson grantee

a deed of 3i0 acres of land in fee dated the 8th day of the 7th month i689 was delivered and acknowledged by Richard Noble — grantor to moses Masley Grantee

a deed of mortgage for 3i0 acres of land in fee dated the 9th day of the 7th month i689 was delivered and acknowledged by — moses Masley grantor to Richard Noble Grantee

a deed of one Tract of land about ioo acres in fee dated the io^th day of the 7th month i689 was acknowledged and delivered by Thomas Coverdale Grantor to Henry Siddall Grantee

Constables appointed for the Succeeding yeare

ffor {
the upper part of the River Peter Worral
the falls Joseph Chorley —
the Lower part of the river Thomas Green
the middle lotts John Rowland atteſted
the upper part of neshaminah James Paxſon
the lower part of Neshaminah John White
}

Estreat Thomas Revel convicted before Joſeph Growdon of Curſing
197 by his owne Confeſſion & therefore fined for the ſame 5ˢ
action The action between John Swift plt & Philip Conway deft the

declaration read

Anſwer read

requeſt was made by the plt that the deft might purge him ſelf of the
Treſpaſs whereof he Stands accuſed wᶜʰ the deſetd to Conde

Anſwer cendd to

deft　　　　Philip Conway atteſted declared that he had Said he knew who
had kild the Colt of John Swift (declared for) but upon him
atteſtation declared that he knew nothing neither directly
nor Indirectly of the killing of the ſd Colt neither did he ever
of his owne knowledg know that John Swift had any Colt
Kild

Iſſue　　⎧ & for Tryal he the ſd deft put him on the Cuntry & ſo did
Joyned⎨ the plt wherefore the Sherrife is Commanded to return
venire　⎩ i2 honeſt & lawfull men &c.

　　　　Jury　Joſuah Hoops　Jon Palmer　william Dark　⎫
　　　　　　　Joſeph English　Tho Tunneclif　Samuel Dark　⎬atteſted
　　　　　　　John Naylor　James Paxson　John Hough　⎭
　　　　　　　Joſeph milner　John Rowland　John Wood —

witneſſes to the declaration

　　　　　　　Edmund moore ⎫
　　　　　　　Job Houle　　⎬ attested
　　　　　　　Philip Parker ⎭

requeſt made to the Court that a wittnes to a will made by
Daniel Hawkins might be examined it haveing relation
to a Tract of land left by Said Hawkins unto Thomas
Coverdale wᶜʰ ſaid land was by Said Coverdale Conveyed
to Henry Siddall & the deed thereof this day acknowled

Anſwer -ged in Court to which the Court gave
attestation　John Clement being atteſted doth Say that he
Saw the Said will bearing date the 30ᵗʰ day of the
ioᵗʰ month 1688 Sealed & delivered by Said Hawkins
& further Saith that the ſd Hawkins did give his land
to the Said Coverdale & his heires forever

adjourned the Court for one houre

ordered by this Court that Richard Ridgway or his aſſignes
do Receive the mony due from Joſeph Growdon & Stephen
Newel upon the account of the negro
　　　　　　　& that the ſd Richard Ridgeway have an
order Signed by Some one Juſtice for to Impower him

to receive the Same, the Said Ridgway haveing this day
in open Court promiſed to anſwer all the Charges that has
been out upon the negro & allowed by the Court ____

198

ordered that a requeſt be drawn to the Govrnr that a regiſter
may be appointed in this County for the probat of wills and
granting letters of Administration that people be not put to
the extrordinary Charge of going to Philadelphia ____

a deed of 50 acres of land in fee dated the firſt day of the 7ᵗʰ
month i689 acknowledged and delivered by Richard Wilſon
grantor to John Gibbs Grantee

a deed of about 90 acres of land in fee dated the 8ᵗʰ day of the 4ᵗʰ
month i688 acknowledged and delivered by Luke Brindley — ˙
grantor to Peter Worrall Grantee

Isaac Burges being Calld none appearing agt him the Court diſcharges
him paying his fees

Jury returned Calld over Say they are not agreed therefore
were returned back againe

Grand Jury Ezra Crosdel James Sutton James Crosley

John Clement Stephen Beakes Luke Brindley ⎫
Jon: Brearley Rich Wilſon Tho: Stakehouſe ⎬ atteſted
ſenr: ⎪
Henry Siddal Andrew Heath ⎭

petit Jury return againe not agreed wherefore the Court returned
them back

Recognizance John Swift being bound by Recognizance to ——
appeare at this Court appeared accordingly & nothing appearing
agt him the Court discharges him

Recognizance Philip Conway being bound to appear at this Court
& to be of good abearing in the meane time appeared —
accordingly & nothing appearing agt him the Court diſcharges
him paying his fees

action John Swift plt ⎫
agt ⎬ both appeared
Philip Conway deft ⎭

Jury ⎱ Returned do Say they find for the deft
verdict ⎰

adjourned the Court untill to morrow morning at 8 a Clock

action Tho: Revel plt————————————⎤ Revel & Taylor ⎱
          agt   ⎬ appeared ——   ⎰
    Richard Thatcher & Ifrael Taylor defts ⎦

declaration was

Iffue Anfwer read the plt defends & for tryal puts him felf
Joyned on the Cuntry & So doth the plt wherefore the Sherrif is
venire Commanded to Caufe to Come i2 honeft & Lawfull men &c.

199

witneffes to prove the Said declaration

> Grace Lang horn Thomas Preift Corin ⎤
> Benjemain Jones Ezra: Crosdel ——   ⎬attefted
> Richard Thatcher Senior —— —— —— ⎦

Recognizance   Richard Thatcher appeared according to Recogniz

grand Jury   brought in a bill agt: Richard Thatcher Junior
              Ignoramus

grand Jury prfented Richard Thatcher for bringing in a dead
    hog to the houfe of Ifrael Taylor upon the firft day of
    the weeke

over Seeres of the High was nominated & appointed for the
              Succeeding yeare

for

the

⎧ the upper part of Neshaminah Henry Paxson ⎤
⎪ the lower part Henry Bircham —————   ⎪
⎨ the other Side of nefhaminah Tho: Hardin   ⎬
⎪ the Lower part of the River John Cook ——   ⎪
⎪ middle lotts Randle BlackShaw ————   ⎪
⎩ the upper part of the River Wm: Clows —— ⎦

Judgmt   given & it is adjudged that John Swift in the action
    he brought agt: Philip Conway Shall pay Coft of Court

Judgmt   given & it is adjudged that Philip Conway for the lye he

told in Jon Swifts Case whereof he was Convicted by his
owne Confeſſion before this Court that he Shall pay —

Eſtreat   2ˢ : 6ᵈ

grand jury brought in presentments about the roades in this
County

ordered that the over Seers of the high ways take Care
to repaire the roads preſented by the grand jury

action Tho Revel agt Ric Thatcher & Iſrael Taylor

Jury } Returned Say they find for the plt thirty Shillings
verdict } damage with Coſt of Suite

Iſrael Taylor abuſed the Jury being examined about it he made
Submiſſion & acknowldgmt of his fault wherefore the
Jury deſired the Court to paſs it by

for Contempt of the Court by Rich Thatcher Junior & abuſes by
him done to Tho : Revel & for Suſpition of takeing a
hog that was none of his owne the Court Commits him into
the Sherrifs Custody untill he finds Suſitient Suerties for his
Comitment   appearance at the next Court & to be of good abearing in
the meane time

Charles Brigham being Calld none appearing agt him the
Court diſcharges him paying his fees

a deed of 50 acres of land in fee dated the ioth day of the 7th mo:
i689 acknowledged & delivered by Nicholas waln grantor
to William Hearſt grantee

200

Judgment given & it is adjudged that Richard Thatcher and
Israel Taylor Shall pay to Thomas Revel 30ˢ damages
with Coſts of Suite according to jurye verdict & that Execution
Issue accordingly

ioth

adjourned the Court to the iith month next

The iith day of the ioth month i689 Several Juſtices
met but no busines preſenting no Court was then
held

action   Isaac Burges plt

agt

Randle Blackſhaw deft

      deferred untill another Court by

      Conſent

County Court Bucks ſs:

Penſylvania

At a Court of Quarter Seſſions Held by the authority of William & Mary king & Queen of England &c in the name of William Penn Proprietor & govrnr of the afforeſd Province & Countys annexed at yᵉ: Court houſe for the Said County the i2ᵗʰ day of the first month i689 being the ioᵗʰ yeare of the — Propryetors Govermt

The Justices Present

Joſeph Growdon   Willm Biles
willm yardley   Henry Baker
Nicholas waln   John Brock
wm: Beakes   Sherrife
Phinehas Pemberton   Cl: Com:

actions

John Shippey plt

agt

Israel Taylor deft

   plea of Caſe

Jos Growdon plt

agt

Tho Hutchins deft

   plea of Caſe

   demurred

Tho Revel plt

agt

Israel Taylor deft

   plea of debt

Arthur Cook plt

agt

Joſeph Croff deft

   plea of Caſe

   withdrawn

Gilbert wheeler plt

agt

Luke Brindley deft

   plea of Caſe with drawn

Grand Jury

201

Rich Hough   Joseph Clows   John Palmer   ⎫
Nathaniel Harding   James Moone   Thos Brock   ⎪   attefted
Rich Ridgway   Sam^ll Dark   Andrew Ellot —   ⎬   —
Jeffry Hawkins   Andrew Heath   Jofeph Englifh ⎪
wm Dark   Jofeph Milner   Henry Pointer   ⎭

Estreat Thomas Coverdale for Comeing into Court drunk the
  Court fines him in 5ˢ

Commitment   Paterick Conway & Philip Conway being Calld and
  Security required of them to anfwer the Several Complts —
  brought agt them wch they refufed wherefore the Court
  Commits them into the Sherrifs Custody untill further ordr

a deed of 200 acres of land in fee dated the 24 day of the 3
  month i689 was acknowledged & delivered by Samuel
  Burges & Randle BlackShaw grantors to Rich Lundy Grantee
a deed of 100 acres of land in fee dated the i0^th day of the i2^th
  month i688 was acknowledged & delivered by Jofeph
  Growdon Grantor to Claws Jonfon Grantee

Complt being made by Derick Clawson that formerly he delivered
  to Arthur Cook and James Harrifon three wolves two of
  them bitches & one dog & that he hath but Received in
  part towards them 7ˢ the Court being Satiffyed of the truth
  hereof by Arthur Cooke one of the Juftices of peace for this
  County

ordered that the fd Clawson be paid what remaines due to him out
  of the firft mony that Comes to hand to the Receivors of
  the publique Stock

notice from John Blackwell not to pay Quit Rents to any
  but Robt Turner or his Subftitutes read
adjourned the Court for one hour
A deed of Some land for a mill pond in fee dated the 20th day of
  the 9th month i689 was acknowledged & delivered by
  william Beakes attorney to John otter Grantor to —
  ffrancis Roffill Grantee

Conftables nominated & appointed for the lower part be
  tween Nefhaminah & Popueffin Samuel Allen Junr:
  for the upper part thereof Jon: purflone attefted

Estreat   William Clows & Thomas Kirle being Summonced to
        appear on the jury this Court the Sherrif being atteſted
        declared they had lawfull Summonce they not appearing
        accordingly the Court fines them in 3ˢ apeice

                            202

Causual death of Ann Hawkins prſented by yᵉ Corronor to this Court
        to be by a fall from a mare She rid upon occationed by
        another horſe that was tyed to her tayle going by the way
        on the Conterary Side of A tree wᶜʰ Cauſed the mare Suddenly
        to Stop So that Shee fell from the ſd mare & was killd
prſentments brought in by the Grand Jury
        agt Rich Thatcher for abuseing his father
        Iſrael Taylor for abuseing the Jury Caling them for Sworn Rogues
        & saing to Tho: Tunneclif that he wold knock him on the head
        Wm: Beakes for keeping bad fence

    the High Way between the fferry houſe & newtowne

    Andrew Ellot for ſelling bear without Lycence

    Henry Marjorum for Selling Liquors

    Thats its neceſſary the County be devided into Townſhips

    that the former Tax be gathered & that there be
    another Tax raiſed for defraying Such neceſſary Charges
    as the former Shall fall Short

    adjourned to 8 in the morning

grand jurys prſentmt agt: Paterick Conway & Philip Conway

Bucks ſs: i2ᵗʰ i 1689
                            ──────
                            mo

(1)   The Jurrors for the propryetory & Govrnr by the king &
Queens authority do prſent Paterick Conway & Philip Conway
of the afforesaid County that on or about the laſt day of the iiᵗʰ month
laſt paſt did breake open the houſe of Wm ffisher in the County of
Philadelphia and from thence did take Steale and Carry away —
Several goods to the value of foure pounds and fiveteen —
Shillings agt the king & Queens peace & againſt the ſtatute
law in that Case made & provided

            John Swift proſecutr

Wm ffisher } witneffes attefted
Samuel Vofe }

pleading   A true bill_____

upon wich they were arrained & pleaded not guilty & for tryal
    put them Seves upon the Cuntry

(2)   Bucks fs: The i2ᵗʰ $\frac{i}{mo}$ $\frac{1689}{90}$

The Jurrors for the propryetory & Govrnr by the king &
    queens
authority do prsent Philip Conway for fraudulently takeing &
    ftealing
one mare being the goods of the propryetory & govrnr about
    the i3
day of the firft month laft paft to the value of foure pounds
    agt the
king & queens peace & agt the Statute law in that Cafe made
    & —
Provided

John Swift profecutor

Pleading   nicholas Randle Micheal Bucher witneffes___ A true bill
            to wᶜʰ he pleaded not guilty & for tryal put him felf upon
            the Cuntry

Bucks fs: The i2ᵗʰ $\frac{i}{mo}$ $\frac{1689}{90}$

203

(3) The Jurrors for the propryetor & govrnr by the king & queens
     authority do prfent Paterick Conway of the afforefaid —
     County for fraudulent Takeing & Stealing one half hide
     of lether to the value of Ten Shillings in or about the
     ioᵗʰ month laft paft being the proper goods of Charles thomas
     of the County of Philadelphia agt the king & queens —
     Peace & Conterary to the Statute law in that Cafe made &
     Provided   Charles Thomas profecutor }
                     William ffisher witnefs   } attefted

pleading   a true bill

To which he pleaded not guilty & for tryal put him
Self upon the Cuntry

Bucks ſs: The i2th i   1689
                      ‾‾‾‾‾‾‾‾
                       mo   90

(4) The Jurrors for the propryetory & govrnr by the king &
    queens authority do prſent Paterick Conway and Philip
    Conway of the County aforeſaid for that on the Second
    day of this Inſtant by violent aſſault & force they took
    away from the perſon of william ffisher one Colt to
    the value of Twenty Shillings being the proper goods
    of william Penn Propryetory & govrnr agt the king
    & queens peace & Conterary to the Statute law in that
    Caſe made & provided

              william ffisher proſecutor ⎤
              John Swift ──────────────── ⎬ wittneſſes atteſted
                                          ⎦

            The evidence of George Burton taken before
            William Markham
    Secretary & one of the Juſtices
            of peace for Philadelphia County

                    A true bill ‾‾‾‾‾‾

pleading

    To which they pleaded not guilty & for Tryal put them
    Selves upon the Cuntry

(5) Bucks ſs: The i3 day of the i   1689
                                      ‾‾‾‾‾‾‾‾
                                       mo   90
    The jurrors for the propryetory and govrnr by
    the king & queens authority do prſent Richard Thatcher
    Junior of the afforeſaid County for fraudulently takeing
    and Stealing one hog being the proper goods of John
    Purſlone in or about the 4th or 5th month laſt paſt to the
    value of one pound agt the king and Queens peace and
    Conterary to the Statute law in that Caſe made & provided

              John Purſlone proſecutor ⎤
              Thomas Revel ──────────── ⎬ witnesses attested
                                        ⎦

pleading   A true bill

    To which he pleaded not guilty & for tryal put him ſelf on
    the Cuntry

motion being made by william Biles the Receivor of the Publique Stock

of the County that there was Several neceſſary Charges of the County
to defrayed as the fees of the Councell & assemblymen
killing of wolves &c: & that he had no Effects in his hands
whereupon the grand jury prſented the neceſſity of haveing a
new Tax raiſed

Jury ⹀⹀⹀⹀⹀ Joſuah Hoops John wood william Ellet ⎫
             Thomas Stakehous John Allen Stephen Beaks ⎬ atteſted
             Henry Hulestone wm: Paxson wm Taylor ⎪
             Rich: Lundy Tho: Hardin Ezra Crosdel ⎭

no Chalenges made by the priſoners agt any of them

witneses   upon the firſt Indictmt agt Paterick Conway & Philip Conway

william ffisher atteſted doth Say that about the latter End of Janu
     -ary being at the houſe of Philip Conway in order to ſeek a
     mare of his that was loſt after he found he he returned
     home againe at which time he found his houſe broken up and
     his Cheſt unlocked & the key in the lock wch key at his going
     away he hid under his beds tead and none knew of the —
     hideing of it there Save Paterick Conway who was prſent —
     when the key was hid & that upon Search for his Goods
     he found part of his goods in Philip Conways houſe viz: one
     Inke horn

Samuel voſe atteſted doth Say that on the laſt day of January
     at night being to have the hay of william ffisher went to the ſd
     ffishers houſe for Some of the hay where he found all
     well on the next morning he went againe for more hay
     where he found a man & horſe had been about the houſe
     he followed the Track in the Snow between 3 & 4 miles
     & as he did apprehend the Track did lead towards the houſe
     of Philip Conway & further Saith not

James Paxson atteſted Saith that he being Conſtable Searched
     the houſe of Philip Conway where was found an Inkhorn
     which william ffisher owned to be his & futher Saith not

Grand Jurys prſentmts ı3 day ı ı689   adjourned for ı houre
                       mo   90

Bucks ſs: wee the jurrors for the body of the County do prſent it
     to the Court thats its neceſſary that a Tax be forthwith made
     for the defraying the requiſit Charge of the County as paying the
     Councel & aſſembley.mens fees what is allready due to them &
     allowed by law & for killing of wolves &c.

jury returned do Say that Paterick Conway & Philip Conway is not
 guilty of breaking up the houfe of william
 ffisher

205

(3) agt Patrick Conway for ftealing half a hide of lether

Charles Thomas attefted doth Say in decemb laft paft Paterick Conway
 & he Came to walter fforeft mill with lether at which time he
 Sold the Said Paterick i Side of lether & the remameing pte
 of his lether he left out of doores for Some time 2 or 3 days
 & faid Thomas Telling over his lether he mift one fide
 there of & after Some time willm ffisher told Said Thomas
 he Saw 2 fides of lether in Philip Conways houfe & that
 Paterick Conway told Said ffisher that Charles Thomas gave
 him one & Sold him the other

willm ffisher attefted doth Say he Saw 2 fides of lether in Philip
 Conways houfe & that Paterick Conway told him that he
 bought one of them of Charles Thomas & that he gave
 him the other

Jury returned Say Paterick Conway is guilty of ftealing the fide
 of lether from Charles Thomas

action

 John Shippey plt ⎤
     agt ⎬ both appeared
 Ifrael Taylor deft ⎦

declarat read

Anfwer read

Iffue Joyned for tryal both put them Selves upon the Cuntry

 venire wherefore the Sherrifeis Commanded to Caufe to Come
    i2 honeft & Lawfull men &c —

Jury ———— John wood William Ellet Tho: Stakehoufe ⎤
    John Allen Stephen Beakes Henry Hudlestone ⎬ attested
    Willm Paxson Willm Taylor Rich Lundy —— ⎪
    Thomas Hardin Gilbert wheeler Ezra Crofdel ⎦

william Biles Jofeph Croffe attefted for the plant

Richard Thatcher Junr: John Purstone attefted for the deft

adjourned untill tomorrow morning at 7 a Clock

Grand Jury bring in theire prſentments

The i4ᵗʰ day of the $\frac{\text{i}}{\text{mo}}$ $\frac{1689}{90}$

prſent Iſrael Taylor for Receiveing a Stolen
hog from Rich Thatcher Junʳ on the firſt day of
the weeke

alſo prſent Henry Marjorum for ſwearing by god
the i3 day Inſtant

Iſrael Taylor being Calld into Court upon the prſentment for the abuſe
done to Thomas Tunneclif he Confeſt the fact whereupon the
Court ordrs he give bond for his appearance at next Court &
to keepe the peace in the meane time

206

Recognizance Iſrael Taylor oblidges him Self in 8 £ to be payd to the —
propryetory & govrnr his heires & Succeſſors to be levyed on his
lands & tenements goods & Chattles & this upon Condition yᵗ:
the ſd Taylor appeare at the next Court of Quarter Seſſions
to be held for this County & to keepe the peace in the meane time

action John Shippey agt Iſrael Taylor

jury returned do Say they find for the plt with 4ᵈ damages & Coſt

verdict   of Suite

a deed of i50 acres of land in fee dated the ioᵗʰ day of february
$\frac{\text{i689}}{\text{90}}$ was acknowledged and delivered by Robt Heaton

attorney to Henry fflower grantor to Thomas Harding
grantee

Henry Marjorum being Calld to anſwer the grand Jurys prſentmts
for Selling Liquors deſired to have what was done paſt by
& for the future he wold for beare

Henry Marjorum upon the prſentmt of the grand Jury for Swearing
by god Submitted to the Court for wᶜʰ the Court fines him
Eſtreat   in 5ˢ

(2)   Indictmt agt Philip Conway for ſtealing a mare of the propryetors

Jury calld over objected agt Gilbert wheeler

Jury ———— John Wood Robt Haton Tho: Stakehoufe
         Stephen Beakes John Allen wm Paxfon
         Anthony Burton wm: Taylor Tho: Hardin   }attefted
         Rich Lundy Wm Ellot Henry Hudelfon —

John Swift attefted doth Say that he tooke up a mare Suppofed to be
about 3 yeares of age unmarked of Colour mealy mouthed
about 4 yeares paft in the 2nd month next of wch mare he gave
notice to the raingers but he refufed to take her & that he fpoke
to James Harrifon the Govrnrs Steward to have bought her to
wch James Harrifon gave way but put no price upon her upon
which he eare marked her with a half peny cut on the under fide
of the nearror eare wch Said mare he Saw Several times —
Since in Philip Conways Cuftody but more perticulerly about
3 weeks ago & about the i3 day of the $\dfrac{\text{i}}{\text{mo}}$ $\dfrac{1688}{9}$ & that Since
then he Saw the Same mare with her Eare marke Changed —

Nicholas Randle attefted doth declare the aforefd markes & takeing
up of the fd mare unmarked & of the Ear marke John Swift
gave her & of his aquainting the raingers with her & further
Saith that about a yeare after the mare Strayed away from

207

from the Said Swifts House Philip Conway told him he wold have
the fd mare & Several times after that he Saw the faid
mare in Said Conways Cuftody & perticulerly about 2 weekes
ago or 3 weekes in harnes at Philip Conways house & Since
then in Philip Conways feild & further Saith that when he
Spoke with Conway about the Said mare he the fd Conway
Said he wold have her

Micheal Bucher attefted doth say that he was prfent at the
takeing up of the fd mare by Jon: Swift as aforefaid & y^{t}:
Shee had the marks & Colour as before teftefyed & y^{t}:
he Saw the fd mare feveral times in Said Conways —
Cuftody & that he Saw fd Conway ride on her about
2 yeares ago & that he Chalenged the mare & fd Conway
thereupon rid away from him that John Swift marked her
with a half peny Cut as aforefd

(4th) Indictemt agt Paterick Conway & Philip Conway for forceably
       takeing a Colt from willm ffisher being the
       Propryetors

Jury atteſted being the Same laſt mentioned
william ffisher atteſted doth Say he has order to take up a Colt
-by Capt: Markham belonging to the govrnr which he according
-ly he did & when he had the Colt in his yard the 2ⁿᵈ day of
this Inſtant Paterick Conway & Philip Conway Came to his
houſe & demanded the Colt the Said ffiſher refuseing to deliver
it Paterick Conway knoct him over in the meane time
Philip Conway tooke away the Said Colt

George Burſton atteſted before william Markham Secretary the
3 day of the firſt month i689 Saith that yesterday he was at the
                          ————
                           90
houſe of willm ffisher and that he Saw a Colt tyed in the
yard the ſd ffiſher telling the deponant that he had taken up
the ſd Colt & was ordered by Capt = Markham to bring him to towne
being unmarked aſter wᶜʰ Came into the yard one Paterick
Conway & Philip his brother & said the Colt was theires &
though they were Charged to the Conterary yet they let the ſd
Colt looſe & Carryed her away & the ſd ffiſher going to —
prvent them by putting up the barre either Struck or thruſt
him backward over the fence & forced the mare & Colt
over him
_____
              Taken before Wm Markham Secretary
                the day above ſaid
whereas the Sherrife wm Beakes & Phine: Pemberton Clark hath
made it appeare that there is due to them for fees three pounds
nine Shillings foure pence from Richard Thatcher & that he the
ſd Thatcher refuſed to pay the Same

                                                          208
jury returned
    do say that Philip Conway is Guilty of Stealing one mare whereof he
        ſtands

verdict   Indicted
_____

They alſo Say Paterick Conway & Philip Conway are Guilty of takeing
forcably one Colt from wm ffiſher whereof he ſtands indicted

(5) Indictmt agt Richard Thatcher for Stealing one hog the goods of
        John Purſlones

    Jury atteſted

John Purſlone atteſted Saith that he loſt a hog of Colour neare White abo
    about 2 yeares of age with a Slit in the further eare & that
    he doth Suſpect Richard Thatcher Junr Stole the Said hog &

that about the Same time he loſt the Said hogg another hog
of his Came home cut Croſs the noſe

Thomas Revel atteſted doth Say that about the beginning of harveſt
laſt Richard Tatcher Junior brought a hog to the houſe of —
Iſrael Taylor of Colour neare white Some what red on the
Sholders but whether it was Sanded or blood he knows not
one of the eares had a Slit in it whether he knew not w^{ch}
hog the ſd Richard Thatcher told him was two yeares old or upward

Iſrael Taylor atteſted doth Say that Richard Thatcher Junr did
bring to his houſe a hog of white Colour with one or both —
Sholders Sanded Some time afore harveſt & that he told ſd
Taylor he wiſht he had not brought the ſd hog for he doubted it
was his fathers hog

A deed of 250 acres of land in fee dated the i3 day of the firſt month
i689 was acknowledged and delivered by Iſrael Taylor —
grantor to william Biles for the uſe of John Coates Grantee

Jury returned

verdict ——— do find Richard Thatcher guilty of ſtealing a hog

action

Thomas Revel agt Israel Taylor

declara read

Iſſuing ⎱ Anſwe read
Joyned ⎰ the deft him Self on the Cunty & So doth plt therefore the

venire   Sherrife is Commaned to Cauſe to Come i2 honeſt & Lawful men
              &c:

Jury atteſted

Joseph Growdon Ezra Croſdel ffrancis Roſſill witneſes atteſted

Jury   ⎱ returned do Say they find for the plt with 6^d damages & Coſts
verdict ⎰ of ſuite

adjourned for one houre

adjourned untill tomorrow morning at 8 a Clock

Judgment given & it is adjudged that Richard Thatcher for
Stealing one hog Shall make 3 fold Satiſfaction to the owner
& be whipt on his bare back 2i Stripes

209

Judgmt awarded in the Cafe Shippey agt Taylor that the Said
    Ifrael Taylor Shall pay the Said John Shippey 2 £ io^s with
    4^d damages & Cofts of fuite

Thomas Revel in open Court declared that Ifrael Taylor had
    Satisfyed him what was awarded him by the Jurys verdict
    & defired Judgment in the fd Case to be fufpended

ordered that Execution Iffue agt the goods of Richard Thatcher
    for the aforefd fees due to the Several officers aforefd if he does not
    take Speedy Courfe to Satisfye the Same

Recognizance Richard Thatcher Junior oblidges him felf in
    20 £ to the propryetory & govrnr his heires & fucceffors to
    be levyed on his lands & Tenemts goods & Chattles &
    this upon Condition that he be & appeare at the next
    Court of Quarter Seffions to be held for this County & to
    be of good abearing in the meane time

Recognizance Thomas Hutchins became bound to the proprye
    tor &c in the Sum of Ten pounds before Jofeph
    growdon for the appearance of one Ellenor Manarte
    (a vagrant woman) at this Court but Shee appeared

Estreat   not wherefore the fd Hutchins forfeited his recognizanc

Judgment awarded upon the 2nd Indictment & it is adjudged
    that Philip Conway for Stealeing one mare being the goods
    of Govrnr Penn Shall make three fold Satisfaction being
    i2 £ to be levyed on his goods or Lands & be whipt on his
    bare back 39 Stripes & be banifhed out of this Govrmt
    not to return againe on penalty of one hundered
    pounds it being the 3 offence whereof he is Convicted

Judgmt Given & it is adjudged that Paterick Conway & Philip
    Conway for takeing away by force and violent affault from
    William ffisher one Colt the proper goods of Govrnr Penn
    Shall make foure fold Satisfaction being foure pounds —
    to be levyed on theire goods or lands & that Paterick —
    Conway be whipt on his bare back i5 Stripes & Philip Conway
    one Stripe both in the Sight of the people

Judgmt given & it is adjudged that Paterick Conway for —
    Stealing one half hide of lether the proper goods of Charles —
    Thomas Shall make 3 fold Satisfaction being 30^s to be
    Levyed on his goods & Chattles & for want of goods & Chattles

to be & remame bondman unto íd Charles Thomas untill he
be Satisfyed the íaid 30ˢ & to be whip on his bare back i5
Stripes in the íight of the Court & people

ajourned to the 20ᵗʰ day of this Inítant month

210

Bucks ís: At a Court held by adjournment the 26 day of
                the firít month i690

                    Justices príent

                    Arthur Cook   william Biles

                    willm yardley   Nicholas waln

                    Henry Baker   John Brock

                    willm Beakes Sherrife

                    Stephen Beakes Deputy Sherrife

                    Phinehas Pemberton   Cl: Com:

          Several acctts & requeíts this day brought in from
       them that have Served in Councill & aífembley that they
    may be Satisfyed what the law allows them for theire —
       attendance this Court with the approbation of the Grand jury —
       have Thought good to order that a Tax be raiíed for —
       the defraing the neceííary Charge of the County & it is

ordered   therefore ordered that a Tax be forth with raiíed of 300 £
          on the males and lands according as the law directs & that
          the Collectors after named Collect the Same with in theire —
          Several diviííions as may be rated on them for theire íhares
          & give an acctt of theire lands & males within theire Several
          deviíions viz

   for ⎧ above the falls to John woods: Joíeph Milner
        ⎪ thence to the Govrnrs Stephen Beakes
        ⎪ thence to ne íhaminh & up the íame to Robt Halls plantation
        ⎪ James Boyden junior
        ⎨ thence up the Creek to the upper moít land taken up ton —
        ⎪ Neshamina Thomas Rowland
        ⎪ middle lotts william Dark
        ⎪ Between neshaminah & poqueííin to the upper part of —
        ⎪ Joíeph Growdons land Samuel Allen junior
        ⎩ thence to the upper moít lands taken up Henry Pointer

ordered that an acctt of lands & males be returned to the Juſtices
the 23 day of 2ⁿᵈ month next at the Court houſe

adjourned the 23 day of the 2ⁿᵈ month next

no Court held according to adjournmt the 23 day of the 2ⁿᵈ month

Pennsylvania

County Court Bucks ſs:

211

action   At a Court of Quarter Sessions held by

wm: Thomas ⎤   ⎤ the king and Queens authority in the name of
   agt   ⎬ plea of ⎬ Willm Penn Propryetor and govrnr of the
Andrew Heath ⎦ Caſe ⎦ afforesaid Province & Counties annexed at the
     with drawn   Court houſe for the Said County the iiᵗʰ day of
                         the 4ᵗʰ month i690

The Justices prſent
Wm Biles   Nicholas Waln
Henry Baker   Jon: Brock
Wm yardley   vic: Com:
Phinehas Pemberton   Cl: Com:

returned the death of John ackerman that he was drowned accidentely
the iiᵗʰ 3 1690
        mo

Recognizance Israel Taylor being bound to appeare at this Court
appeared accordingly & none appearing agt him the Court
diſcharges him

a deed of 6 acres of land in fee dated the 4ᵗʰ day of the 4ᵗʰ month
i690 acknowledged & delivered by william yardley attorney
to Samuel Burges grantor to willm Biles & Joſuah Hoops
grantees for the uſe of them Selves & Tho: Janney and
Richard Hough Grantees

a deed in fee for 300 acres of land dated the i8ᵗʰ day of the i2ᵗʰ mo:
i689 acknowledged and delivered by willm Beakes grantor to
Thomas Tunnclif attorney to Jon worrilow & walter ——
worrilow in Truſt for the uſes therein expreſſed

meſſage from the assembley that there is due from this County to the
Clarks of the assembley i: £ 7ˢ 0ᵈ & deſired that Care be taken
to anſwer the Same

ordered that the Same be pd out of the County ſtock when it
comes in

whereas Tho: Rowland as ordered laſt Court to bring in an acctt
of the lands & males within his deviſion appointed & that he
is Since dead & now that deviſion now thought too large
for one man its therefore

ordered that wm Hearſt from the lower ſide of Robt Halls ———
plantation to new Town & Shadrach walley from thence
to the upper moſt land taken up do give an acctt of the lands
& males Taxable

agreed that if Iſrael Taylor bring in an acctt of all lands ſurveyed
Seated or unſeated with in the limits of this County att or
before the next Court & the Same acctt be Juſt & true faire
drawn out that then the ſd Iſrael Taylor have 20ˢ for
his paines diſcounted out of the Tax to be raiſed

whereas there is occation for a Corronor a boy being lately
drowned & none being Commiſſionated for this County

ordered that wm Biles Ar: Cooke & wm yardley take Care to Endeavor yᵗ
a Corronor & Regiſter be appointed in this County

212

ordered that the Said prſons request the Councill that the upper Roade
for the upper moſt plantations in this County be layd Through
Philadelphia County

Complt being made by John Cartor that his brother Edward Cartor
doth not allow him meate & apparrel

ordered that Arthur Cook & wm: Biles forthwith take Care about
it & ſee for what time the ſd Jon was placed to him by the
orphans Court & endeavor to redreſs the Complt

18 _4_ 1690 execution granted agt Paterick & Philip Conway in wm ffiſhers
mo   Caſe re turnd
adjourned to the ioᵗʰ 7ᵗʰ mo next execut the 30 _4_ 1690 p wm
                                                mo   yardley
                        30ᵗʰ _4_ 90 execution in Swifts Caſe dated
                               mo

                        for 10 £: 3ˢ: 3ᵈ returnd executed ſame day
                                                p wm yardley

Pensylvania

County Court Bucks ſs:

actions Entered
7th day 6 1690
    mo

John Jones by his attorney Samuel Carpentr

Paterick Robinſon Joſhu ffuller & Jon: Swift plt

agt

Jos Holden deft in an acctt of debt 66 £ : 8ˢ : 06ᵈ

Attachmt granted the i9th day of the 6th month i690 agt the goods of
Joſeph Hold in the Caſe afforeſaid by Arthur Cook

Return thereof executed the 2iᵗʰ day of the 6th month i690
p wm yardley Sherrife

action Entered
23 day of the 6
    mo
1690

John Duplovie plt

agt

Joſeph Watson deft

in an action of debt 15 £ : 16ˢ : 07ᵈ

Attachment granted the 2i day of the 6th month i690 agt: the goods
of Joſeph Holden in the Caſe afforeſaid by Arthur Cook

Return the 30th 6 i690 executed p wm yardley Sherrife
    mo

action Entered
23 day of 6
   mo
1690

Philip Richards plt

agt

Joſeph Holden deft

in an action of debt

Attachment granted the 2i day of the 6th month i690 agt: the goods
of Joſeph Holden in the Caſe afforesaid by Arthur Cooke

Return 30th 6 1690 executed p wm: yardley Sherrife
    mo

action Entered
24 6 1690
  mo

Iſrael Taylor plt

agt

Tho: Brock Ralph Boome
John Stetton ffrancis Roſſill
mathew miller — — —

defts

in an action on the

Caſe Sum 8 £

Summonce granted 26ᵗʰ $\frac{6}{mo}$ 1690 agt: ſd defts p John Brock

Return 30ᵗʰ $\frac{6}{mo}$ executed the ſd Summonce p wm: yardley ſherrif

action Entered ⎱ Policarpus Roſe plt
26ᵗʰ $\frac{6}{mo}$ i690 ⎰   agt

                John Pidcock deft

Summonce granted in ſd Caſe 26ᵗʰ $\frac{6}{mo}$ i690 agt ſd deft p Jon Brock

Return 29ᵗʰ $\frac{6}{mo}$ 1690 executed ſd Summonce p wm yardley ſherrife

Summonce for witneſſes in ſd Caſe granted 26ᵗʰ $\frac{6}{mo}$ 1690 for

213

John Lee & his wife Rachel martha Lee & Robt Benſon

Return 28 & 29ᵗʰ $\frac{6}{mo}$ 1690 Summonced the ſd p wm yardley Sherrife

action Entered ⎱ Gilbert wheeler plt
26ᵗʰ $\frac{6}{mo}$ 1690 ⎰   agt   ⎰ in a plea of Caſe

                John Pidcock deft

Sumonc granted in ſd Case for ſd deft 26ᵗʰ $\frac{6}{mo}$ i690 p Jon Brock

Return the 29ᵗʰ of the $\frac{6}{mo}$ 1690 executed p wm yardley Sherrif

Actiou Eutered ⎱ Iſrael Taylor plt
the 26ᵗʰ $\frac{6}{mo}$ i690 ⎰   agt   ⎰ in a plea of Caſe

                John Shippey deft

Sumonc granted for ſd deft: 26ᵗʰ $\frac{6}{mo}$ i690 p Jon Brock

Return 29ᵗʰ $\frac{6}{mo}$ i690 executed p wm yardley ſherrife

Summonce granted for wm Roles witnes in ſd Case the
26ᵗʰ $\frac{6}{mo}$ i690

Return 29ᵗʰ $\frac{6}{mo}$ i690 executed the ſd ſum p wm yardley ſherrif

action Entered ⎫ John wood plt ⎫
the 28ᵗʰ $\frac{6}{mo}$ — ⎬   agt: ⎬ in a plea of Caſe
1690 ⎭ John Butler deft ⎭

attachment granted the 28ᵗʰ day 6 mo in ſd Caſe p Jon Brock

Return 29 & 30 day $\frac{6}{mo}$ i690 executed p wm yardley ſherrif

action Entered ⎫ mary Beakes Adminiſtratrix to her late
the 28 $\frac{6}{mo}$ 1690 ⎭ huſband wm: Beakes by her attorney

Samuel Beakes plt————⎫
agt   ⎬
Jonathan Eldridge deft ⎭

Arreſt granted agt ſd deft the iiᵗʰ $\frac{4}{mo}$ 1690 p wm Biles

Return the iiᵗʰ $\frac{4}{mo}$ i690 Taken into Cuſtody

action Entered ⎫ John wood plt ⎫
28ᵗʰ $\frac{6}{mo}$ i690 ⎭   agt   ⎬ in a plea of Caſe
John Swift deft ⎭

Sumonce granted the 28ᵗʰ day 6ᵗʰ month 1690 p Jon Brock

return 29th $\underline{6}$ 1690 executed p wm yardley
$\qquad$ mo

Pensylvania

Bucks ís: 214

At a Court of Quarter Seſſions held by the
king & Queens authority in the name of
Willm Penn Propryetory & Govrnr of the
afforeſaid Province & Counties annexed
at the Court houſe for the afforeſaid County
the ioth of the 7th month i690

The Justices Present

Joseph Growdon Wm Biles
nicholas Waln Henry Baker
John Brock
Wm: yardley Sherrife
Phinehas Pemberton Cl Com:

Comitment William Evans for Suspition of being Conferate
with Joseph Trivitham in a felonious act the Court Commits
into Safe Cuſtody untill further ordr

adjourned untill 9 o Clock in the morning

action Jon Jones by his attorneys
$\qquad$ agt   } plea of debt
Joſeph Holden ————————

appearance Paterick Robinson & Jon Swift Attorneys to ſd Jones
appeared & the deft by his attorney Hugh Marſh appeared

declaration Read

A Coppy of the ſd Attorneys power & a Certificate of the back
thereof Read

Bonds Read & proved

bill read & proved by atteſtation of John Swift & Henry Pointer

defts attorney declared he had nothing to bject why Judgmt
might not paſs

Judgmt awarded & it is adjudged that Joſeph Holden ſhall
pay to Jon Jones or his attorneys the ſum

of thirty pounds Silver monys
as alfo the Sum of Six pounds eight Shillings Six pence
with Intreft for the thirty pounds from the firft day of the
3 month i690 with Cofts of fuite to which the defts attorneys
affented

ordered by the Court that Paterick Robinson becom bound
upon Record in Court in 100 £ that Jon Jones Shall ratiefye
what he and other attorneys has done in relation to the
afforefaid action

---

obligation   215

Patrick Robinson oblidges him Self his heirs executrs
and administrators to the Juftices now on the —
bench being Jofeph Growdon William Biles Tho: Janney
Nicholas waln Henry Baker & John Brock theire
Executors and adminiftrators in the Sum of one —
hundered Pounds to be levied on his lands Tenements
goods and Chattles Conditioned for the procureing of
an authentick power from Jon Jones or that the fd
John Jones his heires Executors or adminiftrators in
i2 months time do Rate fye what fd Paterick ——
Robinfon & the reft of the attorneys of John Jones
has done or Shall do in relation to an action of
debt for 36 £ : 8ˢ: 06ᵈ now brought agt Jofeph
Holden   **PAT: ROBINSON**

Action   John Duplovie ⎫
                agt   ⎬plea of debt
      Jofeph Holden — ⎭

plt appeared by his attorney Paterick Robinfon
his letter of attorney to Impower him produced
deft appeared by his attorney Hugh marfh
his letter of attorney to Impower him produced

debt accknowledged by the defts attorney

Judgmt Given & it is adjudged that Jofeph Holden Shall
pay to John Duplovie the Sum of thirtteen pounds
pounds eighteen Shillings Seven pence half peny
i3 £ : 18ˢ 7½ᵈ (the Said attorney haveing promifed to
allow what Shall be further made appeare paid upon
acctt)
if any be & that Execution Iffue accordingly to fd
Judgmt

Action Philip Richards plt ⎫
                agt   ⎬ in a plea of debt
       Jofeph Holden deft ⎭

Paterick Robinfon his attorney appeares
letter of attorney produced to prove the fame

Hugh marsh attorney afforefd appeares

declaration read

Anfwer the faid defts attorney acknowledges the debt

Judgmt Given & it is adjudged that Jofeph Holden fhall
pay to Philip Richards the fum of Ten pounds Two
Shillings & three pence 10 £ : 2ˢ 3ᵈ (the fd plts attorney
promifeing to allow what Shall be further made appeare
paid on acctt) & that execution Iffue accordingly

                                 216

action John wood plt ⎫
          agt   ⎬ in a plea of Cafe both appeared
John Swift deft ⎭

declaration read

Anfwer he doth owe the takeing up the negroes

the matter refferred to the bench

Judgmt given and it is adjudged that John Swift Shall pay
to John wood one pound five Shillings & that fd Swift fhall
alfo pay Coft of fuite

action Samuel Beakes attorney to Mary Beakes plt ⎫ both
                        agt ⎬ in a plea of debt ⎭ appeared
Jonathan Eldridge deft ⎭

declaration read

Anfwer he ownes the debt

Judgmt Given & it is adjudged that Jonathan Eldridg Shall pay to
the plt the Sum of Two pounds Three fhillings Seven pence
with Cofts of Suite

which Said Sum of Two pounds three fhillings Seven pence

willm Embley in open Court declared he wold pay to the plt or attorney in three months time

willm Biles promifed to pay the fee of the fd Cafe

a deed of 72 Square Rods of land in fee dated the 4th day of the 7th month i690 acknowledged & delivered by Thomas Janney grantor to Jofuah Hoops & wm yardley for the ufe of them Selves & the reft of the grantees

adjourned for one houre

a deed in fee of 200 acres of land dated the io th day of the i2th month i689 by Phinehas Pemberton grantor unto mary Radclif widow of the grantee

a deed in fee of 250 acres of land dated the 8th day of the 7th month i690 acknowledged & delivered by willm Clows & marjory Clows Grantors to Jofeph Clows Grantee

a deed in fee of 250 acres of land dated the 8th day of the 7th month i690 was acknowledged & delivered by Joseph Clows grantor to willm Clows Grantee

grand jury attefted

Samuel Dark wm Ellot wm Hayhurft
Tho: Tunneclif Shadrach walley John Palmer
Jofuah Hoopes Andrew Heath Joseph Clowes
Jonathan fcaife Andrew Ellot Jon Lee
Jonathan Walters Henry Paxfon peter Worral
Jon white

Indictmt Bucks fs: the jurrors for the body of this County do prfent
Thomas Brock for extortion in ferriage the 8th day of this Inftant
the 7th month Conterarly to the ftatute law in that Cafe made & provided
to wich prfentmt he pleaded Guilty

217

a deed of 500 acres of land in fee dated the 9th day of the 7th month i690 acknowledged and delivered by John Rowland grantor to Gilbert wheeler Grantee

a deed of 360 acres of land in fee dated the 15th day of

November in the firſt yeare of the reigne
of willm & mary king & Queen of England &c: acknow
ledged & delivered by wm Biles attorney to John
Cuff grantor to Samuel Beakes grantee

a deed of 60 acres of land in fee dated the 20ᵗʰ day of the
6ᵗʰ month i690 acknowledged & delivered by Joſeph
Growdon grantor to Thomas Scot grantee

action Israel Taylor plt

   agt:

Thomas Brock ffrancis Roſſill John Stedon ⎫
             ⎬
Ralph Boome & mathew miller defts ⎭

Iſrael Taylor appeared

Thomas Brock ffrancis Roſſill & Jon: Stedon appeared on
behalf of them Selves & the reſt

declaracon read

Anſwer they Confeſt to the declaracon & Sayd that they wold
pay the plt. 5 £ : ioˢ : 00ᵈ with Coſt of ſuite

replye Iſrael Taylor ſaid it Shold Content him & Craved
Judgmt for the Same

Judgmt given & it is adjudged that the ſd defts Shall pay
to ſaid plt Iſrael Taylor 5 £ : 10ˢ : 00ᵈ with Coſts of
Suite & that execution Iſſue accordingly

Cornelius Empſon Craved in open Court that wm: Embley might
be his attorney to proſecute an action of debt
agt Joſeph Holden for 8 £ Silver mony

allowed the ſd request

wm Evans being examined about a hors found in the
Cuſtody of Joſeph Trivetham Said that he lent the ſd
Trivetham the horſe

adjourned untill 8 a Clock tomorrow morning   £   s   d

Execution drawn to be ſigned for John Jones for the levying of 36 : 8 : 6
& 2 £ : 3ˢ : iᵈ Coſts on the Goods & Chattles of Joſeph
Holden

action   Cornelius Empson
                    agt   } Cafe of debt for 8 £ Silver mony
          Joseph Holden

appeares by his attorney wm: Embley

Joseph Holden appeares by his attorney Hugh Marſh
    declarcon Read

Anſwer he ownes the declaracon & Confeſſes the debt

218

Judgment Given and it is adjudged that Joſeph
    Holden Shall pay to Cornelius Empſon the Sum of eight
    pounds Silver mony with Coſts of Suite & that Execution
    Iſſue accordingly

Iſrael Taylor
          agt   } plea of Cafe both appeared
John Shippey —

declaracon Read

Anſwer that he owes the plt 33ˢ & will pay Coſts of Suite
plt declared that the Same pd to him will Satisfy him

Judgmt Given & it is adjudged that John Shippey Shall pay
    Thirty Three Shillings with Coſts of Suite & that execu
    -tion Iſſue accordingly

grand Jury prſents Joſeph Trevithan formerly of this County
    for fraudulently takeing and Carrying away from the houſe
    of Joſeph Growdon the 8ᵗʰ day of this Inſtant the 7ᵗʰ
    month one broad Cloth Coate i paire pluſh breeches one
    womans Cloake being the proper goods of the ſd Joſeph
    Growdon to the value of five pounds Conterary to the
    king & Queens peace & the Statute law in that Cafe
    made & provided &c:

Pro ſecutor Joſeph Growdon

wittneſſes Tho: ffox John Hawkins atteſted

This bill found

Joſeph Trevithan to the Said Indictmt pleaded not Guilty & for
    Tryal puts him Self upon the Cuntry wherefore the Sherrife is
venire   Commanded to Cauſe to Come i2 honeſt & Lawfull men &c:

Jury—Thomas Stackhouſe Senr Jos. milner Stephen Beakes ⎫
wm Paxson   John Croſdel   Edmund Lovet ——————— ⎬ atteſted
wm:Taylor   wm: Dark Henry Marjorum ——————— ⎪
John Penquoit   Henry Pointer   Jon: Swift ——————— ⎭

Thomas ffox atteſted Saith that upon the 8ᵗʰ day of this Inſtant
    month the ſd Trevithan Came to the houſe of Jos: Growdon
    & Said Jos: Growdon had ſent him for Cloths for he & his
    wife had faln in the River meaning the ſd Jos: Growdon &
    wife & that they wanted them & thereby obteined from
    the negro woman i Cloth Coate i paire pluſh breeches i —
    Cloake for a woman & further Saith not

219

John Hawkins atteſted Saith that upon monday laſt being the 8ᵗʰ
    Instant he Saw the Said Trevithan at the houſe of
    Jos: Growdon & that He Saw the ſd Trevithan have
    upon his horſe i Cloth Coate i paire of pluſh breeches &
    one womans Cloak wᶜʰ under pretence of Joſeph
    Growdons being wet in the River he had obtained from t
    the negro woman

action   policarpus Roſe ⎫
         agt   ⎬ with drawn by order of the plt
    John Pidcock ⎭

Conſtables ⎧ above the falls Joſuah Hoops
          ⎪ below to penſberry Jos: Chorley
          ⎪ middle Lotts wm: Duncan
          ⎨ the upper pte of Neſhaminah John white
   ffor   ⎪ the upper pte of the other ſid of Neſhaminah Jon:
          ⎪   purſley
          ⎪ the lower pte on the other side Samˡˡ Allen Junr
          ⎩ the lower pte of the River Tho: Green

Jury returned do Say the ſind Joſeph Trevithan as he is
    Charged in the prſentment

prſentmt agt Tho: king for de fameing Joan the wife of
    ffrancis Searl found to be a true bill to wᶜʰ ſd king
pleaded not guilty & for Tryal put him Self upon the Cuntry

venire where the Sherrife is Commanded to Cauſe to Com &c. i2
honeſt
& lawfull men &c

Jury before mentioned Atteſted

Hugh Marſh Atteſted doth Say that in or about the 3 month laſt
paſt Says he heard Thomas king Say there was a witch neare
by being askt who it was Said he Suſpected Francis Searls
wife for She was an ugly ile favored woman & he did beleive
her to be one

Robt marſh atteſted Says he heard Tho: king Say that there was
a witch hard by

action John Wood ⎫
        agt   ⎬   plea of debt plt appeared
John Buttler ⎭   deft appeared not

declaracon Read

Rich Richway atteſted doth Say that he knows that John wood
did deliver a Conſiderable Quantity of Wheate & that he beleives

220

ſd Buttler owed John wood at his going away above 20 £ : to
the beſt
of his knowledge 2i or 22 £ as he heard John Butler Say &
further
Saith John Buttler promiſed Cattle for the Said Corn

Joſeph wood atteſted proved every article of the acctt

Judgmt Given by default & it is adjudged that John Buttler Shall
pay to John wood the Sum of five pounds ii^s with three pounds
damages & Coſts of Suite & that Execution Iſſue accordingly

Jury Returned finds Thomas king Guilty of defameing Joan
the wife of ffrancis Searl in Saying he beleived She was a
witch

Gilbert wheeler in open Court promiſed to pay the fees of pollicarpus
Rose action
———

action Gilbert wheeler plt ⎫
        agt   ⎬   plea of Caſe both appeared
John Pidcock ⎭

declaracon Read

Anſwer he defds & Saith he owes nothing & for Tryal puts
him Self upon the Cuntry & plt Likewiſe wherefore the —
venire Sherrife is Commanded to Cauſe to Come &c: i2 honeſt & lawfull men
&c

Jury before mentioned atteſted

acct brought & in & atteſted to by the plt & plea of debt proved
by Jos: Hollinshead atteſtation
jurys
verdict we find for the plt with Coſt of ſuite

adjudged that John Pidcock Shall pay to Gilbert wheeler 2 £ : 14ˢ: 00ᵈ
with Costs of Suite & that Execution Iſſue accordingly

a deed in fee of 296 acres of land dated the i2ᵗʰ day of the firſt
month $\frac{1689}{90}$ was acknowledged and delivered by Henry —

marjerum grantor to John Clark Grantee

Judgmt Given & it is adjudged that Thomas king Shall pay Coſts
of ſuite & be bound to keep the peace & to appeare at the next
Court of Quarter Seſſions

Recognizance Thomas king acknowledges him Self
Indebted to the propryetor & govrnr in the Sum of Ten pounds
to be levied on his lands & Tenements Goods & Chattles &

that upon Condition that he Shall appeare at the next Court
of Quarter Seſſions & to keepe the king & Queens peace in the
meane time

adjourned to 8 a Clock in the morning

none appearing agt Wm Evans the Court diſcharges him
paying his fees & Costs

221

Judgmt given and it is adjudged that Joſeph Trevithan upon his
Indictment Shall make double Satiſfaction which is he Shall
Pay to Joseph Growdon Ten pounds and that Joseph Growdon
Shall pay the Coſts and fees the Goalers fees excepted and
whereas the Said Trevithan hath not eſtate to anſwer the ſd
Judgmt it is adjudged that the ſd Trevithan for the Same
Shall Serve the Said Joſeph Growdon one yeare and a
Quarter except he doth Serve very well & faithfully

one yeare then to be free at the yeares End to wich
Judgment both Joſeph Growdon & the ſd Trevithan declared
theire Satiſfaction

John Pidcock being Called appeared and declared Pollicarpus Roſe
had made him Satiſfaction

Policarpus Roſe appeared & nothing appearing agt him the
Court discharges him paying his fees

over ſeeres of the High ways

> above the falls Ruben Pownal
> below to the Govrnrs Joſeph Chorley
> the Lower part of the River Richard Wilſon
> the Lower part of Neſhaminah Derick Clawſon
> the upper part of Neſhaminah wm Hayhurſt
> the middle lotts ———— ———— John Webſter
> the Lower part beyond Neſhaminah walter fforrest
> and Sa. Allen
> for the upper part of the Same Tho: Harding

Adjourned to the 7th of the 8th month next

Executions agt the Goods and Chattles of Joſeph Holden Jon
Duplovies Caſe in Philip Richards Caſe in Cornelius Empsons Caſe
were granted the i9th day of the 7th mo: i690

no Court then Held no buſines prſenting & Returned by the Sherrif
the 29th of the 7th mo 1690

action   peter Jenings plt ⎫
          agt   ⎬ plea of Case   no goods or Chattles to
      Tho. Fox deft ⎭   be found wm yardley

Sumonce dated the i2th day 7 mo 1690 granted by Jon Brock

return that the ſum was executed the 20th day 7 1690 by
                                                  mo

                              wm: yardley Sherrife

action   John Teft plt ⎫
          agt   ⎬ in a plea of Caſe
      Thomas ffox deft ⎭

Sumonce granted 20th day 7 1690 p wm Biles
                            mo

    return

action Joſeph ffarrington plt ⎫
        agt   ⎬ in a plea of debt
John Thatham deft   ⎭

Sumonce Granted 27th day $\frac{7}{mo}$ 1690 p wm Biles

return Sumonced the 29th $\frac{9}{mo}$ 90 p wm yardley Sherrife

                                                    222

action Thomas Tunneclif plt ⎫
        agt   ⎬ in a plea of Caſe
John Lee deft —— ——⎭

ſummonce Granted 27th $\frac{9}{mo}$ 1690 p wm Biles

return executed the 20th day of $\frac{9}{mo}$ i690 p wm yardley Sherrife

Execution granted agt: the Goods & Chattles of John Pidcock the
  29th $\frac{7}{mo}$ i690 by Jos: Growdon to Satisfye a Judgmt
obteined by Gilbert wheeler the io th day of the 7th mo aforeſd

execution granted agt the Goods & Chattles of John Buttler
  the 14th day of the 9th month i690 by John Brock to Satisfye
  a Judgmt obteined by John wood agt ſd Butler the io th day of the
  7th month laſt paſt

Bucks ſs:

            At a Court of Quarter Seſſions held by the king
            & Queens authority in the name of Willm Penn
            Propryetor & Govrnr of the afforeſd Province &
            Counties annexed at the Court houſe for the ſd
            County the io th day of the io th month being the 2nd
            yeare of the king & Queens Reign & io th yeare
            of the propryetorys govrmt i690

               The Justices Present

               Tho: Janney   willm Biles
               Nicholas waln   Henry Baker
               John Brock
               John Cook Corronor
               wm yardley Sherrif
               Phinehas Pemberton Cl: Com:

Grand Jury attefted

Jonathan Scaife   John Hough   James Paxson————⎫
John Smith   Henry Pawlin   Stephen Newell ————⎪
John Towne   Tho: Stakehoufe fenr   Tho: ⎪
    Stakehoufe Jnr ⎬
wm Hearft   Ezra Crofdel   John Crofdel ———— ⎪
Henry Hudleftone Shadrach walley Jos: Milner —— ⎪
Henry Marjerum   Richard Lundy ———————— ⎭

action Peter Jenings ⎫
        agt ⎬ Cald but neither appeared
   Tho: ffox — ⎭

223

action John Teft ⎫
        agt: ⎬ both Called but neither partie appeared
   Tho ffox —— ⎭

action Jos: ffarrington ⎫
        agt ⎬ J: ffarringto appeard
  John Tatham ⎭   Jon Tatham appeared not

Requeft being made by John Tatham to refpite the
    action makeing it appeare that he was Sick & Indif
    -pofed & not able to make his appearance Edward —
    Hunlock & Rich Bafnet engaged for his
    appearance at the next Court to anfwer the action
    without further Summonce or procefs

accidental death of John Stotton returned & read

adjourned the Court for one houre

action Tho: Tunneclif ⎫
        agt ⎬ both appeared
  John Lee ——— ⎭ action with drawn

Tho: Tunneclif agreed to pay half the Charge

Grand Jurys prfentmt agt Ifrael Taylor

Pensylvania

County Court Bucks fs:

The Jurrors for the body of this County do prfent Ifrael

Taylor for takeing Stealing killing & Converting to
his owne ufe about the beginning of 9ᵗʰ month in
the yeare i689 one heifer of Colour red the end of
her taile white haveing a Crop on the further eare
being about one yeare and a half old & worth about
forty Shillings being the proper goods of John Naylor
Conterary to the king & Queens peace & the ftatute
Law in that Cafe made & provided
John naylor profecutor

Richard Thatcher   ⎫
                        ⎬ witneffes attefted
Bartholemew Thatcher   ⎭

we the jurrors do find this bill
to wᶜʰ. Said Taylor pleaded not Guilty & for Tryal put
pleading him Self upon the Cuntry wherefore the Sherrif is
venire   Commanded to Caufe to Come before the Court 12
        honeft & Lawfull men &c:

224

Jury   Jofuah Hoops   Stephen Beakes   Sam: Dark ⎫
          John wood   wm: Ellet — Henry Paxson   ⎪
                                                      ⎬ attefted
          wm Dark   Jacob Hall — wm: Beakes   ⎪
          wm Paxson   Samuel Beakes   Andrew Ellet   ⎭

Rich Thatcher attefted doth Say that being at work at Ifrael
    Taylors in the fall Laft was i2 months he Saw Ifrael
    Taylor give the heifer of Jon naylor bread Several
    times & he the Said Taylor Sd: to the fd Thatcher Come
    let us kill this heifer: but at that time he left the fd
    Taylors houfe for want of provifions & in a few days after
    Ifrael asked the fd Thatcher to Come againe for he had
    Provifions enough & he Came there & Saw in the Celler
    of fd Taylor in a brl Several peices of Smal meate
    & he Saw then the hinder part of A hide of Colour red &
    the end of the taile white & he Saw the fd Taylor bury the
    fd piece of a hide & that about io or i2 weekes ago the
    fd Thatcher underftanding that he was under Suspition
    of being Guilty of affifting in the killing of the fd heifer
    he the fd Thatcher went to the fd Taylors houfe and afked
    the fd Taylors wife what heifer it was that was killed
    and who killed it & She Said Benjemame Jones & Israel
    kill'd her & that Shee beleived it was naylors heifer

Bartholomew Thatcher atteſted doth Say Last fall was Twelve
months he Stayd at Israel Taylors al night & he Saw
Israel Taylo's wife dreſs Some meate wch he Thought
was young heifer beefe & before that time the heifer of
John Naylor was wanting

The will of Rich Thatcher being delivered into Court it was
ordered that Phinehas Pemberton Should keep it till
further ordr

adjourned the Court for one houre

verdict Jury Returned do Say Israel Taylor is not guilty
of the fellony whereof he ſtands Indicted

a deed in fee of 200 acres of land dated the 3 day of the 9th
month i690 acknowledged & delivered by Joſuah Hoops
attorney to Joſeph Engliſh Grantor to Samuel Dark
grantee

Grand Jury prſents the want of Standard for Juſt weights &
meaſures
& the want of the County to be devided in to Town ſhips &c

The Executions before mentioned both returned Satiſfyed

225

Wm: Biles acknowledged in open Court that he had Received
full Satisfaction from Derrick Jonſon for one bl
mare with a long Taile & dule back with Some —
white haires in her forehead & a half peny Cut on the
further eare, wch Said mare the ſd Derrick is allowed
to take up when he Can find her & her Increase that
Shall Lawfully appeare to be long to her & that he the
ſd wm: Biles will warrant the ſd mare & her Said
Increaſe to the ſd Jonſon & defend from all perſons

Reported to this Court by John Brock that Richard Thatcher
did Confeſs he owed to Derrick Jonſon the ſum of
one pound eight Shillings & that it was to be pd in good
wheate & that it was adjudged by the ſd Jon
Brock that the ſd Sum Shold be accordingly pd
with Coſts wch ſd Judgmt is approved of by this
Court & thereupon ordered that execution Iſſue accordingly

Judgmt Given & its adjudged that John Naylor Shall pay Coſts
of Suite & that execution Iſſue accordingly

Israel Taylor promifed to pay the fees in both actions —
wherein Revel was Concerned agt: him to the officers

adjourned the Court to the 20th day of this month to the
houfe of Thomas Janney

8th io   1690
mo

Execut agt: Thater for fees 3£ 9s: 4d returned i3 io   90
mo

i2 io   i690 execu agt íd Thatcher & Taylor for 14£ 14s: 6d returnd —
mo   i6th io   1690
mo

i2 io   1690 execu agt íd Thather for 1 £ i6s returnd
mo

At A Court held by adjournmnt the 20th day of
the ioth month i690 at the houfe of Tho: Janney

Tho Janney: wm: Biles
Nicholas Waln   Jon: Brock
wm yardley   Sherrife
Phinehas Pemberton Cl: Com:

Richard Thatcher being bound in 20 £ to appeare at this
Court none appeareing agt him the Court difcharges him

action John Brock plt
agt   } act of debt plt appeared
Gilbert wheeler deft } the deft appeared not —

decl read

bill read

wm Biles appeared on íd Wheelers acctt & Said that
Gilbert Wheeler was before him this day & Confeft the
bill mentioned in the declaration

226

John Brock Confeft he had Red in pte of the íd bill 1 £: 10s 9d

Judgmt Given & it is adjudged that Gilbert wheeler Shall pay
to John Brock 4 £: 5s: Dt & 5s damages with Cofts of fuite
& that execution Iffue accordingly

whereas the Sherrif hath mad return of the executions out agt

the goods & Chattles of Jos: Holden for the Several Sums
obtained by John Duplovie Philip Richards & Cornelius
Empſon that there is no Goods or Chattles to Satiſſye the ſd
debts & that the perſons have requeſted to have execution
agt the ſd Holdens Land it is ordered by this Court that
execution Iſſue agt: the lands of the ſd Holden to Satiſſye
the Several Judgmts: obteined by the affore ſd perſons

whereas the Grand Jury did prſent the neceſſity of haveing the
County devided into Town Ships it is ordered that Henry
Baker Thomas Janney wm: Biles Phinehas Pemberton
Arthur Cook Edmund Bennet James Boyden Nicholas
waln Joſuah Hoops John Rowland Jos: Growdon Sam[ll]
Allen & that they meete together the day before the
next Court at the Court house & then & there devide
this County into Town ſhips that the Same may be prſented
to the next Court to have the approbation thereof

whereas the Grand Jury prſented the neceſſity of haveing
weight & meaſures Equall according to law its referred
to be further Conſidered of

adjourned to the ii[th] day of the firſt month next
the 3 executions aforesaid granted agt Holdens Land dated
the 20th   day   ii   1690
$$\overline{\text{mo}}$$

Bucks ſs: County Court the ii[th] $\dfrac{1}{\text{mo}}$ $\dfrac{\text{i690}}{1}$

Action Entered the 20th $\dfrac{9}{\text{mo}}$ i690

Joſeph ffarrington plt

      agt: plea of Debt for tryal at the $\dfrac{\text{io}^{th}}{\text{mo}}$

John Tatham deft   Court but the tryal was reſpited

untill this Court becauſe of the deft then Sickneſ

action Entered the i $\dfrac{\text{i2}}{\text{mo}}$ i690   1690

John Smith plt

agt

Thomas Peirce deft

i5th day $\frac{ii}{mo}$ an arrest granted at the ſuite

of wm Biles agt John Pidcock

15th $\frac{ii}{mo}$ i690 attachmt granted at the

ſuite of wm Biles agt the goods of
John Pidcock

action Entered 16th $\frac{i2}{mo}$ i690

Theſe withdrawn againe
by wm Biles

Zacharia Whitpaine plt

agt

Gilbert wheeler deft

plea of debt

227

Sum Granted 16th $\frac{i2}{mo}$ 1690

return executed the i6th $\frac{12}{mo}$ i690 p wm yardley Sherrife

with drawn

action Entered the 23 $\frac{i2}{mo}$ i690

Thomas Revel plt agt Israel Taylor deft plea of Caſe

Summonce granted 23 $\frac{i2}{mo}$ i690

return 27 $\frac{i2}{mo}$ 90 p wm yardley

Sum for wittneſſes dated 24th $\frac{i2}{mo}$ 1690

return

action Entered 24th $\frac{i2}{mo}$ 1690

Andrew Heath plt

agt

wm Beakes deft

in a plea of Treſpaſs

Sum granted 24th $\frac{i2}{mo}$ 90

return 25th $\frac{i2}{mo}$ 90 p wm yardley

Sum for witneffes dated 4th $\frac{i}{mo}$ 1690 return 10th $\frac{i}{mo}$ 90

action Entered 25th $\frac{i2}{mo}$ 90

wm yardley plt
    agt   & Robt Marfh   in an action of debt
Hugh Marfh deft

Sum granted 20th $\frac{i2}{mo}$ 1690 return 27th $\frac{i2}{mo}$ 90 p w: yardley

action Entered 25th $\frac{i2}{mo}$ 1690

Thomas Janney by his attorney Jon: neild plt
    agt
Jon Lee & Jofeph Milner defts in a plea of debt

Sum granted the 25th $\frac{i2}{mo}$ i690 return 25 $\frac{i2^{th}}{mo}$ 90

with drawn by ordr of Tho: Janney

action Entered 25th $\frac{i2}{mo}$ i690

Tho: peirce plt
    agt   in a plea of Cafe
Jon pidcock deft

attachmt. granted 22 $\frac{ii}{mo}$ 90 .

return buck fkin 3 doe fkins 2 Guns 30^{lb} of red Lead

Penfylvania   228
Bucks fs: At a Court of Quarter Seffions held by the king & Queens

authority in the name of wm Penn propryetory & govrnr
of the Said Province & Counties annexed at the Court
houſe for the ſd County the ii^th day of the i i690 being
                                              mo
the ii^th yeare of the propryetorys Govrmt

The Justices then prſent

Arthur Cooke   Joſeph Growdon
Nicholas waln & Henry Baker
wm yardley Sherrife
Phinehas Pemberton Cl. Com:

action Jos: ffarrington plt ⎫
                        agt ⎬ both appeared & deſired
John Tatham deft   ⎭ one houres time before
    the matter be brought to tryal allowed by
    the Court

action Thomas Revel agt Israel Taylor neither appeared

action Andrew Heath ⎫
              agt   ⎬ both appeared decl read
wm Beakes ───────────⎭

deft defends the force for tryal puts him Self upon the

Anſwer

    Cuntry & ſo doth the plt wherefore the Sherrife is Commanded
venire to Cauſe to Come i2 honeſt & Lawfull men &c

Jury—John Swift   Henry Pointer   wm: Dark   ⎫
    Joſuah Hoops Tho: ſtackhouſe ſen^r Henry Paxſon ⎬ atteſted
    wm Paxſon   James Paxſon   John Rowland   ⎪
    Edmund Lovet   wm Taylor   Jos kirkbride   ⎭

action wm yardley agt Hugh & Robt marſh plt appeared the
defts appeared not wherefore the Court ſuſpends the action untill
to morrow

action Andrew Heath agt: wm Beakes

decl proved by the Evidence of James Sutton Joſeph
    Henbry Tho: kirle george Cockrum Joſeph ⎫
    Stewards Tho Tunneclif Ann Ellot Sarah Biles ⎬ atteſted
    Jon Wood Andrew Ellot all of them ———————⎭

adjourned for one houre

adjourned untill tomorrow morning at 9 a Clock

verdict Jury finds for the plt Andrew Heats 3 £ damages &
    Coſts of Suite

229

action Jos: ffarrington agt John Tatham both appeared
    declarat read Anſwer read for Tryal put them
    Selves upon the Cuntry
    wherefore the Sherrife is Commanded to Cauſe to Come
    i2 honeſt & Lawfull men &c

The Jury afforeſd atteſted

    decla: read

    Anſwer read

    obligation read & Confeſt by the deft

    award read & Confeſt by the deft

Jury do say they find for the plt＿＿＿

    John Tatham Craved an appeale

    adjourned the Court for one houre

A deed of Mortgage of 400 acres of land by John Pidcock
    grantor to Edward Hunlock Grantee dated the io[th] of the
    i2[th] mo: i690 with a Schedule thereunto annexed was
    tendered in open Court by ſd Hunlock to Said Pidcock to
    be acknowledged according to law in open Court wch
    Said Pidcock refused to do without Shewing any Cauſe
    for his ſo refuſeing

action John Smith agt Tho: Peirce both parties appeared
    & refferred the Caſe to the bench

action Tho: Peirce agt John Pidcock both appeared

declaracon read

Aníwer he ows nothing & for tryal puts him Self upon the Cuntry & ío doth the plt
wherefore the Sherrife is Commanded to Caufe to Come i2 honest & Lawful men &c

Jury attefted

declaration proved by the atteftations of Tho: peirce gilbert wheeler Policarpus Rofe ____

Jury finds for the plt 20ˢ with Cofts of fuite

adjourned the Court to 9 to morrow morning

wm yardley agt Hugh & Robt marfh both appeared

declaracon read bill obligate read

Answer the defts ownes the bill to be theire acts & deeds

Thomas Peirce produced a difcharge under Jon Smiths hand in full & the Said Peirce promifed in open Court to pay & discharge all Cofts & fees ____

230

adjudged by the Court that the action agt fd Peirce be with drawn

Judgmt given in Heaths Cafe agt Beakes according to verdict and that execution Issue accordingly

Judgment given & it is adjudged that John Tatham pay to Jofeph ffarrington 50 £ & Cofts of Suite

Difference

after Judgmt Given both parties Refferred to the Juftices on the bence what Shall be adjudged in Equity to be abated on the penalty

Judgmt given & it is adjudged that John Pidcock Shall pay to Tho Peirce 20ᵇ & Cofts of Suite & that execution Iffue accordingly

Tho: Revel agt Ifrael Taylor both Calld but neither appeared

adjourned for one houre

i3 _i_ i690 whereas Joſeph ffarrington & John Tatham ———
  mo
    refferred to the Juſtices on the bench what the Judg in ———
    Equity the ſd John Thatham Shall pay to the ſd ffarrington
    in full Satisfaction of the afforesaid Judgmt whereupon the
    ſd Juſtices do Judg award & determine that the ſd Jon
    Tatham Shall pay to the Said ffarrington Twenty eight
    Pounds in Silver mony or in good merchantable wheate
    at Silver mony Price in one months time after the day
    of the date hereof & further that the ſd John Tatham
    Shall pay to the Respective officers the ffees due to them by
    reason of the afforesaid Judgment & upon payment of the
    Said mony that the Said Parties Shall Seale each other General
    releaſes & yᵗ if the Said John Tatham Shall faile payment of the
    Said mony as above expreſſed that then execution Iſſue ———
    according to the Judgment firſt obteined & further it is expreſſed
    that the ſd John Tatham Shall make payment to the ſd Joſeph
    ffarrington or his attorney at the ffurry houſe over agt Bur
  -lington
    george Browne being Calld upon his Recognizance being
    bound for aſſaulting & abuſeing wm Biles one of the Juſtices
    of peace for this County upon his examination Confeſt that
    he puſhed him twice with his hand whereupon the Court gave
    Judgmt & it is adjudged that the ſd george Brown Shall give
    bond for his appearance at next Court & to be of good —

231

    abearing in the meane time & Shall pay a fine of 20ˢ
    to be diſposed of as the Juſtices hereafter Shall think
    fit

    George Brown acknowledges him Self Indebted to the
    Propryetor & Govrnr in 10 £ to be levyed on his lands &
    tenements goods & Chattles & this upon Condition for
    his appearance at the next Court & to be of good ———
    abearing in the meane time

adjourned untill tomorrow morning at 9 a Clock

    whereas the perſons appointed to devide the County have
    not done it is ordered that the ſd perſons meete to
    gether on the 20ᵗʰ day of the 2ⁿᵈ month next to devide
    it into town ſhips

    adjourned the Court unto the 20ᵗʰ day of the 2ᵈ month next

23 $\frac{i}{mo}$ execut agt Rich Thather in Iſrael Taylors Caſe dated &

$\frac{1690}{i}$ returnd

no buſines prſenting there was no Court held in the 2nd month

County Court Bucks ſS:

action Entered the 20th $\frac{i}{mo}$ $\frac{169i}{2}$

Daniel Cox by his attorney John Tatham ⎫
            agt   ⎬   plea of debt _____ ⎭
Gilbert wheeler

Summonce dated 26th $\frac{3}{mo}$ 169i return — 29th $\frac{3}{mo}$ 169i

action entered 2i $\frac{i}{mo}$ 169i

Gilbert wheeler plt ⎫
            agt   ⎬ in a plea of Slander
John Tatham deft ⎭

Summonce dated the 26th $\frac{3}{mo}$ 9i

arreſt granted the 14th $\frac{3}{mo}$ i69i agt Henry Boucher at the

ſuite of Joſeph knight

Returnd the 29th $\frac{3}{mo}$ i69i not to be found p wm yardley Sherrife

action Entered the 23 $\frac{3}{mo}$ i69i ⎫   Arreſt dated 25 $\frac{3}{mo}$ 9i

Joſeph England plt ⎫   ⎬   Returnd 5th $\frac{4}{mo}$ 169i taken
            agt   ⎬   ⎭
Lawrence Parker deft ⎭ into Custody by Wm Yardley Sherrife

the above action with drawn by Philip England i0th $\frac{4}{mo}$ 9i action Entered the 25th $\dfrac{3}{mo}$ 169i

Thomas Hudſon by his attorney Jon white plt

agt $\Big\}$ Summons dated the 26th $\dfrac{3}{mo}$ 1691

Jacob Hall deft return dated the 29 $\dfrac{3}{mo}$ 169i

withdrawn by ordr of wm Biles

232

action Entered the 25th $\dfrac{3}{mo}$ i69i

Joſeph Chorley plt $\Big\}$
agt   in a plea of Case ⌐
marjery Claws deft.   Summonce dated 26th $\dfrac{3}{mo}$ i69i $\Big\}$ withdrawn by
order of
Joseph Chorley

action Entered the 25 $\dfrac{3}{mo}$ i69i

John Tatham plt $\Big\}$
agt   plea of Caſe $\Big\{$
Joseph Growdon deft
Summonce dated the 26 $\dfrac{3}{mo}$ i69i
Return dated the 30th $\dfrac{3}{mo}$ i69i

action Entered the 25th $\dfrac{3}{mo}$ i69i

Thomas Revel plt $\Big\}$
agt   action of debt $\Big\{$
ffrancis Roſſill deft
Sum: Dated 25th $\dfrac{3}{mo}$ 169i
Return dated 30th $\dfrac{3}{mo}$ i69i

action Entered 25th $\dfrac{3}{mo}$ 169i

John otter plt $\Big\}$
agt   action of debt $\Big\{$
ffrancis Roſſill deft
Summonc dated 25th $\dfrac{3}{mo}$ 169i
return dated 30th $\dfrac{3}{mo}$ 169i

action Entered 26th $\frac{3}{mo}$ i69i

Thomas Brock plt $\left.\begin{array}{c} \\ \text{agt:} \\ \\ \text{ffrancis Roffill deft} \end{array}\right\}$ in a plea of Cafe $\left\{\begin{array}{c} \text{Summonc dated 25}^{th}\ \frac{3}{mo}\ 169i \\ \\ \text{Return dated 30}^{th}\ \frac{3}{mo}\ 169i \end{array}\right.$

arreft granted the 25th $\frac{i2}{mo}$ 1690 agt Ralph Sidwell at Tho Brocks Suite

returnd the 29th $\frac{3}{mo}$ i69i not to be found p wm yardley
Sherrife

· County Court Bucks ſs: Penſylvania

at a Court of Quarter Seſſions held by the authority
of wm: & mary king & Queen of England &c: & in the
name of <u>wm</u> Penn Propryetor & Govrnr of the
Said Province & Countys annexed the i0th day of the
4th month i69i

The Justices then Prſent

Arthur Cook   Joseph Growdon   wm Biles
Nicholas waln   Henry Baker   John Brock
John Cooke Corronor
wm yardley Sherrife
Phinehas Pemberton Cl: Com:

George Brown Continued on Recognizance untill
next Court

233

Judgment Given by wm Biles one of the Juſtices of Peace
for this County between Iſrael Taylor plt & Richard
deft: whereupon it was adjudged that Richard Thatcher
Shold pay Israel Taylor 3^s 9^d & thirty apple trees or
for want of the apple trees the Said Thatcher to pay Ten
Shillings Inſtead thereof wch Judgment by this Court is
allowed & its adjudged that execution Iſſue accordingly

action John otter agt: ffrancis Roſſill both appeared

declaracon read

bond read

Anſwer deft owned the bond

plt declared that he deſired nothing but Ten pounds with
the Intreſt Since it was due ____

A proclamation agt vice from the Govrnr read

action Tho: Revel agt ffrancis Roſſill both appeared

declarcon read

bill read

Anſwer the deft owned the debt but not the damages

reply the plt declared that the debt without damages
wold Satiſfye him

action Tho: Brock agt ffrancis Roſſill both appeared

declaracon read

Ansſer the deft owned the debt but not the damages

reply the plt declared that the debt without damages
wold Satiſfye him

Judgmt given and it is adjudged that ffrancis Roſſill
pay to John otter Ten Pounds with Intreſt Since it was
due & Coſts of Suite & that execution Iſſue accordingly

Judgmt Given & it is adjudged that ffrancis Roſſill pay to
Thomas Revel Seven pounds one Shilling three pence
& Coſt of Suite & that execution Iſſue accordingly

Judgment Given & it is adjudged that ffrancis Roſſill pay to
Thomas Brock Ten pounds nineteen Shillings & five ——
pence with Coſts of ſuite & that execution Iſſue accordingly

action Daniel Cox agt Gilbert wheeler deft appeared the
plt by his attorneys Ed: Hunlock george Hutchinſon

declaration read   & Tho: Revel ——

Anſwer the deft & defends & Says he owes nothing upon the
bond & for tryal puts him Self on the Cuntry & so doth
the plt

wherefore the Sherrif is Commanded to Caufe to Come i2 honeft & lawfull men &c

Jury John Swift Henry Pointer Jonathan Scaife⎫
    Jofuah Hoops
    Stephen Beakes wm Beakes Tho:⎬ attested
    Stakehoufe Andrew Ellot
  Sam^{ll} Dark wm: Dark wm: Paxfon James⎭
  ·Paxfon

Bond read & owned by the deft

234

george Hutchinfon James Hill & Bernard Devonifh attefted Prove bond to be fealed while the fd Deft in Dures

action John Tatham agt Jofeph Growdon plt appeared

John Tatham appeared by his attorney Edward Hunlock

george Hutchinfon & Tho: Revell aforefaid who Say they are not Informed any thing Concerning the fd action & therefore defired a Continuation thereof untill the next Court

deft Craved a non fuite with Cofts

wherefore it is adjudged that John Tatham not appearing nor Informing his attorneys Concerning the fd action he Shall be non fuited & pay the Cofts

Jury returnd in the Cafe Cox agt wheeler finds for the deft with Cofts of Suite

Judgmt Given & it is adjudged that Daniel Cox pay Cofts of Suite

action Gilbert wheeler agt John Tatham plt appeared & deft by his attorney aforefaid & both plt & deft defired the fd action to be Continued untill next Court

adjourned for one houre

adjourned to the i6th 7 next
              ——
              mo

County Court Bucks fs: Penfylvania

action Entered for Tryal Last Court but Suſpended by Conſent
untill this

Gilbert wheeler plt
agt:
John Tatham deft } in action of Slander { withdrawn by the plts ordr

action Entered the 29th $\frac{6}{mo}$ 169i

Stephen Beakes agt George Brown in an action of Caſe

Summonce granted 29th $\frac{6}{mo}$ 169i return dated 4th day $\frac{7}{mo}$ 9i

action Entered the 29 day $\frac{6^{th}}{mo}$ i69i

Stephen Beakes agt Joſeph Steward } in an action of Caſe

Summonce dated 1^{ſt} of the 7th mo 169i return dated 3 day $\frac{7}{mo}$ 169i

action Entered the 31: $\frac{6}{mo}$ 169i

John Tatham plt agt Gilbert wheeler deft in an action on y^e Caſe

Summonce dated i $\frac{7}{mo}$ i69i return dated 4: day $\frac{7}{mo}$ 169i

235

action Entered the 3i $\frac{6}{mo}$ i69i

John Tatham plt agt Joſeph Growdon deft action of the Caſe
Summonce dated the i $\frac{7}{mo}$ 169i return dated 3 $\frac{7}{mo}$ 169i

action Entered the 3i $\frac{6}{mo}$ 169i

Jame Bleake by his attorney Chriftopher Snoden plt ⎤
agt
John Clawson in a plea of Cafe ───────────── ⎦

Summonce dated the i $\frac{7}{mo}$ 9i return dated the 3 day $\frac{7}{mo}$ 9i

Bucks fs: Penfylvania

        At a Court of Quarter Seffions held by the
        king & Queens authority in the name of
        wm Penn Propryetor & Govrnr of the
        afforesaid Province & Counties annexed
        at the Court houfe for the afforefd County
        the 16th day of the 7th month being the 3
        yeare of the king & Queens reigne &
        iith yeare of the propryetorys Govrmt i69i

        The Justices prfent

            Arthur Cook   Joseph Growdon
            Thomas Janney   Henry Baker
            Wm yardley Sherrif
            Phinehas Pemberton Cl: Com:

a deed of a peice of meadow land about five acres in fee
dated the 14th day of the 7th month i69i was delivered
and acknowledged by James Moone Senior & James Moon
Junr: grantors to Samuel Dark grantee

Grand Jury

        Henry Margerum Tho: Stakehoufe wm Buckman
    Thomas Rogers Shadrach walley James Paxfon   wm Paxfon
    Andrew Heath   Jos: kirkbride   Hugh Marfh   Andrew Ellot
    Abraham Cox   John white   Samll Burges all attefted

action Gilbert wheeler agt John Tatham both appeared &
    defired the action to be Suspended for one houre wch was
    allowed by the Court

236

action Stephen Beakes agt Jofeph Steward plt appeared but
    the deft appeared not but it was alleadged by Richard Hough

that the occation of his abfence was by reafon of a
refference of the Cafe had been difcourfed between the
Parties wherefore by Confent it is refferred untill another
Court

Stephen Beakes affigne to Jon Jonfon agt George Brown both
appeared the declaration read

Anfwer read alleading the plt had no power by law to bring the
Said action & therefore Craved anon Suite wch was
granted by the Court

Judgmt given & it is adjudged that Stephen Beakes Shall
Suffer anon Suite & pay Cofts of Court

george Brown acknowledged what there was owing to Jonfon aforefd
being 26 bufhells of wheate with Intreft & promifed to pay the
Same to Stephen Beakes before the next Court of Quarter
Seffions

adjourned for one houre

grand Jurys prfentments

we prsent wm: Beakes for Stoping the paffage by the river fide
that doth damnifye the neighbours

we allfo prfent the high way from the falls to South hampton to
be Cleared & the bridge by James Paxfons allfo the bridge that
Comes from wm: Bians to be repaired

we prfent Abraham wharley for keeping unlawfull ——
Swine that hath damnifyed the Inhabitans of new Town

we allfo prfent the neceffity of way from new Town to the
mill & Burlington fferry

       Henry Margerum fforeman

over feers of the high ways

for above the falls	——————	Ruben Pownal
from { thence to the govrnrs	——————	Edward Lucas
{ thence below to nefhaminah	———	Richard Wilfon
for { the Lower pte of nefhaminah		James Paxson
{ the middle Lotts	————	James moone
{ the other fide of nefhaminah Jon: Gilbert & Sam: Allen Junr		
{ South hampton	——————	Tho: Hardin

Tho: Brock attefted Saith that Chriftopher Snoden defired the action
agt John Clawfon to be Stayed this Court

237

Apprizers appointed untill further order

Sam{}^{ll} Dark   Jofeph kirkbride & John Rowland

george Brown being bound to appeare at Laft Court was
Continued & therfore defired this Court to difcharge who
was accordingly difcharged from his recognizance

action Gilbert wheeler agt John Tatham with drawn by
ordr of fd plt

action Daniel Cox by his Attorney John Tatham with —
drawn by ordr of fd Tatham

Conftables for this County are ftill Continued untill further
order

action John Tatham agt Jos: Growdon both appeard &
Jofeph Growdon made Claime of the benefit of the
law for magiftrates & Councillmen becaufe the time
was but Short & therefore was not prepared for tryal
& therefore time was allowed untill next Court

adjourned untill 8 a Clock tomorrow morning

whereas the grand Jury prfented at a Court held the i2{}^{th} day
of the firft month i689 the neceffity of haveing a Tax
raifed to pay the Councill & affembly men for theire
attendance already paft & other publique Charge of
the County it was accordingly ordered by a Court held the
26 1   90 that a Tax of 300 £ be raifed according to Law on
mo
the lands & males of this County for the ufes aforefd &
that returns be perfected according to former order of lands
& males & now ordered that duplicites be made thereof to every
Collector for
raifcing the fd mony

george Philips being taken up for a run away by Tho: Brock
& brought before this Court being Searched was found in
his Pocket one purs in w{}^{ch} was foure pounds 9{}^{d} Silver

mony & one bras 9ᵈ bit who upon his examination ——
Confeſt that he had taken the ſaid mony in the night time
out of the Cloſet of Denis Linſtone with whom he had
lived about 3 months as alſo one paire of gloves wᶜʰ ſd
gloves he the ſd Philips Confeſt the tooke out of the ſd Cloſet

Judgmt Given & it is adjudged that the ſd George Philips Shall
make Satiſfaction to the parties greived as the Law requires
by Servitude that he the ſd George Philips have 15 ſtripes
on his bare back well layd on now in Sight of the Court
& that he be Confined in the Sherrifs Cuſtody (untill his —
maſter have notice hereof) & that he be not delivered

238

to his Said maſter without ordr from Joſeph Growdon to whom
this Court referrs the ſd Denis Linstone to treat about the ſaid
George Philips freedom or Servitude being obteined as is ſd
Conterary to law

ordered that the ſd mony be kept by the Clerk as alſo the Gloves
& that after all Charges fees & Coſts are deducted that the
remaineing part be delivered to the owner thereof

adjourned to the 9ᵗʰ: 10ᵗʰ month next

action Suſpended Laſt Court untill this Court ⎱ with drawn by the ⎱
John Tatham agt Jos: Growdon plea of Caſe ⎰ plts ordr —— ⎰

action Entered 23 $\frac{9}{mo}$ 169i

Joſeph Growdon agt John Grey alls Tatham ⎱   ⎱ with drawn by
in a plea for Treſpaſs done —— —— ⎰   ⎰ the plts ordr
Summonce Granted 23 $\frac{9}{mo}$ i69i ——————

action Entered 23 $\frac{9}{mo}$ 169i

Joſeph Growdon agt John White in a plea of Treſpaſs ⎱ with drawn
⎱ by the plts
Summonce Granted 23 $\frac{9}{mo}$ i69i —————————⎰ order

action Entered 23 $\frac{9}{mo}$ 169i

Joſeph Growdon agt Edward Cartor in a plea of Treſpaſs } withdrawn by the plts ordr

Summonce Granted 23 $\frac{9}{mo}$ 169i ___ ___ ___

action Entered 23 $\frac{9}{mo}$ 169i

Joſeph Growdon agt: Henry Hudleſton in a plea of Treſpaſs } with drawn by the plts ordr

Summonce granted the 23 $\frac{9}{mo}$ i69i ——————

action Entered 23 $\frac{9}{mo}$ 169i

Joſeph Growdon agt Tho: Stakehouſe Ju^{nr} in a plea of Treſpaſs } withdrawn by the plt ordr

Summonce granted the 23 $\frac{9}{mo}$ i69i ——————

County Court Bucks ſs: Penſylvania

At a Court of Quarter Seſſions held by the authority of wm & mary king & Queen of England &c & in the name of wm: Penn Propryetor & govrnr of the province of Penſylvania & Counties annexed at the Court houſe for the afforeſd County the 9th day of the i0th month being the 3 yeare of the king & Queens Reigne & iith year of the Propryetors Govrmt i69i

The Juſtices Preſent

Thomas Janney   wm Biles   Henry Baker   Jon Brock
wm yardley vice Com:
Phinehas Pemberton Cl: Com:

239

The mony found upon George Philips wch was delivered to Phinehas Pemberton to be kept for the owner there

of untill the owner was known being Two pounds ten
Shillings nine pence & one bad 9ᵈ bit being what —
remamed of the whole Charges being deducted out of
the whole for takeing him up & other fees then Contracted
was delivered to Arthur Cook by the Said Phinehas
Pemberton which this Court doth allow of & difcharges
the fd Phinehas Pemberton of the faid Sum of 4 £ 9ᵈ &
one bras bitt the fees & Charges being 30ˢ & payd as
appeares in Court by fd Phinehas Pemberton
whereas there has none Com'n to Complaine agt geo:
Philips for any mifdemeanor Committed by him the
Court by Confent of the boy has put him to Henry Baker
for 6 months time to See in the meane time what
may be alledged agt him

adjourned to the 9ᵗʰ i next
                      ───
                      mo

28 ii 169i Jofeph Holdens land taken in execution to Satifye the debt
───   ──── & Cofts
mo

of Jon: Duplovie Philip
                    Richards
& Cornelius Empfon

County Court Bucks fs: Penfylvania

Juftices prfent

                at a Court of Quarter feffions held by the king
Jos: Growdon
                & Queen authority in the name of willm Penn
wm Biles
                Penn Propryetor & Govrnr of the afforefd
Nicholas waln
                Province & Counties annexed at the Court
Henry Baker
                house for the afforefd County the 9ᵗʰ day of the
wm yardley fherrif
                firft month being the 3 yeare of the king and
P. Pemberton Cl Com
                Queens Reigne over England &c & i2ᵗʰ yeare
                of the propryetors Govrmt i691

Atteftation of Samᵘ overton attefted doth Say that he lent
2 Chaines to John Clows & that he never Re but one of

the faid Chaines either from the Said Clows or any other
perfon directly or indirectly Since that time
Dunkin williams & his Son william william williams being
bound over to this Court upon Complt of Jofeph Growdon
& his baile defireing to be difcharged declareing they will
not Stand bound any longer & the fd Dunkin williams
Craveing untill another Court to prepare him felf for
tryal wch is allowed the Court Commits them into Cuftody
untill they Shall give Suffitiont fuerties for theire appearance
at next Court & to keep the peace in the meane time
John Bown & Ralph Boome Complt of george Philips
It appearing that Sd Philips by John Bown and fd Boome unto Denis
Linck who lives out of the Province its ordered that Jon: Bowen
Shall difcharge Ralph Boome & Reinburs what Denis Linck
has pd towards the price he was to give for him & that Ralph Boone
difcharge the Linck & that the fd Geo: Philips Shall ferve the fd
John Bowen two yeares from this day in Confideration of

240

the damage done to him by Sd Philips & that he the fd John Bowen
Shall pay to Henry Baker for what Cloths he hath bought for
him what they may be Judged to be reafonably worth & to this
the parties declared theire Satiffaction

adjourned to the 8th day 4th month next

2nd 3 month i692 the Land of Jofeph Holden taken in execution was
appraifed by

County Court Bucks fs: Penfylvania   i2 men at eighty pounds

At a Court of Quarter Seffions held by the authority of
wm & mary king & Queen of England &c and
in the name of Willm Penn Propryetor and
govrnr of the Said Province & Counties annexed
at the Court houfe for the Said County the 8th day
of the 4th month i692 being the 4th yeare of the
king & Queens Reigne & i2 yeare of the propry
etors Govrmt

The Justices Present

Jofeph Growdon   w^{m} Biles
Nicholas waln   Henry Baker
John Cook   Corronr
Phinehas Pemberton Cl: Com.

a deed of 27 acres of Land in fee dated the 6th <u>2</u>   i692
mo
acknowledged & delivered by Phinehas Pemberton attorney
to Jofeph English Grantor to Thomas Brock Grantee

a deed of 500 acres of land in fee dated the 8th day of the
i0th month i69i was acknowledged and delivered in open
Court by John Rowland Grantor to Henry Baker Grantee

a deed of Two hundered acres of Land in fee dated the i0th day
of the 4th month i692 was acknowledged and delivered in
open Court by John Cook attorney to Samuel Allen Grantor
to John Baldwin Grantee

a deed of five hundered acres of land in fee dated the 16th day of
the 7th month i69i was acknowledged and delivered by
Jofeph Chorley attorney to Jacob Hall grantor to william Biles
attorney to Thomas Hudson grantee

a deed in fee for Two hundered acres of land dated the 8th day of
the 4th month i692 was acknowledged and delivered by —
Samuel Allen Grantor to Samuel Allen his Son grantee

a deed in fee for 200 hundered acres of land was acknowledged and
7th 4   delivered unto John Balwin by Samuel Allen grantor for the ufe
mo
1692   of his grand daughter Elizabeth Pegg dated the 7th day of the 4th
month i692

241

Complt being made agt Ralph Boome for Some extravagant
Speeches he Submitting to the Court it was ordered that
he Shold pay to the wittnes foure Shillings & other Cofts
of Court

Willm Dunken being bound to this Court to appeare to anfwer
the Complt of Joseph Growdon defired the fd Court to —
Sufpend the tryal untill another Court for that his
wittneffes were not in readines wch was affented to by
Jofeph Growdon

a deed of one hundered and Twenty acres of land in fee
dated the 8th day of the 4th month i69i & of two rods
through the Land added in breadth to the lines mentioned

was acknowledged and delivered by Richard Ridgway
grantor to Samuel Beakes grantee

Corronors Inquest Concerning the death of Ellizabeth Chappel
taken before John Cook Corronor the i5th day of the
3 month i692 was this day returned into this Court
that her death was Cafual by falling of her horfe into the
water or nefhaminah Creek

Corronors Inqueft Concerning the death of an unknown
perfon found neare the mouth of nefhaminah Creek
the 8th day of the 3 month i692 taken before John
Cooke Corronor the i2th day of the fd 3 month laft returned
into this Court willfully murthered Suppofed to be ————
murthered about 6 weekes afore the fd veiue

upon a due examination of things it appeared that a Confidera
ble Quanty of blood on the wall and on the bed of one —
Derrick Jonfon als Clawson about the Suppofed time that
the above murthered perfon loft his life was difcovered
& the Said Derrick refufed to give any account how
the Said blood Came there whereupon this Court Commits
him the fd Derrick Clawfon als Jonfon into Safe Cuftody
of the Sherrif untill he Shall be delivered by due
Courfe of Law

Derrick Jonfon als Clawfon being examined Saith he ————
Shewed the blood on the wall to Edward Lane & his brother
Claws Jonfon & to mary Boydon he also Saith there was no
blood on the bed but what was bled by a man that Came to
Thrafh for him 3 yeares ago & that he had Spoke of the blood
fully as much as it was

Corronor John Cook Saith that when he went to veiue the
blood he perceived that it had run in Several Streames
down the boords on the wall wch Streames Continued
untill they went behind the planks that lay on the ground floore

242

Brighta the wife of Said Derrick Saith that the blood Seen on
the wall was difcovered between day and sun rifeing & that
there was a Sheete hanged on the out Side of the bed in manner
of a Curtaine & that there was no blood on the bed being
asked when the put fresh Straw in the bed Shee Said Shee
was not Certaine but Shee thought about the latter end of
march or beginning of apprill laft

Adjourned the Court to the i4th of the 7th month next

action Entered the 29th $\frac{6}{mo}$ 1692

wm Biles agt Gilbert wheeler in a plea of Cafe ⎫ with drawn
Summonce granted ditto return date 2 $\frac{7}{mo}$ 92 ⎬ by the
⎭ plts order

action Entered the 29th $\frac{6}{mo}$ 1692

Stephen Beakes agt Gilbert wheeler in a plea of Cafe ⎫ withdrawn ⎫
⎬ by the ⎬
Summonce Granted ditto returnd dated 2 $\frac{7}{mo}$ 1692 ⎭ plts order ⎭

action Entered the 30th $\frac{6}{mo}$ i692

Edward Antill Leasor to Jon whitpaine by his attorney willm
Nichols plt ⎫
agt ⎬ in an action ejectione firme
John Teſt ouſter deſt ⎭ the endorſement & declaraction Served &

Read on the premiſes the 2^d $\frac{7}{mo}$ i692

Penſylvania County Court Bucks ſs: P Sam^{ll} Beakes Sherriſe
 At a Court of Quarter Seſſions held by the king &
 Queens authority in the name of willm Penn propry
 etor & govrnr of the afforeſaid Province & Counties
 annexed at the Court houſe for the Said County the
 i4th day of the 7th month being the 4th yeare of the
 Reigne of willm & mary king & Queen of England
 &c & i2th yeare of the propryetors govrmt i692

The Justices Present

 Arthur Cook Joseph Growdon
 wm: Biles Nicholas waln Henry Baker
 John Cook Corronor
 Samuel Beakes vice: Com:
 Phinehas Pemberton Cl: Com:

Willm: Nichols Letter of attorney from Edward Antill proved

action Edward Antill Leaſor to John whitepaine appeared by his attorney willm Nichols —

It appearing that this action was not brought according to for -mer method the Court was not willing to admit the tryal but

243

but Gilbert wheeler then poſſeſt of the premiſes prayed that he might be admitted deft & that the action might be brought on not with Standing they had varyed from the former method & So did plts attorney whereupon the Court gave way & ordered the Tryal accordingly Shold be permitted to Paſs & thereupon the Iſſue was Joyned

defts –⟩ pleaded not Guilty as to Come with force & armes but as
anſwer⟩
as to the Trepaſs defends the force for that the ſd Antill Leaſor did Enter upon the premiſes as a diſſeiſor

replye And the Said Edward Antill by his Said Attorney replyes that he did not Enter as a diſſeisor & this he deſires may be enquired of by the Cuntry & So doth the deft in like manner where

venire for the Shrrif is Commanded to return a Jury ——

Jury — Richard Hough Robt Heaton James Paxson ⟩
John Rowland Edmund Lovet Joseph Kirkbride ⟩
John white Samll Dark Stephen Beakes —— ⟩ atteſted
Joſeph Milner Job Bunting Thomas Brock ——⟩

declaracon read

Anſwer read

a deed from Gilbert wheeler unto Edward Antill of the prmiſes read & owned by Gilbert wheeler

Two letters read Said to be from Gilbert wheeler to Said Edward Antill owning mony due to be payd to Said Edward Antill but the Said Letters were not owned nor disowned by ſd Wheeler the one dated Decemb the 18th 1686 the other dated august the 10th 1689

a deed for 200 acres of land in fee dated the 20th day of the —
9th month 1690 was acknowledged and delivered by ——

Hugh marſh & Anthony Morgan grantors to Joſias Hill grantee

A Mortgage dated the 20th day of the 9th month i690 for the ſd
200 acres of Land acknowledged and delivered by Joſias——
Hill grantor to Anthony Morgain grantee

adjourned the Court untill tomorrow morning at 8 a Clock

Petition of Evan Prothera Concerning George Philips servitude
read

Petitioner refferred to treat with John Bown for the Said Philips
time of Servitude & if done to Content of all parties the Juſtices will
rateſye the agreement

ordered that it be aſſented to that if the Said Evan Prothera do make
reaſonable Satiſfaction to John Bowen his peſent maſter & that
the Said John Bowen & George Philips be agreeing to the Same that'
then the Said Evan Prothera have him the remainder of the time
he is to Serve the Said John Bowen by order of Court or for what
leſs time the ſd George Philips & Evan Prothera Can agree for

244

Thomas Bowman atteſted doth Say that after Edward Antill had
attached the goods of Gilbert wheeler to his knowledg Gilbert wheeler
Stood in So much feare of Edward Antill that he durſt not Come at
York for a time except privately untill that he had given him a
mortgage of his land

Conſtables above the falls Ruben Pownall ——		over ſeeres of the highways	
from	thence to the govrnrs Edward Lucas —	for the ſd Places	
	thence below Neſhaminah Rich Wilſon	Peter worrall	
		Stephen Beakes	
		wm: Dungan	
for	Neſhaminah Tho: Stakehous ſen^r —	Henry Pawlin	
	middle lotts — Edmund Lovet ——	Abraham Cox	
	the other ſide neſhaminah Jon: Gilbert	Sam^{ll} Allen	

Jury return in Antill agt wheeler Caſe brought in theire verdict
for the plt

an appeale preſently there upon requeſted by the deſt to the next
Provincial Court in Equity wch was then by the Court allowed of &

adjudged that he the ſd deſt giveing Security to proſecute the ſd appeale & pay Coſts ought to have an appeale

By Conſent & on requeſt to the Court of both plt & deſt that the ſd appeale might be deferred to the Provincial Court in equity wch Shold happen in Spring next wch was allowed of by the Court & ordered that Security be taken accordingly

Recognizance memorand that Gilbert wheeler & Robt Cole both of the afforeſd County Came before this Court & acknowledged them Selves to be Indebted to Edward Antill of new York Gent in the Sum of fifty pounds Currant mony of this Province to be payd to the ſd Edward Antill for true payment whereof they grant for them ſelves theire heires executors & administrators that the Said Sum be levyed & recovered from their lands & tenemts goods Chattles & heriditaments of them the Said Gilbert wheeler & Robt Cole theire heires executors & administrators & aſſignes whereever they be found

Condition and this upon Condition that the Said Gilbert wheeler Shall appeare at the provincial Court wch Shall be held for this County in the Spring next & then & there Shall proſecute his appeale wch is taken in equity with effect & if he be Caſt in the Said Court Shall not only pay all the Coſts and damages he Shall be Caſt in at the ſaid Court but alſo all the Coſts & damages of this prſent Court

a deed in fee of 240 acres of land dated the 8 day of the 4th month i692 was acknowledged & delivered by Henry Baker grantr to Job Bunting grantee

A deed in fee of 60 acres of land dated the 7th day of the 4th month i692 was acknowledged & delivered by Robt Heaton attorney to Jon Auſtin grantor unto Nicholas waln grantee

245

Roads whereas the former ordr for laying out the road from the upper plantations upon Delaware to the Landing at the ferry houſe agt Burlington was not obſerved & that Some of the pſons ordered are removed its therefore now —

ordered that Henry Baker Ruben Pownal Joſeph Milner Enoch yardley Jacob Janney Richard Hough Abraham Cox & Edmund Lovet or any 6 of them do lay out the ſaid Road & give an acctt thereof to the next Court

Town Ships whereas there was encouragemt formerly (for the deviding of this County into Town Ships) from the Councill

& that thereupon there was an ordr from the Court to pti
culers for devideing the Same & that it was not pformed accord
ingly its therefore now ——

ordered that Arthur Cook Joſeph Growdon John Cook Tho:
Janney Richard Hough Henry Baker Phinehas Pemberton
Joſuah Hoops wm Biles Nicholas waln Edmund Lovet
Abraham Cox & James Boyden or the greater number of
them meete together at the meeting houſe at neſhami
-nah the 27ᵗʰ day of this Inſtant & devide this County
into Town Ships

adjourned this Court to the meeting houſe at Neſhaminah
to the 27ᵗʰ day of this Inſtant month i692

At a Court held at the meeting houſe at Neshaminah
the 27ᵗʰ 7   1692
       mo

Justices Present

Arthur Cook Joseph Growdon
Thomas Janney Nicholas waln Henry Baker
Samˡˡ Beakes vic Com:
Phinehas Pemberton Cl: Com:

whereas it was ordered formerly that this County Shold
be devided into Town ſhips according to ſd ordr the ſd perſons
by this Court ordred did this day meete & devided the
Same as ffolloweth

the upper moſt Town Ship being Calld makeſeild to begin at
the upper moſt plantations & along the river to the upper
moſt part of John woods Lands & by the Lands formerly belong
-ing to the Hawkinses & Jos: kerkbrid & wid Lucas Land &
So along as neare as may be in a ſtreight line to fetch in Joſuah Hoops
    land

the Town ſhip at the falls being Calld *
begin at Penſbery & So up the River to the upper ſide of Jon
woods Land & then to take in the Hawkins Jos kerkbride & the
wid: Lucas Land & So the land a long that Creek Continueing
the ſame untill it takes in the land of Jon Rowland &

---

* Pemberton omitted to say what it was called.

246 †

& Edward Pearſon & so to Continue till it Com with Penſbury
Land then along Penſbury to the place of begining
Then Penſbury as its layd out
below Penſbury its calld Buckingham & from Penſberry to to follow
   the river
to neſhaminah then up neſhaminah to the upper ſid of Robt
Halls plantation & to take in the Land of Jon Town Edmund
Lovet Abram Cox & So to Penſbery & by the ſame to the
place of beginning
the middle Town to be Calld middleton to begin at the upper ſide of
Robt Hall Land * * * inah to New Town & from
thence to take in * * * John Hough Jonathan
Scaiſe & John * * * Jon * * * Land & ſo to take
in the back part * * * by theire land to the
place of begining * * *
new Town & wrights * * * one Town Ship
all the Lands between Neshaminah & Poqueſſin & So to
the upper ſide of Joſeph Growdons Land in one & to be
Called Salem
South Hampton & the Lands about it with warminſter one

Whereas there was a Tax formerly ordered its now ordered
that the ſame be forth with raiſed & that warrants be Iſſued
to the Conſtables of every deviſion for the doing thereof
& that when Rec it be pd to Arthur Cook Joſeph Growdon ——
Nicholas walne and Sam: Beakes that the publique Charges of
the County may be defrayed

ordered that the Receivors be accountable to every Court of
Quarter Seſſions from time to time as they Rec any mony

adjourned to the next 3 day at the Court houſe

              Penſylvania   247

Bucks ſS: the 4ᵗʰ day of the $\frac{8^{th}}{mo}$ i692 at a Court of Quarter

Seſſions held by adjournmt

: The lower third of pages 246 and 247 have been clipped away.

Derrick Clawſon als Jonſon deſired that he might have
libertie on baile for his appearance

whereas it was Suppoſed in the beginning of this Court yᵗ:
the Said Derrick Shold have been brought to Tryall
forth with but the Judges beleiving it to be more diſcretion
—all to deffer the Tryall untill Spring to See if Some
thing further might not be diſcovered Concerning the
Suppoſed murther & * * * winter Seaſon &
the prison Inconvenienced * * * Seaſon Thought good
to ordr that baile be * * * his and his wifes appearance at the
next Court of Quarter Seſſions to be held for this County

N
_____

memorand: that Derrick Clawſon als Jonſon acknowledges him
Self Indebted to be propryetor & govrnr in 100 £ and
Claws Jonſon in 50 £ & Peter Rambo in 50 £ to be levyed
on theire goods & Chattles Lands & tenements where
ever they be found

and this upon Condition that the ſd Derrick Clawſon & his
wife Shall appeare at the next Court of Quarter Seſſions
to be held for this County in the firſt month next &
to be of good abearing in the meane time

i4ᵗʰ day of the 8ᵗʰ month i692 the land of Joſeph Holden taken in execution

adjourned to the tenth of the firſt month next   Sold to Joseph
growdon at
action Entered the 23 day 9   i692   Seventy Seven
̄̄̄̄̄̄̄̄̄̄̄mo   pounds by
Sam Beakes Sherrif

John Nichols by his Attorneys Phinehas
Pemberton & Henry Baker

agt

Bartholemew Joſeph & Amos Thatcher executors
of theire ——

father Richard Thatcher in a plea of debt— ——— - -

248

Summonce * * *

Summonce for Joſ * * * 9   i692
̄̄̄̄̄̄̄̄̄̄̄mo

action Entered the 2 * * * proven by witneſſes dat

Tho: Brock plt * * * with drawn
　　　　agt
Richard Bartho * * *　　　　　　⎫
Sum Dated 26ᵗʰ * * * Thatcher defts　⎬　in a plea of debt
　　　　　　　　　　　　　　　　　⎭

Sum: for Jon * * * & white & Anthony Banks witneſſes
dated to 29ᵗʰ $\frac{9}{mo}$ * * * drawn

action Entered 23 $\frac{9}{mo}$ * * *

wm: Biles plt _ _ _ _ * * *　　dated 28ᵗʰ $\frac{9}{mo}$ 1692
　　　　agt
Ralph Boome deft　　　　　witnesses ditto 29ᵗʰ

action Entered 26ᵗʰ $\frac{9}{mo}$ * * *

Joſeph Chorley plt ⎫ * * *
　　　　agt　　　　⎬ * * * Sum dated 29 $\frac{9}{mo}$ 1692
Edward Lucas deft ⎭

Arreſt granted agt Henry Greenland dated 4ᵗʰ $\frac{9}{mo}$ i692 at

the ſuite of Richard Thather plea of Caſe

returnd executed the 4ᵗʰ day 9 month i692 & baile taken

p Sa: Beakes vic: Com:

　　　　　　　　　Penſylvania
County Court Bucks ſs:

　　　At a Court of Quarter Seſſions held by the king and
　　　Queens authority in the name of Willm Penn ——
　　　Propryetor & Govrnr of the afforeſaid Province and
　　　Counties annexed at the Court houſe for the Said County
　　　The i4ᵗʰ day of the $\frac{i0}{mo}$ 1692

　　　　　　The Justices Present
　　　　　Wm: Biles Nicholas Waln Henry Baker
　　　　　Samˡˡ Beakes Sherrif
　　　　Phinehas Pemberton Cl: Com:

Adjourned to the houfe of Jofeph Chorley

a deed in fee for 340 acres of Land dated the 2nd day of the
9th month i692 acknowledged & delivered by wm Biles
attorney to Ellizabeth Bennet grantor to Nicholas waln grantee

[249] *

action Entered Jos: * * * Lucas both appeared

declaracon read
Anfwer not guilty & for * * * felf on the Cuntry
& So doth the plt wher * * * 3r &c:
Caufe to come i2 honeft * * *

Jury John Rowland * * * Samll Dark Peter Worral
   James moone John Pan * * * wm: Paxson } all
   Andrew Ellot Jofeph Cr * * * wm: Dungan } attested

wittnefes to the fd * * *
   Robt Cole = * * * John Clark * * * Tho: peirce wm: Taylor
   James yates Tho: Cole * * * Poole all attefted
   adjourned the Court * * *

verdict the Jury retu * * * by deft with Cofts

A deed in fee of * * * dated the i2th day of the
   7th month i692 was acknowledged & delivered by Rich
   Lundy grantor to ff * * * grantee

An appeale requefted by Jofeph * * * Chorley But the pretended
damages not being 10 £ Sterling the Jury declaring they
had veiued the ox & that he was so little harmed by the
Shot that the Said Chorley needed not to have loft 2 days
work for any harm the ox had Received by the Same
as alfo the deft: Craved the Benefit of the law that
where the debt or damage is pretended to be above —
five pounds & it prove undr that in Such Cafe the plt
Shall Loofe his action wherefore the Court Saw no Caufe
to grant him an appeale

Judgmt Given & it is adjudged the Jofeph Chorley pay Cofts
& that execution Iffue accordingly

---

* Page 249 is numbered at the bottom of the page.

Richard Thatcher
         agt   } both Calld but neither appeared
Henry Greenland

adjourned the Court to the 8th day of the firſt month next

Penſylvania County Court Bucks ſs:

              At a Court of Quarter Seſſions held by the authority
              of wh & mary king and Queen of England &c:
              & in the name of wm Penn Propryetor and
              & Govrnr of the ſd Province & Countyes ——
249   annexed at the houſe of Samll Beakes the
              8th day of the i month i692 being the 4th yeare
$$\frac{}{3}$$
              of the king & Queens Reigne & i3 yeare
              of the Propryetors Govrmt ———

[250]*

* * *

* * * berton Cl: Com:

adjourned the C * * *

Wm: Duncan being * * * appeared
* * * ance none appearing
agt him the Court * * * paying his fees

Robt Benſon being bound * * * Recognizance appeared
none appeareing * * * the Court discharges him paying
fees

Stephen Newell being summonced to Court for Selling a
Servant out of the province alleadged that he had not
Sold him but lent him to Service for Some time & that
he wold bring him back in 3 months

a deed of 5½ acres of land in fee dated the 8th day of march
i692 acknowledged & delivered by Thomas Green and —
Rachel his wife grantors to Thomas Brock Grantee

a deed of 5½ acres of land in fee dated the 8th day of march
i692 acknowledgcd and Delivered by Thomas Green and
Rachel his wife Grantors to Anthony Burton Grantee

---

*Page 250 is numbered at the bottom of the page.

Richard Thatcher being Committed into Cuſtody on Suſpition
of ffelony being Calld requeſted his Tryal might be defferred
untill further time & that in the meane time he might be
let to baile wᶜʰ is left to the diſcretion of the Juſtice wᶜʰ
Thatcher Shall applye him Self to with his baile ____

Job: Houle being bound by Recognizance to this Court further Complt
Comeing agt him by Tho: Brock he is Continued untill the next
Court ____

Job Houle acknowledges him Self Indebted to the propryetor &
govrnr in Ten pounds to be Levyed on his lands & tenemts
goods & Chattles & this upon Condition that he appeare at the
next Court & Anſwer the Complt of Tho: Brock

adjourned to the i0ᵗʰ Inſtant at i0 a Clock in the morning

250

[251]*

* * *

* * * that wm: * * *
ke Care ab * * *

adjourned the * * *

At * * * nment at the Court
houſe * * * unty the i4ᵗʰ day 2
                              ——
                              mo

i693 * * *

* * * Present
* * * on Wm Biles
* * * Henry Baker
Sam * * * kes Sherrif
Phin * * * Pemberton Cl: Com:

action John Addington plt ⎫
       agt   ⎬ in a plea of Caſe withdrawn by
John Hewett def ____ ⎭ the plts ordr

A deed in fee for 250 acres of land Dated this i4ᵗʰ day of
the 2ⁿᵈ month i693 acknowledged & delivered by Israel

_____

*Page is numbered at the bottom of the page.

Taylor Grantor to James yates Grantee

Tho Lacy being bound by Recognizance to appeare here
being Charged with geting mary Roles with Child appeared
accordingly

mary Roles being examined about the Same declared that
Thomas Lacy had got her with Child & Said he lay with her
Several times one time was the firſt day afore Iſaac page
dyed wᶜʰ is Said to be about the middle of the 9ᵗʰ month
laſt & that he lay with her but once afterwards & that was
about i3 or i4 weekes from this time

ordered that the ſd Thomas Lacy give bond to anſwer the ſd Complt
at the next Court

N

memorand Thomas Lacy acknowledges him Self Indetted to the
Propryetor in 10 £ & Iſrael Taylor in 5 £ to be levyed theire
lands & Tenements goods & Chattles & this upon Condition for the
appearance of the ſd Tho: Lacy at the next Court to anſwer
the aforeſd Complt of mary Rowles

Hugh marſh declared that Iſrael Taylor had arreſted him —
and that he deſired a Special Court wᶜʰ was granted him
he being about to depart out of the province

251

[252]*

[The upper 2/5 of the page is missing]

agt him the Court * * * paying his fees

adjourned for one * * *

Bucks ſs: Penſy * * *

          The Jurors * * * pryetor & Govrnr by the king and
Queens authority * * * Richard Thatcher for that he Some
time before 18ᵗʰ day * * * of the 12ᵗʰ mo: laſt paſt did Steale and
     fraudulenᵗ
-ly take away one * * * mare with a blaze in her face & a Snip
on her noſe & one of Colt of a black Colour belonging to the ſd mare
being the proper goods of ffrancis white being worth foure pounds

*Page 252 is numbered at bottom of the page.

Conterary to the king and Queens Peace & the Statute law in that
Cafe made & provided

ffrancis white Profecutor
Robt Benfon   Jon Clark
Jon Crofdel   Jon: Penquoit
Jofeph Chorley ―― ――
} witneffes attefted

a True bill

grand Jury John Swift Thos Hardin Jofuah Hoops geo: Brown
Jos: Milner Job Bunting Abraham Cox Sam^ll Dark
Henry Paxfon Jonathan Scaife Jofeph kirkbride
ffrancis Roffill James Paxfon wm: Beakes Jon: Palmer
} attefted

Richard Thatcher being Calld appeared according to recognizance
ordered that he be taken into the Sherrifs Cuftody untill ――
further ordr

adjourned for one houre   252

[Upper 1/3 page missing]

[253]*

* * * the fd Thatcher * * * e mare that was in
* * * fdels pafture
Robt Cole attefted doth * * * Saw Richard Thatcher
when he brought a black * * * the River with a mare
Colt of blackifh dun * * * ge Starr in her face
and a Snip on her nofe & * * * further eare & fome
notches in the other but what he * * * Certaine & he afked
Said Thatcher where he had the Said mare and he Said he bought
her of an eaft Jerfey man on the road between Daniel
Brinfons & Doctor greenlands & that Jon Richardfon and
John Houghton were prefent when he bought her & the
Said Thatcher Confeffes it was the Same mare that he
sold to John Clark

John Crofdel attefted doth say Richard Thatcher Came to fee
the mare in his brothers pafture & that Said Thatcher Confeft
it was the mare he Sold to John Clark & that he knowns
that ffrancis white or his mother bought the Said mare of Thomas ―
Stakehoufe Junr

---

*Page 253 is numbered at the bottom of the page.

Jon Penquoit atteſted Saith the Same

Derrick Clawſon appearing to this Court according to recog
nizance the Court diſcharges him & his Suerties of the ſd
recognizance

John Gilbert being accuſed with begating a baſtard Child on a negro
girl of the widow fforreſt wᶜʰ ſd Gilbert deneyed & it appearing
by the examination of the ſd girl that Shee is disagreeing in
her relation both as to the time & Cercum ſtances
its therefore ordered that She be whipt & have i5 Laſhes on
her bare back   253

[All the foregoing pages are in the hand of Phineas Pemberton. Beginning with 254
the hand changes to that of Robert Cole.]

                                    Pennsilvania   254
Bucks vid:

            At a Courte of Quarter ſeſſions held by yᵉ king &
            Quens Authority at the Courte houſe of the sd
            County the 14 day of June 1693 beinge ye ffiſte
            yeare of thayer Maggestis Reigne

        The Justices psent   Gilbard Wheeler
                              Jos: Woode
                              John Brocke
                                  Robt Cole Clarke

Ordered That Clouſe Johnston & Mary Boydon beforth
            wᵗʰ sent ffor to give in Bonnds ffor thayer
            apearance at yᵉ Next Coarte to Teſtifie all they
            now Conseuring ye Blood that was seene upon
            Derick Johnstons Wall in May 92
    Tho: Leacy Caled to Answar yᵉ Complaynt of Mary Roales
            Leacy not apeared
    Mary Roales Caled to procute yᵉ Complaynt against
            Tho: Leacy Not apeared
                            Ordered
            That yᵉ Complaynt stand upon Record till next
            Coarte

Ordered That Wm Tayler Putt up Rayles about yᵉ Courte
            houſe stayers & Rayles about yᵉ Table ffor wᶜʰ he
            is to have 16/ to be pd by sd Wheeler

Ordered a New Table to be made by Wm Taylor for
   wch he is to have 15/ to be pd by Robt Cole

The. Courte rajornes tell y^e 13 of Sep^t 93

Bucks vid: 255   Pennsilvania

Att a Courte of Quarter Sesions held by the kinge &
Quens Authority at the Courte houfe of y^e County aforesd
the 13 day of Sep^t 1693 Being y^e iiiii of thayer maigestys
Reaigne ___

The Justises Present	Gilbart Wheeler
John Brocke	Jo: Wood
John Swifte	Henry Poyntar
Tho: Brock Shreefe	Robt Cole Clark

Grand
Jury The Grand Jury attested Wm Doyles fforeman
      James Paxton Henry Paxton Wm Paxton Wm Hofte
      John Crosdall John Pinck White Jobe Buntinge
      Sa: Coatts   Wm Darke   Shadraich Woolly   Jos: Millenor
      John Parseley Henry Hudelston ___

Tho: Brocke } Complaynent
Jos: Chorly } Chorly Apearing according to his racognefens
                and Nothing Ap'ing against him is Clered

Jo: Wood   } Complaynent
Mary Chorly } Jos: Wood makes Complaynt of seavaroll abuses
                done him by Mary Chorley y^e Courte suspends thayr

Judgmen^t   at this tim & rajourns for 2 owers
            The Courte seetts & ye Grand Jury Caled noa present
            ments Courte rajourns tell next moring

   Sep^t 14   The Courte seets & Chofes Petar White Constable
            ffor Middletown Antho: Burton for Buckinham
            An: Heath for mackefeld Nick: Randalph for Southhampton
            John Clarke ffor Crockhorne ___
overseeyers Tho: Williams Buckingham & ffrances Rosale
highways Gorge Brown for Crockhorne Wm Paxton for —

Midd Sam: Aleine for Bensalame Jo: Webstar
for Southhampton John Clowefe for Mackfeld

deed   Abraham Beake grantor acknowledges a deede of Land
bearing date y^e i3 of Sep^t 1693 of 300 ackars of Land
* * *
* * *

Bucks vid: 256   Pennsivania

Att a Courte of Common Peafe he^{l}d by ye kinge & Queens
Authority at ye Courte Houfe of ye sd County Sep^t ye i4 day
1693 and ye 1111i yeare of theyer Maytis Reaigne

The Justises Present Gilbart Wheeler   John Brocke

Jos: Wood   John Swife   Henry Poyntor

Jos: Wood   } plt in an actyon of Debt
Henry Hudellston } Deft ye actyon Caled thay boath apered

Henry Hudelston in open Court acknowledgs Judgmen^t
ffor his Bonnd

Lewifs Lavally } plt
John Pownd } Dff boath apered ye Declarcyon read

The Daf^t saith hee is not Guilty in manner & fforme
& soa puts himselfe upon ye Country   Jo: White atorney
    for plt
The plt in Licke manor   Pettar morow saith y^t John pownd
                      did ack: y^t hee had ye bill of Lews
                      Lavally &
                      Left it weet in his window Rodger
                      Murfey swore ye same

Iffue } The Jury atested Henry Marjoron John White
Joyned } Edward Carter Tho. Green An: Burton James Moon se^r
        Tho: Shackhars Henry Hudelston Bartho: Thathar
        Wm Darke Jo: Millner Ruben Pownar

Wm Biles } plt upon two acktyons they Boath Comm to Courte
Jo: Pidcock } Dff and desaireth y^t ye actyons may Continew upon
    racord tell next Courte of Comon pleafe

Jo: Pidcock } plt
Wm Biles } Dff ye actyon Caled they boath Com in to Courte &
    desiareth y^t ye actyon may Continew upon racord
    tell ye next Courte of Comon pleafs

The Jury raturned & ffind for yᵉ Dtt John Pound
John White Atorney for yᵉ plt moved ffor an apell
    to yᵉ present Courte
wᶜʰ was Granted & yᵉ plt & Deff in yᵉ meane time agreefe
Wm Beaks Coms into Courte & John Murfyn his Sarvaint
& Wm Beaks doas acknowledg yᵗ provided his man Murfen
dufe behave himselfe dutyfully he will give him one yeare
of his sarvice & Murfeyn doas declear he has 4 years
from yᵉ 15 day of Mo: Next but on is to be alowed

Mary Beaks ⎱ Coms in to Courte & acknowledges a deed in ffee of
Steven Beaks ⎰ 300 Akars of Land to Wm Beaks bearing date yᵉ 9 day

Sam: Beaks ⎱ of yᵉ 11 moᵗʰ yᵉ 4 yeare of kinge James yᵉ 2ᵈ Reaigne
Abra: Beaks ⎰ The Court rajorns tell yᵉ 2ᵈ day of yᵉ 7ᵗʰ month

257

Bucks ſs: At a Court of Quarter Seſsions held by yᵉ kinge &
        Quens authority at yᵉ Courte houfe neare yᵉ ffalls
        the seconde Wednsday of yᵉ monnth of Decʳ 1693
        and yᵉ ffifte yeare of thayer Majestis reigne

    The Justices Present   Gilbart Wheeler

        John Brocke   Jos: Woode   John Swifte
Tho Brocke   Tho: Lacy stood bound by racognefence to answar ye
        Com of M Roles Cald Not
Shrefe   apeared Isarale Taylor security
        ffor Lacy Cald Not apered for wᶜʰ they forfeett thayer
Robt Cole   Racognisence
  Clarke

        The Grand Jury Caled & atested Johnathan Scafe
        Jos Millar John Pamar John White Tho: Cearll
        Tho: Tannclefte John Hugh ffrances Rofell
        Wm Cluse Wm Darke James Paxton Henry Paxton
        Jobe Bownton John Pursly Tho: Thakorf

        Adiorned the Court tell 8 acloke in yᵉ moring

    1 The Grande Jury raturns caled & all
        answar they doa prasent grate Nafsity of a Carte
        Roade to be laid out from Newtowne to yᵉ ferry
        houfe Tho: Stackhoufe Senior Sam: Coate Steven
        Willson Jobe Bunting Wm Buckman Wm Smith

John Cowgell being men ordred by this Courte to
Leay out ye roade

2 The Grand Jury have in discorsed ye Leate trasurar
doa finde savarall Just debts due to ye County & y^t thare
are savarall persons in arare of ye late tax thay doa
prasent ye Nefsity of Collecting the same & alsoa
raqueste ye Court y^t warrants be Isued forth for ye
parfecting of it

3 According to ye Leat acte of Genarall afsembly ffor ye
defraying of Nefsary Charges as ye provincall Judges
& allsoa ffor ye destroying of woolfes wee thare fore do
present ye Nefsity of Raifen the some of Thirty pounds
to defray ye Same & wee raquefit this Courte that two
Safe and honest men be chofen to putt ye s^d Some
* * *

258 And that the s^d two men be accountable to this Court
and the Country viz: ye grandiury Soa often as nede shall
requiar

4 wee do^e alfoa p^rsent ye nefsesity of a road to be laide
out ffrom Henry Bakers to John Pidcoks
Ordared y^t men be apoynted to Leay out a roade from
the uper side of Jos: Woods Lande to Henry Bakers —
& Soa to ye Linkers poynte men apoynted by ye Courte
John Pidcoke Henry Maryorom John Brocke Jacobe
Jeney Wm Clufe Tho: Tanyclefte
The Grand Jury doa prefent Gilbart Wheeler for
takeing extortion for ferrige

The Courte mets and apoynts a privat seisons to Consider
of ye Bill delivered by ye Grande Jury to be
at Gilbarte Wheelers ye ffirste day of January
Next

A deed in ffee of 50 Akars of Lands dated ye 10 day
of ye 10 Month 1689 was acknowledged & delivered in
open Coarte by John Gibbs Grantor to Rich: Willson
Grantee

Att a Coarte of Common pleafes held by ye kinge &
Quens athourity at ye Courte houfe of ye s^d County
Buks fs ye 13 day Decr 1693

Justis Present　　Gilbart Wheelar
Jos: Woode　John Brocke　John Swifte
Robt Cole　Clarke

Mary Beaks plt ⎱ The action caled thay Both apeare y^e —
Jos: Charlly Defts ⎰ daclaratyon rad ye Bonde read ye Covenan^t
& Mary His wife　in ye daclaratyon ye patten of ye Land mentyoned
in ye Covenante and it was proved
in Courte y^t ye D^{tt} hade Noa Aísetts of Akarm
ans In his hands save ye Tracte Lande
mentyoned in ye Morgadg

Thare ffor ye Dft acknowledge Judgment in open
Coarte for 48 £ deb^t & fourten pounds in trest wth
Cost of sute to be Leavied on ye Lande of Akarman
According to Lawe

259

Buks ís　At a privat sesions held at Gilbart Wheelars Jenuary
the 1 day　4　by ye Justis of the County whear it is
⎯⎯
93

ordared that the Clarke gives publique Notife to
the in habitents of this County by Nayleing up 4
Bills at ye most publique pleafses of ye County to
deasiar all parfons y^t are Consarned in ye County
to apear ye 2^d wednsday of March next at ye
Courte houfe of ye s^d County to put a finell end and
to deschardg the arrears layd to ye Charge of ye
County by ye fformar Councell and afsembly
That thare be awarant Isued out for ye Collecting
the arears of ye ould tax of this side & ye ffarthar
side Neashamony & y^t thare be anew tax of 7^d p
pounde upon ye reall & parsonall eastate & 6/ by y^e
Powlle of all Not Capable of beinge othar ways
taxed from 16 years to 60 years to be Collected by
Tho: Brocke High Shrefe ye County & Broug^t
in to ye Next County Courte
And that Notis be given to y^e in Habitents of
the siteing of y^e orphants Coarte
John Caws Ralfe Bons & wife y^e Hayers of Rich
Thathar Nick: Walen James Delworth —
And: Hearth
Att a Courte of Quorter Sisins hild by y^e

Kinge & Quens athourity at y^e Courte
Courte houſs of the County aforsᵈ 14th of 1 mo $\frac{1693}{4}$

The Justis present Gilbert Wheeler
Jos: Woode   John Brocke   John Swife
Henry Poyter Tho: Brocke Shreefe
Robᵗ Cole Cla

Stephen Nowell Being being bounde by
racognesence to appear to y^e Complaynt of
ralfe Cowgell upon his Complaynt yᵗ hee did
suspecte y^e sᵈ Nowell to have stolene a mare
Cowlte of his ye sd Nowell apears & ye Grande
Jury being Impeneled & atested did not find
ye bill where upon Nowell was Clered payin
fees

(260)

The Names of the Grande Jury as they was
Atested Was Jos: Whoops fforman
Johna: Scafe   Wm Beaks   Tho Curll
Jon- Hugh   And: Eliott Tho Rodgers
Jon Rowland   ffrances Rosalle
Wm Dungan   Wm Eliott   Wm Darke
Ruben Pownor   Enocke yardly
John Gilbart   John Baldwn
Wm Clowfe   John Palmar

Danill Gardnar Being bound by racognisence
by Gilbert Wheeler Justis to answar ffor his
Contempt against John Clarke when hee Came
to sarve awarant one hime, upon Gardners
Submision y^e Courte Clears him payin his
ffees   The Courte Calls & ratiurns tell y^e 2ᵈ
Weednsday of Mon^th of June 94

Att acurte of Com pleafs held at ye Courte
houfs y^e 14 day 1th Month $\frac{1694}{3}$ by y^e Kinge &

Quens authority The Justis Present
Gilbart Wheeler   Jos: Woode   Jo: Brocke
Jo: Swifte   Henry Poynter   Tho: Brocke
Shreefe   Robt Cole Clark

The Coarte caled & raiurned to yᵉ 2ᵈ Weednsdy
of the Monᵗ of June 1694
June yᵉ

Noa Courte this month —— ————
Sepᵗ the   Noa Courte by rason of yᵉ Shrefe
Leay very secke at Philidalph
Decʳ ye   Noa Courte by rason of Exterordn
ary Beade Weathar *

Bucks ſs:

261†   At a Court of Quarter ſſeſſions held by the kings
authority in the name of William penn abſolute
proprietary & Governor: of the province of penſyl
vania and Counties annexed the i2ᵗʰ day of the
fourth month 1695 being the 7 yeare of the
kings Reign &   of the proprietarys govermt
over the ſd province &c.

The Juſtices preſent
Gilbert wheeler Joſeph Wood
John Brock   John Swift
John Cook Corroner
Tho: Brock Sherrif

a deed in fee for 300 acres of land dated the 20 __1__ 1694 was
acknowledged and   mo
delivered by Saml Beakes attorney to William Beaks
& his wife Ellizabeth Beaks grantors to John ſnowden
grantee

a deed of Joynture dated the i8ᵗʰ __i2__ 1689 made by Wm —
mo
Beakes of the above mentioned three hundered acres
of land to John worrilow & walter worrilow in truſt

---

*This is the last entry in the hand of Robert Cole.

† Beginning with this entry Phineas Pemberton resumed his county clerkship and so
continued until the 14ᵗʰ day of the first month 1699 , the last entry in his hand.
1700

for Elizabeth worrilow theire fifter & now wife of the fd
wm: Beakes was furrendered in open
Court by Saml Beakes
attorney to John worrilow aforefd furviveing truftee
unto the above named John fnowden by order of fd
wm Beakes & Ellizabeth

Mary fcaife being examined about her haveing of a baftard
born on her body acknowledged the fame & faid
James Heaton was the father of it

ffined The Court adjudged to pay a fine of three pounds for
Commiting fornication

payment of the fame was promifed by Jonathan fcaife
father of the fd Mary

adjourned to the 7 mo next
at ufual day

262

Grand Jurys prfentmts brought in

we of the Grand Jury do prfent the kings roade through the
Timber Swamp neare Saml Burges & fo along the road to
middle Towne

and James Heaton for haveing a baftard Child by Mary
the daughter of Jonathan Scaife —

And the neceffity of haveing a ftandard in this County for
wett and dry meafures and alfo for weights

and Tho Brock for not bringing in his acc^{tts} to this Court
Concerning the late tax for which he was made Collector

And the roade between Henry Bakers and the ffalls
a return made of the Roade from the upper planation to the — —
ferry againft Burlington
ffirft from Richard Houghs Plantation by a line of marked
trees
to the falls meeting houfe and from thence to the Cold
Spring —
by a line of marked trees & fo down the old Road to the fferry

By Richard Hough   Ruben Pownal   Jofeph Milner
Enoch yardley Henry Baker formerly appointed to
lay out the fame

Action   ffrancis Jones plt ⎫
           agt   ⎬ plt appeares
    Robt Cole deft ⎭ deft being Calld appeared not

Joſeph Wood Soninlaw to the ſd Defte haveing formerly had an
attachment upon the pipe ſtaves mentioned in the plt Declarcon
being upon the land of the ſaid Jos Wood he the Said wood here
in Court declares that the action Grounded upon the ſd attachment
is with drawn and that he diſclaimes any property in the ſd pipe
Staves and that the said plt may take them away when
he pleaſes according to the ſd Deft Robt Coles deſire Certefyed to
this Court by the afforeſd wood and Gilbert wheeler

Judgmt   Therefore it is Conſidered that the ſd plt Shall recover agt the
      ſd deft the ſd pipe staves or value thereof with Coſts of ſuite

action   wm Rakeſtraw plt ⎫ both appeared
           agt   ⎬
    Tho Terry deft ⎭ the deft made anſwer he had not ſeen
                    or heard that any Complt was Entered
                    agt
                    him whereupon the Court Granted the
                    deft
                    a non ſuite

action   wm Rakeſtraw plt ⎫ both appeared but the plt withdraw his
           agt   ⎬
    Robt Cole deft — ⎭ action

Court adjourned untill the 4ᵗʰ day 9 month next

263   Bucks ſs: Att a Court of Quarter ſeſſions
              held by the kings authority in the name Willm
              Penn Proprietary & Governor of the Province of
              Penſylvania at the Court houſe for the ſaid County
              the iiᵗʰ day of the i0ᵗʰ month being the   yeare
              of the kings reigne   of the Proprietarys —
              govrmt i695

The Justices preſent

                  Willm Biles   Richard Hough ⎫
                  John Swift — — — — — — —⎬

                  Samll Beaks Sherriff
                  phinehas pemberton Clerk Coun:

The Court adjourns into the house of Joſeph Chorley

a deed of Two hundered thirty Six acres of land in fee dated the 12 day of the 6th month i694 acknowledged and delivered by Joſeph Chorley attorney to Charles Biles Grantor to Abell Janney Grantee

a deed of foure hundered and eighty acres of land in fee dated the 20th day i2 mo: 1693 acknowledged and delivered by — Abel Janney Atorney to John Hornor to Grantor Phinehas Pemberton Grantee

a Certificate of Joan the wife of James Moones being alive Signed in Court Shee being then Preſent

The preſentment agt James Heaton Continued untill next Court and ordered that a warrant Iſſue that he be apprehended to give bond for his appearance at the next Court ——

Accounts of Tho: Brock late Sherrife this day preſented but not being perfected and no grand Jury preſent they are returned and ordered that they be brought to the next Court and That a warrant Iſſue from Some of the Juſtices to Impower the said Tho Brock to levye What is in arreare of the County Taxes

ordered that the Clerk write to Joſeph wood to bring or ſend the County records that he hath in his hands

Sent the Said order by Andrew Heath Conſtable who being returned brought three paperbooks 2 of them Covered with Sky-Coloured paper marked No: 1: 2: and another paper book of Robt Coles writeing in ffo: haveing thereon write only ſeven ſides all the reſt blank and Said that the ſaid Joſeph wood Said that was all that was in his Cuſtody

The Court adjourns for one houre

(264)

Reported to this Court by John Swift that the land of Philip Conway was formerly taken in Execution to Satiſſye the Several Judgments of Court and that the Same has not been ſold and diſpoſed of So as to aſſure thoſe now poſſeſt of it a ſuitable — title Its therefore ordered that Execution be againe Iſſued

Comley—Robt Heaton with his Son in law Henry Comley appeared in Court this day and declared the ſaid Comley to be of age &

defired to have in thofe bonds given to Court on his behalf —

ordered thereupon that the Clark make fearch after the bonds &
records yet remameing in the late Clerk Robt Coles hands
& when the bonds relateing to Said Comley are had and —
obtained that he deliver them to Robt Heaton to be ——
difpofed of to his ufe as foone as may be —

Reported to this Court by Tho Brock that ffrancis Roffill left to the
poore of this County Certaine Sums of mony to be payd
by his Executor Samll Carpenter & that the faid Samll
Carpenter is willing to pay it to Such from time to time as this
Court Shall recommend to be neceffitous & therefore its —

ordered that the Clerk write to Said Samll Carpenter ——
acquaint him that Edward Doyal & James Sutton are neceffi-
-tous & that if he pleafe to lett them have fifty Shillings —
a piece that they have need of it

a deed in fee of 248 acres of land dated the i0ᵗʰ day $\frac{i0}{mo}$ 1695

acknowledged and delivered by Job Bunting Grantor to
Stephen Twineing Grantee

adjourned untill the iiᵗʰ $\frac{1}{mo}$ next

Bucks fs:

265   At a Court of Quarter Seffions held by
the kings authority in the name of Willm
Penn absolute proprietarie and governr —
of this province and Territorys thereunto
belonging at the Court houfe of the faid
County the i1ᵗʰ day of the i mo: $\frac{i695}{6}$

The Juftices present

Jofeph Growdon Willm Biles
Henry Baker Richard Hough
Samll Beakes Sherrife
Phinehas Pemberton Cl: Com:

—a deed in fee from Thomas William Grantor of Two hundered —
acres of land in fee dated the 2 day 9ᵗʰ month —

i695 was by him acknowledged and delivered
unto Abraham Cox Grantee

a releaſe from the Governor of a fine Impoſed by
the Court on mary the daughter of —
Jonathan Scaiſe produced in Court by her father
as ffolloweth

Penſylvania

Locus　whereas the daughter of Jonathan Scape of Bucks
ſigil　County Stands ffind upon Record of the Said County in
the Sum of three pounds I do forgive Releaſe and —
acquit her of the Said fine witneſs my hand & seale
this 26 day of october i695

Wm Markham Govr
undr wm Penn abſolute
Recorded by order of Court　Proprietor

prſentmt agt: James Heaton for haveing a bastard Child

Bucks ſs: 9ᵗʰ 　8　 i695
mo

The Jurrors for the proprietary and
govrnr by the kings authority do prſent James
Heaton for haveing a baſtard Child by mary —
daughter of Jonathan Scaiſe Conterary to the kings
peace and the Statute law in that Caſe made and
provided &c.

pleaded　not Guilty & for tryal put him ſelf upon the Cuntry whereupon

venire　the Sherrife was Commanded to return a Jury wᶜʰ according
=ly he did

Jury　Peter Warrall　Henry Marjorum　John Croſdell ⎫
James moon　John Smith　Edmond Lovet　　　⎬ atteſted
Ruben Pownal　wm Dark　John Palmer　　　　⎪
Edward Pearſon　ffrancis Tunneclifᵗ　Ed: Lucas ⎭

prſentmt proved by mary Scaiſe　Thomas Stakehouſe Junr —
and Jonathan Scaiſe

Court adjourned for an houre & a half

action Arthur Cooke plt ⎫
          agt   ⎬ in a plea that he render to ſd plt
    ffrancis Collins deft ⎭ Seventy pounds damage for want
                             of pforming Sundry Covenants about
                             building both plt & deft appeared
declaracon Read

Anſwer   the deft anſwered the Complt was true & deſired Judgmt —
          might be entered accordingly

Judgmt — Therefore it is Conſidered that the Said plt recover agt
          the ſd deft the Said Sum of Seventy pounds with Coſt
          of Suite

— a deed of Two hundered acres of land in fee dated the
          Tenth day of the firſt month i695   acknowledged and
          delivered by Nicholas Waln grantor to John ſtakhouſe
          grantee

     verdict Jury returned give in verdict we do find James =
          Heaton guilty of begeting a Child of mary Scaife

     a deed-of-one hundered acres of Land in fee dated the fourth
          day of the eleventh month i695 acknowledged and
                                          ——
                                           6
          delivered by prudence Betridge grantor to George
          willard Grantee

     a deed of Elleven acres of land in fee dated the Twentieth
          day of the Twelfth month i695 acknowledged .
                                        ——
                                         6
          and delivered by Phinehas Pemberton
          Attorney to Joſeph Engliſh Grantor to Thomas —
          Brock & Anthony Burton Grantees

     a deed of Elleven acres of land in fee dated the Twentieth
          day of the Twelfth month i695 acknowledged and —
                                         ——
                                          6
          delivered by Phinehas Pemberton attorney to Joſeph
          Engliſh Grantor to Peter white Grantee
          William Rakestraw plt: ⎫
action {   agt: ⎬ in an action of detenuce ⎫
          Gilbert Wheeler deft. ⎭ both appeared ——   ⎭

     a deed of   of land in fee dated the   day

of the month i69   acknowledged and delivered
by John Rowland Grantor to Arthur Cook Grantee

decleracon read Complaineing agt Gilbert G wheeler for detaineing
of 33 buſhells of barley & 6i bushells of oates of the plts

Anſwer   he detaines it not & of this put him ſelf upon the Cuntry & ſo
venire — doth the plt whereupon the Sherrife is Commanded to return a
Jury wch he accordingly did

267

Jury—Henry Marjorum John Crosdell James Moone —— ——
John Smith Edmund Lovet willm Dark ———— ——
Joſeph Kirkbride Edward pearſon ffrancis Tunneclift
Edward Lucas Enoch yardley John ſiddall atteſted

declaracon: proved by the Evidence of Phinehas Pemberton
Richard Hough Peter Worrall Thomas Janney Jnr
Ruben Pownal John Palmer ————
Thomas Brock all atteſted

a deed–of Two hundered acres of land in fee dated the
firſt day of february i695 acknowledged & delivered
by Joſeph wood attorney to Thomas ffaireman
grantor to John Swift Grantee ————

a deed of Sixty acres of land in fee dated the 29th day of
May i695 acknowledged and delivered by Joſeph
Wood attorney to Iſrael Taylor Grantor to John ——
Swift Grantee

a deed– of one hundered Seventy three acres of land in fee
dated the i4th day of the 2 month i693 acknowledged
and delivered in open Court by willm Biles Grantor —
to Samuel Beakes Grantee

a deed– of one hundered acres of land in fee dated the Tenth
day of the Sixth month i695 acknowledged & delivered
by willm Croſdel & John Croſdell Grantors to Jonathan
Scaiſe Grantee

a deed of one hundered and Seventy acres of land in fee dated
the i2th day of the Tenth month i694 acknowledged
and delivered by william Croſdell & John Croſdell ——
Grantors to Robt Heaton Junr Grantee

a deed– of Two hundered acres of land In fee dated the 20th

day of the 9th month i693 acknowledged and ——

delivered by John Cook attorney to John Green Thomas Green & katherine

Green Grantors to Thomas Brock attorney to Joſeph Large grantee

a deed of Sale & mortgage for Two hundered acres of land in fee dated the 2nd day of the 9th month i694 ——— acknowledged & delivered by Phinehas Pemberton attorney to Joſeph Large grantor to John Cook ——— attorney to Samuel Carpenter grantee

a deed of one hundered and Twelve acres of land in fee dated the firſt day of the firſt month $\frac{i694}{5}$ acknowledged and

delivered by Phinehas Pemberton attorney to Randel Blackſhaw Grantor to Ralph Cowgill Grantee

a deed of fifty acres of land in fee dated the Tenth day of the firſt month $\frac{1695}{6}$ acknowledged and delivered by

Clement Dungan grantor to Joſeph Large Greantee

Judgment given upon the verdict brought in againſt James Heaton for haveing a child by Mary Scaiſe & it is

fine adjudged that he pay a fine of three pounds & ffees

Court adjourns to the houſe of Joſeph Chorley

268

Complt being made by the overſeer of the high way of Make feild that peter Worral neglected to bring his teame to the high ways when he had notice ſo to do by the ſd officer & that the makeing a bridg was there

order–by left undone its therefore ordered that Peter —— worral do lead the wood for the bridg & help to lay it up or pay a fine of 25^s

order—— whereas divers attempts have been made to bring
about the arrears of aſſembley & Councell mens
the fees fees to Some Certainty & that Som Compenſati-
of on may be made to Such as have been at an ——
members extrordinary Charge by theire long attendance there
of -in its ordered that the Juſtices meete together
Council at the Court houſe the i8th day Inſtant to treat
& with thoſe Concerned & ſee what will Satiſye them

Affembly & give an acc^{tt} thereof to the next County Court
to be then further Confidered of by the Grand
Jury.

Complt being made by Jofph Large of his poverty requefted
request the Courts recomendation to Saml Carpenter ——
Executor to ffrancis Rossill late of this County deceafed
to have a Share of the Legacy left by Said
Roffill to the poore of this County whereupon
order– it was ordered that the Clerk do write to faid
Saml Carpenter to let him have three pounds of
the fd Legacy

verdict The Jurys verdict in the action wm Rakestraw
agt Gilbert wheeler was find for the plantf with
cofts of Suite

Judgmt: whereupon the Court awards Judgment that the deft
pay to the Said plaintf   ⎱ & that Execution Iffue
the faid fum of 4£ with Cofts ⎰   accordly

Complaint being made that Some perfons do oppofe the laying
out the Cart way from the mill Dam to the landing
at the fferry in Buckingham its there fore ——

ordered that Henry Baker Peter worral nicholas waln
and John wilfford & Enoch yardley or any three
of them do lay out the fame upon a Straightline
& make return thereof to the next Court

> Adjourned the Court untill the 18th
> day Inftant at the Court houfe

— — — — — — — — — — — — — —

269 At a Court held by adjournment the 18 day of the
firft month 1̄6̄9̄5̄
6

The Juftices prefent

William Biles Richard Hough John Swift

Samuel Beaks Sherrife

Phinehas Pemberton Cl: Com:

adjourned to the houfe of Jofeph Chorley

addrefs being made to this Court by Phinehas Pemberton

about the
Sale of
Adkifons
land

on behalf and at request of Jane formerly the
wife of Thomas Adkinson but now wife of Willm
Biles requefting the
approbation of this Court for the difpofeing & Sale of three
hundered acres of land given to her by her Said
late hufband Thomas Adkifon by his laft will and
Teftement dureing her natural life & after her ——
deceafe to his three Sons Isaac william & Samuel
Adkifon alfo acquainting the Court how that the fame
might be fold for a full value & the aforefaid william
Biles declared that at the requeft of his fd wife Jane
& for the benefit of her fd three fons had by her firft
hufband he had Condicended to quit his Claime and
Intreft in it dureing his fd wifes life & wold Raise for
the Same ninety pounds and Intreft for the
refpective Sums or Shares due to the fd Sons of ——
Tho: Adkinfon as they Shold Severaly attaine to theire
feveral ages   They feveraly
acquiting theire Claime or title to the faid land and
premifes as they shold severaly Re: theire parts & ——
shares of the faid mony & Intreft viz: To Ifaac Adkinfon
at the age of 2i yeares thirty pounds & the Intreft thereof
to william Adkinfon the like fum of thirty pounds with the
Intreft thereof when attained to the age of 2i yeares
to Samuel Adkinfon the like fum of thirty pounds with
the Interest thereof when attained to the age of 2i yeares
and this Court haveing fuly Confidered that the faid
ninety pounds is a full value for the lands & that the
Sale there of will much Conduce to the bettering and ——
Improveing the faid Childrens Eftate & be divers ways
advantagious to them this Court adjudged that the
Said Land be fold and the mony Secured as aforefd

270

what was
done about
the members
of Council
& assembleys
fees

Whereas it was ordered laft Court that the Juftices Shold
meet this day and affertaine the Councill and
affembley mens fees that have been at extrordinary
Charge in theire Long fervice & have as yet had
no Compenfation for the Same which they accordingly
did but few made appearance here this day to make demand & therefore it was beleived much was not
expected but haveing difcourft with thofe prefent they
were found to be moderated & feemed Rather to

Seek to have an end put to the Said affaire then
theire own Intreſt & Cold not perceive but that if
the Grand Jury wold make Some ſuitable preſents
to thoſe that had been at an extrordinary Charge
by Reaſon of theire long Continuance in the ſaid
places that it wold put an end to it
   adjourned to the ioth of the 4th month next

— — — — — — — — — — — — — —

Bucks ſS:

At a Court held by the kings authority in the —
name of william penn abſolute proprietarie and
govrnr of the province of penſilvania and Counties
annexed at the Court houſe for the aforesaid — —
County the ioth day of the 4 month i696

The Juſtices present

Joseph Growdon William Biles ⎱ Juſtices
  Henry Baker Richard Hough ⎰
    John Cook Corronor
    Sam¹ Beaks Sherrif
    Phinehas Pemberton Cl: Com:

Eſtreat

John Snowden being Summoned to ſerve on the
Jury this Court & for his non appearance according
to Summons the Court fines him in five shillings

grand Jury
atteſted —

Jonathan Scaife Joſuah Hoops Samuel Dark
James paxſon John Brock Joſeph Wood
Henry Marjorum Joſeph millner
                    Thomas Hardin
willm Paxſon John palmer Richard wilſon
Joſeph Clows Andrew Ellot
                Thomas ſtakehouſe Jnr
william Smith Joſeph kirkbridge all atteſted

271

—A deed of partition of the moiety of Twenty Two acres of land in
    ffee dated
    the Sixteenth day of the firſt month 1695 was acknowledged
    and delivered by peter white & Ellizabeth his wife grantors
    to Anthony Burton & Thomas Brock grantees

—a deed of portion of the other moiety of the fame Twenty acres
of Land in ffee dated the faid fixteenth day of the firft month
1695 was acknowledged and delivered by Anthony Burton
& Thomas Brock grantors to peter white Grantee

—A deed–in ffee for fifty acres of Land dated the 30 day of decemb
i695 acknowledged & delivered by Thomas Brock attorney
to Matts kan Hance Loyke Elizabeth Johnfon and——
katherine Johnfon Grantors to Breta Johnfon grantee

—A deed–in ffee for one hundered acres of land dated the 4ᵗʰ day of
feptember 1695 was acknowledged and delivered by Thomas
Brock attorney to Thomas ffaireman Grantor to Dunken——
williams grantee

—A deed in ffee for Two hundered forty six acres of land dated the
17 day of the 3 month acknowledged and delivered by John
Town Attorney to Ralph ward & Thomas Jenner grantors
unto Thomas Stakehoufe Unior Grantee

—An Indenture of partion for the moiety of ii acres of land in ffee
dated the 8 day of the 4 month 1696 was acknowledged
and delivered by Thomas Brock grantor to Anthony——
Burton grantee

—An Indenture of partion for the other moiety of the faid ii acres
of land in ffee was acknowledged and delivered by Anthony
Burton grantor to Thomas Brock Grantee

—A deed–in ffee of foure hundred and fifty acres of land taken in
Execution to
fatifye the debts of Jofeph Holden bearing date the eighteenth
day of the 2 month was acknowledged and delivered
in open Court by Samuel Beaks the then fherrife Grantor
to Jofeph Growdon Grantee

—A deed ffor the abovefaid foure hundered and fifty acres of
land in ffee dated the 30 day of the firft month 1694
was acknowledged and delivered by Jofeph Growdon
grantor to John naylor Grantee

—A deed of Two hundered thirty fix acres of land in ffee dated
the 8 day of the fourth month 1696 was acknowledged
& delivered by Samuel Beaks grantor to John——
neild grantee

—The former Record of Court againe allowed and approved
in Relation to Thomas Adkifons Lands & fecurity given

in Court at the fame time for the Confideration mony by
william Biles unto Phineas Pemberton & Richard Hough
in truft for the heires of faid Akdifon —— ——

—A deed of Three hundred acres of land in ffee dated the Tenth
day of the fourth month one Thoufand fix hundered ninety
fix acknowledged and delivered in open Court by william
Biles and Jane Biles his wife grantors to george Biles grantee

Execution agt Gilbert wheeler in willm Rakeftraws Cafe returned
fully Levyed according to the Contents thereof by Samuel —
Beaks fherrife

272

Complaint being made by Jofeph Chorley & mary his wife of feveral
abufes done to them by Richard Thatcher & Bartholemew
Thatcher as that they did ftrike the faid Chorley & his
wife in the faid Chorley's houfe to the fheding of Blood
which fact the faid Richard Thatcher & Bartholomew —
Thatcher Confeft to be true & fubmited to the Court where
upon the Court fines them Richard Thather in in forty
ffine   fhillings & Bartholemew Thather in Twenty fhillings to
be paid to the proprietor & govrnr & that they be bound
to theire good behaviour for one yeare

Recognizance Richard Thatcher acknowledged him felf Indebted to the
proprietor & govr willm Penn the fum of Twenty pounds
& the faid Bartholemew Thather acknowledged him felf
Indebted to the faid proprietor in Ten pounds to be Levied on
theire Lands & tenemants goods & Chatles under Condition
that he the faid Richard Thatcher Shold be of good abearing
towards the faid proprietarie & all the kings fubjects for one
whole & yeare

requeft   George Heathcoat & John fiddal defired the matter in diference
between them might be fufpended untill the next Court

Recognizance Bartholemew Thatcher acknowledged him felf Indebted
Twenty pounds & Richard Thatcher in Ten Pounds to the
proprietor & Governor willm pen to be
levied on theire lands & tenemants goods & Chattles under
Condition that fhold be of good abeareing towards the fd
proprietarie & all the kings fubjects for one whole yeare

adjournment   adjourned untill 9 a Clock to morrow morning

Holdens } whereas the eftate of Jofeph Holden was formerly taken in —
Eftate } Execution to fatiffye the feveral debts due from the faid Holden
to his Creditors and the accts thereof are not as yet brought in
of the faid eftate by Samuel Beakes Sherrife it is therefore

ordered that the said fherrife do bring in an acctt thereof & of
what monys is in the hands of Jofeph Growdon & how
much is paid out of the faid eftate to anfwer the feveral —
Judgments of the Court

adjournment   adjourned the Court for one houre

Grand jurys prefentments

(1) we the jurrors for the body of this County do prefent the
great neceffity of a roade to be layd out from new Towne
to the landing at Gilbert Wheelers for the fervice of In
ha bitants both of new Town & the neighbourhood on this fide

(2) we do prfent the overfeer or fupervifor for the falls townfhip[2]
for neglecting the high roade to mend the fame—(viz:) the —
road leading from Gilbert wheers to midle Townfhip —

(3) Alfo we do prefent the neceffity of Clearing & mending the road
that's layd out from Henry Bakers to the ferry over agt Burling

(4) Alfo we do prfent the neceffity of a rate to be made through
out this County of three half pence per pound[s] & heads
according
ly according to the law provided in that Cafe viz: after the

273   the manner of one peny p pound and six fhillings p
head for the defraying of neceffary Charges of the
faid County and alfo that a Collector in every Townfhip
be Chofen to Collect the fame & that Two honeft fub-
ftantial men be Chofsen to be receivors in order to —
which we propofe Jofuah Hoops william Paxfon
Samuel Dark & Jonathan fcaife & that any two
of them which the Court fhall think fitt may ferve
to Receive and pay all fuch mony as fhall be Collected
& payd to them by the order of the Court & grand jury
and that the faid Receivors Shall be accountable
when & fo often as the Court & grand jury fhall
fee meet.

(5) alfo we do prefent Ralph Boome & Jofeph Croffe
for unlawfull takeing & Carrying away a black
walnut Logg of Claws Jonfon Edward Lane and Willm

Howard & John Jonſon from John Bowens Landing
at the bottom of neſhaminah Creek

road — prſent-ment of a road from Wrights Town to the
Landing at the ferry agt Burlington brought in

roade — The road from the mill pond to the Landing at the
fferry afforeſd agt Burlington prſented to be Layd
as ſtraight as may be

order — upon the prſentment of the neceſſity of a Cartroad
from newtowne to the landing at Gilbert wheelers
the Court appoints willm Buckman Joſuah Hoops
Jonathan ſcaiſe william Dark & Jon Hough
to lay out the ſame

petetion of Iſaac Burges declareing his want of releiſe

ordered that Juſtice Growdon Inſpect his neceſſity & ——
allow him what is fit for a preſent ſupplye

preſentmt upon the Grand jurys prſentmt of Ralph Boome
& Joseph Croſſ unlawfull takeing away of a black
walnut Logg belonging to Claws Jonſon Edward Lane
wm Howard & John Jonſon from John Bowens
Landing at the bottom of neſhaminah Creek

deftes pleaded not guilty & for tryal put them ſelves on the Cuntry

venire ſherrif is Commanded to return a jury wᶜʰ was accordingly
done

jury   ptr worrall   Robert Heaton   Henry Hudleſtone
    willm Croſdell   peter White   willm Buckman
    John pidcock   Jeremiah Langhorn   Wm Taylor
    John neild   Andrew Heath   Abraham Cox all

atteſted

John Bowen Lucy Boare Henry Bowen Margret
matthews atteſted for the plants:

ordered by the Court that the Juſtices meet the 22 day of
this Inſtant to aſſeſſ the Tax at the Court houſe
prſented by the grand jury neceſſary to be raiſed.

A deed of Two hundered and fifty acres of land in fee dated the
274 eight day of the fourth month one Thouſand ſix hundred
ninety ſix acknowledged and delivered by Henry ——
marjorum Grantor to Henry Baker grantee

verdict   jury finds for the plt Twenty shillings with Cost of suite

Judgmt   Given and it is adjudged that the said Joseph
Cross and Ralph Boome pay accordingly & that Execution
Issue accordingly

ordered   that peter worral & Enoch yardley & Henry Baker or any two
of them lay
out the road from the mill dam to the Common Landing at
the ferry

adjournment   adjourned to the 22 day of this Instant month

Bucks ss: At a Court held by adjournment the 22 day of the $\frac{4}{mo}$

1696

Justices then present

william Biles Henry Baker Richard Hough
Sam^{ll}: Beakes Sherrife Phineas Pemberton Cl. Com:

accounts of Thomas Brock hath been in pte examined but find the
orriginal Tax book is wanting that was made under the
Commis
-sion of Benjamaine fletcher & no Recipts of any mony paid
by the
said Brock late Sherrife to be found therefore the said acc^{ts}
are defferred untill —
an other time and its   ·

ordered   that Sam^{ll} Beakes the prsent Sherrife do speake to John Swift
one of the Justices under that Commission and enquire of him
for
the orriginal Tax book & the Acc^{tts} brought in by said Brock
to the grand jury that the said acc^{tts} may be brought in & psected
at the next Court

Tax   whereas the grand jury last Court prsented the necessity of
raiseing a —
Tax of three half pence pte on the Clear value of real
& psonal estates & 9^d p pole on those that are not
otherwise rated according as the law directs in that Case
for the defraying of necessary Charges of the aforesaid County
ordered & agreed that the several Inhabitants be valued as they were
in the last tax except where there is manifest Cause

to the Conterary & that all such as are Taxable that have
beene heretofore omitted be entered in this Tax & that
this be regarded & altered by the Clerke as he fhall find
any error or omiffion made now in this Court in the
tranfcribeing of the faid Tax

petition of Ifaac Burges in relation to a debt due to him from
his brother Sam^ll Burges was read and the Court ——

appoints Jofeph kirkbride to fpeake to faid faml Burges & advife
him to reffer the mater in diferenc to Indiferent men to
be by them Chosen but if he fhall refufe the faid advice then
then willm Biles & Richard Hough do take what further
Care is fitt to accomodate the matter in diference as may
be found moft expedient & expeditious

adjourned for one houre

ordered that the Clerk write the Tax faire over agt next Court
275   & after allowance thereof to draw out duplicates of every
Townfhips Tax respectively

Collectors ordered for the feverall Townfhips

for

Buckingham   Anthony Burton
ffals — — — — Samll Beakes
makefeild — — Jofeph milner
middle Town ——
new Town ——
wrights Towne
& Lands adjacent
⎫ wm Crofdel

Benfalem — — John Gilbert
fouth hampton & Lands adjacent } John Cuttler

ordered   that Jonathan Scaife & Samll Darke be receviors
of the County Tax to be difpofed of as the Court fhall
appoint

—A deed of Several lotts of land (in Buckingham) in fee dated fixteenth day of the fourth month i696 acknowledged and
delivered by willm Crofdell attorney to Thomas Brock
Anthony Burton peter
white & Elizabeth his wife grantors to phineas pemberton
grantee

—A deed of one lott of land in fee (in Buckingham) dated the Twenty ſecond day of the fourth month one Thouſand ſix hundered ninety ſix acknowledged and delivered by Anthony Burton grantor to phineas pemberton Attorney to ſamll Bowne grantee

—A deed of one lott of land in fee (in Buckingham) dated 22 day of the 4 month 1696 acknowledged and delivered by —— Anthony Burton grantor to willm Croſdel grantee

—A deed of one lott of land in fee (in Buckingham) dated 22 day of the 4 month 1696 acknowledged and delivered by Anthony Burton grantor Henry Baker grantee ——

A deed — of ſeveral lotts of land in fee (in Buckingham) dated the ſixteenth day of the fourth month 1696 was acknowledged and delivered by Anthony Burton Attorney to the peter white & Elizabeth white his wife grantors to Phineas pemberton Attorney to ſaml Carpenter — grantee

adjournment   adjourned to the 9th day of the 7 month next

Bucks ſS: 276

At a Court of Quarter ſseſſions by the kings authority in the name of william penn abſolute proprietarie and govrnr of the province of penſylvania and Territories thereunto belong -ing at the Court houſe for the Said County the 9th day of the 7th month 1696.

The Juſtices present

Joſeph Growdon   Henry Baker ——
Richard Hough   John Swift
Samll Beaks Sherrife
Phineas Pemberton Cl: Com: —— ——

roade — peter worrall Enoch yardley &c make return — that they have laid out the road from the mill — Dam in Buckingham to the Common landing by the fferry houſe upon a ſtraight line

roade — 3 day of the 7 month 1696 we whoſe names are hereunder written being appointed by order of the

laſt Court to lay out a roade (viz a Cart roade from
new Town to the fferry at Gilbert wheelers pur-
ſuant to the ſaid order we accordingly have met —
together and Layd it out according to the beſt of
our underſtanding (viz) from new town to the Creek
Commonly Called the old mans Creek or Core Creek by
a line of marked trees from thence to James ſutton
by a line of marked trees from thence to ſtony hill —
by a line of marked trees from thenc by the houſe
of widow Lucas or ſome of that familys by a line
of marked trees from thence by a line of marked
trees into the kings roade that leads to philadel-
-phia from Gilbert wheelers & from thence to the
ffalls along the kings roade

requeſt   In order to effect the ſaid roade we deſire
the Court wold be pleaſed to give out ordr that the
ſaid road may be Cleared with as much expedition
as may be for the uſe & benefit of all the ——
Inhabitants Concerned

witnes our hands

    will Buckman
    Joſhua Hoops
    Jonathan ſcaiſe
    John Hough

Tax   againe allowed and a warrant signed for the ——
277   Collecting thereof

Conſtables Choſen

| ffor | Buckingham ffalls — — — makefeild — — middle Towne & towns adjacent | Clement Dungan Daniel Gardner Thomas kirle John Croſdel — |
| | Bensalem Cum ſouthhampton —— & places adjacent | John Cuttler |

overſeers of the high ways

for —
{
Buckingham   John Baldwin & Edmund Lovet

makefeidl ——— Thomas Janney Junr

ffals — — —   John Rowland

midle Towne   } willm Crofdell
& places adjacent }

Benfalem &
fouthhampton &   }— John Webster
places adjacent
}

—A deed— of Two hundered and fifty acres of land in ffee —
dated the fourth day of the fourth month 1694
acknowledged and delivered by Jofeph Chorley —
Attorney to John otter grantor to Henry Baker
grantee

—A deed— of Two small parcells of land in ffee dated the
14 day of the i2ᵗʰ month i693 acknowledged &
delivered by phineas pemberton attorney to
Randle Blackfhaw grantor to Jofeph kirkbride
grantee

—A deed   of five hundered acres of land in ffee dated the
23 day of july i696 acknowledged and delivered
by Jofeph kirkbride grantor to phineas pemberton
for the ufe of Gideon ffreborn grantee —

adjourn ment   adjourned to the 9ᵗʰ of the i0   next
                                               ——
                                               mo

278

Bucks ís: At a Court of Quarter feffions held by the kings
authority in the name of william Penn abfolute
proprietarie and Govrnr of the province of
penfylvania & Territories thereunto belong
-ing at the Court houfe for the faid County the
9ᵗʰ day of the i0ᵗʰ month being the 8 yeare
of king willm: the 2ⁿᵈ of his raigne over —
England &c. annoquoe dm: i696

The Juftices prfent

Jofeph Growdon willm: Biles Henry —
Baker Richard Hough John Swift ——
Sam¹ Beakes Sherrife
Phineas pemberton Cl: Com:

—A deed— of Two hundered thirty five acres of land in fee dated
the firſt day of the 10 month i696 acknowledged and
delivered by willm Darke grantor to John Dark grantee

—A deed   of five hundered acres of land in fee dated the Twenty
seventh day of the 4ᵗʰ month i696 acknowledged and
delivered by phineas pemberton attorney to Samll
Bown grantor to Samll Beakes attorney to Richard
willits gardian to Hannah willits his daughter grantee

—A deed— of one lott of land in fee (in Buckingham) dated
the 8ᵗʰ day of the i0ᵗʰ month i696 acknowledged
and delivered by peter white & Elizabeth white wife
of the Said peter grantors to Joſeph Growdon Grantee

An Indenture of ſale & mortgage in fee for Two lotts of
Land in Buckingham dated the 9ᵗʰ day of the i0ᵗʰ
month i696 acknowledged and delivered by ——
Thomas Brock grantor to Stephen nowel Grantee

—a deed of fifty acres of land in fee dated the 9ᵗʰ day of the
fourth month i696 acknowledged and delivered
in open Court in the ſaid County by Clement Dungan
grantor to Edward Doyle grantee

—a deed of one hundered fifty five acres of land in fee dated
the ninth day of the 10ᵗʰ month i696 acknowledged
and delivered by John webſter grantor to ſamuel
Burges Junr grantee

—a deed of fifty acres of land in fee dated the firſt day of
the 10ᵗʰ month 1696 acknowledged & delivered by
Thomas Dure grantor willm Darby grantee ——

—A deed of one hundered and ſix acres of land in fee dated
279   the fourth day of September 1694 acknowledged and
delivered by phineas pemberton Attorney to Henry
Burcham and margret Burcham his wife grantors
to James Boyden Junr attorney to willm Hughs —
grantee

—A deed–of the ſaid one hundered and ſix acres of Land in fee
dated the 9ᵗʰ day of September 1696 acknowledged &
delivered by James Boyden attorney to Willm Hughes

grantor to Daniel Done Attorney to Thomas Bills —
grantee

action — Arthur Cook agt Tho. Rogrs they both appeared and
defired the fame might be fufpended untill next Court

adjournment   adjourned untill tomorrow morning at
9 a Clock

certificate of Jofiah Blackfhaws being alive Signed — —

Richard Thatcher being Committed for breaking the peace was
Called & Confeffed the fact & fubmitted to the Court —
whereupon the Court

ordered ordrs that he give fureties for his
appearance at the Court to be held in the i0ᵗʰ month
in the yeare 1697 & to be of good abearing in the
meane time and to be Comitted to prifon untill he
pforme the fame

The Court alfo awards judgment that he had forfeited
his former recognizance

grand jury Jofuah Hoops wm Paxfon Ezra Crofdel James paxfon
Jofeph kirkbride George Brown Willm Biles Jof: wood
ftephen Sands Richard wilfon Ralph Cowgill John fmith
John Snowden wm Dark all attefted ——

grand juries } we present Jofeph Smalwood for prophane fwearing
prefentments }

we prefent the bridge on Widow Lucas land in the roade
leading from the falls to new Towne

we prefent the neceffity of a bridge over Core Creek
leading from new Town to the fferry

we prefent the neceffity of mentaineing the way from
middle towne to the falls

Bucks fs: The jurors for the proprietarie & govrnr by the kings
authority do prfent ftephen nowel for entering into the houfe
of peter white the 2i day of 7 month laft paft & did then and
there violently affault with Batterie the wife of faid peter white
& the wife of the faid ftephen nowell & did alfo open a Cheft &
ffelonoufly take out of the faid Cheft about five pounds of filver
mony and one filver fpoone & one filver Chaine the Chaine &
fpoone

280   the proper goods of peter white Conterary to the kings peace
       and the ftatute laws in that cafe made & provided

       peter white profecutor   Ellizabeth white ⎱ wittneffes
                                          Ellizabeth nowel ⎰

vera billa   we find this bill

pleaded — not Guilty & for tryal put him felf on the Cuntry where

venire   upon the fherrife was Commanded to return a jury w^{ch}
          was done as ffolloweth

Jury — Gilbert wheeler Henry Marjorum Jeremiah Langhorn —
       Stephen Beakes ffrancis Tunneclift James moone fenr —
       John Brock faml Coates Wm Darby james Yates
       Saml Hough James moone junr all attefted

   wittneffes Ellizabeth white & Ellizabeth nowel proved the prfentmt
             agt ft nowel

Complaints about the Tax redreffed

   ordered   that phineas pemberton examine the accts of Tho: **Brock**

Recognizance   Richard Thatcher did acknowledg him felf Indebted to
          the proprietary & govrnr in the fum of 20 £ & Jofeph
          Thatcher in the fum of 10 £ to be levied on theire lands
          and tenements goods & Chattles and this upon Condition
          that the faid Richard Thatcher Shall appeare at the
          Court of Quarter feffions to be held in the i0th month
          in the yeare 1697 and not to depart the Said Court
          untill he Shall have licence fo to do & to be of good
          abearing in the meane time

   verdict — we of the jury do find Stephen nowell guilty of ftrikeing
          of Elizabeth white in the houfe of peter white figned
          in the behalf of the jury by Gilbert wheeler foreman

   judgment given and it was adjudged that Stephen nowell Shold
          pay the Coft of Court & that Execution iffue accordingly
          and that he give fuerties for his appearance at the
          next Court of Quarter feffions to be held for this County
          & to be of good abearing in the meane time

---

*This page is numbered twice.

Recognizance   Stephen nowell acknowledged him felf Indebted
to the proprietarie & govrnr wm Penn in the fum of
20 £ & george Duncan & James moone Junr each in
10 £ to be levied on theire lands and tenements goods &
Chattles and this upon Condition that the faid ftephen
nowell Shall appeare at the next Court of Quarter —
feffions to

petition —of Edward Doyal Read feting forth his want of releife

ordered   that Samll Beakes pay him out of the County Levie
the fum of

fatiffaction on a Judgment obtained by willm Rakeftraw againft
Gilbert wheeler was made appeare in Court by a rect
under faid Rakeftraws hand dated the 2 day of the $\frac{5}{mo}$

i696 in Samull Beakes the fherrifs Cuftody

ordered   that the Several Collectors do pay the mony they
$\overline{281}$ Receive on the late County Tax to Saml Dark
or Jonathan Scaife & take theire or either of
theire Receits for So much mony as they pay and
that the faid Saml Dark & Jonathan fcaife —
bring the Said mony to the next Court then and
there to be difpofed of by the Court for the —
defraying the neceffary Charges of the County
to what other ufes it was raifed

adjourned to the 9th day of the firft month next

Bucks fs:

At a Court of Quarter feffions
held by the kings authority in the
name of willm penn proprietarie
and governr of the province
of penfylvania and Territories
thereunto belonging at the Court
houfe for the aforefaid County the
10th day of the firft month being
the 8th yeare of the king reigne
and 17 yeare of the proprietaries
govrmt over the faid province 1696
$\overline{7}$

The Juſtices present

william Biles   Henry Baker
Richard Hough

Jonathan Scaiſe   Corronor
Samll Beaks Sherriſe
Phineas Pemberton Cl: Com:

Commiſſ   Corronors Commiſſion read

—A deed— of five Thouſand acres of Land in fee dated
the ninth day of the firſt month $\frac{1696}{7}$ acknowledged

and delivered by willm Biles Attorney to Thomas —
Hudſon grantor to Stephen Beaks attorney to
willm Lawrence John Talman Joſeph Thorn Samuel
Thorn & Benjemaine ffeild grantees

—A deed   of Two hundered and fifty acres of land in fee dated
the 5ᵗʰ day of the firſt month $\frac{1696}{7}$ was acknowledged

and delivered by phineas pemberton Granto unto
Stephen Beakes for the uſe of william kenerley and
his heires Grantee

282

—A deed —of one hundered and Twenty five acres of
Land in ffee dated the eight day of the Tenth month
one Thouſand Six hundered ninety Six acknowledged
and delivered by Joſuah Hoops grantor to Daniel
Hoops Grantee

+A deed   of Six hundered and Sixteen acres and Two thirds of
an acre in ffee dated the Twenty firſt day of the eleventh
month one Thouſand Six hundered ninety Six was
acknowledged and delivered by Henry Baker —
Grantor to peter worral Attorney to John Harriſon
Grantee

A deed of Twenty five acres of land in fee dated the —
Twenty firſt day of the Eleventh month one Thouſand
Six hundered ninety Six acknowledged and —
delivered by william Biles attorney to Thomas
Hudſon Grantor to peter worral Attorney to
John Harriſon Grantee

—A deed of foure hundered acres of land in fee dated the
Twentieth day of the eight month one Thouſand
Six hundered ninety Six acknowledged and
delivered by John Smith Attorney to Arthur Cooke
and John Cook Grantors to John Circuit grantee

—A deed of one Thouſand and fifty acres of land in ffee dated the
Twenty firſt day of the eleventh month one Thouſand
Six hundred ninety Six acknowledged and —
delivered unto peter worral Attorney to Matthias
Harvie grantee by william Biles Attorney to
Thomas Hudſon grantor

—A deed of Two hundered ninety Six acres of land in ffee
dated the firſt day of the Tenth month one Thouſand
Six hundered ninety Six acknowledged and delivered
by Joſeph Chorley Attorney to John Clark grantor
unto Joſeph milner Grantee

—A deed of one hundered and Seventy acres of land in fee
dated the Tenth day of the firſt month one Thouſand
Six hundered ninety Six acknowledged and delivered
by Robert Heaton Junior Grantor to Jonathan
Scaiſe Grantee

—A deed of Two hundered Thirty Six acres of land in ffee
dated the Sixth day of the firſt month one Thouſand
Six hundred ninety Six acknowledged and
delivered by Abel Janney Grantor to Richard
Hough Grantee

—A deed of Two acres of meadow land in fee dated the
ninth day of the fourth month one Thouſand ſix
ninety Six acknowledged and delivered by
Enoch yardley grantor to Ruben pownal grantee

—A deed of fifty acres of land in ffee dated the fifth of
283 the firſt month one Thouſand Six hundered ninety
Six acknowledged and delivered by Joſeph Chorley
Attorney to Elixabeth Bennet grantor to Thomas
yardley Grantee

—A deed of eighteen acres and a half of land in ffee
dated the Sixth day of the firſt month one Thouſand
Six hundered ninety Six acknowledged and
delivered by John white Grantor to John Smith
grantee

—A deed of nine acres and a Quarter of land in fee dated —
      the eighth day of the firſt month one Thouſand Six
      hundred ninety Six acknowledged and delivered
      by John Smith grantor to John Town Grantee

—A deed of about foure acres and a half in fee dated the
      eight day of the firſt month one Thouſand ſix
      hundred ninety Six acknowledged and delivered
      by John Smith Grantor to Phineas pemberton
      Attorney to Thomas muſgrave grantee

—A deed of a Small lott of land in ffee dated the ninth
      day of the firſt month one Thouſand Six hundered
      ninety Six acknowledged and delivered by John
      Town Grantor to Henry Baker partner to ſamuel
      Carpenter grantee

—A deed of Two hundered and ninety acres of land in ffee
      dated the firſt day of the firſt month one Thouſand
      Six hundered ninety Six acknowledged and —
      delivered by Randol Blackſhaw
      grantor Jose: kirkbride grantee

—A deed of eight hundered acres of land in ffee dated firſt
      day of the firſt month one Thouſand Six hundered
      ninety Six acknowledged and delivered by Randol
      Blackſhaw grantor to Joſeph kirkbride for the
      uſe of nehemiah Blackſhaw Son to the
      Said Randol grantee

—A deed of Two hundered acres of land in ffee dated the
      firſt day of the firſt month one Thouſand Six hundered
      ninety Six acknowledged and delivered by Randol
      Blackſhaw grantor to Joſeph kirkbride for the uſe of Abraham
          Cowgill and nehemiah
      Cowgill ſons of Ralph Cowgill grantees

    ordered & the ſaid Randol Blackſhaw ordered the ſaid deed
      after recorded to be delivered to the ſaid Joſeph
      kirkbride to be by him kept untill the Said Abraham
      and nehemiah Shold Come of age

—A deed of one hundered and Twelve acres of land in ffee
      dated the firſty day of the firſt month one Thouſand
      Six hundered ninety Six acknowledged and —
      delivered by Ralph Cowgill grantor to Joſeph kirkbride
      grantee

284

A deed— of four hundered and eighty acres of land in fee
acknowledged and Delivered being dated the
fourth day of december one Thoufand Six —
hundered eighty nine by Henry pawlin grantor
to Richard Burges Grantee
and the feale of the faid deed being Imperfect
& broken he the faid Pawlin did amend and new
make the Said feale in open Court before the
delivery there of

the death of Richard Atthary returned by the corronor
to be a natural death

affeffors chofen for the ffollowing yeare John Gilbert Jonathan Scaife
Jofeph milner
Edmund Lovet Samuel Dark Henry Baker

Complaint being made by John Siddal that George Heath
coate had taken out of his houfe feveral goods by
vertue of a warrant of fearch and refufed to profe
cute or bring the faid matter to A hearing the he
was bound fo to do neare a yeare agoe by recog
-nizance and that he the faid fiddal had given
his Attendance at Every Court to make his defence
& therefore Craved an order from this Court to
have his goods reftored to him againe whereupon

its ordered the Said Complaint appeareing
to be true that the Conftable in whofe Cuftody
the faid goods are do reftore the faid goods fo
taken to the faid John fiddal he the faid fiddal
paying the ffes was Cleared by proclamation —

ordered that the Collectors and Receivors of the County Tax
give theire Attendance here and pay in the mony
Collected by them the firft day of the 2 month next
adjourned the Court to the firft day of the
of the Second month next enfueing

At a Court held by adjournment the ift
day of the 2 1697
mo

The Juſtices preſent

william Biles   Henry Baker
Richard Hough   John Swift
Samˡ Beakes   Sherrife
Phineas Pemberton Cl: Com:

adjourned the Court to the houſe of Joſeph Chorley

Grand Jury Joſuah Hoops   John palmer   Edmund Lovet
   Abraham Cox John Rowland   James Boyden Junr
   Robt Heaton   Henry Hudleſtone   Enoch yardley
   William Duncan   Stephen Beakes   James moone
   Joſeph Milner   John Gilbert   Samuel Dark
   John Grifith   all Atteſted

$\overline{285}$ accounts made up in open Court with divers perſons about
               wolf heads

    adjourned the Court for one houre

    accounts more made up with divers perſons about wolfs
         and the accounts returned to Saml Dark

    accounts about wolves Ballanced about Wolves
         with Joſuah Hoops John palmer Henry * * *

    accounted with John Swift & he was then debtor
         to the County as may appeare by the account
         in Saml Darks hand 1£ i5ˢ 3ᵈ
    and that Jos Growdon had detained in his
    hand from John Gilbert the Collector of
    Benſalem Tax 5£ –9ˢ –0ᵈ

makefeild Tax amounted ii£ : i4ˢ : 3ᵈ being a * * *
    made the 4   1696 to defray the neceſſary
          mo
    Charges of the County

Recognizance Stephen newel & George Duncan * * *
    diſcharged therefrom being bound to appeare
    at this Court

Stephen newel appeared to proſecute in a Caſe agt
    Claws Johnſon according to a recognizance
    as he Saith Taken before Joſeph Growdon

and it being the Second time of his appearance
& no recognizance returned the Court diſchar
ged him from the ſame

—a deed of Two hundered and fifty acres of land in fee
dated the Twelfth day of the i month $\frac{1696}{7}$

acknowledged and delivered by John Cartor
grantor to John Smith grantee

—a deed of a lot of land in Buckingham in fee dated the
25 day of october acknowledged & delivered by
John Smith grantor to Richard Burges grantee

—a deed of Two hundered & ninety acres of land in fee dated
the 22 day of March $\frac{i696}{7}$ acknowledged and

delivered by Saml Beaks attorney Iſrael Taylor
grantor to John Griſith grantee

—one Indenture of mortgage and ſale of the above mentioned
Two hundered and ninety acres of land was
acknowledged and delivered by John Griſith
aforeſaid mortgageor to Abraham Cox attorney
to the aforeſaid Iſrael Taylor mortgagee

presentments of the Grand Jury   (286)
we of the Grand Jury of the County of Bucks do preſent the
neceſſity of repaireing the bridge between this County &
the County of philadelphia on poqueſin Creek

The i day $\frac{2}{mo}$ 1697

we do alſo acquaint the Court that we wold have phineas
pemberton and Arthur Cook each of them to have eight
pounds paid them out of the County Tax in full for theire
Service and Attendance in Council & aſſembley or any
diſburſements thereupon provided they give diſcharges
to the County in full upon the acceptance & Receipt there
of

we alſo wold have Joſeph Growdon to have Six pounds
payd accordingly he accepting the Same & diſchargeing
the County accordingly in full for his ſervice attendance

& other difburfements in or about the Council or —
affembley
phineas pemberton declared then in Court that he
wold accept the Same & accordingly difcharged the
County whereupon it was

ordered that william Crofdel Collector of the Tax in the
middle Townfhip Should pay to the faid phineas pem
berton eight pounds out of the Said Tax —

ordered that Saml Beaks Collector of the Tax in the
ffalls Town Ship pay to the administrators of wm
Beaks eight pounds fourteen Shillings foure pence
being the ballance of an acc^{tt} due to faid Beaks
in his life time for difburfements about the
building the Court houfe &c:

The petition of the Inhabitants of Benfalem about laying
out of a road to the fferry at Dunk williams deffered
for the prefent

—a deed one hundered & fifty acres of land in fee dated the
10th day of the $\dfrac{3}{mo}$ 1689 acknowledged & delivered by
phineas pemberton Attorney to Edward Smith grantor
to Jofeph kirkbride grantee

ordered that Arthur Cook be payd out of the County levyes
the Sum of eight pounds according to the grand Juries
requeft he difcharging accordingly

and That Jofeph Growdon be payd Six pounds on
the fame Terms

adjourned untill the 9th of the 4 month next

Bucks ff: 287

At a Court held in the name of William — — —
penn proprietarie of the province of penfylvania
and Counties Annexed at the Court houfe for the — —
aforefaid County the 9th day of the 4th month 1697

Juftices present

Joſeph Growdon william Biles   Henry Baker
Richard Hough John Swift
Jonathan Scaiſe Corronor
Samuel Beake Sherrife
Phineas Pemberton Cl: Com:

The Grand Jury Joſua Hoops foreman

Anthony Burton Edmund Lovet Abraham Cox
   Stephen wilſon
Henry Margerum John Brock John white
   Thomas Brock —
Peter worral Thomas Stakehouſe William Hayhurſt
   James moon
John palmer ffrancis white John Snowdon
   Shadrach walley
William Duncan willm Dark Ruben pownal
   John Stakehouſe

⎫
⎪
⎪
⎬ all Atteſted
⎪
⎪
⎭

26th 3 / mo   Action Entered

Iſaac merriot plt ⎫
     agt ⎬ in an action upon the Caſe
Samuel Jerrom deft ⎭

Bucks ſſ   Theſe are by the kings authority in the name of william penn
Locus   proprietarie and govrnr to require thee to Arreſt the body of
Sigilli   Samll Jerrome if found in they Balywick and him Safely keep
Arrest   and have at the next Court to be held at the Court houſe for the
      aforeſaid County the 9th day of the 4th month next as well to anſwer
the Complt of Iſaac Merriot of Burlington in weſt Jerſey merchant
in a plea on the Caſe as to abide the Judgmt of the ſd Court
and make return hereof and of thy doings herein at the sd Court
faile not at thy perril and for thy ſo doing this Shall be thy —
ſuffitient warrant given under my hand and Seale of the County
the 27th day of the 3 month i697

To Samll Beakes Sherrife of the ſaid   William Biles
County of Bucks theſe

Bucks ſſ By vertue of the within the body of Samuel Jerrome was return } Arrefted the 27th day of the 3 month i697 p

Samll Beakes fherrife

Declaracon Bucks ff

> Ifaac merriot plt
> agt
> Samuel Jerrome deft } in a plea upon the Cafe

Ifaac Merriot of Burlington in weft Jerfey Complts
agt Samll Jerrome for that whereas the Said deft Stands
Juftly Indebted to the fd plt in the Sum of Six pounds Six fhillings
and ten pence half penny Currant Silver mony being due to the
Said plt for divers goods wares and merchandizes by him

290* Sold to the Said Defte for which he the Said Jerrome did affume and
faithfully promife to pay all which the fd plt aver notwithftanding
the
Said deft: his promife and Affumption not regarding but
Endeavoring
and fraudulently Intending him the Said plt in this behalfe Craftely
and Subtilly to deceive and defraud hitherto hath refufed and
Still doth refufe the Same to pay whereupon action doth accrew to
the fd plt and Craves Judgmt of this Court agt the fd Samll Jerrome
for the fd Sum of Six pounds Six fhillings and ten pence half peny
with thirty Shillings damages and Coft of fuite &c:

action Called both plt and defend appeared

declarcon read

Judgmt} The Said Samuel Jerrome Confeffed he owed unto the Ifaac
Confeft} merriot the Said Sum of Six pounds Six Shillings ten pence
half penny

Judgmt & } { whereupon Judgmt was awarded for the Said Sum and that
Execut
Execucon } { Iffue accordingly & for Coft of fuite
awarded
accordingly }

A deed in ffee of Three hundered acres of Land bearing date the the
i5[th]

*There is no page numbered 288 or 289. Page 290 follows page 287.

day of the firſt month 1696/7 was delivered by John Smith grantor unto Henry Baker grantee

A deed in ffee of foure hundered acres of Land dated the i7th day of the third month i697 was delivered by John Shaw and George Willard grantors unto Phineas Pemberton Attorney to william Smith grantee

A deed in ffee of Six hundered and   acres of Land dated the firſt day of the 2nd month 1697 was delivered by Joſeph Growdon grantor to william Duncan grantee

Adjourned   Adjourned the Court unto the houſe of Joſeph Chorley at 10 a Clock in the morning   wm: Markham govrnr preſent

A deed in fee of five hundered acres of Land dated the 4th day of the i0th month i696 was delivered by Joſeph Chorley Subſtitute Attorney to Thomas ffaireman Attorney to his brother Robt fairman grantor unto Joſeph Growdon grantee

A deed in fee of one hundered acres of Land dated the 6th day of the firſt month i696 was delivered by Joſeph Chorley Attorney to Edward Evans grantor unto Joſeph Growdon grantee

A deed in ffee of ninety acres of Land dated the 9th day of the 4 month i697 was delivered by Phineas Pemberton Attorney to grace Langhorn Jeremiah Langhorn william Biles Junr and his wife Sarah Biles grantors unto William Paxſon grantee

A deed in ffee of three hundered acres of Land dated the i7th day of may 1695 was delivered by John Rowland Attorney to Robert webb and his wife Elizabeth webb grantors unto william Buckman grantee

Action entered the 26 day of the 3 month i697

Joſeph Engliſh peter white Elizabeth his wife
Thomas Green and Rachel his wife plts —
            againſt
Richard noble defendant - - - - - - - -

in an action upon the Caſe

Action being Called peter white one of the plts appeared and produced
        A letter
        of Attorney from the Reſt to appeare on theire behalfs
        defendant Called but appeared not

Complaint being made agt John Rowland for neglecting his duty
        in Collecting the Tax he being made Collector of A provincial
        Tax for the Townſhip at the ffalls

Exam : he being Called to anſwer to the Said Complt Confeſſed that he
        had not Collected any part thereof nor paid in the monys as
        the Law in that Caſe directs and that he was not ffree to Collect
        it

ffine- whereupon the Court fines in three pounds to Levied on his
        goods
        and Chattles

ordered thereupon that Samuel Beakes Sherrif be Collector of
        the Said Tax for the Said Townſhip at the ffalls

        John Rowland in his defence about not Collecting the ſd
        Tax haveing Spoke an untruth in the Court and for telling
        one of the Juſtices that he Spoke falsly the Court demanded
        of him to appeare at the next Court to —
        make anſwer to the Same and he acordingly promiſed
        to appeare

    action Entered the 26ᵗʰ day of the 3 month i697

        Iſaac Norris plt
                agt   } in an action upon the Caſe
        Samuel Jerrome deſt

Arreſt thereupon granted the 27ᵗʰ of the ſd mo i699
                                   3

    Return of the Sherrife thereupon

        Bucks ſſ By vertue of the within the body of Samll
        Jerrome was Arreſted the 27ᵗʰ day of the 3 month i699

Action } Iſaac norris & ptner plts } appeared by his Attorney
Called–} Saml Jerrome deſt   } appeared

        declaracon being read Bucks ſſ Iſaac norris plt } in a plea
                                 agt   } upon the
                       Saml Jerrome deſt}   Caſe

Iſaac norris of philadelphia merchant Complains agt —
Samuel Jerrome for that whereas the ſd deft Stands Juſt
-ly indebted to the plts in the Sum of Ten pounds five
teen Shillings nine pence half peny Currant ſilver mony
of the province of penſylvania being the ballance of an —
account of divers goods wares and merchandizes Sold by the
Said plts to the ſd deft an acc^{tt} whereof under the plts hand
herewith in Court to be produced may appeare all wch the
ſd plts do aver And tho the plts have often requeſted the ſaid
deft to have made payment to them of the ſaid Sum in full —
ballance of the ſd account never the leſſ the ſd deft hath refuſed
neglected and deneyed the Same to pay Still doth whereupon –

292   action doth accrew to the ſd plts and Craves Judgmt of this —
Court agt the Said Samuel Jerrome for the Said Sum of Ten
pounds fiveteen Shillings and nine pence half peny with foɾty
Shillings damages and Coſt of Suite &c:

Judgmt }   The Said Samuel Jerrome Confeſſed that he owed to the ſd
Confeſt }   plts the aforeſd Sum of Ten pounds fiveteen Shillings nine
pence half penney

Judgmt
&
Execution   } Whereupon Judgmt was awarded with Coſt of Suite and that
awarded   Execution Iſſue accordingly
accordingly }

Adjourned the Court for one houre

obligation   ⎫ Joſeph Growdon and John Swift promiſed in open Court to
to pay mony   ⎬ pay to Iſaac norris & partner theire Executors or
to Iſaac   ⎭   Adminiſtrators
norris &c: the Sum of Eight pounds on account of the Samll Jerrome
pt of the   in the ninth month next Enſueing
                 And the ſd Joseph Growdon and John Swift did likewiſe

Judgmt—   ⎫ promiſe to pay to Iſaac merriot his Executrs or Adminiſtrators
obligation   ⎬ the Sum of Six pounds and Coſt of Suite in three yeares
to pay—   time to be paid Quarterly by Equal portions
mony on the
aforeſd Judg
mt to Iſaac
merriot   ⎭

obligation
to serve in
Confideration
of the afore
fd mony—

In confideracon whereof the Said Saml, Jerrome obliged
him felf to ferve the Said Jofeph Growdon and John Swift or –
theire Affigns Two yeares for the Said mony by them fo to
be paid

we of the grand Jury for this County do by feverall Complts
for want of the ferry at Gilbert wheelers not being kept
do prfent the neceffity of haveing A ferry kept at Jofeph —
Chorleys which is a Convenient place and he doth promife to –
keep and Attend the Said ferry and A flat and Cannoes
always ready for to Attend the fd ferry fo that there be no
other place of ferriage allowed within three miles of the fd
Jofeph Chorleys

grand
Jurys—
prefentments

Likewife we prefent the neceffity of A ferry at nefhamina
Creek to be kept at John Baldwins which is nearrer to —
philadelphia from the ferry at Buckingham by 2 or 3 —
miles then the other ferry or way of rideing and John
Baldwin will keep a flat for to ferry horfes at reasonable
termes as the Cuntry Shall think fit he haveing the —
priveledg aforefaid alowed him

we Likewife prefent the bridg and the Roade that comes
from new town to the falls for want of repaire

we Likewife prefent the neceffity of gathering the arrears
of Taxes due from the County by the next Court and to
be paid into the Court or to whom they fhall authorize
to Receive the fame

we Likewife prefent the necessity of John Brock haveing his
mony that is due to him from the County Several yeares —

293

we Likewife prefent that no perfon or perfons Shall Sell rum
    or any
other Liquor by Small meafures to be drunk in theire houfes
without A license from the govrnr

grand
Jurys
prfent
mts –

we Likewife prefent Andrew Heath for Selling of Rum by —
Retaile and Richard Burges for the like offence of felling
Liquor by Small meafure

It was Likewife prefented as neceffary and A petition
drawn that we might have a Town layd out at Bucking
ham neare the old ferry and was prefented to the govr

-nr and Council being Signed by all the grand Jury and by about 20 pſons more

The Court adjourns to 2nd weekly fourth day in the 7ᵗʰ month next

Actions Entered for the 7ᵗʰ month Court next

24ᵗʰ   6   1697 ffrancis white plt
mo
     agt   } in an action upon the Caſe
     Stepehn newel — —

25ᵗʰ   6 i697 Summonce granted agt ſd newell ditto a ſummonce for witneſſes
mo
     with drawn by the plts order

24ᵗʰ   6   1697 John Town plt — —
mo
     agt   } in an action upon the Caſe
     Stephen newell deft

25   6   Summonce granted agt ſd newel in ſd action
mo

24ᵗʰ   6   1697 — — Thomas Hudſon plt
mo   agt   in an action upon the Caſe
25   6   Sumonce } Samll Hough deft } This action with drawn by ordr
mo
     in ſd Case —

of the plts attorney wm Biles

26 6 mo 1697 Gilbert wheeler plt
     agt   } in an action upon the Cafe —
     John Heeſum deft

26   6   1697 Arreſt granted agt John Heeſum
mo
by vertue whereof the Sherrif returned him Arreſted the 27ᵗʰ   6   97
     mo

Action Entered the 26ᵗʰ   3   1697
     mo

peter White &c: plts ⎤
          agt   ⎬ in an action upon the Cafe —
Richard noble deft ⎦

Attachment was thereupon granted then Returnable to the next Court
    by Saml Beakes then Sherrife dated 26ᵗʰ day 3 month 1697

return thereupon was made in the following words or words to
    the fame Effect viz

Bucks ff by vertue of the abovefaid the Land of Richard noble
    Lying in the Townfhip of Buckingham Conteineing about
    300 acres was Attached the 26ᵗʰ day of the 3 month 1697
                               p Samll Beakes fherrife

Bucks ff At a Court of Quarter Seffions held in the name of
_294_   william penn proprietarie and Govrnr of the pro-
        -vince of penfylvania and the Counties annexed
        at the Court houfe for the aforefd County the 8ᵗʰ
        day of the 7ᵗʰ month 1697

                Juftices prefent
    Henry Baker Richard Hough John Swift
    Jonathan Scaife Corronr
    Samll Beakes Sherrife
    Phineas Pemberton Cl: Com..

Apprizors ⎰ appointed Jofeph milner Edmund Lovet Anthony Burton all
Attefted ⎱

Action   peter white and as Attorney ⎤
Called   to Jofeph Englifh Thomas green ⎬plts ⎤ appeared
          and his wife Rachel — — —⎦   ⎬
                  agt   ⎦
       Richard noble — — — — defts ⎦ appeared not

A Deed In fee of about Ten acres of Land dated the firft day of
        the Seventh month 1697 was delivered by —
        matthias Harvie grantor to Jofeph milner grantee

A Deed in fee of one hunered Ten 110 acres of Land dated
        the 30ᵗʰ day of the 6ᵗʰ month 1694 was delivered by —
        Phineas Pemberton Attorney to Charles Read and Anne his

wife grantors unto John Rowland Attorney to Thomas Rogers Grantee

A Deed in fee of the above said one hundered and Ten acres of Land Dated the i2ᵗʰ day of the i0ᵗʰ month 1694 was delivered by John Rowland Attorney to the above named Thomas Rogers grantor unto Edmund Lovet grantee

A Deed in fee of A lott of Land in Buckingham dated was Delivered by Thomas Brock grantor unto Jonathan — Scaife Attorney to walter pomphray grantee

A deed in fee of one hundered ninety three acres of Land dated the 10ᵗʰ day of the first month 1694 was Delivered by Samuel Beakes Attorney to John Rowland and his wife priscilla grantors unto Phineas Pemberton Attorney unto Arthur Cook grantee

A Deed in fee of Six hundered acres of Land Dated the 3 day of the Sixth month i697 was Delivered by Jonathan Scaife Subftitute Attorney to Samuel Carpenter and Phineas Pemberton Attorneys to Thomas Mufgrave grantor unto Samuel Beakes Attorney to valentine Hudleftone grantee

A Deed in fee of one hundered and Ten acres of Land dated the 7ᵗʰ day of the 7ᵗʰ month 1697 was Delivered by Edmund Lovet grantor unto John Rowland grantee

Court adjourns untill the 5ᵗʰ day of the 8ᵗʰ month next

Action — David powel plt   action Trefpafe upon the Cafe
Entered — agt
9ᵗʰ 7   97 — Richard Davies deft
mo

Attachment thereupon granted i0ᵗʰ 7   i697
mo

return that the Lands of fd Davies was Attached the 25ᵗʰ day 7   1697
mo

(295)

At A Court Held by Adjournment the 5ᵗʰ day of the eight month 1697

9ᵗʰ 7 1697 action

——
mo

Entered

David powel plt

agt

Richard Davies deft

action Trefpafe upon
the Cafe ————

Juftices prfent

Joseph Growdon william Biles   Henry Baker
Richard Hough John Swift
Samuel Beakes Sherrife
Phineas Pembert Cl: Com:

grand Jury Attefted — —

A Deed in ffee of eighty acres of Land dated the firft day of the 6ᵗʰ month
1697 was Delivered by Jofeph Growdon Grantor unto Thomas knight
grantee

A deed of foure hundered acres of Land in fee dated the firft day of the 6ᵗʰ
month
i697 was delivered by Jofeph Growdon grantor unto francis Searl
grantee

A Deed of Twenty five acres of Land in fee Dated the firft day of the 8ᵗʰ
month i697 was Delivered by william Biles Attorney to Thomas —
Hudfon grantor unto Richard Hough grantee

A Deed of Sixty one acres and A half of Land in fee dated the 5ᵗʰ day of the
eight month 1697 was Delivered by Thomas Stakehoufe Junr grantor
unto Ezra Crofdel grantee

A Deed of fifty one acres and A half of Land in fee dated the 8ᵗʰ day of the
10ᵗʰ month 1696 was delivered by Jofeph kirkbride grantor unto
peter webfter grantee

A Servant boy his name being Neel Grant was prfented to the Court by his
mafter Jofeph kirkbride to have his age adjudged and the Court
according
-ly did adjudg him to be thirteen yeares of age the firft day of the
fifth month Laft paft and that he Serve his Said mafter according to Law
And the Said Jofeph kirkbride promifed to give to his Said Servant
at the expiration of his terme as the Law directs

A Servant boy his name being John Weire was prfented to the Court by
his mafter John Duncan to have his age adjudged and the Court —
accordingly did adjudg him to be thirteen yeares of age from this
day and that he Serve his Said mafter according to Law

And the Said John Duncan promifed to give to his Said Servant
at the Expiration of his terme of Servitude as the Law directs

Court adjourns for one houre

A Deed of three hundered acres of Land in fee dated the 7ᵗʰ day of the
7ᵗʰ month i697 was Delivered by william Buckman grantor unto
John Shaw grantee

A Deed of two hundered and three acres of Land in fee dated the firft
day of the 8ᵗʰ month 1697 was by william Crofdel grantor Delivered
unto
John Crofdel grantee

ordered that Duncan Williams have A Lycence to keep ordinary to pay 24ˢ

ordered that Thomas Brock have A lycence to keep ordinary to pay 24ˢ

A Deed of one hundered acres of Land in fee unto william Smith and
of Two hundered acres of Land in fee unto Ralph Boome bearing
date the firft day of the Sixth month 1697 was Delivered by —
Samll Beakes Attorney to Samuel Carpenter grantor unto the
Said william Smith and Ralph Boome grantees

ordered that Jofeph Chorley have a Lycence to keep an ordinary & to pay 24ˢ

296

A Deed of Two parcels of Land Conteing foure hundered and ninety acres
in fee
dated the fourth day of Auguft 1696 was Delivered by Phineas
Pemberton Attorney to James wood grantor unto Jofeph Growdon
Attorney to Jofeph kirle grantee

A Deed of Two hundered and forty Six acres of Land in fee dated
the i day of the 6ᵗʰ month i697 was delivered by Phineas Pemberton
Attorney to Jofeph paul grantor unto John Shaw Attorney
to George willard grantee

A Deed of a lot of Land in Buckingham In fee dated the i day of the 7ᵗʰ
month 1697 was Delivered by Thomas Brock grantor unto
Saml oldale grantee

A Deed of a Lot of Land in Buckingham in fee dated the i day of the 7ᵗʰ
month 1697 was delivered by Thomas Brock unto Edward
mayos grantee

grand Jurys prfentments { we the grand jury do prfent James Alman for
breaking the peace

on Saml Beakes & John Addington Sherrife &
Conftable in Executing
a warrant on the goods of John Rowland

Action   John Town plt
Called   agt   } in an action upon the { plt appeared ——
          Stephen newel deft }   Cafe   { deft appeared not }

Action } Gilbert wheeler plt
Called }   agt   } in an action upon { plt appeared ——
          John Heefum deft }   the Cafe   { deft appeared not }

Action was continued at the plts requeft untill another Court

Action } David powel plt
Called }   agt   } in an action upon { plt appeared ·
          Richard Davies deft }   { deft appeared not }

grand Jurys prfentmts Adjourned the Court untill tomorrow morning at
    9 a Clock

we the grand jury do prfent the neceffity of raiseing a Tax of
one peny p pound to defray
the County Charge   Jofuah Hoops foreman

John Heefum being accufed of Swearing by the name of god
upon his Examination Confeffed the fact

ffine   whereupon the Court fines him in Ten fhillings

Conftables   appointed to Serve for the Succeeding yeare

for —
Buckingham — — — — John Baldwin
ffalls — — — — — — Samuel Burges
makefeild — — — — — John Dark
middle Town
new Town & } — — — ffrancis white
wrights Town
Benfalem — — — — — nicholas vandegricft
Southhampton & } - — Henry walmsley — —
warminfter — —

overfeers of the High was for the enfueing yeare

$$
\text{for} \begin{cases}
\text{Buckingham} \relbar\relbar\relbar\relbar \begin{cases} \text{Thomas Brock} \\ \text{Edmund Lovet} \end{cases} \\
\text{falls} \relbar\relbar\relbar\relbar\relbar\relbar\relbar \\
\text{makefeild} \relbar\relbar\relbar\relbar \text{ Joſeph kirkbride} \\
\left.\begin{array}{l}\text{middle Town} \\ \text{new Town \&} \\ \text{wrights Town}\end{array}\right\} \begin{array}{l}\relbar\relbar\relbar \text{ Joſeph milner} \\ \relbar\relbar\relbar \text{ Henry Hudleſtone}\end{array} \\
\text{Benſalem} \relbar\relbar\relbar\relbar\relbar \text{ ffrancis Searle} \\
\left.\begin{array}{l}\text{South hampton \&} \\ \text{warminſter} \relbar\relbar\end{array}\right\} \relbar\relbar\relbar \text{ John Eaſtbourn}
\end{cases}
$$

grand Jurys prſentmt

> we the grand Jury do prſent the neceſſity of the executing a warrant directed to
> phineas Pemberton bearing date the 28th day of may 1697 for the laying out of a conve
> nient Road from the falls to philadelphia and from wrights town to Dunk williams on —
> delaware river and that Reasonable Charges be paid him out of the ſtock —

297

> ordered That phineas pemberton Survey and Lay out the Road between the falls and John Gilberts and alſo the Town of Buckingham according
> to the warrant to him directed with the aſſiſtance of John Surket Samuel Beakes Joſeph Chorley Thomas Brock John Baldwin Saml Allin John Gilbert nicholas vandegreift and as many of the Juſtices as Can well be there

> ordered That phineas pemberton Survey and Lay out the Road from wrights Town to neſhaminah meeting houſe and from Thence to Joſeph Growdons and thence to branch out the one way to — — the ford at Allin foſters over penipecce the other from — Joſeph Growdons to Duncan williams according to a warrant to him Directed from the Govrnr

> ordered that william Smith william Buckman James yates Robert Heaton Henry Huddleſtone Jeremiah Langhorn aſſiſt him therein

> ordered that the Said Phineas Pemberton be paid for Surveying and Laying out the Said Roads and Town out of the County Levies after the Same is done

Adjourned the Court for one houre

accounts of the County when Thomas Brock was made Collector of
the Tax was by Said Brock made up in open Court and it then —
appeared there was due to Said Brock from the County 12^s: 3^d

action Robt Lucas plt   ⎫ whereas Complt was made to william Biles
        agt   ⎪ one
  Richard Thacher deft ⎬ of the Juſtices of the peace for the aforeſd
                  ⎪ County
                  ⎪ how that Richard Thatcher was Indebted
                  ⎭ to him

the ſpliting of foure hundered of Railes whereupon the ſame
being made appeare to the ſaid juſtice of peace he gave Judgmt
that the Said Thatcher Shold Split the Said Railes wch being —
Judgmt reported to this Court upon further Examination thereof did Confirm
the Said Judgmt

A Deed of one hundered two and a half acres of land in fee dated the
    ist day of the 7th month i697 was Delivered by mahlon Stacy
    and Henry Baker Attornes to John nichols and Elias nicholas
        grantors
    unto Joſeph Chorley grantee

ordered that Gilbert wheeler have a lycence to keep ordinary & to pay
    30^s
Adjourned to the 2nd weekly 4th day in the 10th month next

Action Entered the 2i day of the 9th month 1697

    Saml Beakes plt   ⎫
        agt   ⎬ in an action upon the Caſe
    Richard Thatcher deft ⎭

Arreſt granted thereupon agt the ſd deft the 22 day 9   1697
                                       mo

Return Bucks ſſ by vertue of the within the body of Richard
Thatcher was Arreſted the 30th day of the 9 month 1697 p me
                                  Samll Beekes Sherrife

Bucks ſſ

298   At a Court of Quarter Seſſions held in the name
of william penn proprietarie of the province of
penſylvania and Territories thereunto belonging

at the Court houſe for the aforeſaid County the 8th
day of the i0th month 1697

The Juſtices preſent

Joſeph Growdon william Biles Richard Hough

Samuel Beakes Sherrife

Phineas Pemberton Cl: Com:

Court Adjourned to the houſe of Joſeph Chorley

Aſſault & Battery	Thomas Archer being Committed to priſon for aſſaulting & beating Thomas Brock being Examined thereupon Confeſt the fact and Submitted to the Court whereupon the Court Commits
Submitted to the Court	him into the ſherrifs Cuſtody untill give Suerties for his appearance the next Court and to be of good abearing in the meanetime and also^² the Court fines him
fine	Twenty Shillings

A Deed in fee of Two hundered forty five acres of Land dated the 7th day of
December 1697 was delivered by Joſeph Growdon grantor unto
Claws Jonſon grantee

A Deed in fee of Two hundered forty one acres of Land dated the firſt day
of the 5th month i697 was Delivered by Joſeph Growdon grantor
unto Leonard vandegreift grantee

A Deed of Two hundered and fifteen acres of Land in fee dated the —
firſt day of the 5th month 1697 was Delivered by Joſeph Growdon
grantor unto nicholas vandegrieft grantee

A Deed of one hundered and Six acres of Land dated the firſt day of the
5th month i697 was Delivered by Joſeph Growdon grantor unto —
ffrederick vandegreift grantee

A Deed of Two hundered Seventy one acres of Land in fee dated the
firſt day of the 5th month 1697 was Delivered by Joſeph Growdon
grantor unto Johannes vandegreift grantee

A Deed of one hundered and Six acres of Land in fee dated the firſt
day of the 5th month i697 was Delivered by Joſeph Growdon
grantor unto Jacob Groesbeck grantee

A Deed of one hundred and Six acres of Land in fee dated the firſt
day of the 5th month 1697 was delivered by Joſeph Growdon
grantor unto Barndt virkirk grantee

A Deed of Three hundered acres of Land in fee dated the 3 day of
the 10ᵗʰ month i697 was Delivered by John Rowland grantor
unto Daniel Burges grantee

A Deed of a lot of Land in fee lying in Buckingham dated the 7ᵗʰ
day of the 10ᵗʰ month 1697 was Delivered by John Town —
grantor unto Saml Beakes Attorney to Rebecca wilfford grantee

ordered that Phineas Pemberton Send the will of Richard Thatcher unto
the Govrnr being Regifter general

Action   David powel plt   ⎱   the plt appeared by his Attorney
                agt   ⎰   Andrew Heath
           Richard Davies Deft   the Defendant appeared not — —

                                                         299

Action ⎱ peter white for him Self and as Attorney for Jofeph ⎰ appeared
               Englifh   ⎰
Called — ⎰ Thomas Green and his wife Rachel plts — — —
           Richard noble deft appeared not — — — — — —
     default haveing been made three times

               Adjourned the Court untill 9 tomorrow morning

Declaracon being read is as follows

Bucks ff Jofeph Englifh peter white and Elizabeth his wife Thomas
     green and Rachel his wife complaines agt Richard noble of the
     Said County yeoman Adminiftrator of the Eftate which was of —
     Saml Clift late of the Said County hufbandman deceased of A —
     plea that whereas the Said Saml Clift in his Lifetime (to wit)
     on the 23 day of the 9ᵗʰ month in the yeare of our Lord 1682
     being very weake in body but of perfect Sence and memory
     did make his laft will and Teftament in writeing and after
     he had bequeathed Some Legacyes he thereby declared that as
     for his proper Eftate and houfeing and alfo his goods liveing &
     dead he freely gave unto his Son Jonathan Clift whome he
     left his Executor defireing Chriftopher Taylor and Richard noble
     to be his Truftees and over Seers for his Said Son as by the
     Said Laft will and Testement more fully appeares and fhortly
     after dyed after whofe deceafe the Said Christopher refufing to
     meddle with the Said Truft Adminiftracon of the Said Teftators
     goods & Chattles with his will annexed was Committed to the
     Said Richard noble by vertue whereof he the id deft did —
     poffeff him Self of the Said Teftator Samll Clifts Eftate real —
     and perfonal to the value of above Seventy Six pounds but

hath not diſtributed the Said Eſtate according to the direction
of the Said will nor rendered any account of his Adminiſt
ration Either to the ordinary or Regiſter general as he —
ought to have done and the plts in fact Say that the ſaid
Jonathan Cliſt Dyed Inteſtate haveing no Iſſue now Living
after whoſe deceaſe the Said Samll Cliſts Eſtate ought of
right to be diſtributed amongſt the plts being the next of
—kin or relation to the ſd decedents Samuel and Jonathan
Cliſt nevertheles the ſaid deft (Though often requeſted —
hath not delivered or given up the Said Eſtate to be diſtributed
as aforeſaid but detained and doth detaine the ſame in
his own hands and Converted to his own uſe to the plts damage
of 200£ and thereof they bring Suite &c:

The will of Samll Cliſt and ⎱ by which it appeared that there was due
the Inventory read ⎰   to the —
to the plts from the ſd Defts as he is Adminiſtrator of the ſd Cliſts,
Eſtate the Sum of thirty five pounds eight Shillings Six pence

Ralph Boome being then upon the plantation and Lands of Richard noble
the plts Crave that he may be Called into Court and ordered to
ſhew
if anything for Self he hath to Say or knoweth wherefore the
ſd plts ought not to have execution of the Lands of Richard
Noble then in

300   the poſſeſſion of the Sherrife as in the return of the Attachmt
So as
afore mentioned Attached
whereupon the Said Ralph Boome came and Said that he held the aboveſd
plantation and premiſes by vertue of an agreemt made by his
wifes
former huſband (namely John Allen) with one moſes maſley to
whom the ſaid premiſes was Sold by the ſd deft noble and by the
ſd masley mortgaged and reconveyed to the ſd deft for ſecurity of
the Conſideracon mony
whereunto the plts replye and produce A letter which the ſd Deft
Sent from
England unto Edmund Bennet intimateing that the ſd maſley
had not
wherewith to pay the Said mortgage mony therefore he the ſd
Deft
was Conſtrained to take back the Land and plantation aforeſd
inſtead
of his mony and So gave order to ſd Bennet to ſell the Same

All which being Seen by the Juſtices here fully underſtood

It was Conſidered by the Court that the Said plts Shall recover agt the
deft the Said 35 £ : 8ˢ-6ᵈ with Coſt of Suite and Shall have
Execucon for the Same to be Levied on the lands Tenements
and plantation (of the ſd Deft in the Townſhip of Buckingham
according to the Sherriffs return of the Attachment) So as aforeſd
Attached

And the Said peter white for him Self and the reſt of the plts did find
Suffitient Security to reſtore the ſd Lands unto the ſd Deft if he
with
in one yeare and a day Shall and will come and verefie by due —
Courſe of Law that the aforeſd plts theire action aforeſd ought
not
to have and mentaine (as ffolloweth)

Be it remembered that peter white for him ſelf and Elizabeth his wife
and for Joſeph Engliſh his father in law and for Thomas Green &
Rachel his wife did produce ffrancis white and John Smith for his
Security who recognized them ſelves (to wit) the ſaid peter
white in —
Sixty pounds and the Said ffrancis white and John Smith in —
Twenty pounds apeice to be levied on theire Lands and Tennemts
goods and Chattles for the uſe of Richard noble Adminiſtrator of
Samll Clift Deceaſed
upon Condition that if the Said Richard noble Shall come intoany of
the County Courts that Shall be held for the ſd County of Bucks
with
in one yeare and A day now next enſueing and diſprove or by
due Courſe of Law avoyd the damages So recovered by the ſaid
Joſeph Engliſh peter white and Elizabeth his wife Thomas
Green &
Rachel his wife as aforeſaid that then the Said Recoverers theire
heirs Executors or Aſſigns Shall reſtore the Lands and Tennemts
goods and Chattles which hath been Attached as aboveſaid and
Shall be taken and ſeized in Execucon to Satiſfy the ſaid recovery

A mortgage of the Lands and plantation Henry Baker now lives upon
was —
delivered by ſaid Baker mortgagor
unto phineas pemberton Attorney to Richard walter of Barbadoes
mortgagee   .

A Deed of Two hundered fifty Two acres of land in fee dated the firſt

day of the 8th month i697 was Delivered by Henry Baker grantor
unto Stephen wilſon grantee

Action ⎱ John Town plt ⎱ plt appeared and deſired the action to
Called ⎰   agt   ⎰ be with drawn
        Stephen newel deft

Adjourned the Court to the Court houſe

301

A Reconveyance of a Tract of land in fee of Six hundered and Sixteen
    acres and
    Two thirds of an acre wch was formerly granted by Henry Baker
        to John
    Harriſon was by the Said Harriſon reconveyed in fee and the
    Said Reconveyance was delivered by Joſeph milner Attorney to
        the ſd
    John Harriſon grantor unto the Said Henry Baker grantee

A Conveyance of Twenty five acres of Land in fee wch was formerly
        Conveyed to
    John Harriſon by Thomas Hudſon was reconveyed in ffee by ſaid
    Harriſon to Said Hudſon wch reconveyance was Delivered by —
    Joſeph milner Attorney to Said John Harriſon reconveyor
    unto the Said Thomas Hudſon by his Attorney william Biles

Action ⎱ Gilbert wheeler plt ⎱   ⎧ the plt appeared
Called ⎰   agt   ⎰ in an action upon ⎨ the deft did not appeare
        John Heeſum deft   the Caſe   ⎪ when Called but francis
                                                  ⎪ Tunneclift his ſecurity
                                                  ⎩ appeared and petitioned

to the Court as followeth that whereas he according to the baile –
    given did Attend with the deft & the action was Continued at the
    requeſt of the plt & the deft being now of the province prayed
        that the
    action might be Continued untill another Court

But it appearing by the Records of the Court that the ſd deft did not
    appeare when the action was Called and the plt Craveing Judgmt
    the Court rejected his petition

Declaracon being read as ffolloweth viz

Bucks ſſ Gilbert wheeler Complaines agt John Heeſum in a plea that
    he render unto him Ten pounds foure ſhillings & one penny w^{ch}
        he

unjustly detaines from him and for that whereas the faid John –
Heefum gave his bill under his Hand dated the 20 day of the 5ᵗʰ
month i697 to pay to the Said Gilbert wheeler the Said Sum of
Ten pounds foure Shillings and one penny upon demand as may
appeare by the Said bill herewith in Court to be produced as alfo
he the Said John Heefum hath bought and had at Sundry times
Since the date of the Said bill in meate drink and Lodging from
the fd Gilbert wheeler to the value of Seventeen fhillings foure
pence yet not withftanding the Said mony being in the whole —
Eleven pounds one fhilling and five pence hath been divers times
demanded from the Said John Heefum yet he hath hitherto
   refufed
to pay the Same and ftill doth refufe whereupon the Said Gilbert
wheeler brings this action and Craves Judgment of this Court –
agt the fd John Heefum for the Said Sum of Ten pounds foure
Shillings and one penny as alfo for the faid Sum of Seventeen
Shillings and foure pence with damages and Coft of Suite &c:

The bill mentioned in the aforefd declaracon read

witnefes Richard Bull ⎱ attefted to the truth thereof
            william Taylor ⎰

The Account alfo read and Gilbert wheeler Attefted to the truth thereof
   and that he Cold not give any Credit towardd the fd bill or the
   fd account

It was Confidered by the Court that the Said plt Shall recover agt
   the Said John Heefum the Said Sum of Eleven pounds one
   Shillings and five pence with Coft of Suite and that Execution
      Iffue
   accordingly

Action ⎱ Samll Beakes plt   both appeared and defired that the
Called ⎰   agt   action depend
         Richard Thatcher deft   ing between them might be reffered to
                                      be arbitra
                                    ted by william embley Jofeph wood and
                                       George
                                    Brown and both declared they wold
                                       ftand to theire
                                    award or the award of any two of
                                       them to
                                    wᶜʰ the Court affented

302   whereupon the Said Arbitrators takeing upon them the Said Charge
       report

to the Court that they have awarded the Said Richard Thatcher Shall pay to
the Said Samll Beaks the Sum of Two pounds and both plt and deft -- declared theire Satiffaction therewith

whereupon the Said Samuel Beakes defired Judgmt of the Court for the Same and that Execution might Iffue accordingly

wherefore It being Confidered by the Court that the Same Judgment of the arbitrators was done according to theire request and Satiffaction the Court awarded Judgmt that the Said Richard Thatcher Shold pay to the Said Samll Beakes the Said Sume of forty Shillings and that Execution Iffue accordingly

Richard Burges being brought into Court Selling of his wife and other mifdemeanors and Contempts

The Court Committs him the Said Burges into the Sherrifts Cuftody untill he Shall find Suerties for his appearance at the next Court and to be of good abearing in the meane time

James Alman being prefented by the grand Jury Laft Court for — hindering the Sherrife and Conftable in the due execution of theire office and the Said Alman being brought before the Court and the Said prefentment read to him he Submitted to the Court

whereupon the Court difcharged him paying his fees

Recognizance   Richard Burges acknowledges him Self Indebted to the proprietarie
in the Sum of thirty pounds and Henry Margorm of the aforefd —
County and Andrew Heath of the Same in Ten pounds apeice to be —
Levied on theire Lands and Tennements goods and Chattles
And this is upon Condition that the Said Richard Burges Shall appeare at the next Court of Quarter Seffions to be held for this
County then and there to anfwer Such matters of mifdemeanor as
Shall then and there be objected againft him and to abide the Judgmt
of the Said Court and to be of good abearing in the meane time

A Deed of the moiety of the Land plantation and other premifes in fee mentioned

in the Said deed Dated the 4th day of the 10th month i697 was—
Delivered by Robert Lucas grantor unto his brother Edward
    Lucas
grantee

A Deed of Two hundered forty foure acres of Land and premifes with
    Some exceptions in the Same in fee dated the 6th day of the
    i0th month
    1697 was Delivered by Elizabeth Lucas Giles Lucas and
    Edward Lucas
grantors unto Robert Lucas grantee

ordered that the Sherrife get the Court Staires repaired or made new
    and Two of the windows of the Court houfe glazed and one of
    them Shut up and the north end plaftered and that the Same
    be pd
for out of the County ftock

Recognrz Thomas Archer Acknowledges him felf Indebted in Twenty
    pounds and Edward
    Doyl in five pounds unto the proprietarie to belevied on their
    Lands
    and Tennements goods and Chattles
    And this is upon Condition that the fd Thomas Archer Shall
    appeare
    at the next Court of Quarter Seffions to be held for this
    County and to
    be of good abearing in the meanetime

upon Complt of Samll Beake Sherrife agt Richard Thatcher how
    that the
    Said Thatcher Stood in debted to him the fum of Two pounds –
    Seventeen Shillings and eight pence due to him for fees in
    fundry Cafes

303

    before this Court and Craved Judgmt of this Court
whereupon the Court being full Satiffyed of the Same Iwas
    Confidered that
    the Said Samuel Beakes Shold recover the Said Sum of
    2£ : 17s : 8d and
    that Execution Iffue accordingly

ordered that phineas pemberton write to Samuel Carpenter Executor
    of

ffrancis Roffill that it is the Courts requeft that he wold
pay to Edward Doyl Twenty Shillings and to James Sutton
Twenty
Shillings out of the Legacy left to the poore of this County
by the
Said ffrancis Roffill

Adjourned the Court unto the Second weekly fourth day in
the firft month next

Action Entered the 2i day of the i2ᵗʰ mo: $\frac{1697}{8}$

Richard Burges plt agt Henry paxfon deft in a plea

Summonce thereupon granted the 22 day of the i2ᵗʰ month 1697/8

Bucks ff   At a Court of Quarter Seffions held in the name
of William Penn proprietarie and Govrnr of the
province of penfylvania and Territories thereunto
belonging at the Court houfe for the aforefaid
$\frac{7}{}$
County the 9ᵗʰ day of the firft month i698

Juftices prefent

Jofeph Growdon william Biles   Richard Hough

Samuel Beakes Sherrife and deputy Cl: Com:

Action   David powel agt Richard Davies Continued untill next Court
at the requeft of plt and
deft   Court ajourns to the houfe of Jofeph Chorley one houre
hence
whereas there was an Ececution granted ffor the Leviing of the
fum
of Eleven pounds one Shilling five pence which Gilbert
wheeler —
recovered by Judgmt in a Court of Quarter Seffions held for
the afrefd
County the 8ᵗʰ day of the 10ᵗʰ month laft paft with 2£ : 11ˢ: 6ᵈ
with Coft of
Suite

Return upon the Said Execution was made viz

Bucks ff There is no Effects of goods nor Chattles of yᵉ with in
John —

Heeſum to be found with in the aforeſd County

The 9th of $\frac{i}{mo}$ $\frac{1697}{8}$ p me Saml Beakes

whereas execution was granted agt John Rowland for the
    Leviing of A
    fine of three pounds Impoſed upon him the 9th day of the 4th
        month laſt
    paſt dated the 20th day of the ſd 4th month

Return was made upon the ſd Execution as followeth

    Bucks ſ̃ by vertue of the within there is taken one Cow of the
        Goods of
    . John Rowland the 7th day of the 6th month i697
                                p Saml Beakes ſherrife

    Bucks ſ̃ The above ſaid Cow was Sold at an out cry unto
        Thomas Brock
        for Two pounds and Two ſhillings the 9th day of the i0th
        month i697
                                p Saml Beakes Sherrife

grand Jury Joſuah Hoops John palmer willm Dark John Croſdel ⎫
    Jeremiah Langhorn   John Smith   Stephen Beakes   ⎪
        Samll Hough —   ⎬
    Daniel Done   Enock yardley   willm Duncan   Stephen   ⎪
        Twineing —   ⎪
    Thomas kirle   James moone — all of them Atteſted   ⎭

304

A Deed of A Certaine Tract of Land in fee dated the 14th day of
    february i697
    was Delivered by Joſeph wood Attorney to Elizabeth Bennet
        grantor
    unto Joſeph Taylor Subſtitute Attorney to Barbery Blayden
        grantee

A Deed of Sixty acres of Land in ſee Dated the 9th day of the firſt
    month
    1698 was Delivered by John Scarbrough grantor unto Thomas
    Bayns grantee

Action } Richard Burges plt }
Called }   agt   } in A plea { both appeared
           Henry paxſon deft }

declaracon Read

Anſwer the plt Saith he is not Guilty and thereof for tryal puts him
      ſelf
      upon the Cuntry and So doth the plt whereupon the ſherriſe is
venire   Commanded to return A Jury

Jury Thomas Stakehouſe   Joſeph kirkbride   } all
     Edward Lucas
James yates John Scarbrough Robt Heaton   }
     Thomas Bayns
Clement Dungan Joſeph milner   Samuel Dark }
     wm: Dark Jos: Wood   } atteſted

Declarcon againe Read

Action Continued at the requeſt of the plt & by the Conſent of the
     Deft untill
     the next Court

Complt was made by Henry paxſon that Richard Burges Did not take
     Suitable Care to mentaine his wife

Anſwer the Said Burges promiſed the Court to allow his wife such &
     So much as this Court Shall order him towards a mentainance

A Deed of about Sixty acres of Land be it more or leſs in fee dated
     the 9th day of the 8th month i697 was Delivered by Joſuah Hoops
     Attorney to James Dilworth grantor unto Thomas Stakehouſe
     Attorney to
     martin wildman grantee

Information being given to the Court agt Richard Thather the he had
     Sworn and Curſed & otherwiſe broke the kings peace
ordered that A warrant be Iſſued out to apprehend the ſaid Thatcher
     to make anſwer to the Same

Court Adjourned untill 8 a Clock in the morning

grand Jurys prſentment brought in agt nathaniel walton
     nathaniel walton being Called appeares
     Barndt virkirk proſecutor appeared

preſent ment as follows being read

Bucks ſſ we the grand Jury for the body of the County do prſent nathaniel
walton for takeing and Converting to his own uſe onw Sow Swine
of the proper goods of Barndt virkirks the i8ᵗʰ day of the i2 month
i697 Conterary to the kings peace and Law of this province

Joſuah Hoops   foreman

prſoner being Arraigned pleaſed not guilty and for tryal put him
ſelf upon the Cuntry whereupon the Sherrife was Commanded to
venire   return Twelve honeſt men of the neighbourhood
Jury   Thomas ſtakehouſe Joſeph kirkbride Edward Lucas James Yates
John ſcarbrough   Robert Heaton   Thomas Baines   Clement
Dungan
Joſeph milner   Samuel Dark   william Dark   Joſeph Wood
all Atteſted

The prſentment proved by Barndt virkirk and John Gilbert both Atteſt

Jury Returned   Adjourned the Court for one houre

prſoner brought to the barr

305

Jury   ⎰delivers in theire verdict we find the prſoner guilty as he ſtands –
verdict-⎱Indicted

It is therefore Conſidered by the Court that nathaniel walton pay to
Barndt virkirk Twenty foure Shillings he being therewith ſatiſfyed
and the Coſt of Suite and that Execucon Iſſue accordingly

Andrew Heath being prſented by the Jury ſubmits to the bench
whereupon
the Court fines him 10ˢ and Discharges him paying the fees

nathaniel walton Discharged by proclamation

Adjourned the Court untill the i4ᵗʰ day of the 2 next
mo

10ᵗʰ day 1 1697 Execucon granted agt the Land of Richard noble in Engliſh
mo 8
and whites Caſe returnable to Seventh month Court next

Action Entered the 26ᵗʰ i 1698
mo

Thomas kirle plt   ⎫
        agt   ⎬ in an action of Treſpas upon the Caſe
Andrew Heath deft   ⎭

Arreſt thereupon granted agt the body of Andrew Heath the 29th day $\frac{1}{mo}$ 1698

return made by Samll Beakes Sherrife that he had taken the body of the ſd
Heath the 30th day of the $\frac{1}{mo}$ 1698

At a Court held by Ajournment the i4th day of the
2nd month 1698

Juſtices preſent

Joſeph Growdon william Biles Richard Hough
Samuel Beakes Sherrife and Deputy Cl: Com:

Action Called

Thomas kirle plt
        agt   } in an action of Treſpaſe { plt appeared }
Andrew Heath deft   } upon the Caſe   { deft appeared }

Declaracon read

Anſwer that the plt did not pforme on his pte whileſt he the deft was
in a Capacity to pforme and that he is now diveſted of his Truſt and
Cannot performe the Conditions menconed in the ſd Declaracon and
of

Iſſue – this puts him Self upon the Cuntry and So doth the plt whereupon
the

venire – Sherrife is Commanded to return Twelve honeſt men of the vicinage
by whom the Truth of the matter may be the better known –

Jury – Samuel Dark   Robt Heaton   Thomas Stakehouſe
        John palmer   all
Jeremiah Langhorn   william Dark   Stephen Beakes
        Ralph Cowgill
william Duncan   John neild   william Croſdel   Atteſted
        Joſeph Chorley

Declaracon Read as follows

Action of Treſpaſs in Caſe agt Andrew Heath Treſpaſſer to Thomas kirle plt
and the Said Thomas kirle Compts that the ſd Andrew Heath by his
promiſe and agreement made with the Said Thomas kirle the 9th day
of the 10th month 1697 did bargaine and Sell unto the Said Thomas –
kirle his Heirs and Aſſigns forever Two hundered and fourteen acres
of Land part of the Land on which the Said Andrew Heath did
then live

to be Laid out at the back part of the aforeſd Lot for and in
Conſideracon
of the Sum of forty five pounds Currant ſilver mony of this province
of penſylvania to be paid unto the Said Andrew Heath his Heirs or –
Aſſigns and untill the Said time of payment to pay Lawfull Intreſt
for the
Same from the 25 day of the firſt month Called march laſt paſt in
part
of which Sum of forty five pounds the ſd Thomas kirle did then
and there
pay the Said Andrew Heath the Sum of Six Shillings which he the
ſd Andrew Heath

306   Received as Such and promiſed he wold make unto the Said Thomas
      kirle
a good title to the Said 214 acres of Land all which the Said Thomas
kirle is ready to prove and make appeare in Court yet notwiſtanding
the promiſes the ſaid Andrew Heath Craftily and fraudulently
    Intending
to Deceive the ſaid Thomas kirle hath refuſed and hitherto
doth refuſe to layout the ſaid Land or ſuffer it to be done unto the ſd
Thomas kirle or to make him a title to the ſame though often
thereunto required whereby the ſd Thomas kirle ſaith he is worſe
and hath damage to the value of ninety pounds and therefore
&c: Craves Judgmt of this Court for the ſd Sum with Coſt of ſuite

Anſwer   ⎫
Andrew Heath ⎬ for his plea agt kirl Saith
   ⎭

           That being requeſted by his Daughters in Law
to sell the Said 214 acres of Land &c: he acknowledges the
    Conditions in
ſd Declaracon menconed and was accordingly on ſd 25ᵗʰ day of
    march
laſt paſt ready to have pformed the Conditions but ſd kirle the plt –
brought neither deed to be ſigned nor Conſideracon mony nor –
offered any Security for the ſame and ſince the ſd Andrew is –
diveſted of his Truſt and is in no Capacity to pforme the Conditions
&c: and of this put him ſelf upon the Cuntry and ſo doth the plt

witneſes Atteſted Andrew Ellot ⎫
           & ⎬ for the plt –
Joſeph Henbery ⎭

⎧ John Gilbert   Jonathan ſcaiſe
⎨ Edmund Lovet ſtephen Beaks
⎩ Andrew Ellot wm Buckman

Aſſeſſors appointed for this preſent yeare – – –

Court Adjourned for one houre

Recognizance Richard Thatcher being Called upon his Recognizance
      appeared not
      the Court being informed that he was Sick ordered that he —
      appeare at the next Court

one Letter of Attorney from Thomas Hudſon to Impower william Biles
      to ſell his Land in this province bearing date the i8 day of Auguſt
      was brought before the Court and was there approved and allowed

Jury returned

      verdict finds for the plt i5 £ Damages with coſt of ſuite
      Appeale from which verdict the deft appealed to the next provincial
         Court in Equity

Recognizance Andrew Heath and Richard wilſon became bound unto Thomas
      kirle in the Sum of fifty pounds on Condition that the ſd Andrew
      Heath Shall proſecute his appeale at the next provencial Court
      and pay the Charge of the ſd Court if he Shall be Caſt

Action ⎫ David powel agt Richard Davies neither plt nor deft appeared
Called ⎬   when Called
               Court Adjourns untill the 2ⁿᵈ wekly 4ᵗʰ day in the 4
                     next   mo

action entered the 31 day 3 1698 Joſeph Chorley agt Henry warwin
      action upon   mo

      the Caſe Replevin thereon granted

Bucks ſſ

Sherriſs return
that he had replevined
on horſe of sd warwins
and ſummonced ſd
warwin to appeare at
the next Court –
dated the 1 day of the
4th month 1698 –

} At a Court of Quarter Seſſions held in the name

of william penn proprietarie and Governor of the

province of penſylvania and Territories thereunto –

belonging at the Court houſe for the aforeſd
    County the

8th day of the 4th month 1698

The Juſtices present

8th month 1698

Samll Jerrome plt
agt
Andrew Heath deft

}

william Biles Henry Baker   Richard Hough
    John Swift
Jonathan Scaife Corronor
Samuel Beakes Sherrife
Phineas Pemberton Cl: Com:

Arreſt granted
with drawn ___ }

Juſtices Commiſſion Read

proclamation from the Govrnrs for the Apprehending of all
    pirates
privateers and Sea rovers was read

307

A Deed of one hundered acres of Land in fee dated the firſt day of the –
    10th month i697 was Delivered by Jane Chapman grantor unto willm
    Smith grantee

Adjourned the Court for one houre

petition of James kirkham agt his maſter Samuel oldale read
    the ſd Samll oldale being Called in Court and Examined upon the
    Same and the Juſtices being fully informed thereof the Conſidered

order the premiſes and ordered that Said oldale Receive his Said ſervant
    kirkham againe into his Service and defray his Charges dureing
    his Sickness and pay the Said kirkham wages for the time he —
    Served according to his agreement

A Deed of three hundered acres of Land in fee Dated the iith day of

the 10th month 1697 was Delivered by Jonathan Scaife attorney
to Richard Burges and his wife Elizabeth grantors unto Iſrael
morris and Edmund Cowgill grantees

A Deed of Two hundered forty foure acres of Land in fee Dated
the 12th day of the 8th month 1697 was Delivered by william Croſdel
Attorney to James Dilworth grantor unto Robert
Heaton grantee

A Deed of three hundered and forty acres of Land in fee Dated the firſt
day of the 10th month 1697 was Delivered by Saml Beakes –
Attorney to nicholas waln grantor unto Robert Heaton grantee

A Deed of Two hundered eighty Six acres of Land in fee Dated the 8th
day of the fourth month i698 was Delivered by James paxſon   ·
grantor unto his william paxſon grantee

A Deed in of five hundered acres of Land in fee Dated the i2th day of
the 8th month 1697 was Delivered by Samuel Beakes Attorney
to Daniel Jones grantor unto Daniel Smith grantee

Joſeph Smalwood being bound over by Recognizance to Appear at this
Court for beating and abuſeing his wife and it appearing to this
Court that he had ſince threatened her to do her further miſheiſe

Comitmt the Court Commits him into the Sherrifs Cuſtody untill he give —
Security for his appearance at the next Court and to be of good
abearing in the meane time

Richard Thatcher being Called into Court upon his Recognizance
it being made appeare by the Teſtemony of James mills &
John Clark that he Swore 4 times by the name of god the
fine   Court fines him in 20^s and orders that he pay Coſts

Action	Joſeph Chorley plt	in an action upon	plt appeared
	agt	the Caſe	
Called	Henry warwin deft		deft appeared not

Action Continued untill the next Court being the firſt default

Adjourned the Court unto the houſe of Joſeph Chorley

Same Examinations taken about venables and Barrets Land

Adjourned the Court untill the 14th day of the 7th month next

308

Actions Continued untill the next Court

Action Joſeph Chorley plt ⎫
                  agt   ⎬ in an action upon the Caſe
        Henry warwin deft ⎭

Actions entered for the next Court 20th day of the 4th month <u>1698</u>

        ffrancis white plt ⎫ ,
                  agt   ⎬ in an action of Treſpas upon the Caſe
        James Alman deft ⎭

Replevin thereupon granted the 20 day of the 4 month 1698

Sherrifs return that he had Attached one gelding

    Entered the 13 day 6th month 1698

        Thomas Gardiner plt ⎫
                  agt   ⎬ in an action of Treſpaſs and Aſſault
        Samll oldale deft -- ⎭

Arreſt thereupon granted the 13 day of the 6th month 1698

        return made Samll oldale was Arreſted the i3 day <u>6</u> 1698
                                                           mo

                p Samll Beaks ſherf

    Entered the 13 day <u>6</u> i698
                         mo

        Thomas Gardiner plt ⎫
                  agt   ⎬ in an action of Treſpas upon
        Chriſtopher Snowdon deft ⎭ the Case

Arreſt thereupon granted the i3 day of 6th month i698

Return Chriſtopher Snowdon was Arreſted the 16th day of the
    <u>6</u> i698
    mo

    Entered the 30 day of the 6th month 1698

        Edward Hunlock plt ⎫
                  agt   ⎬ in an action of Treſpaſs upon the
        John pidcock deft ⎭ Caſe

    Summonce thereupon granted

return that he was Summonced

Entered the 30th day 6th month i698

    John grey als Tatham plt ⎤

              agt   ⎬ in an action of Debt

    Robt Cole & ⎫

    Joſeph wood ⎭ defts ⎦

    Summonce thereupon granted

return that Joſeph wood was ſummonced Robt Cole not to be found

Entered the 30th day 6th mo 1698

    John Grey also Tatham plt ⎤

         agt   ⎬ in an action upon the Caſe

    Joſeph Growdon deft – ⎦

    Summonce thereupon granted the 2 day 7th mo 1698

    returned ſummonced

Entered the i day of the 7th mont 1698

    James Alman plt ⎤

        agt   ⎬ in an action upon the Case

    John Rowland deft ⎦

    Summonce thereupon granted

    return that he was Summonced

309

Bucks ſſ   At a Court of Quarter ſeſſions held in the name of william penn proprietaries and — Govrnr of the province of penſylvania and Territories thereunto belonging at the Court houſe for the aforeſaid County the i4th day of the 7th month 1698

The Juſtices preſent

Joſeph Growdon william Biles Richard Hough John Swift

    Jonathan Scaife Corronor

    Samull Beakes Sherrife

    Phineas Pemberton Cl: Com:

grand Jury Joſhuah Hoops Peter worral John Surket willm Duncan
John Croaſdel Robt Heaton Ruben pownal william Buckman

atteſted   Samll Coates Jeremiah Langhorn John white Giles Lucas –
Thomas kirle william paxſon william Hayhurſt all atteſted

Return of an Execution granted agt the Goods Chattles and Land of
Richard Thatcher to Satifye Two Judgmts obtained by Samll –
Beakes as ffollows –

Bucks ff by vertue of the within Execucon the Land of Richard
Thatcher Lying neare neſhaminah Creek at or neare the pines –
was taken the 3 day of the 7th month i698

p Saml Beakes ſherrife

Return of an Execution granted agt the Lands of Richard noble
to Satiffie A Judgment obtained in A Court held for this –
County the 8th day of the 10th month Laſt paſt as follows
by Jos Engliſh peter white and Elizabeth Thomas Green and Rachel

Bucks ff   Theſe are to Certefie that I have Cauſed the meſſuage
Land and plantation with in mentioned to be apprized by –
Twelve honeſtmen of the neigh bourhood as within I
am Commanded which meſſuage Lands and plantation remaines
unſold for want of buyers and I am ready to Deliver the ſame
premiſes to the Creditors as within I am required the Reſidue of
the Execucon of this writ Lyes in a schedule Certefied under
my hand the Twenty ninth day of auguſt 1698

valued by the apprizors at 200£   Samuell Beakes ſherrife

A Deed of three hundered acres of Land in fee Dated the 1 day of
the fifth month 1698 was Delivered by Joſeph Chorley Attorney
to william Smith grantor unto Thomas Brock grantee

A Deed of a lot of Land in Buckingham about eight acres in fee
Dated the 1 day of the 6th month i698 was Delivered by –
Thomas Brock grantor unto Phineas Pemberton Attorney
to Samuel Carpenter grantee

Adjourned the Court for one houre

310

A Deed of Two hundered acres of Land in fee Dated the 2 day of the
2nd month 1698 was Delivered by Clement Dungan

Thomas Dungan Jeremiah Dungan and John Dungan
grantor unto walter pomphray grantee

A Deed of one hundered acres of Land in fee Dated the 22 day of the
5th month 1698 was Delivered by Clement Dungan Jeremiah
Dungan and John Dungan grantor unto Thomas Dungan
theire brother grantee

A Deed of five hundred eighty Two acres of Land in fee Dated the
7th day of the iith month 1698 was Delivered by John fwift
Attorney to Thomas ffaireman grantor unto James plumley
grantee

A Deed of Two hundered and fifty acres of Land in fee Dated the 28th
day of the 3 month 1698 was Delivered by John Swift
Attorney to James Jacob grantor unto nicholas Randol
grantee

A Deed of Two hundered and fifty acres of Land in fee dated the
30th day of July i696 was Delivered by John Swift Attorney
to phillip Howel mary peart and Thomas peart grantors
unto James Jacob grantee

A Deed of Two Lotts of Land in ffee Lying in Buckingham Dated
the 5th day of the 5th month 1698 was Delivered by Anthony
Burton grantor unto Jeremiah Dungan grantee

Recogniz: Jofeph Smallwood appeared in Court according to his Recognizance but the Court did not think fitt to difcharge him untill
they had further Considered of it

Action John Tatham plt
Called   agt   } in an action of debt { plt appeared
         Robert Cole   Jofeph wood
             &   } deft   appeared
         Jofeph Wood

The Declaracon being Read the Said Jofeph wood one of
the plts Confeffed that there was due to the Said John –
Judgmt Tatham from his father in law Robt Cole for which he the fd
wood ftood bound with his fd father in law to the fd plant the
Sum of Sixty five pounds fiveteen fhillings foure pence
It was Therefore Confidered by the Court that the Said
plt Shold recover agt the fd Defts the Said Sum of 65£ : 15s : 4d
with Coft of fuite and that Execution Iffue accordingly

Action   Thomas Gardiner plt ⎫   ⎧ plt ⎫
                agt   ⎬in an action of Trespaſs⎱ ⎰ & ⎬appeared
          Samuel Oldale deft   ⎭   & aſſault — — —⎰ ⎱ deft ⎭

declaracon Read whereupon the defts Attorney Inſtits upon the ſtatute
2i James i2 but waived pleading the general Iſſue as the ſtatute –
directs but after Some debate both parties agreed to deferr any
further proceedings untill tomorrow morning

Adjourned the Court untill 9 a Clock in the morning

311

At which time the ſd plt and Deft being Called and both appeared
and. Some things being offered agt the Tryal the Caſe In this
Court the Court thereupon Continued the action untill the Juſtices
Shold adviſe thereupon and the Defts baile is Continued to anſwer
to the action and to abide the Judgmt of the next Court

Action   Thomas Gardiner plt ⎫   ⎧ plt ⎫
Called   agt   ⎬in an action ⎱ ⎰ & ⎬both —   ⎫
          Chriſtopher Snowden deft⎭ upon the Caſe ⎱ deft ⎭appeared ⎰

The Same things being offered agt the Tryal of the ſd action
in this Court as in the other this action was alſo Continued
untill the Juſtices Shold adviſe thereupon and the baile in like –
manner Continued Except they put in other baile

Action ⎱ John Grey alis Tatham plt⎫   ⎧ plt ⎫
Called ⎰   agt   ⎬in an action ⎱ ⎰ & ⎬both appeared
          Joſeph Growdon deft - - ⎭ upon the Caſe ⎱ deft ⎭

Declaracon being read and the action depending upon Some accts
both plt and deft requeſted that the accts might be firſt audited
and Requeſted that Thomas Revel and willm Biles may have the
auditing of the ſd accts and that if they Cannot agree thereupon
Edward Shippen may have the Concluſion thereof of wᶜʰ the
Court Allowed and
ordered accordingly and that they make report of theire doings therein
unto the next Court to be held here in the next 10ᵗʰ month –

action   Edward Hunloke plt ⎫   ⎧ plt ⎫
Called   agt   ⎬in an action of Treſpas⎱ ⎰ & ⎬appeared
          John pikcock deft   ⎭ upon the Caſe   ⎱ deft ⎭

Declaracon read and the deft acknowledged that he had the goods &
Chattles declared for of the Eſtate of Bowmans and promiſed
to yeild up the Same to the plt he the ſd plt paying the funeral
Charges of the ſd Bowman and Attendance in his Sicknes and
The Court haveing heard the premiſes Conſidered that the
plt Shold recover agt the deft the Eſtate of the ſd Bowman
that Came to the hands and poſſeſſion of the ſd deft in the life
time of the ſd Bowman and at his deceaſe and that the plt
Shold pay to the ſd deft nine pounds five Shillings Six pence
for funeral Charges and that the deft deliver up all writeings
books papers or accounts that were in his hands or poſſeſſion
or that he Cold get into his poſſeſſion that did any way relate
to the ſd Thomas Bowman deceaſed and that the deft pay Coſt
of ſuite

And the ſd deft promiſed to yeild and deliver up what he had in
his poſſeſſion to the plt or his order Except the books papers or,
other writeings which he had and thoſe he promiſed to deliver to
willm Biles one of the Juſtices of peace then upon the bench
for the uſe of the ſd plt

Court adjourns for one houre

A Deed of Three hundered and fifty acres of land in fee dated the 25th
day of April 1698 was Delivered by Samll Beakes Attorney
to Henry flower grantor unto Thomas Hardin grantee

312

| Action
Called | James Alman plt
agt
John Rowland Deft | in an action of Treſpas
upon the Caſe | plt
&
deft | appeared |

declaracon Read the plt and Deft deſired that the actions depending might
be arbitrated by Joſeph kirkbride and James paxſon to wch the —
Court Conſented and appointed Richard Hough as umpire to End
what they Cold not agree upon viz the arbitrators and they
promiſed
to pforme what they Shold award (viz the plt and deft) relateing
to the ſaid Complt then brought into Court by the plt & deft And
the Court
ordered that the ſd awarders make report of theire doings therein
unto the next Court to be held in the 10th month next

Action ⎫ ffrancis white plt ⎫
Called ⎰   agt   ⎬ in an action of Trefpas ⎰ plt & deft ⎬ appeared
James Alman deft ⎭ upon the Cafe

Declaration read as follows

> ffrancis white Complaines agt James Alman of the County of
> Bucks aforefaid in an action of Trefpafs upon the Cafe for that
> whereas the Said ffrancis white was poffeffed of one nag or gelding
> about foure yeares of age neare a Cheftnut Coulour with a Small
> blaze down
> his face being parted neare the middle with other Coloured haire
> a little white Spot on the fitlock upon the right foot behind –
> a Smal half penny Cut neare the middle of the right Eare
> upon the under fide and branded whileft he was out of the Cuftody
> of the fd plt: worth three pounds Ten fhillings which nag or
> gelding
> doth properly belong to the faid plt
> and Altho the faid deft was fufitiontly
> informed thereof yet notwithftanding
> the Said James Alman devifeing to deceive the fd plt: of the fd
> nag or gelding
> him did take keep ufe and Convert to his own ufe Conterary to
> the ftatute Laws of this province whereupon the fd plt Saith he
> is damnified three pounds Ten
> Shillings and thereupon produceth this fuite and Craves Judgmt
> of this Court for the fd damages and Coft of fuite &c:

Anfwer the deft pleaded not guilty and for tryal puts him felf upon the
Cuntry and fo doth the plt whereupon the Sherrife is Commanded

venire to return Twelve honeft men of the neighbourhood by whom
the truth of the matter may be the better known

Jury ⎫ Jofeph milner Anthony Burton Henry Margerum Edmund
returnd ⎬ Lovet
Attefted ⎭ Edward Lucas walter pomphray William Dark John Shaw –
John Stakehoufe Jacob Janney Thomas Janney all attefted

wittnefes Attefted for the plt

> Elizabeth white Attefted doth Say as to the horfe declared for She
> knew him from a Colt and that Shee knew his Sucking of her
> Son ffrancis Whites mare

> peter white Attefted doth Say that he knew him from a Sucking
> Colt and that he hath a Small blaze down his face and a Smal

White Spot upon his nofe of a Chefnut Colour about the latter
End of this Summer foure yeares of age

John Cartor Attefted doth say he knew the fd horse from about
a month old and that he hath know him all along untill this
time being about foure yeares of age of a Chefnut Colour with a
blaze
down his face parted in the middle of the face with haire of the
Colour of his body

313

william Codery Attefted doth Say that he being Servant to the fd plt he
knew
of the takeing up the mare and the Colt the Colt being the horfe
now
declared for and that he took Care of it and gave it meale one ─,
winter, and that he helped to marked it with a Smal half peny cut
under the right Eare and to the Colour and blaze as above

John plumley Attefted doth Say that he knew the horfe from a Colt and
that he was always Called by the name of ffrancis white Colt and
afterward by his horfe and alfo Spoke to the Colour and blaze as
above

witnefes Attefted for the deft

william Biles Junr: Attefted doth Say that he Chalenged the horfe
when
he was a Colt and that he had fo done and known him yearly
Ever fince and did take him up and brand him and that he ─
heard ffrancis white Say that the horfe that he now Claimes
to the beft of his knowledg had Two half peny cuts

John Biles Attefted Say that he Eare marked a Colt which is as ─
likely to be the Same horfe now in Controverfie as its poffible
a Colt Can be like to a horfe

Samll Beakes Attefted doth Say that about the 22 or 23 day of the
5th mo: laft paft being at ffrancis whites there was A young
mare that fd white told him was marked at the fame time
when the aforefd horfe was Eare marked which marked with
Two half peny cuts and he afked why they were diferently
marked and Said white Said that he might know them the one
from the other

Jeremiah Dungan Saith that he knew george Biles mare and knew

Shee was Drowned and Saw the Colt and it was lame & poore

Edward Mayos Attefted Saith he and John Cook riding up Cooks run found a Colt that was fo weak and poore it Cold not Stand tho they helped it up whereupon faid Cook Said it was George Biles Colt and knockt it on the head and kild it becaufe they thought it Cold not live

John Addington Attefted Saith that william Biles Chalenged a horfe at grace Langhorns of about 3 years of age that was then unearemarked

Richard Thatcher Attefted Saith that George Biles Told him his Colt had mealy Sides and muffel

verdict Jury returned finds for the deft:

Grand Jury Complaines that Clement Dungan and John Gilbert Collectors of the late Tax have not brought in theire duplicates and made up theire accounts of the Tax its therefore

ordered that warrantes be Iffued for bringing in the fd Collectors to this Court to anfwer the fd neglect

A Deed or Indenture } of the moiety of Sundry Lots and parcels of Land mils and buildings premifes and appurtenances therein mentioned in fee Dated the 3 day of the 7th month i698 was Delivered by — Phineas Pemberton Attorney to Samuel Carpenter grantor unto Henry Baker grantee

The Counter part thereof was Likewife delivered by the aforefaid — Henry Baker unto the aforefaid Phineas Pemberton for the ufe of the aforefaid Samuel Carpenter

314

Action Called } Jofeph Chorley plt— agt Henry warwin deft } in an action upon the Cafe { plt appeared / deft appeared not

It being the Second Default

A Deed of Three hundered acres of Land in fee Dated the firft day of the 7th month 1698 was Delivered by Henry Baker grantor unto william Biles grantee

Recogniz: george Randol being Called upon his Recognizance appeared nothing further appearing againſt the Said george Randol the Court diſcharges him paying his fees

grand Jurys preſentmts

Ralph Boome prſented for aſſaulting the Sherrife and Conſtable in the Execution of theire office

Bucks ſſ we the grand Jury haveing veiued the County accounts and do find the County in debt and do preſent the neceſſity of raiſeing one peny the pound Tax for defraying the Charge

Joſuah Hoops foreman

The neceſſity of A road from Thomas kirls houſe to the kings road

The neceſſity of Every freeholder to have a diſtinct Eare mark

Bucks ſſ we the grand Jury for the body of this County do preſent ffrancis
white for ſtrikeing John Addington one blow

Joſuah Hoops foreman

A Deed of one hundered and fifty acres of Land in fee dated the 25th day of the 4th month i698 was Delivered by Samll Beakes Attorney to Bartholemew Thather and Joſeph Thatcher grantors
unto Robt Heaton grantee
Samll Beakes Complaines againſt John Stork how that he was taken up as A run away and has made an Eſcape from him and

Complt – how that there was fees due to him and others for the takeing of
him up to the value of 2£ –5ˢ –6ᵈ as p his pticulers wᶜʰ
was allowed of by this Court and the Court awarded Execution
agt: the goods and Chattles of ſd Stork for satisfyeing the ſd Charge

over ſeeres of the high ways appointed for the Succeeding yeare

Buckingham	Thomas Brock
ffalls _ _ _ _ _ _ _	Joſeph kirkbride
makefeild _ _ _ _	Joſeph milner
middle Town _ _ _	Henry Hudleſtone

new Town
&   } James yates
Wrights Town

Benſalem _ _ _ _ ffrancis ſearle

Southhampton
&   } John Eaſtbourn
Warminſter

Conſtables for the ſucceeding yeare

Buckingham — — — Thomas yardley
ffalls — — — — peter webſter
makefeild — — — Thomas Janney
middle Town — — Edward Cartor
new Town
&   } _ _ _Samll Hough
wrights Town

Benſalem — — — nicholas vandegreift
Southhampton & warminſter John Eaſtbourn

315

ffrancis white being prſented for Strikeing John Addington
one blow

Submitted to the Court

Whereupon the Court diſcharged him paying his ffees

Court Adjourns untill the Last Inſtant

Actions Continued untill the next Court

Action   John grey als Tatham plt
agt   } in an action upon the Caſe
Joſeph Growdon deft

Thomas Gardiner plt
agt   } in an action upon the Caſe
Chriſtopher Snowdon deft

Thomas Gardiner plt
      agt
Saml oldale deft –   } – in an action of Trefpafs & affault

Jofeph Chorley plt
      agt
Henry warwin deft –   } in an action upon the Cafe

Action Entered the i day i0 month 1699 Wm Biles Junr plt

                                       agt   } in an action upon the Cafe

Summonce granted ii[th] day   Elizabeth Burges deft

with drawn the 14th day by the plts ordr

Bucks ff –   At a Court of Quarter feffions held in the
name of william penn proprietarie & Govrnr
of the province of penfylvania and Territories
thereunto belonging at the Court houfe for the
aforefaid County the i4[th] day of the i0[th] month
1698

The Juftices present
    Jofeph Growdon william Biles Richard Hough
    Jonathan Scaife Corronor
    Samuel Beakes Sherrife
    Phineas Pemberton Cl: Com:

Court Adjourns to the Houfe of Jofeph Chorley

grand Jury Robt Heaton Peter worral John Hough Henry paxfon
       Stephen Twineing John Surket Thomas Stakehoufe Andrew–
Attefted – Ellot Enoch yardley Jeremiah Langhorn Thomas knight –
       Thomas Bayns william paxfon John palmer Jofuah Hoops all
       Attefted

Jofeph milner Anthony Burton walter pomphray Thomas
       Janney
william Dark Edmund Lovet Edward Lucas Jacob Janney —
John Shaw Henry Margerum John Stakehoufe James moone –
being bound by Recognizance to appear at this Court to
       Anfwer

theire Illegal proceedings being Impaneled on a Jury the Laſt -
Court for tryal of a Caſe then depending between ffrancis white
plt and James Alman deft

being Called they all appeared

316 And upon their Examination thereupon they acknowledged and
    Confeſſed
that being devided in theire oppinions Cold not agree upon a verdict
haveing debated the Caſe part of A day and the moſt part of the night
they Condecended to See which way it Cold go by Lot and thereupon
Cauſed the Conſtable John Dark to Caſt a peice of mony in his
hat but deney'd that the verdict was brought in upon the Lott but
that they afterward agreed upon the verdict and accordingly
brought the Same verdict in to Court which Caſting of the lot had
been agreat trouble to them that they had ſuffered Such a thing
amongſt them and that they had payd So much money as had -
given Satiffaction both to the plt and deft and parties Concerned
whereupon ffrancis white George Biles &c: were Called into the
Court and declared the Jury had given them ſatiſfaction and
that they were no way hurt or damnifyed by the said verdict

Adjourned the Court for one houre

Adjourned until tomorrow morning at 8 a Clock

The Said Jury men being againe Called in to court they declared
as before and Submitted to what the Court wold do to them for
the Said offence and So they did all being Called anſwered one
by one that they ſubmitted to the Court
John Dark the Conſtable who Attended the Jury at the Same time
and Caſt the mony in the hat being bound by recognizance to —
appeare at this Court being Called appeared Likewiſe and Confeſt
the fact and Submitted to the Court

It was Conſidered by the Court that they Sold be fined as followeth

Joſeph milner Shold pay a fine of 2£ — 10^s — 0^d
   Anthony Burton—a fine of _ _ _ 2 —10 —0
   Henry Margerum a fine of _ _ _ _ 2 —10 —0
   Edmund Lovet a fine of _ _ _ _ _ 2 —10 —0
   Edward Lucas a fine of _ _ _ _ 2 —10 —0
   walter pomphray a fine of _ _ _ _ 2 —10 —0
   James moone a fine of _ _ _ _ _ 2 —10 —0
   willm Dark a fine of _ _ _ _ _ 2 —10 —0
   John Shaw — a fine of _ _ _ _ 2 —10 —0

John Stakehoufe a fine of _ _ _ _ _ 2 _ _ 10 _ 0
John Stakehoufe a fine of _ _ _ _ _10 _ _ 10 _ 0
John Stakehoufe a fine of _ _ _ _ _ _ 2 _ _ 10 _ 0
Jacob Janney — a fine of _ _ _ _ _ 2 _ _ 10 _ 0
Thomas Janney a fine of _ _ _ _ _ 2 _ _ 10 _ 0

in all — 30 _ _ _ _   _ _

And the Court fines the Said John Dark in 10ˢ

And alfo awards that they and Every of them pay theire respective ffees

A Deed of five hundered acres of Land in fee with divers goods and Chattles Dated the 10th day of the 10th month 1698 was Delivered by Henry paxfon and Elizabeth Burges grantors unto James plumley and John plumley grantees

A Deed of foure hundered ninety Two acres of Land in fee dated the 10th day of the 10th month

Abigaile Milles being bound over by Recognizance to appeare at this Court being Called appeared accordingly

And be accufed by Stepen Beakes for felonioufly takeing from him fundry goods to

317

the value of foure Shillings Sixpence and upon her Examination Confeffed

the fact and Submitted to the Court

whereupon the Court considered that the Said Abigaile miles Shold pay to the Said Stephen Beakes foure fold being i8ˢ and fees of Court

| Action
Called | John grey als Tatham plt
agt
Jofeph Growdon deft — | in an action upon
the Cafe | plt appeared
deft appeared not |

The Deft Said he ought to have a non Suite but being he beleived that the River being frozen was the occation of his not being there he therefore wold not take the advantage but is Contented it may be Continued whereupon the Court Continued the fd action untill the
next Court

Adjourned the Court for one houre

Action ⎱ Thomas Gardiner plt ⎱ in an action ⎱ plt appeared by
Called ⎰   agt   ⎱   ⎰   his
        Chriftopher Snowdon deft ⎰ upon the Cafe ⎰ Attorney David
                                                    Lloyd
                                                 ⎰ deft appeared not

The Deft baile Craved that in as much as they lived on the other
fide of the River and the River being frozen up that he Cold not
Come over that the action might be Continued untill the next
    Court
wch was accordingly Continued by the plts Attorneys Confent and
the baile was likewife Continued

Action ⎱ Thomas Gardiner plt ⎱ in an action ⎱ plt appeared
Called ⎰   agt   ⎱ of Trefpafs ⎰ by his Attorney David
         Samll oldale deft   ⎰ and affault ⎰   Lloyd
                                               ⎰ deft appeared

But the action was Continued at the requeft of the plt & deft —

Action ⎱ Jofeph Chorley plt ⎱   ⎱ plt appeared —
Called ⎰   agt   ⎱ in an action upon ⎰
         Henry warwin deft   ⎰   the Cafe   ⎰ deft appeared not

The declaracon Read as ffollows

Jofeph Chorley Complaines agt Henry warwin of Eaft Jerfey
    in a
plea of Cafe for that whereas the Said Henry warwin did take
one brown bay ftone horfe to the value of foure pounds being
the proper goods of the Said Jofeph Chorley which horfe the
    faid
warwin did Convert to his own proper ufe whereupon the faid
plt Commences his Suite and Craves Judgmt of this Court
for the fd horfe with damages and Coft of fuite &c

The Declaracon proved by Richard Thatcher James Acreman
and Saml Beakes

The Juftices haveing heard and underftood the premifes it
was Confidered that Jofeph Chorley Shold recover the horfe
declared for with Coft of Suite

John Grifith being Chofen Conftable for Southhampton &c:
    pleaded
his age and defired to be excufed and the Court accordingly —
Excufed him

John Eaftbourn appointed in his ftead for the fucceeding time
Grand Jury, brought in theire prfentments

Bucks ff we the grand Jury for the body of this County do prfent
Henry Baker for not repaireing the way where the waft water
runs neare bucks mill dam being intolerable paffing both for
foot and horfe

318 we alfo prefent Jofeph kirkbride for being defective in his office
in not repaireing the way that Leads from the falls to
nefhaminah
in the falls Townfhip

upon the Complt of peter webfter we prfent the neceffity of his
haveing Convenient way from his houfe to the kings road
Robt Heaton foreman

we alfo do prfent Jofeph Smalwood for violently beating and
Intolerably abufeing his wife

we alfo do prfent Geo Randol for beating and Intolerably
abufeing
of his grand Child

we alfo prfent the neceffity of A bridg to be made over the Creek
Commonly Called Cooks Creek on the road from the falls to
Buckingham
Robt. Heaton foreman

we do alfo prfent the neceffity of another houfe of
Entertainemnt
and accomodations for man & horfe at the Court time to be
kept at Saml Beakes houfe

we do alfo prfent Jofeph Chorley for Selling beare by unlawfull
meafure
Robt Heaton foreman

Jofeph Chorley being prfented by the grand Jury for Selling
beare by unlawfull meafure Submitted to the Court
Samll Beakes allowed to keep ordinary

Gilbert   Jofeph Gilbert being brought before the Court upon the
Complt of nicholas williams was ordered to give Security for
Recogniz   his appearance at the next Court to anfwer the fd Complt
Jofeph Gilbert acknowledge him felf Indebted to the proprietarie
in the Sum of Twenty pounds and John Gilbert his father in

Ten pounds to be Levied on theire Lands and Tenemts goods & Chattles

And this is upon Condition that the Said Jofeph Gilbert Shall appeare at the next Court of Quarter Seffions to be held for the aforefd County to anfwer the Complt of nicholas williams

willms   nicholas williams acknowledged him felf Indebted to the
Recogniz proprietarie in the Sum of Ten pounds to be Levied on his goods and Chattles Lands and Tennemts

And this is upon Condition that he appeare at the next Court of Quarter Seffions to be held for this County to profecute his — Complt agt Jofeph Gilbert

Judgmt   Samll Beakes requefted the Court to grant him Execution for
and   ffees due to him and the Jury about Serveing the Execution
Execut   in the Cafe Englifh white & green agt noble
awarded his Demand according to his account being 6£ –i0ˢ –6ᵈ whereupon the Court awarded that Execution be Iffued agt the fd plts for foure pounds in pte of the Said ffees

upon the prfentment of peter webfters neceffity of a road from his Houfe to the kings roade The Court appoints Saml Dark Henry margerum willm Dark James paxfon & John Rowland to Lay out the fame

The Court adjourns to 2ⁿᵈ weekly 4ᵗʰ day in the firft month next

Actions Continued untill the next Court   319

John grey als Tatham plt
        agt   }in an action upon the Cafe
Jofeph Growdon deft – –

Thomas gardiner plt
        agt   } in an action of Trefpafs and Affault
Samll oldale deft

Thomas gardiner plt
        agt   } in an action upon the Cafe
Chriftopher Snowdon deft

Actions Entered agt the next Court

Action Entered the 4ᵗʰ day of the i2ᵗʰ month 1698

mahlon Stacy plt
agt
Joſeph Chorley deft
} in an action of debt

Summonce granted thereupon

Action Entered the 4th day of the i2th month 1698

Samll oldale plt
agt
Joſeph Chorley deft
} in an action upon the Caſe

Attachment granted thereupon the 4th day i2 month i698

Action Entered the 4th day i2 month 1698

william Biles plt
agt
Joſeph Chorley deft
} in an action upon the Caſe

Attachment thereupon granted the 4th day i2 month 1698

with drawn the ſd action by the plts ordr the 20th day of the ſd month

Action Entered the 4th day i2th month 1698

John Scarbrought plt
agt
Joſeph Chorley deft
} in an action upon the Caſe

Attachment thereupon granted the 4th day i2th month i698

with drawn the ſd action by the plts ordr the 20th day of the ſd month

Action Entered the 4th day i2 month 1698

Joſeph kirkbride plt
agt
Joſeph Chorley deft –
} in an action upon the Caſe

Attachment thereupon granted the 4th day i2 month 1698

with drawn by the plts ordr the 20th day of the ſd month

320

Action Entered the 6th day of the i2th month 1698
9

Gilbert wheeler plt ⎫
      agt   ⎬ in an action of debt
Joſeph Chorley deft ⎭

Attachment granted thereupon the 6th day of the 12th mo $\frac{1698}{9}$

with drawn by the plts ordr the 20th day 12 month

Action Entered the 6th day 12th month 1698

John Scarbrought plt – ⎫
      agt   ⎬ in an action upon the Caſe
Joſeph Smalwood deft ⎭

Attachment thereupon granted the 6th day i2th month 1698

Return Attached one bright bay mare and a Colt about
2 yeares the 27th i2 month $\frac{1698}{9}$

                                  p Saml Beakes ſherrife

Action Entered the 6th day i2th month 1698

willm Embley Thomas Lambert & ffrancis
    Davenport   ⎫
Executrs of John Lambert deceaſed plts agt ⎬ in an action
Joſeph Chorley deft — — — — — — — — — ⎭ of debt

Attachment granted thereupon the ſame Day

with drawn by the plts ordr the 20th day of the ſd month

Action Entered the 7th day i2 month i698

James Acreman plt ⎫
      agt   ⎬ in an action upon the Caſe
James Alman deft ⎭

Arreſt thereupon granted the ſame day

Action Entered the   day of the   month 1698

Peter worral plt ⎫
      agt   ⎬ in an action upon the Caſe
ffrancis Tunneclift deft ⎭
with drawn

Action Entered the 9th day i2th month i698

> John Snowdon plt
>   agt   } in an action upon the Cafe
> Jofeph Chorley deft

Attachment granted thereupon the fame day

with drawn by the plts ordr the 20th day i2
                                            mo

Action Entered the 15th day i2th month 1698   321

> Phineas Pemberton plt
>   agt   } in an action upon the Case
> Jofeph Chorley deft

Arreft granted thereupon the Same day

with drawn by the plts ordr the 20th Inftant

Action Entered the 17 day of the i2 month 1698

> John and Elias nichols plts } in an action upon the Cafe for a
>   agt   }   fum
> Jofeph Chorley deft   } under forty Shillings

warrant granted thereupon to apprend the Said Jofeph Chorley to
        bring him
        before a Juftice of the peace to anfwer the fd Complt: the i7th
        day 12
            mo

The fame day the fd Chorley was brought before Richard Hough
        one of
        the Juftices of peace for the aforefd County where fd Joseph —
        Chorley owned that he owed the mony to the plt mentioned in
        the warrant aforefd

whereupon the Said Juftices of the peace ordered payment thereof
        to the Complainant

Action Entered the i4th day i2 month 1698

> Ifaac Norris plt
>   agt   } in an action upon the Cafe
> Jofeph Chorley deft

Arreſt granted thereupon the Same day

return the body of Joſeph Chorley was Arreaſted the i5ᵗʰ day of the
　ſd month

　　by Samll Beakes Sherrife

Action Entered the 17ᵗʰ day i2ᵗʰ month 1698

　　John nichols and Elias nicholas Leaſors to Anthony Burton ⎫
　　Leaſee by theire Attorneys mahlon Stacy and Henry Baker ⎭ plts

　　　　　　　　agt

　　Thomas Brock auſtor in an action Ejectione firme

Summonce & Declaracon of the Ejectmt read and delivered to **Joſeph**
　　.Chorley
　　the 17ᵗʰ day of the ſd month by Samll Beakes ſherrife

Action Entered the i5 day i2ᵗʰ month 1698

　　Jeffery Hawkins plt ⎫
　　　　agt　　　　　　⎬ in an action upon the Caſe
　　Joſeph Chorley deft ⎭

Arreſt granted thereupon the i5ᵗʰ day of the Same month

with drawn the 20ᵗʰ of the ſd month by the plts ordr

　　322

Action Entered the i5ᵗʰ day i2ᵗʰ month i698

　　Stephen Beakes plt ⎫
　　　　agt　　　　　　⎬ in an action upon the Caſe
　　Joſeph Chorley deft ⎭

Arreſt granted thereupon the Same day

with drawn by the plts order the 20ᵗʰ Inſtant

Action Entered the i5ᵗʰ day i2ᵗʰ month i698

　　Samll Jennings plt ⎫
　　　　agt　　　　　⎬ in Caſe under forty Shillings
　　Joſeph Chorley deft ⎭

warrant granted the i5ᵗʰ day of the ſd month to anſwer the ſd Complt
　　and

the debt he owned to be due before Richard Hough one of the Juſtices of peace for the ſd County who ordered payment thereof the ſd day

with drawn by the plts ordr the 20ᵗʰ Inſtant

Action Entered the i5ᵗʰ day i2ᵗʰ month 1698

> Iſaac Merriot plt
>   agt   in Caſe under forty Shillings
> Joſeph Chorley deft

A warrant granted thereupon the Said day month & yeare to anſwer the ſd

Complt and the ſd debt he the ſd deft owned the Same day to be

due to the ſd plt before Richard Hough one of the Juſtices of peace

for the ſaid County who at the ſame time ordered payment thereof

with drawn by the plts ordr the 20ᵗʰ Inſtant

Action Entered the i6ᵗʰ day of the 12ᵗʰ month i698

> James ffox plt
>   agt   in an action upon the Caſe
> Joſeph Chorley deft

Arreſt thereupon granted the ſame day

with drawn by the plts order the 20ᵗʰ day of the ſd month

Action Entered the i7ᵗʰ day i2ᵗʰ month 1698

> Andrew Ellot plt
>   agt   in an action upon the Caſe
> Joſeph Chorley deft

Attachment granted thereupon the Same day

with drawn by the plts order the 20ᵗʰ Inſtant

Action Entered the day month i698

> Joſeph Chorley plt
>   agt
> Samll Beakes deft

with drawn by the plts order the 9ᵗʰ $\dfrac{\text{i}}{\text{mo}}$ $\dfrac{1698}{9}$

323

Action Entered i8ᵗʰ day i2ᵗʰ month i698

John Cartor plt
agt
Bartholomew Thatcher deft ⎬ in an action upon the Cafe

Arreſt granted thereupon the 2i day of the ſd i2ᵗʰ month
return not to be found

Action Entered the 2i day i2ᵗʰ month i698

Joſeph kirkbride plt
agt
Bartholomew Thatcher deft ⎬ in an action upon the Cafe

Arreſt granted the Said day

Return not to be found

Action Entered the 2i day i2 mo 1698

Joſeph Chorley plt
agt
Elizabeth Burges deft ⎬ in an action upon the Cafe

Summonce granted thereupon

with drawn by the pls order

Action Entered the 8ᵗʰ day of the i month 1698

Joſeph Chorley plt
agt
John Hornor deft ⎬ in an action upon the Cafe

Arrest thereupon granted the ſame day

Bucks ſſ   At a Court of Quarter Seſſions held in the name
of william penn proprietarie of the province
of penſylvania the 8ᵗʰ day of the firſt month
at the Court houſe for the aforeſaid County
Anno Dij $\dfrac{1698}{9}$

The Juftices prfent

willm Biles Henry Baker Richard Hough John fwift

Jonathan Scaife Corronr
Saml Beakes Sherrife
Phineas Pemberton Cl: Com:

grand Jury Jofuah Hoops John Surket Edward Lucas william Smith
Stephen Twineing John Cowgill John Crofdel Thomas Hardin
Henry Margerum John Rowland John Smith Robert Heaton
Saml Allin willm Hayhurft Saml Coates all Attefted

Ralph Boome being Called upon his prfentment Submitted to the Court
whereupon the Court Difcharged him paying his fees

Henry Baker being prfented Laft Court for not repaireing the road
where the waft water of the mill dam at Buckingham overflowed
promifed to repaire the Same when the weather prfented but faid
he expected the Cuntrys Affiftance

324

Jofeph kirkbride being prfented Laft Court for neglecting to get the
high
ways repaired in the ffalls Townfhip promifed to take Speedy Care
to get them repaired

upon the prfentment of the neceffity of A bridg over the Run Called
Cooks
Run or Creek the Court ordered that the overfeers of the high
ways Summonce the inhabitants of the Townships of the ffalls &
Buckingham to make a bridg over the fd Run

Jofeph Chorley being prfented Laft Court for felling beare or ale
by Small meafure Submitted to the Court and thereupon the
Court difcharged him paying his ffees

Adjourned the Court for one houre

A Deed of A Tract of Land about Two hundered and fifty acres in fee
dated the Twenty ninth day of the i0th month i698 was Delivered
by Peter white grantor unto John Headley grantee

A Deed of Three hundered acres of Land in ffee Dated the 28th day of
the i0th month 1698 was Delivered by Samuel Beakes Attorney
to John white ffrancis white willm White Jofeph White and

Benjemame white grantors unto theire brother peter white grantee

A Deed of Two hundered and fifty acres of Land in fee Dated the ii day' of march 1695 was Delivered by John white grantor unto peter white Attorney to his mother Elizabeth white grantee

grand Jury prſented John pidcock for beating and wounding James verrier

pleaded not guilty and for Tryal put him ſelf upon the Cuntry whereupon the Sherrif is Commanded to return 12 honeſt men of the neighbourhood whereby the truth of the matter may be the better known

Jury william paxſon Joſeph Clows Enoch yardley willm Duncan

Stephen Beakes Andrew Ellot Henry Hudleſton Ruben pownel

Jeremiah Langhorn wm Biles Junr: willm Ellot John Hough

all Atteſted

bill read as ffollows

County of Bucks for the Court held in the ſd County the 8th March $\frac{1698}{9}$

we the grand Jury for the body of ſd County do preſent John pidcock

of the ſd County yeoman for that he the ſd pidcock did on or about the 2i

day of January Laſt paſt wilfully and malitiouſly in his own houſe within

the Juriſdiction of this Court violently aſſault knock down beate & abuſe

James verier of the Said County maſon So that his head was extreamly

Swelled Cut and battered to the great hazard of his Life and very much to his

damage all which is againſt the peace of our Soveraigne Lord the king his

Crown and Dignity and againſt the Laws of this province in that Caſe made & provided

A true Bill Joſuah Hoops foreman

peaded not guilty

willm Smith Attefted Saith that John pidcock Struck James verier on
the
head firft with a peice of a Loafe of bread and after broke a
ftoole upon
him and after gave him a blow upon the head with a ftoole &
further
Saith not

325

A Deed of Two Tracts of Land being three hundered acres in fee dated
the 29th day of the 4th month i698 was Delivered by peter —
white Attorney to John white
and wife grantors unto ffrancis white grantee

A Deed of Two hundered acres of Land in fee Dated the 29th day of
the 4th month i698 was Delivered by Samll Beakes ——
Attorney to Elizabeth white peter white ffrancis white Jofeph
white Benjemaine white and william white grators unto ——
John white grantee

A Deed of Two hundered and fifty acres of Land in fee Dated the 5th
day of the
3 month 1697 was Delivered by Samuel Beakes Attorney to Sarah
Clows and her hufband Edward Bennet grantors unto Richard
Hough
grantee

A Deed of Six hundered acres of Land in ffee dated the 14th day of
the 3 —
month 1684 was Delivered by John Swift Attorney to Allin ffofter
and his wife mary grantors unto James plumley Attorney to
Thomas
ffaireman grantee

A Deed of five hundered eighty Two acres of Land in fee Dated 26th
day of the
ii th month 1698 was Delivered by James plumley grantor unto
John   9
Swift Attorney to John morris grantee _____

A Deed of one hundered and eighteen acres of Land in ffee dated the —
6th day of the i0th month 1697 was Delivered by Samll Allin —
Attorney to Nicholas waln grantor unto John Town grantee

A Deed of one hundered acres of Land in fee dated the i2th day of the 7th
month 1692 was Delivered by william Hayhurft Attorney to
Thomas

ffaireman grantor unto Samuel Allin grantee

Adjourned the Court untill 9 a Clock tomorrow morning

A Letter of Attorney from Samel Beakes to his brother willm Beakes acknowledged by the Said Samel Beakes to be his act & deed

A Deed of Twenty five acres of Land in fee Dated 8th day of the i2[th] month 1698 was Delivered by willm Biles Attorney to
       Thomas 9
Hudſon grantor unto Richard Hough grantee

A Deed of Twenty five acres of Land in ffee dated the 7th day of the i2[th] month i698 was Delivered by willm Biles Attorney to Thomas Hudson grantor unto Henry Baker grantee

A Deed of five hundered acres of Land in ffee dated the 6th day of the firſt month 1688 was Delivered by phineas pemberton
          9
Subſtitute Attorney to Richard Davies grantor unto Joſeph — Growdon grantee

A Deed of Two hundered acres of Land in fee dated the 10th day of the 8th month i698 was Delivered by Joſeph Chorley Attorney to Iſabel Cutler grantor unto william paxſon grantee

A Deed of a Smal peice of Land about three acres in fee Dated the 12th day of the 10th month i698 was Delivered by Barndt virkirk grantor unto Leonard vandegreift grantee

A Deed of about thirty Two acres of Land in fee dated the i2[th] day of the 10th month i698 was Delivered by ffrederick vandegrieft grantor unto Barndt virkirk grantee

(326)

A Deed of one hundered ninety Seven acres of Land in fee Dated 20th day of
the i2[th] month 1698 was Delivered by william Hayhurſt Attorney
    to   9
william Croſdell and John Croſdell grantors unto John Cowgill grantee

A Deed of one hundered acres of Land in fee Dated the 6th day of the i2[th] month 1696 was Delivered by Richard Thatcher (Attorney Samuel Beakes) grantor unto John Scarbrough grantee

Edward Hunloke Complained agt John pidcock how that according to A former Judgmt of Court wch he the Said Hunloke obtained agt the Said pidcock he had not performed neither to deliver the affets of Thomas Bowman deceafed nor to pay the Court Charges and — Therefore Craved Execution agt the fd pidcock whereby the Said Judgment may be fullfilled

whereupon the Court ordered that Execution Iffue agt the eftate of the Said John pidcock for one pound eight Shillings and Ten pence half peny charges of Court and for all the bookes papers writeings or other Eftate the faid John pidcock hath got in his Cuftody of the faid Thomas Bowman

Jury Returned and Called over

John pidcock Called appeared

verdict we find John pidcock guilty of the Crime whereof he ftands Indicted

Judgmt   It was therefore Confidered by the Court that John pidcock Shold pay

fine   A fine of Ten fhillings to the Govrnr and give Security for his good abearing toward James verier and all the kings fubjects

Jofeph Chorley being Called upon his Recognizance appeared and the Court orders that he give Security for his appearance at the next Court and for his good abearing in the meane time and — Commits him into the Sherrifs Cuftody untill he Shall performe the fame

Adjourned the Court for one houre

A Deed of   of Land in fee dated the day of the month 169   was Delivered by Jofeph Growdon grantor unto James Bond grantee

A Deed of one hundered acres — — — of Land in ffee dated the — 3 day of the i month 1698 was Delivered by Jofeph Growdon grantor unto Stephen Sands grantee

A Deed of Two hundered and Two acres of Land in ffe with fome Exceptions dated the 16th day of the 12th month $\frac{1698}{9}$ was Delivered

by Jofeph Growdon grantor unto william Beale grantee

A Deed of Two hundered and fifty acres of Land and premifes in fee Dated

the 10th day of the i2[th] month <u>1698</u> was Delivered by Samuel
9

Beakes Attorney to Jonathan Scaife grantor unto John Hough
grantee

A Deed of Two hundered and nine acres of Land in fee
dated the Tenth day of the i2[th] month <u>1698</u> was Delivered by
9

Samuel Beakes Attorney to John Dawſon and his wife martha
and Ann Clarke grantors unto Henry Bowen grantee

A Deed of three parcells of Land in fee Dated the 1 day of the firſt
month
<u>1698</u> was Delivered by Joseph kirkbride grantor unto his father
9

in law Randol Blackſhaw grantee

327

A Deed of the aforementioned three parcells of Land in ffee with Some -
proviſoes Dated the 2nd day of the i month i698 was Delivered
by Randol Blackſhaw unto his Son nehemiah Blackſhaw —
grantee

The Counterpart of the Said Deed or Indenture bearing Equal date
therewih was Delivered by nehemiah Blackſhaw unto his father
Randol Blackſhaw

A Deed of one Thouſand and fifty acres of Land in fee Dated the 8th day
of the 12th month 1698 was Delivered by willm Biles Attorney to
Thomas Hodſon grantor unto matthias Harvie grantee

Joſeph Gilbert being prſented by the grand Jury for feloniouſly takeing
Sundry goods out of the houſe of nicholas williams

pleaded to the Said preſentment not guilty and for tryal put him
ſelf
upon the Cuntry whereupon the Sherrife is Commanded
to return —
venire   12 honeſt men of the neighbourhood whereby the truth of the
matter
may be the better known

Jury returned william paxſon Enoch yardley william Duncan Stephen
Beakes
Andrew Ellot Henry Hudleſton Jeremiah Langhorn william
Biles Junr

William Ellot Ruben pownal John Hough John Snowdon all
Attested

bill read

*we the Jurrors do find Joseph Gilbert guilty of ffeloniously
entering into
the house of nicholas williams and from thence takeing and convert
ing to his owne use several goods to the value of foure Shillings —
Eleven pence

Bucks ff we the Jurrors for the body of this County do prsent Joseph Gilbert
for going into the house of nicholas williams and takeing away —
Several goods thence Conterary to the kings peace and Statute
Laws
of this province &c

a true bill — Josuah Hoops foreman

presentment proved by the affidavit of Joseph Saterthwait

Jury returned and Called over & the said Joseph Gilbert brought to the
barr
delivered theire verdict in writeing as ffollows

we the Jurrors do find Joseph Gilbert Guilty of ffeloniously
entering into
verdict the house of nicholas williams and from thence takeing and
Converting
to his own use Several goods to the value of foure Shillings Eleven
pence
willm paxson foreman

Commitm^t Court Commits Joseph Gilbert into the Sherrifs Custody untill
further order
The Court thereupon Considered that nicholas williams Shold
recover agt
Judgmt Joseph Gilbert foure fold the value of the Said goods being 19^s —
8^d
and Costs and that the sd Gilbert be at Liberty

prsentmt we the Jurrors for the body of this County do prsent the
neceifity of
a way to be Layd out from James Bonds Stephen Sands and
Issabel
Cutlers to the mill and meeting

---

*This paragraph crossed over in original record.

prſentmt we do prſent James Alman and Benjamain Cook for tyeing of Straw to the tayle of Joſeph Large Horſe and Setting it on fire and Samuel Smith Suffering it to be done in his ſight and upon his plantation

Joſuah Hoops foreman —

they all pleaded not guilty and for tryal put them ſelves upon the Cuntry The Sherrife is therefore Commanded to return 12 honeſt men of the neighbourhood by whom the truth of the matter may be the better known

328 Thomas Terrey ⎫
Jaſper Terrey ⎪ all Atteſted
Lawrence pearſon ⎬
Enoch pearſon ⎭

Jury willm paxſon Enoch yardley willm Duncan Stephen Beakes Andrew Ellot Henry Hudleſtone Jeremiah Langhorn willm Biles Junr: willm Ellot John Snowdon Tho ſtakehouſe Ruben pownall all Atteſted

Jury Returnd give in theire verdict they donot find Benjemaine Cook and Samuel Smith guilty

Iwas Conſidered by the Court that James Alman Shall pay a fine of Twenty Shillings to the Govrnr and pay Coſts

Action ⎧ John grey als Tatham plt ⎫
⎨ agt ⎬ action Continued att the plts requeſt
⎩ Joſeph Growdon deft – – ⎭ & by the defts Conſent

Action ⎧ Thomas Gardiner plt ⎫ the action Continued neither plt nor
⎨ agt ⎬ deft appearing but requeſt that the
⎩ Samll oldale deft ⎭ Same may be Continued

Action ⎧ Thomas Gardiner plt ⎫ the action Continued according to
⎨ agt ⎬
⎩ Chriſtopher Snowdon deft ⎭ requeſt untill the next Court

Recogniz John pidcock acknowledges him ſelf indebted to the proprietarie in the Sum of Twenty pounds and Richard Wilſon and John Scarbrough in Each Ten pounds to be Levied on theire goods & Chattles Lands and Tennements

And this is upon Condition that the Said John pidcock Shall be of good abeareing towards James verier and all the kings fubjects untill the Juftices Shall think fit to difcharge him or untill the next Court of Quarter Seffions

Jofeph Chorley acknowledged him Self indebted to the proprietarie in the Sum of one hundered pounds and willm Crofdel in the fum of forty pounds to be levied on theire goods and Chattles Lands and tennements

And this is upon Condition for the good behavior of Jofeph — Chorley to wards John Hornor and all the kings Subjects & that he appeare at the next Court of Quarter Seffions or untill the Juftices Shall think fit to difcharge him

A Deed of part of Two hundered acres of Land in fee Dated the 16th day of the 9th month 1697 was Delivered by Samll Beakes Attorney to Job Houle grantor unto Hugh Ellis grantee

Adjourned the Court untill the 23 Inftant

Action Entered the 9th day of the firft month 1698

Jonathan oldham plt
        agt   } in an action upon the Cafe
Jofeph Chorley deft

Attachment granted thereupon the fame day

Action Entered the 9th 1 mo 1698

John Swift plt
        agt   } in an action of debt
Jofeph Chorley deft

Attachment granted the fame day

329

Bucks ff   At a Court held by Adjournment the 23 day of the 1 month 16 8
                            99

Juftices present william Biles Henry Baker Richard Hough John Swift
Samuel Beakes Sherrife
Phineas Pemberton Cl: Com:

A Deed of one Thouſand acres of Land in fee Dated the i8ᵗʰ day of November
i697 was Delivered by phineas pemberton Attorney to Iſrael Taylor Joſeph Taylor John Buſby and mary Buſby grantors unto Robt Heaton grantee

A Deed of one hundered acres of Land in fee Dated the i7ᵗʰ day of the i2ᵗʰ month 1698 was Delivered by John Shaw grantor unto George ——9—— willard grantee

A letter of Attorney from Anthony Burton to his brother John Burton was acknowledged to be the act and deed of the ſaid Anthony Burton bearing date this day and the Same Certefied under the hands of the Juſtices and County Seal

petition of Julian kirle Read about away from her houſe to kings road refferred to the next Court

Return of the Road from peter webſters houſe to the kings road read and report made to the Court that it was not layd out to ſatisfaction

ordered that Henry Baker and Richard Hough do veiue the place as it is returned and if it donot Satiſſie all parties Concerned that then they appoint how it Shall be layd out

Action / Called } James Acreman plt agt James Alman deft } plt appeared / deft appeared not }

Action / Called } John Scarbrought plt agt Joſeph Smalwood deft } plt appeared / deft did not appeare } firſt default

Action / Called } Joſeph Chorley agt Elizabeth Burges } plt & deft } neither appeared

Adjourned the Court for one houre

acctt   Gilbert wheeler preſented his account in Court and there appeared to be due to him 5£ – i0ˢ which the Court orders that he have payd to him by the Treaſurror out of the County Stock

Samuel Beakes Requeſted the Court to grant him Judgmt for the — remaineing part of the fees due to him in the Caſe peter White &c:

agt Rich noble and the Court thereupon Confidered that the Said -
Beakes Shold have 20ˢ more then what was formerly allowed him
and that Execution Iffue accordingly and that he take no more —

Adjourned the Court untill the 1 day of the Second
month next

Bucks ff

330

At a Court held by adjournment the
firft day of the Second month 1699

The Juftices prfent
william Biles　Henry Baker　Richard Hough
Samuel Beakes Sherrife
Phineas Pemberton Cl: Com:

Action Called– { mahlon Stacy plt　agt　Jofeph Chorley deft } plt appeared　deft appeared } action debt

Declaracon read

Jofeph Chorley did acknowledge and Confefs that he then Stood
Indebted unto the Said mahlon Stacy the Sum of forty pounds
mentioned in the Said Declaracon

Anfwer made by the plt that he wold not take the advantage of
the forfeiture of the obligation but defired only the forty pounds
principal mony

All which being fully underftood by the Juftices

It was Confidered by the Court that the fd plt Shold recover agt the —
deft the Said forty pounds with coft of Suite and that he Shall —
have execution for the Same — to be Levied on the goods and —
Chattles of the fd deft the aforefd Judgmt was not given untill the
4 mo
Court and may be seen in the minuts of the fd Court

Action Called { John nichols and Elias nichols　by theire attorneys Mahlon ftacy　and Henry Baker ——　agt　Thomas Brock deft — — — — — — — — — — — — — } Leafors to Anthony Burton　Leffee plts }

Jofeph Chorley Came into Court and defired that he might be }
admitted deft which was allowed by the court & plts — — }

plts & deft appared both   action Ejectione firme

Declaracon read

Joſeph Chorley did acknowledg and Confeſs that he had Executed
a Certaine
deed of Sale and mortgage unto the ſaid John and Elias nichols
which proviſoe in the Said deed or Indenture is not performed
on his part and that there is 64£ i3ˢ –0ᵈ due to the Said plts
for which mony the Land mentioned in the Said declaracon lyes —
mortgaged to the ſd plts

Action ⎫
Called ⎭
Abra Hardman ⎫ by
&
Iſaac Norris ⎭ theire Attorneys plts ⎫
Joſeph kirkbride — —
agt
Joſeph Chorley — — — deft ⎭ deft
plt appeared
by his ſd
Attorney
appeared - -
action
upon
the
Caſe

Declaracon Read

Anſwer made by the deft Joſeph Chorley that he did Confeſs and
acknowledg
that he is and ſtands Indebted to the Said plt the Sum of fifty
foure pounds thirteen Shillings being the Sum declared for —

Judgmt   defferred in the foregoing Caſes untill the next Court

action ⎫
under
40ˢ– –
upon
the
Caſe ⎭
John and Elias nichols plts ⎫
agt
Joſeph Chorley deft — — ⎭

Richard Hough one of the Juſtices
of peace reported to this Court how
that Joſeph Chorley acknowledged
him ſelf debtor the plts 39ˢ iiᵈ ½

due for rent of a Certaine parcel of Land and that he had
given it as his Judgmt that the ſd Chorley ought to pay the ſame
and the ſd Chorley againe Confeſſed the ſd Debt to be due to ſd plts
The Court Confirmed the ſd Judgmt and ordered Execution to
Iſſue accordingly

*[331]

*Page 331 is not numbered in the record book.

action ⎫
under ⎬ Thomas Coleman acknowledged that he was Indebted unto
40ˢ - - ⎬ John – nichols and Elias nichols thirty nine Shillings and Eleven
upon the ⎬   pence half
Cafe ⎭ peny
It was therefore confidered by the Court that the fd nichols
        Shold recover —
    agt: the Said Thomas Coleman the fd 39ˢ ii½ᵈ and Cofts and
    that Execution Iffue accordingly

Adjourned the Court to Samll Beakes houfe an houre hence

Action ⎫ Jofeph Chorley plt agt ⎫
Called ⎬ Elizabeth Burges deft   ⎬ plt appeared & defired the action to be
                                  ⎭   with drawn

Action   Jonathan oldham plt ⎫ plt ⎫
                  agt   ⎬ nor ⎬ neither appeared
          Jofeph Chorley deft ⎭ deft ⎭

ordered that phineas pemberton have paid him by the Treafurror five
    pounds towards what is due to him for Laying out the Roads

Adjourned the Court untill the i4ᵗʰ day 4   next
                                        ───
                                        mo
Actions Continued untill the next Court

Action   John grey als Tatham plt ⎫
                  agt   ⎬ in an action upon the Cafe
          Jofeph Growdon deft   ⎭

Action Thomas Gardiner plts ⎫
              agt   ⎬ in an action of Trefpafs and affault
        Samuel Oldale deft   ⎭

Action Thomas Gardiner plt   ⎫
              agt   ⎬ in an action upon the Cafe
        Chriftopher Snowdon deft ⎭

Action John Scarbrough plt ⎫
              agt   ⎬ in an action upon the Cafe
        Jofeph Smalwood deft ⎭

Action James Acreman plt ⎫
                agt   ⎬ in an action upon the Cafe
        James Alman deft ⎭

Action   John and Elias nichols ⎫
         by theire Attorneys —— ⎬plts ⎫
         Henry Baker & mahlon ftacy ⎭   ⎬ in an action Ejectione
                agt   ⎬   firme
         Jofeph Chorley defts — — — ⎭

Action Ifaac Norris plt ⎫
                agt   ⎬ in an action upon the Cafe
        Jofeph Chorley deft ⎭

Action   mahlon Stacy plt ⎫
                agt   ⎬ in an action of debt
        Jofeph Chorley deft ⎭

Action   Jofeph Chorley plt ⎫
                agt   ⎬ in an action upon the Cafe
        John Hornor deft ⎭

Action   John Swift plt ⎫
                agt   ⎬ in an action of debt
        Jofeph Chorley deft ⎭

        332

Action Entered for the fourth month Court next

        Action   Jofeph kirkbride plt ⎫
     entered the   agt   ⎬ in an action upon
   10ᵗʰ 2 1699 Bartholomew Thather deft ⎭   the Cafe
        mo

        Attachment thereupon granted the Same day

        Return there was Attached the 14ᵗʰ day of the 2ⁿᵈ month 1699 in
            the hand of
        Robt Heaton the Sum of thirty pounds being due upon bond the
            25ᵗʰ day
        of the 4ᵗʰ month 1698 as alfo one Tract of Land Lying and
            adjoyneing

to the Land of willm Hayhurſt and one Tract of Land Lying over the

Creek the Quantyty unknown to me was Attached the 10th day of the 3

mo

1699 p e   Samll Beakes ſherrife

Action Entered the i7th day of the 2 month i699

> Edmund wells plt
> agt   } in an action of debt
> ffrancis white deft

Summonce thereupon granted for the deft appearance at the next Court to be

held for this County

Action Entered the i day of the 4th month 1699

> Joſeph Chorley
> agt   } in an action upon the Caſe
> James Alman deft

Attachment granted thereupon the Same day

Execution granted Samll Beakes for fees due to him in the Caſe peter white &c

agt Rich noble dated the 5th day of the 3 month 1699

Return there was taken the mony of peter white the Sum of five pounds thirteen Shillings in full p me

Samll Beakes ſherrife

Action Entered the 25th day of the 3 month 1699

> Richard Thatcher plt
> agt   } in an action upon the Caſe
> willm Huntley deft

Arreſt granted the Same day

Bucks ſſ   At a Court of Quarter Seſſions held in —
the name of william penn proprietarie of
the province of penſylvania and territories thereunto
belonging At the Court houſe for the aforeSaid County

the 14th day of the 4th month i699

The Juſtices prſent

Joſeph Growdon william Biles Henry Baker Richard Hough

Samll Beakes Sherrife and deputy Cl: of the County

proclamation from the govrnr about the Scoth

Laws made the Laſt Aſſembley read

Adjourned the Court for one houre

Action ⎱ Edmund wells plt ⎱ plt ⎱
⎰ agt ⎰ & ⎰ both appeared
Called ⎰ ffrancis white deft ⎰ deft ⎰

333

deft did Confeſs that he owed the plt Thirty pounds and Intreſt for the Same

It was therefore Conſidered by the Court that the plt Shall recover

agt the deft thirty pounds with Intreſt for the Same & Coſt of Suite

being what the plt deſired and that he Shall have Execution for the

Same to be Levied on the goods and Chattles of the Said Deft

Action John grey als Tatham plt ⎱ in an action ⎰ plt appeared not ⎱
agt ⎰ upon the ⎰ ⎰
Joſeph Growdon deft - - ⎰ Caſe ⎰ deft did appeare ⎰

and Said he ought to have a non Suite but however tho he had often

appeared to the Said action yet he was not unwilling that the action

might be Continued untill the next Court to ſee if the plt might then make

his appearance and profecuˑe his action whereupon the Court Continues

the action untill the next court

Action Iſaac Norris plt ⎱
agt ⎰ in an action upon the Caſe ⎰
Joſeph Chorley deft ⎰

whereas the Laſt Court held the firſt day of the 2ᵈ month Laſt paſt the deft

Confeſſed that he was Indebted to the plt fifty foure pounds thirteen

Shillings

It was Conſidered by the Court that the Said Iſaac norris Shold recover

agt the Said Joſeph Chorley the Said Sum of 54 £ : 13ˢ : 00ᵈ and Coſt of

Suite and that the plt Shall have execution for the Same to be Levied on

the goods and Chattles of the Said deft:

Action Mahlon Stacy plt ⎱
     agt   ⎰ in an action of debt
Joſeph Chorley deft

Joſeph Chorley in a Court held the i day of the 2 month Laſt paſt

did Confeſſ he owed & Stood Indebted unto mahlon Stacy the Sum of

forty pounds

It was Conſidered by the Court tha the Said plt Shold recover agt the ſd deft the

Said forty pounds with coſt of Suite and that he Shall have execution

for the Same to be Levied on the goods and Chattles of the ſd deft:

Joſeph Chorley being bound by Recognizance to appeare at this Court

appeared accordingly and was diſcharged paying his fees

Action John nicholas and Elias nichols plts ⎱ plt appeared by theire
         agt   ⎰ ſubſtitute Attorney
Joſeph Chorley deft — — — — — Samuel Beakes who

declared that he had Received 66 £ –13ˢ –00ᵈ and Coſt of Suite in full

Satiſfaction of what was due to the Said plts and thereupon Cancelled

the mortgage & Sale of the Land Sued for in this Court by the ſaid

plts and Delivered up all patents writeings or other evidences Concern ing the Same unto the deft Joſeph Chorley

A Deed of Three hundered and od acres in fee dated the 22 day of the 3ᵈ
month i699 was Delivered by Joſeph Chorley and mary
his wife James Acreman James Heyworth and mary his wife
grantrs
unto Samuel Beakes Attorney to John Harriſon grantee

Adjourned the Court untill 8 a Clock in the morning

Action } Joſeph Chorley plt ⎱ plt appeared — — —   ⎫
Called }   agt   ⎬ Court Continued
        John Hornor deft ⎰ deft appeared not   ⎭ it accordingly
    plt declared his willingness to Continue the
    · action untill next Court

334

Action } John Swift plt   ⎱ in an action ⎰ plt appeared by his
Called }   agt   ⎬ of debt   ⎨ Attorney Samuel Beakes
        Joſeph Chorley deft ⎰   ⎩ deft appeared

And the Said Deft Confeſſed that he owed to the ſd plt Six
pounds
and Intreſt for the Same the plt declared his Satiſſaction
therewith

It was Conſidered by the Court that the Said plt Shold recover
agt the Said deft the Said Sum of Six pounds and Intreſt due
thereupon and Coſt of Suite and that he Shall have execution
for the Same to be Levied on the goods and Chattles of the ſd
deft

Action } Joſeph Kirkbride plt   ⎱   ⎰ plt appeared by
Called }   agt   ⎬ in an action ⎨ his Attorney
        Bartholemew Thatcher deft ⎰ the Caſe   ⎩ Samll Beakes
                                                        deft appared not

Declaracon Read and the account therein mentioned likewiſe proveing
the ſd Declaracon

whereupon the Court ordered that Robt Heaton Garniſhee be ſummoned
to Court to ſee if he have any thing to ſay why the mony Attached
in his hands Shold not pay what is due to the plt

Action }
Called } Joseph Chorley plt ⎤ both appeared and desired the Continuation of the
          agt   ⎬ action untill the next Court and it was accord
          James Alman deft ⎦
ingly Continued

Action }
Called } Thomas Gardiner plt ⎤ neither plt nor deft appeared whereupon the
          agt   ⎬ Court Continues the action
          Samuel oldale deft ⎦

Action }
Called } Thomas Gardiner plt ⎤ neither plt nor deft appeared whereupon
          agt   ⎬ the Court Continues the action
          Christo Snowdon deft ⎦

Action }
Called } John Scarbrough plt ⎤ plt appeared ⎤
          agt   ⎬   ⎬ Second default
          Joseph Smalwood deft ⎦ deft appeared not ⎦

Action }
Called } Richard Thather plt ⎤
          agt   ⎬ action Continued
          willm Huntley deft ⎦

mahlon Stacy appeared in Court and acknowledged he had Received
ffull Satisfaction from Joseph Chorley for the Judgmt
he obtained this Court being forty pounds & Cost of suite

Samll Beakes Attorney to Isaac norris declared that he had
Received 54£ i3ˢ and Cost of suit being in full Satisfaction
of the Judgmt the said Isaac norris obtained this Court agt
Joseph Chorley

ordered that Samuel Beakes be recommended to the governor as A
fit person to keep ordinary

Adjourned the Court untill the i7ᵗʰ day of the 7 month next

335

Actions Continued untill the next Court

          John Grey als Tatham plt ⎤
          agt   ⎬ in an action upon the Case
          Joseph Growdon deft____ ⎦

Thomas Gardiner plt
agt
Samuel Oldale deft
} in an action of Trefpafs and affault

Thomas Gardiner plt
agt
Chriftopher Snowdon deft
} in an action upon the Cafe

John Scarbrough plt
agt
Jofeph Smalwood deft
} in an action upon the Cafe

Jofeph kirkbride plt
agt
Bartholemew Thather deft
} in an action upon the Cafe

Jofeph Chorley plt
agt
John Hornor deft
} in an action upon the Cafe
withdrawn

Jofeph Chorley plts
agt
James Alman deft
} in an action upon the Cafe

Richard Thatcher plt
agt
willm Huntley deft
} in an action upon the Cafe
non fuite granted thereupon

Actions Entered for the Court to be held in the 7th month next

Action Entered the 28th day of the 6th month i699

Enoch yardley plt
agt
Joseph Chorley deft
} in an action upon the Cafe

Attachmt granted thereupon

with drawn the declaracon by the plts order

Action Entered he 28th day of the 6th month i699

Edward Hunloke plt ⎤
    agt ⎬ in an action of Debt
Walter pumphray deft ⎦

Summonce granted thereupon
non ſuite

Action Entered the 3i day of the 6ᵗʰ month 1699

Peter worral plt ⎤
    agt ⎬ in an action upon the Caſe
ffrancis Tunneclift deft ⎦

Attachment granted the 3i day of the 6ᵗʰ month 1699
non ſuite

336

Action Entered the 25ᵗʰ day of the 5ᵗʰ month i699

John Burradel plt ⎤
    agt ⎬ in an action of debt
Richard Thatcher deft ⎦

Arreſt thereupon granted agt the body of Richard Thatcher the 25ᵗʰ
    day $\frac{5}{\text{mo}}$ 1699

Return he had taken his body the 2ⁿᵈ of the 6ᵗʰ month i699
                                  p Samll Beakes
Action Entered the 25ᵗʰ day of the 5ᵗʰ month 1699   Sherrife

George ffiſher plt ⎤
    agt ⎬ in an action of debt
Edward Shaw deft ⎦

Arreſt granted agt his body the body of the deft the 25ᵗʰ day 5 mo i699

Return Taken the i day of the 6ᵗʰ month i699
non ſuite

Bucks ff   At a Court of Quarter Seſſions held
           in the name William Penn proprietaries of the --
           province of penſylvania and Territories
           thereunto belonging at the Court houſe of the afore Said
               County the
           13 day of the 7ᵗʰ month 1699

The Juſtices present

Joſeph Growdon william Biles   Henry Baker
John Swift
Jonathan Scaiſe Corronor
Samll Beakes Sherrife
Phineas Pemberton Cl:Com:

Theſe perſons following being Summonced to ſerve upon the Jury did not
appeare when Called viz John Rowland Stephen Sands Henry
pawlin francis
white Samuel Smih george Brown James Heaton
Thomas Stakehouſe Junr Ralph Cowgill

Edward Doyl the Sherrifs Deputy Atteſted that he
did Summonce allof them to ſerve upon the Jury
this Court

ffines

whereupon the Court fines John Rowland in 5ˢ Stephen Sands 5ˢ——
Henry pawlin 5ˢ francis white 5ˢ Samll Smith 5ˢ george brown 5ˢ
James Heaton 5ˢ Thomas Stakehouſe Junr 5ˢ Ralph Cowgil 5ˢ

Return of the Corronors Inqueſt of the death of James Hagath the ſervant
of John Scot that he Received his death by a blow of John Snowdons
Horſe that he ſtruck him the 5ᵗʰ day of the 7ᵗʰ month 1699 & dyed
the day following the boy being driveing the plow when the horſe
ſtruck
him

Action
Called

{ John Scarbrought plt
agt
Joſeph Smalwood deft }

{ plt appeared
deft appeared not }

it being the 3
default

Declaration Read as ffolloweth viz

John Scarbrough Complaines agt Joſeph Smalwood in a plea that
where
as the Said Joſeph Smalwood did Imploy the wife of the Said John
Scarbrough
to waſh for him his Linnen &c which shee accordingly did to the
value

337

of Twenty Seven Shillings with Several goods delivered to him
as may appeare
by account herewith in Court to be produced as alſo the Said
Joſeph Smalwood

did agree with the Said John Scarbrough to keep and nurſe his
Child for which
the Said Joſeph Smalwood did agree and aſſume upon him Self
to pay foure
Shillings for every weeke he Shold So keep and nurſe the Said
Child with in
the yeare the Said Child was So put to him thirty Shillings in
part where
of the Said Joſeph Smalwood hath paid yet not with ſtanding the
Said
John Scarbrough hath often demanded the Said Joſeph Smalwood
to —
pay what was Due to him for keeping the Said Child and upon
the ſaid
account he the Said Smalwood hath hitherto refuſed and Still
doth refuſe
to pay what is due and therefore the ſd plt Commenceth this
Suite & —
Craves Judgmt of this Court for the Said Twenty Seven Shillings
and
for the nurſing and keeping the Said Child after the rate of foure –
Shillings p week untill the time of holding this Court with
damages and
Coſt of Suite &c

The deft Atteſted the truth of the ſd Declaracon and that he Cold not
give him
any more Credit

It was Conſidered by the Court that the plt Shold recover what
was due to him
for nurſeing the Child & for the goods and waſhing with Coſt of
Suite & that
he Shall have Execution for the Same to be Levied on the
goods and Chattles of the ſd deft

Action } George ffisher plt ⎫   ⎧ plt appeared not
Called }   agt   ⎬ in an action of debt ⎨
           Edward Shaw deft ⎭   ⎩ deft appeared

whereupon the deft Craved a non Suite for that he had not
filed a __ __
declaracon nor appeared to his action

The Court therupon awarded a non ſuite

| Action Called | Thomas Gardiner plt agt Samll oldale deft | plt & deft | both appeared and Craved the Continuation of the action untill the next Court & it was |

accordingly Continued

| Action Called | Thomas Gardiner plt agt Chriftopher Snowdon deft | plt & deft | both appeared and defired the Continuation of the action untill the next Court and it was |

accordingly Continued

| Peter worral plt agt ffrancis Tunneclift deft | the plt appeared deft appeared not | The Court Continues the action untill the next Court |

Adjourned the Court for one houre

A Deed in ffee of i2½ acres dated the 4ᵗʰ day 7 month 1699 was Delivered by
willm Hayhurft grantor unto Henry Hudleftone grantee

A Deed of A parcel of Land be it more or lefs dated the i4ᵗʰ day of the 4ᵗʰ month 1699 was Delivered by James paxfon Attorney to his fon william paxfon grantor unto John Scarbrough grantee

Ordered that Jonathan Scaife have the fees due to him for veiueing the body of Richard Athay who was found dead upon the Road payd him out of the County Stock by the Trefurror

ordered that John Cook late Corronor have the fees due to him for — veiueing the body of John Stotton payd him out of the County ftock by the treafurror

John pidcock being Called upon his recognizance Appeared & the Court difcharged him

338

A Deed of a Lot of Land in fee Lying in Buckingham Dated the iiᵗʰ day of the 7ᵗʰ month 1699 was Delivered by Jofeph Growden grantor unto william Crofdell grantee

A Deed from John Scarbrough of eighty acres of Land in fee dated the 4th day
   of the 7th month 1699 was delivered by him grantor unto Henry Hudleſtone
   grantee

A letter of Attorney from John Scarbrough of London to the aforeſaid John
   Scarbrough his Son Dated the i5th day of october i696 was proven
   in Court

A Deed of foure hundered acres of Land in fee was Delivered by Andrew
   Heath and his Son in law John Richardſon and his wife Joyce
   Richardſon
   grantors unto John Snowdon grantee

A Deed of five hundered acres of Land in ffee dated the 4th day of the 8th month
   i696 being Endorſed on A pattent Dated the 20th day of decembeʀ i690
   was Delivered by John Swift Attorney to Joſeph Jones grantor unto —
   peter Chamberlaine for the uſe of him & his wife Lucy grantees

Complaint being made by peter webſter that the Road formerly ordered by
   the Court to be Layd out from his Houſe to the kings road that is not
   as yet perfected

whereupon the Court orders Peter worral John palmer Joſuah Hoops —
   Thomas Janney Anthony Burton John Siddal to veiue the place
   and if there be need to
   Lay out the Same according to Law

Complt being made by peter Chamberlaine of the want of a road from
   his Houſe to the kings Road the Court orders John Jones, Henry pointer
   Thomas Hardin John Naylor John Eaſtbourne nicholas Randol to veiue
   the place and ground and if there be need to lay out the Same according
   to Law

Complt of Thomas kirle for the want of Aroad from his Houſe to the kings
   road John Palmer Joſuah Hoops Thomas Janney Abel Janney
   Anthony Burton John Siddal are ordered to vieue the Same and
   if there be – need to Lay out the Same according to Law

Action } John Burradel plt_____ } in an action of debt { plt & deft } both appeared
Called }   agt
        } Richard Thatcher deft

The Declaracon Read

Bucks ff   John Burradel Complaines agt Richard Thatcher in an action of
        debt for that whereas the Said Richard Thatcher became bound and
        obliged to the Said John Burradel in one obligation bearing date the
        ii^th day of the 10th month 1697 in the Sum of Twenty pounds for pay
        ment of Ten pounds with Lawfull Intereſt at or upon the 10th day of the i0
        month Enſueing the date thereof and not with ſtanding the Said plt hath
        divers times demanded the Said mony So due the ſd deft hitherto hath
        refuſed and Still doth refuſe the Same to pay whereupon the plt —
        Commenceth this Suite agt the Said deft and Craves Judgmt for the
        Said Sum of Twenty pounds with Coſt of Suite &c

Anſwer the deft Confeſſed to the truth of the declaracon and Said he had —
        nothing to Say agt it

whereupon it was Conſidered by the Court that John Burradel Shold recover
        agt the ſd Deft: the Said Sum of Twenty pounds and Coſt of ſuite
        and that he Shold have Execution agt the body of the ſaid deft
        for payment thereof

Zachariah ſferries being Called upon his Recognizance appeared and
Confeſt he had taken a scread of ſtuf from John Swift to a
Small value nothing further appearing agt him the Court orders him
to pay to ſd Swift 9ˢ 6ᵈ and Charge of Court and is thereupon
        diſcharged

339

Conſtables appointed for the Succeding yeare

ffor
{
Buckingham — — —   Thomas Dungan
ffalls — — — — — — — John Siddal
makefeild — — — — —giles Lucas
middle Town — — — — Edward Cartor
Benfalem — — — — — Abel Hinckftone
South hampon &— } — — John Eaftbourn
warminfter — — —
wrights Towne }
    Cum   } — Saml Hough –
new Town –
} all Attefted

over Seers of the high ways appointed for the Succeeding yeare

ffor
{
Buckingham — — John Surket
ffalls — — — — — willm Biles Junr
makefeild — — — peter worrall
middle Town — — Ezra Crofdel
Benfalem — — — ffrancis Searle
South hampton }
    cum   } — Thomas Walmfley
warminfter – }
new Town }
    cum   } — James yates
wrights Town }

Adjourned the Court untill the i9ᵗʰ day of the 8ᵗʰ month next

Action Entered the 8 day of the 8 month 1699

John Sutton Executor of Jofeph Burden late of Barbadoes
    deceafed by

Samuel Carpenter his Attorney plt ———
        agt
Samuel Burden Son and heire of Samuel-
    Burden
deceafed and ffrancis Rawle Adminiftrator
    of the
goods and Chattles of the fd Samll Burden
    deceafed deft
} in an action of
Covenant

Bucks ff   At a Court of Quarter Seffions held by ——

Adjournment the19ᵗʰ day of the 8ᵗʰ month i699

The Juſtices present
Joſeph Growdon William Biles
Henry Baker Richard Hough John Swift
Samll Beakes Sherrife
Phineas Pemberton Cl. Com:
Conſtables Atteſted

grand Jury William paxſon John palmer Stephen Twineing
  Shadrach walley
 william Smith Edward Lucas Thomas Stakehouſe ſenr
  Jeremiah Langhorn —
 william Hayhurſt Thomas Stakehouſe Junr Ezra Croſdel
 Henry pawlin John Smith Peter worrall Job Bunting
  John Penquoit

All Attested

Charge given

340

Return of the Roads from peter webſters houſe to the kings Road as
 ffolloweth

Bucks ſſ   The 14ᵗʰ day of the 8ᵗʰ month i699

wee whoſe names are under written being appointed by order of
 Court
to Lay out a road for Peter webſter have Layd it out as ffolloweth
 from
a Stake Standing by the fence of peter webſter from thence upon a
Straight line by the Eaſt end of the houſe of Randol Blackſhaw and
from thence Straight to the Road Leading from the ffalls to Southhampton Two poles wide

      Joſuah Hoops John Palmer
      Peter worral Anthony Burton
      Thomas Janney John ſiddall

The 14 of the 8 month 1699

we whoſe names are hereunder written being appointed by order of
Court to Lay out a road for the Conveniancy of Thomas kirle begin
ing at the houſe of Thomas kirle and runing along between
 Thomas

kirle and Andrew Ellot and then between Andrew Ellot and
   Peter worrall
along theire line unto the Road Leading from the falls up the
   River
being two poles in breadth all along

                    Jofuah Hoops John palmer
                    Anthony Burton Thomas Janney
                    John fiddal Abel Janney

Read allowed and ordered to be Entered the abovefd returns

Dure ⎫
   ⎬ george Stone Came into Court and Confeffed him Self to be debtr
&   ⎬   to
   ⎬ Thomas Dure the Sum of thirteen pounds eighteen Shillings and
Ston ⎭ promifed paymt of the Same

A Deed of five hundered acres of Land in fee dated the i8ᵗʰ day of the 8ᵗʰ
   month
   1699 was Delivered by Phineas Pemberton grantor unto george
   ftone
   grantee

A Deed of one hundered and fifty acres of Land dated the 10ᵗʰ day of the i2
   month 1698 was Delivered by Jofeph Growdon grantor unto
   Garret
   van Sand Grantee

a deed of one hundered and fifty acres of Land in fee Dated the 10ᵗʰ day
   of the
   12 month 1698 was Delivered by Jofeph Growdon grantor unto
   Cornelius van Sand grantee

A Deed of ninety acres of Land in fee Dated the i7ᵗʰ day of the 8ᵗʰ month
   i699 was Delivered by Jofeph Growdon grantor unto Thomas
   Stakehoufe Junior grantee

A Deed of one hundered acres of Land in fee Dated the i8ᵗʰ day of the
   8ᵗʰ month 1699 was Delivered by ——————————attorney to
   grace Langhorn Jeremiah Langhorn william Biles and Sarah
   Biles grantors to Thomas Stakehoufe grantee

A Deed of Two Lotts of Land in fee Lying in Buckingham Dated the i8
   day
   of the 8ᵗʰ month 1699 was Delivered by Thomas Brock grantor
   unto Phineas Pemberton Attorney to Jofeph kirkbride grantee

A Deed of Two lotts of Land in fee Lying in Buckingham Dated the

5th day of the 7th month 1699 was Delivered by Thomas Brock grantor unto Richard pearce grantee

A Deed of Two hundered fifty two acres of Land and premifes in fee dated the 17th day of the i2 month i698 was Delivered by ftephen wilfon grantor unto Stephen Twineing grantee

A Deed of one hundered and eight acres be the fame more or lefs Dated the 22 day of Aprill 1699 was Delivered by Samuel Beakes Attorney
to Richard Ridgway grantor unto william Biles Junior Attorney to Daniel
gardiner grantee

(341)

A Deed of the said Tract of Land being about Two hundered and eight acres 10 or 14½ acres be the Same more or Lefs dated the firft day of
the 7th month 1699 was Delivered by william Biles Senr Attorney to Daniel gardiner grantor unto Jofeph Janney grantee

Robert Barry and Irifh boy Servant to James plumley was brought before the Court to have his age adjudged and the Court accordingly ― Judged to be of Ten yeares of age from this day & Serve ―――― according to Law and at the expiration of his terme to have allowance accordingly

Adjourned the Court untill 8 in the morning

An Atteftation of John Bowns read in Court declareing the payment of three pounds to John Pidcock for the Service of negro will done in Eaft Jerfey after the deceafe of Thomas Bowman whofe negro the Said will: was and the John pidcock not makeing it appeare to the Court that he hath payd the Said 3£: to Edward Hunlock Adminiftra
-tor of the Said Bowmans Eftate

wherefore it was Confidered by the Court that the Said Edward Hunloke Shold recover the Said 3£ of the Said John pidcock according to a former Judgmt of this Court which fd Hunlocke obtained agt the fd pidcock being affets in his hands of the fd Bowmans Eftate Except Eleven Shillings which appeared to the Court the fd pidcock
had Layd out in Shooes and ftockings for the fd negro and that he have Execution to Levie the Same on the goods & Chattles of the Said John pidcock for the fd fum of 2£ 9s―

Action Edward Hunloke plt } in a plea { plt & deft } appeared
    agt
  walter pomphray deft

  The Declaracon read

  the affidavit of Robt Stacy read

  Henry Grub &   atteſted an agree mente or an award
  made by the awarders —

  plt & deft agreed to deffer the tryal of the action to the next Court
  if the weather wold then permit if not to the next after that neither
  plt nor deft to take advantage if the weather hindered theire —
  appearance & it was accordingly Continued

Action Richard Thatcher plt – } plt appeared not
    agt
  willm Huntley deft } deft appeared —

  whereupon the deft Craved anon ſuite which the Court granted him

Action Peter woral plt———— } plt & deft } both appeared
    agt
  ffrancis Tunneclift deft

  declaracon read it diſerring about three words from the Coppy the deft
  Craved a non ſuite for the Same which the Court granted him

    Adjourned the Court to Samll Beakes houſe

Action Joſeph Chorley plt } in an action upon the Caſe { plt & deft } both appeared
    agt
  James Alman deft

  Declaracon read

342

Anſwer deft ſays he ows nothing of this puts him ſelf upon the Cuntry

Iſſue and ſo doth the plt

venire whereupon the Sherrife is Commanded to return a Jury

Jury } Peter worral willm Dungan wm Biles Junr John ſiddal
Atteſted } Clement Dungan Enoch yardley John ſcarbrough Thomas
    Coleman

Joſeph Janney James moone Junr Geo Biles wm Croſdel all Atteſted

deſt   offered an account to prove the horſe pd for mentioned in the declaracon

Action   depending upon Some accounts the Court appointed wm: Biles Junr

and wm Croſdel to audit the accounts and the plt & deſt Submitted

the whole Caſe to the Arbitration of the ſd Auditors if they think good to take it upon them

grand jury brought in theire prſentments

prſent Edmund Lovet for his difficiency in his office as Collector of

the County Tax in Buckingham townſhip

we prſent the neceſſity of a Convenient road from John Croſdells houſe to the kings road that Leads from new Town to Buckingham

for the uſe of John Croſdel

we prſent the neceſſity of a road for Ezra Croſdel from his houſe to the kings road which leads from new town to Buckingham

Bucks ſſ   The Jurrors for the body of this County do prſent willm Beatridg and James Jolly for runing away from theire maſter John Swifts Service and feloniouſly takeing with them Two of theire Said maſters horſes to the value of Twelve pounds

Conterary

to the kings peace and the Statute Laws inthat Caſe made and provide

we of the grand Jury do find this bill william paxſon foreman

william Beatridge and James Jolly brought to the barr and the preſentment read wm Beateridg

pleaded guilty

The Court thereupon Conſidered that the Said willm Beatridge Shall Serve the Said John Swift Two yeares after the expiration of the term of his prſent Servitue

And that he Shall have 7 Laſhes upon his bare back and weare a Roman T on his left arme of A yellow Collour according to Law James Jolly

pleaded guilty

It was thereupon Confidered by the Court that the Said James
Jolly
Shall Serve the Said John Swift Two yeares after the —
Expiration of the terme of his prſent Servitude
And that he Shall be Whipt 7 Laſhes upon his bare back and
weare a Roman T on his Left arme of A yellow Collour accord-
ing to Law

Action } John Tatham plt   } in an action upon { plt }
Called }   agt   }   theCafe   { & } both
        } Joſeph Growdon deft }   { deft } appeared

Declaracon } John grey als Tatham late of Tatham houſe neare neſheminah
Read —   } in the
           } County of Bucks in Penſylvania merchant Complaineth
           }   againſt
           Joſeph Growdon of the County aforeſd Gent: in an action
           upon the

343

Cafe for that whereas in the yeare i685 the ſd pltf gave the
faid Deft Credit for
ſundyr goods & merchandizes amounting to Seven pounds
Six ſhillings and
eight pence which Sum the Said Deft aſumed to pay within a
Small time after
the delivery of the Said Goods and merchandizes and lent him
the faid deft
foure books value foure pounds which he promiſed Shortly to
reſtore and —
likewiſe lent him fifeteen pounds Caſh upon his note or letter
under his
owne hand dated at Benſalem the 7th day of   9   i685 to
repay the faid   mo
fiveteen pounds in filver mony at or before the 6th of the i2
next   mo
Enſueing the date thereof with Intreſt for the Same then due
wch Said
Sums of Seven pounds Six Shillings eight pence and foure
pounds —
Charged for the Said Books and the Said Sum of fiveteen
pounds
Lent and Intreſt thereof now due viz fiveteen pounds & eight
ſhillings

for Twelve yeares and Ten months at eight p Cent amount to one &

forty pounds fiveteen ſhillings and eight pence And the ſaid pltf hath

often requeſted the ſaid deft the ſaid Several Sums of Seven pounds

Six Shillings and eight pence due for the ſaid goods & merchandizes

and the Sum of foure pounds for the Said books or the books to be

reſtored and the Said Sum of fiveteen pounds with Intreſt due

and accrewing at the Reſpective times when the ſaid pltf demanded

the Same as above Set forth and declared yet nevertheleſs the ſaid

deft hath Still refuſed & doth Still refuſe to pay the Same or any of the

Said Sums or reſtore the Said books whereupon the ſaid pltf brings

this Suite & Craves Judgmt of this Court for the ſaid ſeveral ſums

amounting in the whole (as aforesaid to one and forty pounds —

fiveteen ſhillings and eight pence Currant ſilver mony of the afore

said province with damages and Coſt of Suite

Anſwer read – } I owe unto the pltf nothing to my knowledg only the foure books
of a Small value I borrowed wch I am ready to reſtore and of this

Iſſue
venire
he puts him ſelf upon the Cuntry & ſo doth the pltf:

whereupon the Sherrife is Commanded to reurn 12 honeſt men of the

neighbourhood whereby the truth of the matter may be known

Jury Called
&
Atteſted –
} John Surket Henry Hudleſtone John naylor Ralph Cowgill
Enoch yardley willm Dungan ffrancis white Richard wilſon
willm Biles Junr: Robt Heaton Junr: John Croſdell James plumley

Declaracon againe Read and the pltf produced the letter menconed there in

The letter read as ffolloweth

Benfalem 7° $\frac{9}{mo}$ i685

my Good friend

prefumeing that it may not difcomode thee I fhall requeft
the favore of thee to fpare me fiveteen pounds which be pleafed to fend
me by the bearror my Servant Philip Daniel and thefe Shall oblige
me to repay thee againe in filve mony at or before the 6th of
$\frac{i2}{mo}$ next enfueing with Intreft and be acknowledged as a great —

kindnes done unto thy much obliged friend   Joseph Growdon

1685

my Refpects to thy good wife the fame to thy felf   }
pray pleafe to send 6th of fugr by the bearror —   }   Idem J G

7th of november i685 Received then of John Grey for the ufe of my

Receipt for   }
the fame —   }   mr Jofeph Growdon the abovementioned fiveteen pounds witnes my
                        hand

philip X Daniel
his   mark

witneffed by us will myers John Tomlinfon

344

The which letter and the Receipt of the mony the deft owned but pleaded that at the fame
time the mony was borrowed the fd pltf was Indebted to him the faid
deft more then the mony mentioned in the fd Letter amounted to upon
the account of a Certaine tract of Land he the faid deft fold the fd pltf

The pltf replyed he had payd for the Said Land & produced Receipts for the Same

The which Receipts the deft owned but pleaded they figned at the requeft of

the pltf before all the mony was paid he the ſd pltf aleadging that
it was requiſit the ſaid Receipts Shold be given at the ſealing and
delivery of the deed or Conveyance of the said Lands and that what
was wanting the ſaid Conſideracon mony he the ſaid pltf promiſed
he wold pay or be accountable for the ſame and that he the ſaid
deft upon the pltf promiſe did ſeal the ſaid Receipts

whereupon the ſaid pltf for proofe of payment of the ſaid Conſideracon
mony to have been made in full according to the ſaid Receipts &
that there was nothing due thereupon to ſd deft produced the
following account

The acctt read as ffolloweth

A porticuler

of the hundered pounds worth of Engliſh goods which I did pay &
Deliver to Joſeph Growdon gent. for one Thouſand acres of Land
(by vertue of an agreement verbaly Concluded between him and
me for the ſame) in July i685 the Reſidue of that purchaſe (wᶜʰ
was one hundered pounds more) being payable in Caſh upon the
Coſts & Charges of which Goods till they were houſd at my Settlement
neare neſhaminah River I was to have allowed me Twenty
pcent: ſterling profit by the ſaid agreemt & no more

	£	s	d
1 Imprims 4 pr mens woſted hoſe at 2ˢ: 4ᵈ p pr	—	-9	-4
2 It: i4 pr ditto Coarſer at i8ᵈ p p —	-1	-1	--
3 It. i ps of fine bengall att — —	--	16	--
4 It: 1 ps ditto Courſed at — — — —	--	14	--
5 It: 2 ps plaine ditto at 12ˢ 6ᵈ p ps	-1	-5	--
6 It: i ps wᵗ Callicoe at — — — —	--	i0	-6
7 It: 1 ps. ditto — — —	--	-9	-6
8 It: Iſarees — — — — — — — —	--	i2	--
9 It: i ps wide blew callico — — —	-i	-3	--
i0 It: i ps blew callico — — —	--	i0	--
ii It: 2 ps blew linnen at 18ˢ p ps —	-i	i6	--
i2 It: i ps wᵗ Linnen at	-i	ii	-3
i3 It i ps wᵗ Ticklingberge	--	i5	.2
i4 It: 24¾ yrds of Hartfords at 6ˢ p yd — —	--	i2	.4½
i5 It 37 Ells Canvas at iiᵈ p Ell — — —	-i	13	-ii
i6 It: 12 yrds broad Cloth at 5ˢ p yrd	-3	--	--
i7 It 2 ps Duffalls at 6£ -3ˢ -5½ᵈ p ps —	12	-6	ii
i8 It i ps fine Cloth Serge — — — —	-3	13	--
i9 It: 3 ps ditto 5iˢ: 4ᵈ p ps	-7	14	--
20 It: 6 ps norwich stuff at 20ˢ p ps — —	-6	--	--
Carrye over	46	i5	5½

	£	s	d
brought over —	46	i5	5½.
It			
2i 2 ps barronits at 30ˢ p ps — — — —	-3	--	--
22 It: 6 pr french fulls at 3ˢ 4ᵈ p pr — —	-1	--	--
23 It: 6 pr mens plaines at 2ˢ 3ᵈ p pr — — —	--	i3	-6
24 It: i pr boys & i ditto girls at 16ᵈ p pr —	--	-2	-8.
25 It: i pr boys ditto at —	--	-2	2
26 It: 5 pr pumps at 7ᵈ pr pr — — — —	--	-2	ii.
27 It: 2 pr more of girls ſhooes at i6ᵈ p pr —	--	-2	-8.
28 It: i ps of Canvas Cont: 65½ Ells at 17ᵈ p El	-4	12	-9
29 It: i ps of scotch cloth Cont: 10 yrds at 16ᵈ p yd — — — —	--	i3	-4
30 It: i ps of fuſtian at —	--	15	--
31 It: 3ˡᵇ Coloured thread at 2ˢ p ˡᵇ: i ditto brown 22ᵈ —	-7	i0.	
32 It: i ps Searge Cont: 20½ yrds at 22ᵈ p yrd —	-i	i7	-7
33 It: i grs bell mettal buttons — — — —	--	-2	-4.
34 It: 2 braſs kettles —	-2	i0	--
35 It: 13ˡᵇ powder & the brl — — — — — .	--	i3	-8
36 It: 14ˡᵇ of ſhot — — —	--	-i	-6
37 It: 6 falling axes at i4ᵈ p ps —	--	i5	--
38 It 6 broad hows at i4ᵈ p ps — — —	--	-7	--
39 It 6 tilling hows at 12ᵈ p ps — — —	--	-6	--
40 It i little how at — —	--	--	10.
4i It i broad ax at — —	--	-3	-6
42 It 3 doz Spoones at 16ᵈ p doz —	--	-4	--
43 It 3 doz more at 20ᵈ p doz — — —	--	-5	--
44 It: 6 Cow bells at 5½ p ps —	--	-2	-9
45 It i Large pewter chamber pot — — —	--	-3	--
46 It : 3 doz ditto of Leſſor ſize — — .	--	-7	-6
Carryed on =	66	-8	--

345

	£	s	d
Sum brought over - -	66	-8	-0

47 It 6 Large podding
difhes at 9ᵈ p ps - - -- -- -4 -6
48 It 6 ditto Leffor fize -- -4 --
49 It i doz Marjerine
plates — — — — -- i2 --
50 It 3 Small bafons i
Large — — -- -8 --
5i It 3 Quart Tankards 4ˢ
p ps — — — — 12 --
52 It 2 Large muggs at 12ᵈ
p ps — — — -- -2 --
53 It 4 Leffor ditto at 10ᵈ
p ps — — — -- -3 -4
54 It 6 half pt bottles at
9ᵈ p ps — — -- -4 -6
55 It 6 Quart pt bottles at
6ᵈ p ps — — -- -3 --
56 It i pr Large
Candlefticks - - - - -- -6 -6
57 It: i Little Sauce pan -- -2 -3
58 It ½ doz tand lether
raines at 7ᵈ p pr -- -3 -6
59 It 2 pr bl ditto at i0ᵈ
p pr — — — -- -1 -8
60 It 3 Twifted 3 plaine
Snuffles at — — -- -3 -6
6i It i pr fterrup lether -- - i -6
62 It 4 pr ftirrup Irons at
ẝ i0ᵈ p pr — -- -3 -4
63 It 2 more of Tand
fterrup lethers — -- - i -6
64 It 2 bridle bitts at 20ᵈ
p pr — — — -- -3 -4
65 It 2 double & 8 fingle
girths — — — -- -4 --
66 It i plufh faddle with
bridle & furniture 1 18 --
67 It 3 hunting fadles ⎱
with bridles &- ⎰
furniture at i3ˢ p ps ⎰ - i i9 --
68 It 12ˡᵇ of 10ᵈ nailes at
4ˢ 9ᵈ p m — — -- -5 -8
69 It 2 m̄ of 8ᵈ nailes at
3ˢ 9ᵈ p m — -- -7 -6

	£	s	d
Sum brought over — —	77	-3	11

other Cofts & difburfe-
ments upon
thefe goods for porter- ⎱
idge Cart- ⎮
age Entering at the ⎮
Cuftome — ⎮
houfe & duties there paid ⎮
for ⎰ 10 -- --
the Same for Lighterige ⎮
to the ⎮
Ship & fraight being ⎮
Computed ⎮
at above 2 Tunn at 4£ & ⎮
for bringing them up to — ⎮
nefhaminah amount to -- ⎰

Twenty p cent fterling ⎱
upon ⎮
the Cofts of the above ⎰
goods is ⎰ i7 -8 -9

	£	s	d
Summa totalis =	i04	12	-8

overpaid

Over paid Mr. Growdon
by the
within Goods - - - -- -4 -i2 -8
as the with in account
makes —
Evident
A true Coppy of the faid
Account

The above goods were delivered
to Mr. Growdon him felf and by
him Called out of the whole Cargoe
July the i8 and i9th 1685 delivered to his
fervant July the 28 1685 (vpage P4i)   – i   i9   – 6
viz: 2 m 10d nailes at 4s 9d p m
& 8 m of 8d ditto at 3s 9d p m wch:
amount to — — — — — — — —

It   i gouge i hammer i Chiffell —   — — – i   – 6
It ½ pt bottle — — — — — —   — — — – i   — —

The prime Cofts at the ftores upon }   77 – 3   ii
thefe goods amount to — — {

The hundered pounds Cafh which I was further to pay him for the faid Land was thus Difcharged

£   s   d

15 4 1685 pag L:37
—
mo
   Then pd Mr. Growdon in ps of } 10 — — — —
8th Ten pounds fterling — —

pd alfo then to him
   Sixty ps of
8th more wch: mr
growdon wold
not alow to be more
then — —
13£ 10s: fterling tho } i3 10 — —
upon an
honeft and juft Efti-
mate of —
theire value they do
amount
to i8s fterling more - -

ii 5 1685 It pd then more to Mr
—
mo
growdon one hundered ps 8th wch
he Contentioufly difputed to be no } 22 10 — —
more then 22£ –10s fterling
nor wold he otherwife alow for
the fame tho 30s sterling more

July the 20th i685 then paid Mr
growdon the refidue of the —
hundered pounds thus viz fifty } 53 i9 – 2
Gineas at one & Twenty fhillings
and Seven pence p ginea wch
makes the fum of — — — — —

Then 10d fterling yet
   wanting
to the ballanceing of
this
account according to } — — — — i0
mr —
Growdons Calculation
and
novel Arithmetick was
dicharged by a bit and
a half

Errors Excepted P me John Tatham

A true Coppy

    100 00 00

overpd in the 2d paymt
30s in the } – 2 – 8 — —
3d payment i8s in the
whole

over pd as above in
goods — —   4 –i2 – 8

over paid in the whole   7 — – 8
     fterling mony

346

objection by the deft to the forefd acctt	To which the deft anfwered that they had never pfected any account —

Concerning the fame but that the Said pltf had framed the
aforefd —

account and that it was a falfe one that it varied from an account
formerly given him by the fd pltf Concering the aforefd Goods
and

requefted the account menconed in the declaracon might be
produced

where upon the fd plt produced the fd account mentioned in the
declaracon

which was read and is as followeth

acct mencond in the decla- con — —	Jofeph Growdon is Debtor unto John Tatham for fundry goods & merchandizes delivered by him unto the fd Jofeph Growdon in the yeare 1685 wch the faid john was

never yet paid for asffollows

	£	s	d
July the i8ᵗʰ 1685 Imprs to a brl of mollofes att — — — — –3		-0	-0
It: then to a gallon of Rum — — — — — — — — — —		-5	--
28 P: 4i – It: to 5 gallon 3 qrts of Rum at 5ˢ p gallon — — — –1		-8	-9
It: to 1/2 lb fugr — — — — — — — — — — — –1		-5	--
Auguft ift It to a fyth — — — — — — — — — — — —		-4	--
Septemʳ i0ᵗʰ It: to a barr of Iron wᵗ 40ˡᵇ delivered to ffr: Rufh p ordr — —		13	-4
octob 26 pg R: 43 It to 2ˡᵇ 30ᵈ nailes at 8ᵈ p lb — — — — —		1	-4
It then to 3ˡᵇ of 20ᵈ nailes and 4ˡᵇ of i0ᵈ at 9ᵈ p lb — —		-5	-3
It: to 6ˡᵇ of fugr delivered to Jofeph fervant by his note — —		-3	--
It: to 2ˡᵇ more delivered to Jofeph him felf at 6ᵈ p lb — — — —		-1	--
novemb 7ᵗʰ It Jofeph is debtr to Cafh lent him at his requeft — and upon his promife by his note to repay it with Intreft in three month — — — — — — — — — — —	15	--	--
It to Intreft for 12 yeares & i0ᵗʰ months now due for the Same at 8 pcent — — — — — — — — —	i5	-8	--

It to 4 books which he borrowed the fame to be
     reftored —
or theire prices at 20ˢ p booke — — — — —   }   4 — —

Sum Total: 4i – 14   : 8

Errors Excepted   p me John Tatham

A true Coppy

He owes me likewife for the mony paid and difburfed by me
for the furveying of the Thoufand acres of Land he Sold me wch
     by
bargaine he affumed to pay as is evident by his Letter in PC: 29
and for half of the Charges for the deed for he haveing a Counter
part or duplicate ought to pay for it which pticulers I fubmit to
your reafonable & Juft Confideracon   John Tatham
due more the 10ᵗʰ of this Inftant September 1699 one yeares
Intreft for the i5 £ viz 24ˢ

A true Coppy

The deft aleadged that divers articles in the foregoing account were
     Charged in the account formerly given towards what was
     due to him for the Thoufand acres of Land

To which the pltf replyed that it was a true account and that he had not
     Charged any article thereof in any other or former account
     and that he was ready to be attefted to the truth thereof

347

whereupon the Said John Tatham the pltf was Attefted and upon his
     Atteftation
     declared that the fore going account was Juft and true & that he
     had not Charged any one article thereof in any former account

The deft thereupon produced an account & afked the pltf whether that
     was his hand writeing

The plt replyed thereto that it was his hand writeing he wold not deny it
     wch Said account so produced by the deft was read & is as
     ffolloweth

Goods Delivered to Joſeph Growdon
as follows — — — — — — —

	£	s	d
4 pr fine mens wostet hoſe at 2ˢ 4ᵈ p pr — —	— —	-9	-4
14 pr mens worſtet hoſe att 18ᵈ p pr —	-i	-1	--
i ps fine Bengall — — — — — —	--	16	--
i ps ditto Coarſer — — — — —	--	14	--
2 ps plaine ditto — — — — —	-i	-5	--
i ps wᵗ Callico — — — — — —	--	10	-6
1 ps ditto — — — — — — —	--	-9	-6
1 ps Iſarees — — — — — —	--	12	-6
i ps wide blew calico — — — —	-1	-3	--
i ps blew calico — — — — —	--	12	--
2 ps blew linnen — — — — —	-i	-ii	-3
1 ps wᵗ Ticklingberge — — —	--	i5	-2
24¾ hartfords — — — — —	--	12	-4½
37 Ells of Canvas at iiᵈ p Ell —	-i	i3	-ii
12 yrds of broad Cloth at 5ˢ p yrd — — — — — — — —	-3	--	--
2 ps Duffalls — — — — — —	12	-6	ii
1 ps fine cloath Searge — —	-2	i3	--
3 ps Searge — — — — — —	-7	i4	--
6 ps norwich stuffs — — — —	-6	--	--
2 ps Barronets 30ˢ p ps — —	-3	--	--
6 pr french ffulls at 3ˢ 4ᵈ p pr	-i	--	--
6 pr mens plaines at 2ˢ 3ᵈ p pr	--	13	-6
pr of boys ſhoes & i of girls at i6ᵈ p pr — — — —	--	-2	-8

		£	s	d
	Shoes att	--	-2	-2
	at 7ᵈ p pr	--	-2	ii
	1s ſhoes at i6ᵈ p pr	--	-2	-8
	65½ Ells at i7ᵈ p Ell	-4	i2	-9½
	h Cont: i0 yrds at i6ᵈ p yd	--	13	-4
		--	15	-
	10 at 2ˢ p pd: & 1 brown at 22ᵈ —	--	-7	i0

ſf the was Eaton by rats or mice or ſuch like it Cold not be read.

ps of ſearge Cont: 20½ yrds at 22ᵈ p yd	-1	i7	-7
1 gr bellmetal buttons — — —	--	2	-4
1 brl molloſes — — — — —	-2	-8	--
ffraight & other Charges — —	-3	-8	--
3 braſs kettles — — — —	-2	i0	--
13 lb powder & the brl — —	--	i3	-8
14 lb ſhot — — — — — —	--	-i	-6
6 felling axes — — — — —	--	i5	--
6 broad hows — — — — —	--	-7	--
6 tilling hows — — — — —	--	-6	--
1 little how — — — — —	--	--	10
1 broad ax — — — — — —	--	.3	-6
3 doz ſpoons 16ᵈ p doz — —	--	.4	..
3 doz more att 20ᵈ p — — —	--	.5	..

Carryed over

	£	s	d
½ Doz Cow Bells — — — — —	--	-2	-9
1 great Chamber pot — — —	--	-3	--
3 little ones — — — — —	--	-7	-6
½ doz Large podding diſhes —	--	-4	-6
½ doz of a leſſer ſize — — —	--	-4	--
1 doz mazerine plates — — —	--	12	--
3 Smal baſons 1 Large — — —	--	8	--
3 Quart tankards — — — —	--	12	--
2 Large muggs — — — — —	--	2	--
4 leſſer ditto — — — — —	--	3	-4
6 ½ pt bottles — — — — —	--	-4	-6

74.13 : 6

	£	s	d
½ doz ¼ pt bottles — — — —	--	4	--
1 pr Large Candle ſticks — —	--	6	-6
1 little ſauce pan — — — —	--	2	-3
½ Doz pare Tand leſer rains —	--	3	-6
2 pr bl rains — — — — —	--	1	-8
i pc bl ſtirrup lethers — — —	--	--	10
3 Twiſted 3 plaine Snuffles —	--	3	-6
4 pr ſtirrup Irons — — — —	--	3	-4
2 double & 8 ſingle girths —	--	4	--
1 pluſh ſaddle with holſters &c	1	18	,-
4 bottles of Rum — — — —	--	5	--
½ ſf ſugr — — — — — —	-1	-5	--
3 lb worth of nailes whereof — delivered 1200 of 10ᵈ nailes at 4 ſ 9ᵈ p m & 200 of 8ᵈ at 3 ſ 9ᵈ p m — —	-3	--	--

delivered more July the 28ᵗʰ —
1685 2 m of 10ᵈ nailes at 4ˢ
9ᵈ p 8 m of 8ᵈ nailes 3 9 — i 10 — —
the 1200 delivered before com
the 200 10ᵈ nailes comes
delivered more 5 gallon &
3 qrts of Rum wch at
5 ſ p gallon comes
It i gouge i hammer & i Chiſſel

this Eaton as before & Cold not be — read

It ½ pt bottle — — — — — — -- -i --

	£	s	d
	12	-5	-6
	74	13	-6
	86	19	--

delivered by my man a ſyth

348

The Court Compareing the aforegoing accounts together it appeared that –
    Several articles in the account mentioned in the declaracon were
    Charged formerly by the pltf in the account the deft produced
    for and towards payment of the Thouſand acres of Land and that
    Some of the articles in the account the pltf produced to prove —
    payment for the Land were augmented above what they were
    at firſt given in unto the deft

Whereupon the pltf then acknowledged that the account about the Land
    was never perfected and was but a Curſory account

The deft aleadged that the Land paid for according to agreement
    there wold be nothing due to the pltf and thereupon produced
    his objections agt the account firſt given in by the pltf to the
    deft and are as ffolloweth

	£	s	d
Imprimis over Charged on nailes Twice ſet to account — —	–3	—	—
overCharged on nailes 200 p m for they ought to be 1200 to each m when as they were but 1000 delivered	—	10	—
over Charged on 5 gallons of Rum being Charged at 5ˢ p gallon the highest rate Sold for here Inſtead whereof I ought to have dollars at 4ˢ 6ᵈ Each or Engliſh goods at 20 pcent advance — — — — — — — — — — — —	— —	i7	–3
over charged on i brl of molloſſes after the ſame manner — — — — — — — — —i	—	—	—
and on 1/2 lb of ſugr — — — — — — — — — — —	10	—	
and on 4 bottles of Rum — — — — — — — — —	–3	—	
over charged on fraight &c — — — — — — — —i	—	—	
to Damages on 2 ps of Duffalls — — — — — — –4	–2	4	
to Damages on 2 ps of Callico — — — — — — —	–5	—	
to ſo much Loſs by 88 £ Received in gineas at 2iˢ 6ᵈ each and other mony Equivalent when as Iought to have by contract Dollars at 4ˢ 6ᵈ each this Loſs at i7ᵈ p £ is	.5	–i3	–4
more loſs on light mony — — — — — — — — —	i2	—	
to a red leather Chaire lent his ant — — — — — —	i5	—	
for Timber by him fallen on my land & Converted to his uſe			
	i8	07	ii

After a full hearing of both parties the Jury went out and the next
morning returned into the Court and delivered in the following
verdict in writeing

Bucks ff

we of the Jury do find for the deft with coft of fuite as witnes
verdict   our hands

John furket fforeman Richard wilfon John naylor willm Dungan
Enoch yardley Robt Heaton John Crofdell Henry Hudleftone
ffrancis white Ralph Cowgill James plumley willm Biles Junr

ffrom which verdict the Said pltf appealed to the next provincial Court
to be held for the aforefd County in Equity and entered into —
Recognizance according to Law to profecute the fd appeale
John Tatham obliges him felf unto william Penn Proprietarie and
Govrnr of this province his Heirs and fucceffors in the Sum of
fifty pounds to be Levied on his goods and Chattles Lands and

349

Tennemts and This is upon Condition that the Said John Tatham
profe
-cute his appeal agt Jofeph Growdon at the next provincial court
to
be held for this County in Equity and to pay all cofts & damages
that
Shall be decreed in the faid Court agt the Said appealant _____

grand Jurys prfentmt

Bucks ff   the 20th day of the 8th month 1699

we of the grand Jury for the body of this County d prfent John
Tatham for Takeing a falfe Atteftation upon the i9th day of the 8th
month 1699 Conterary to the kings peace and ftatute Laws made
&
provided figned by order of the Jury by

william Paxon
foreman i699

action
John Sutton
agt
Burden

*merand to Enter
the date of A deed
Jos Growdon grantr
to Abel Hinckſtone
grantee

† Bucks ſS   350

At A Court of Quarter Seſsions held the by
the Kings Authority in the Name of William
penn proprietʳʸ & Governʳ of the province: of pensilvaⁿⁱᵃ
and terretories thereunto belonging the 12° day
of the first Month Anno Domj: 1700

Juſtices prsent Joseph Growdon   William Biles
                John Swift   Richard Hough
                Samˡˡ Beaks Sherriffe
                phenihas pemberton Cl: Com:

The Grand Jury Atteſted which were

Bucks ſs the 13° day of the 1ˢᵗ mo: 1 __700__
                                        699

wee the grand jury (upon Complaint) do prsent the Neſseſsity of
aroad from the ferry at John Balldwins into the moſt Convenient
place of New town Road leading to Neſhaminy Meeting houſe, as
it may beſt anſwer yᵉ Convenency of the Neighbourhood

Wee Likewiſe prsent John Scarbrough for keeing an
ordinary without lycence

And allso the Neſseſsity of the placeing a Court houſe Near
the Middle of the County which wee eſteem to be Near
  Neſhaminy Meeting houſe   Signed by
                                  Joſhua Hoops fforeman

---

*A small slip of paper loose between pp. 348 and 349.

† The remaining entries in the record are in a different hand from that of Pemberton,
more like that of Jeremiah Langhorn who succeeded him as Clerk of the County.

A deed of   acres of land in fee was acknowledged
    by Anthony Morgan Attorny to Joſias Hill grantor
    unto John Ellett grantee dated the   day of

   A deed of   hundred acres of land in fee was acknowledged
    by Samuel Beaks Attorny to Jonathan Scaiſe grantor
    unto John Rumford grantee dated the   day of

   A deed of five thouſand acres of land in fee dated the   day of
       was acknowledged by William Biles Attorney to
    to Thomas Hudson grantor unto William Lawrence
    and Company grantees

A deed of   hundred acres of land in fee dated the day of
    v   was Acknowledged by William Biles junr. Attorny
    to Samuel Richardson grantor unto phenihas pemberton
    Grantee

    351

A deed of   hundred acres of land in fee was Acknowledged
    by Joseph Growden grantor unto William Baker grantee
    dated the   day of

A deed of   hundred acres of land in fee was Acknowledged by
    Richard Hough grantor unto John Watson Grantee dated
    the   day of

A deed of Mortgage of   hundred acres of land dated the
    day of   was Acknowledged by John Watson Mortgagor
    unto Richard Hough Mortgagee

        Court Adjurned for one hour

    The Grand Jury's prsentm[ts] brought in

Bucks ſs

    The 14th day of y[e] 1st month 1699
                          700

    wee the grand Jurors for the body this County do preſent
    a Neſseſsity of a Road from Joseph Growdon's to the
    Kings Road leading to the falls & Neſhaminy Meeting
    Houſe Signed by   Joſhua Hoops foreman

Bucks ſs the 14ᵗʰ day of yᵉ 1ˢᵗ mo.   1699
                                      ——————
                                        700

Wee of the Grand Jurors for the Body of this County do
prsent Charles Smith (Sojurnʳ amongst us) for
Entering into the Stable of William paxſon Junʳ and
unlawfully takeing an old pare of Stockings, a bridle and
a few old buttons of Samuel Oldale's And allso a horse
of yᵉ sd William paxſons out of his Yard without his leave or
Conſent Signed by   Joſhua Hoops fforeman

Likewiſe wee preſent the Neſseſsity of building a bridge over
Neſhaminy Creeke, And that the Charge thereof, Levied
upon our County exceed not eighty pounds, And that the
Court apoint Tenn Men for to vew & Make Choice of a
place And allso to lett out the worke, And to See the good
accompliſhmᵗ. thereof Six whereof agreeing Shall be thought
Sufficient
          Signed by

                         Joſhua Hoops fforeman

         Court Adjurned untill Eight a Clock tomorrow
         Morning about wᶜʰ time being open

Note: The foregoing Court was held on the 12ᵗʰ day of the 1ˢᵗ month Anno
Dom 1700. The next court recorded was held on 10ᵗʰ day of 7ᵗʰ mo: 1702.
Between these dates are the above presentments and others dated 12ᵗʰ ye
first mo 1702/2, and at the end of sundry, similar & other Court record entries
appears "This Court adjourns till yᵉ usual time in June."

INDEX OF PERSONS

Only one reference is given to a name on the same page.

Abbott, Samuel, 74, 75, 76, 82, 83, 85, 185.
Abbotts, Answer, 84.
Ackerman, 282.
Ackerman, John, 4, 9, 11, 19, 222.
Ackerman, Mary, 38.
Acreman, James, 361, 365, 379, 383, 387.
Adams, Seemercy, 75.
Addington, 178.
Addington, John, 274, 355, 356, 357, 327.
Adkinson, Isaac, 294.
Adkinson, Jane, 294.
Adkinson, Samuel, 294.
Adkinson, Thomas, 20, 32, 75, 82, 294, 296.
Adkinson, William, 294.
Aleine, see Allen.
Allen, Jedidiah, 66.
Allen, John, 104, 202, 214, 215, 217, 332.
Allen, Nathaniel, 32.
Allen, Neamiah, 91, 191.
Allen, Samuel, 25, 75, 89, 130, 149, 164, 169, 190, 236, 242, 262, 266, 328, 370, 372, 373.
Allen, Samuel, Jr., 91, 112, 122, 147, 158, 164, 191, 210, 221, 233, 256, 262.
Allott, Andrew, 188.
Alman, James, 326, 336, 347, 352, 353, 359, 365, 377, 379, 383, 384, 388, 389, 400.
Alsop, Jon, 57.
Andrews, Elizabeth, 48.
Andrews, Francis, 49.
Antill, Edward, 168, 169, 170, 264, 265, 266, 267.
Archer, Thomas, 330, 337.
Athay, Richard, 393.

Atthary, Richard, 312.
Austin, John, 74, 79, 80, 170, 267.

Bainbridge, John 47.
Bains, Thomas, 339, 340, 341, 358.
Baker, Henry, 20, 22, 25, 41, 47, 59, 86, 90, 92, 93, 100, 101, 105, 111, 121, 123, 126, 130, 133, 138, 139, 152, 157, 159, 161, 162, 163, 167, 170, 171, 172, 174, 176, 178, 185, 190, 192, 193, 199, 200, 203, 209, 221, 222, 227, 228, 237, 242, 245, 251, 255, 259, 260, 261, 262, 264, 267, 268, 270, 271, 274, 281, 285, 288, 293, 295, 298, 299, 300, 302, 304, 309, 311, 312, 313, 316, 318, 323, 325, 329, 333, 334, 345, 355, 362, 367, 370, 373, 378, 380, 383, 385, 391, 397.
Baker, William, 415.
Baldwin, John, 71, 164, 262, 283, 304, 321, 327, 328, 414.
Banks, Anthony, 172, 271.
Bannor, Lawrence, 20, 50, 51, 52, 53, 58, 62, 63, 64, 66, 68.
Bannr, see Bannor.
Barrets, 346.
Barry, Robert 399.
Basnet, Richard, 48, 127, 238.
Bayns, see Bains.
Beake, Abraham, 279, 280.
Beakes, Daniel, 195.
Beakes, Edmund, 84, 85, 184, 185.
Beakes, Elizabeth, 284, 285.
Beakes, Ellenor, 95, 195.
Beaks, Mary, 84, 105, 145, 184, 204, 226, 229, 280, 282.
Beakes, Samuel, 140, 141, 145, 164, 167, 171, 172, 174, 176, 179, 181, 226, 229, 231, 239, 263, 264, 268, 269, 270, 271, 273, 274, 280, 284.

285, 286, 288, 291, 293, 295, 296,
297, 298, 300, 301, 302, 304, 305,
308, 309, 313, 314, 315, 316, 317,
319, 323, 324, 325, 326, 327, 328,
329, 330, 331, 335, 336, 337, 338,
339, 342, 345, 346, 347, 348, 349,
352, 354, 356, 358, 361, 362, 365,
367, 368, 370, 372, 373, 375, 378,
379, 380, 382, 385, 386, 387, 388,
390, 391, 397, 399, 400, 414, 415.
Beakes, Stephen, 85, 99, 121, 156,
157, 158, 165, 167, 168, 169, 185,
187, 198, 203, 206, 214, 215, 217,
221, 233, 239, 253, 254, 255, 256,
264, 265, 266, 280, 307, 309, 313,
339, 342, 344, 360, 367, 371, 375,
377.
Beakes, William, 3, 4, 10, 11, 19, 25,
40, 42, 50, 51, 52, 53, 58, 60, 61,
64, 65, 87, 91, 101, 105, 111, 112,
121, 123, 132, 134, 145, 175, 182,
185, 186, 191, 200, 203, 209, 210,
211, 218, 221, 222, 226, 239, 243,
245, 247, 253, 276, 280, 283, 284,
285, 315, 373.
Beaks, William, Jr., 79, 80.
Beal, see Beale.
Beale, William, 201, 374.
Beatridg, Betridge, see Betrice.
Bennet, Edmund, 10, 15, 19, 24, 31,
32, 40, 49, 58, 62, 64, 65, 123,
130, 242, 332.
Bennet, Edward, 372.
Bennet, Elizabeth, 174, 272, 310,
339.
Benson, Robert, 91, 143, 177, 179,
180, 192, 225, 273, 276.
Betrice, Mark, 88, 107, 125, 188.
Betrice, Prudence, 290.
Betrice, William, 401.
Bians, William, 256.
Bills, Thomas, 306.
Bircham, Henry, 20, 32, 93, 109,
193, 207, 305.
Bircham, Margaret, 305.
Black, William, 82.
Blackwell, John, 112, 210.
Bladen, Barbary, 339.
Biles, Charles, 57, 73, 74, 287.
Biles, George, 297, 354, 355, 359,
401.
Biles, Jane, 297.
Biles, Sarah, 134, 246, 318, 398.

Biles, William, 5, 6, 8, 9, 10, 11,
16, 19, 22, 23, 25, 31, 32, 40, 42,
43, 46, 56, 61, 62, 64, 65, 66, 67,
69, 70, 71, 73, 74, 83, 88, 89, 90,
96, 97, 101, 105, 111, 113, 115,
121   123, 124, 126, 128, 129, 130,
131, 135, 137, 138, 139, 140, 145,
151, 152, 153, 161, 162, 163, 164,
165, 167, 171, 173, 174, 176, 178,
184, 189, 191, 196, 197, 200, 203,
209, 213, 215, 219, 221, 222, 223,
226, 227, 228, 230, 231, 236, 237,
240, 241, 242, 243, 248, 250, 251,
259, 260, 261, 262, 264, 268, 271,
272, 274, 279, 286, 288, 291, 293,
294, 295, 297, 300, 301, 304, 306,
309, 310, 313, 316, 322, 325, 329,
330, 334, 338, 342, 344, 345, 348,
352, 355, 358, 364, 370, 373, 375,
378, 380, 385, 391, 397, 398, 414,
415.
Biles, William, Jr., 318, 354, 358,
371, 375, 377, 396, 399, 400, 403,
413, 415.
Biles, William, Sr., 399.
Blackshaw, Josiah, 306.
Blackshaw, Nehemiah, 311, 375.
Blackshaw, Randulph (Randle or
Randol), 20, 33, 84, 89, 101, 103,
109, 112, 184, 189, 200, 201, 207,
209, 210, 292, 304, 311, 375, 397.
Bleake, James, 156, 255.
Blowers, Joseph, 22, 23, 24.
Boare, Joshua, 20, 40, 57.
Boare, Lucy, 299.
Bond, James, 374, 376.
Bons, see Boone.
Boome, Ralph, 141, 143, 162, 163,
164, 173, 224, 231, 261, 262, 271,
282, 298, 299, 300, 326, 332, 356,
370.
Boucher, Henry, 150, 249.
Bowen, Henry, 299, 375.
Bowen, John, 59, 162, 163, 169, 261,
266, 299, 399.
Bowman, Thomas, 3, 266, 374, 399.
Bowman's Estate, 352.
Bown, Samuel, 305.
Bowns, John, 399.
Bownton, see Bunting.
Boyden, James, 20, 22, 24, 32, 42,
130, 171, 242.

Boyden, James, Jr., 121, 221, 305, 313.
Boyden, Mary, 166, 263, 277.
Bradley, Joshua, 67.
Brearley, John, 30, 79, 80, 87, 172, 186, 206.
Brian, William, 191.
Bridgman, Walter, 76, 77, 86, 88, 186, 188.
Brigham, Charles, 103, 110, 202.
Brindley, Luke, 3, 5, 6, 9, 15, 19, 23, 26, 27, 28, 29, 30, 32, 35, 36, 38, 40, 41, 45, 46, 47, 51, 52, 53, 55, 56, 62, 63, 82, 96, 108, 112, 117, 196, 206, 209.
Brinson, Daniel, 4, 11, 16, 17, 32, 34, 37, 59, 68, 180, 276.
Brittan, Lyonel, 10, 20, 22, 32, 47, 58, 63, 99, 198.
Brock, John, 9, 13, 15, 26, 30, 34, 35, 36, 41, 47, 48, 57, 58, 69, 76, 77, 84, 85, 86, 89, 91, 92, 93, 100, 101, 105, 111, 121, 123, 126, 128, 129, 130, 132, 138, 139, 143, 144, 152, 159, 161, 184, 186, 189, 191, 192, 193, 199, 200, 203, 209, 221, 222, 225, 226, 227, 228, 236, 237, 240, 241, 251, 259, 277, 278, 279, 280, 281, 282, 283, 284, 295, 307, 316, 321.
Brock, Thomas, 91, 104, 141, 143, 152, 153, 154, 158, 159, 163, 168, 172, 175, 177, 191, 202, 210, 224, 230, 231, 251, 252, 257, 262, 265, 271, 273, 274, 278, 280, 282, 283, 284, 285, 287, 290, 292, 295, 296, 300, 301, 305, 324, 326, 328, 329, 330, 339, 349, 356, 367, 380, 398, 399.
Brown, George, 32, 137, 152, 156, 157, 158, 182, 248, 251, 254, 256, 257, 276, 278, 306, 335, 391.
Bucher, Michael, 88, 117, 118, 188, 212, 217.
Buckman, William, 76, 77, 93, 193, 229, 255, 280, 299, 303, 318, 326, 328, 344, 349.
Bud, John, 151.
Bull, Richard, 335.
Bunting, Job, 168, 170, 182, 265, 267, 276, 278, 280, 288, 397.
Buntinge, see Bunting.
Burcham, see Bircham.

Burden, 414.
Burden, Joseph, 103, 202, 396.
Burden, Samuel, 97, 99, 100, 103, 104, 197, 199, 202, 396.
Burges, Anthony, 82.
Burges, Daniel, 331.
Burges, Elizabeth, 346, 358, 360, 379, 382.
Burges, Isaac, 108, 206, 209, 299, 301.
Burges, Richard, 178, 181, 312, 314, 321, 336, 338, 340, 346.
Burges, Samuel, 30, 33, 68, 72, 112, 123, 210, 222, 255, 285, 301, 327.
Burges, Samuel, Jr., 305.
Burradel, John, 390, 395.
Burton, Anthony, 98, 177, 197, 217, 273, 278, 279, 290, 295, 296, 301, 302, 316, 323, 350, 358, 359, 367, 379, 380, 394, 397, 398.
Burton, George, 213, 218.
Burton, John, 379.
Busby, John, 379.
Busby, Mary, 379.
Butler, John, 144, 147, 148, 203, 226, 234, 237.

Carpenter, Samuel, 103, 142, 202, 224, 292, 293, 302, 311, 324, 326, 337, 349, 355, 396.
Carter, see Cartor.
Cartor, Edward, 95, 104, 124, 160, 195, 202, 223, 259, 279, 357, 396.
Cartor, John, 70, 71, 124, 223, 314, 354, 369.
Cartor, Robert, 32, 34, 56, 70, 71, 72.
Cartor, William, 56.
Cartr, see Cartor.
Caws, see Clows.
Cearll, Thomas, 280, 283.
Cearll, see Kirle.
Chamberlaine, Lucy, 394.
Chamberlaine, Peter, 163, 394.
Chapman, Jane, 345.
Chappel, Elizabeth, 164, 263.
Chorley, Joseph, 8, 82, 84, 101, 106, 147, 149, 151, 164, 173, 174, 179, 180, 187, 200, 204, 233, 236, 250, 262, 271, 272, 276, 278, 282, 287, 292, 293, 297, 304, 310, 313, 318, 321, 326, 328, 329, 330, 338, 342,

344, 346, 347, 349, 355, 358, 361, 362, 364, 365, 366, 367, 368, 369, 370, 373, 374, 378, 379, 380, 381, 382, 383, 384, 385, 386, 387, 388, 389, 400.

Chorley, Mary, 278, 282, 297, 387.

Circuit, John, 310.

Circuit, see Surket.

Clark, John, 129, 148, 180, 235, 272, 276, 277, 278, 283, 310, 346.

Clarke, Ann, 375.

Clarke's Orphans, 15, 16.

Clawson, Derick, 10, 20, 24, 112, 149, 210, 236, 277.

Clawson als Jonson, Derick, 177, 181, 182, 270.

Clawson, John, 79, 80, 156, 158, 255, 256.

Claypoole, James, 47.

Clement, John, 107, 205, 206.

Clif, Samuel, 44, 331, 332, 333.

Clif, Jonathan, 331, 332.

Clift, see Clif.

Clowes, see Clows.

Clows, John, 7, 8, 32, 47, 57, 162, 260, 279, 282.

Clows, Joseph, 86, 88, 141, 186, 188, 210, 230, 295, 371.

Clows, Margery, 141, 151, 230, 250.

Clows, Sarah, 372.

Clows, William, 98, 109, 112, 141, 197, 207, 211, 230, 280, 281, 283.

Clowse, see Clows.

Cluse, see Clows.

Coates, John, 57, 119, 219.

Coates, Samuel, 278, 280, 307, 349, 370.

Coatts, see Coates.

Cockram, George, 134, 246.

Cockrum, see Cockram.

Codery, William, 354.

Cole, Robert, 170, 180, 267, 272, 276, 277, 278, 280, 282, 283, 286, 287, 288, 348, 350.

Cole, Thomas, 272.

Coleman, Thomas, 134, 135, 382, 400.

Collins, Francis, 290.

Collins, John, 22, 24, 50, 57, 95, 96, 100, 195, 199.

Comley, Henry, 42, 43, 287.

Conway Paterick, 111, 113, 114, 115, 118, 119, 120, 125, 176, 210, 211, 212, 213, 214, 215, 218, 220, 223.

Conway, Philip, 32, 50, 75, 76, 77, 78, 81, 103, 105, 106, 107, 108, 109, 113, 114, 116, 117, 118, 119, 120, 122, 125, 176, 202, 204, 205, 206, 207, 210, 211, 212, 213, 214, 215, 216, 217, 220, 223, 287.

Cook, Arthur, 33, 56, 66, 71, 72, 74, 75, 78, 81, 86, 90, 103, 111, 112, 121, 124, 130, 133, 142, 143, 152, 157, 159, 161, 167, 171, 182, 183, 185, 190, 202, 209, 210, 221, 223, 224, 242, 245, 251, 255, 260, 264, 268, 290, 291, 306, 310, 314, 315, 324.

Cook, Benjamin, 377.

Cook, John, 109, 126, 152, 163, 164, 165, 167, 171, 176, 207, 237, 251, 261, 262, 263, 264, 268, 284, 292, 295, 310, 355, 393.

Cooke, see Cook.

Cotterill, Thomas, 85, 185.

Coverdale, Jane, 75.

Coverdale, Thomas, 105, 106, 107, 111, 134, 135, 204, 205, 210.

Coverdale's wife, 77.

Cowgill, Abraham, 311.

Cowgill, Edmund, 346.

Cowgill, John, 280, 370, 373.

Cowgill, Nehemiah, 311.

Cowgill, Ralph, 283, 292, 306, 311, 342, 391, 403, 413.

Cows, see Clows.

Cox, Abraham, 43, 44, 45, 47, 76, 77, 101, 169, 171, 182, 199, 255, 266, 267, 269, 276, 289, 299, 313, 314, 316.

Cox, Daniel, 150, 154, 155, 158, 249, 252, 253, 257.

Crapp, John, 54, 55.

Crosdel, John, 67, 68, 93, 179, 180, 193, 233, 238, 276, 278, 289, 291, 303, 326, 339, 349, 370, 373, 401, 403, 413.

Crosdell, Ezra, 42, 73, 98, 109, 119, 197, 206, 207, 214, 215, 219, 238, 306, 325, 396, 397, 401.

Crosdell, James, 193.

Crosdell, William, 86, 90, 92, 93, 96, 185, 190, 192, 193, 196, 291, 299, 301, 302, 304, 315, 326, 342, 346, 373, 378, 393, 401.

Crosley, James, 93, 206.

Crosse, Joseph, 111, 115, 209, 215, 298, 299, 300.
Crossley, see Crosley.
Cuff, John, 57, 67, 68, 74, 75, 141, 231.
Cuft, see Cuff.
Cutler, Edmund, 25, 49, 59.
Cutler, Isabel, 373, 376.
Cutler, John, 67, 68, 301, 303.
Cuttler, see Cutler.

Daniel, Philip, 404.
Darby, William, 305, 307.
Dark, John, 305, 327, 359, 360.
Dark, Samuel, 6, 10, 11, 16, 41, 42, 79, 80, 93, 99, 128, 157, 158, 160, 182, 193, 198, 205, 210, 230, 239, 240, 253, 255, 257, 265, 272, 276, 295, 298, 301, 308, 312, 313, 340, 341, 342, 363.
Dark, William, 20, 58, 64, 65, 76, 77, 79, 80, 86, 88, 98, 121, 186, 188, 197, 205, 210, 221, 233, 239, 253, 278, 279, 280, 283, 289, 291, 299, 305, 306, 316, 339, 340, 341, 342, 353, 358, 359, 363.
Darke, see Dark.
Davenport, Francis, 365.
Davis, David, 14, 15, 42, 43, 61, 62, 63.
Davies, Richard, 324, 325, 327, 331, 338, 344, 373.
Dawson, John, 375.
Dawson, Martha, 375.
Dennis, Samuel, 67.
Derick's Indictment, 178.
Devonish, Bernard, 154, 155, 253.
Dickerson, Thomas, 50.
Dilworth, James, 49, 50, 59, 163, 282, 340, 346.
Done, Daniel, 306, 339.
Done, Robert, 48, 68, 82.
Dow, Robert, 67.
Doyal, see Doyle.
Doyl, see Doyle.
Doyle, Edward, 305, 308, 337, 338, 391.
Doyles, William, 278.
Druet, Morgan, 33.
Duncan, George, 308, 313.
Duncan, John, 325, 326.
Duncan, William, 147, 164, 177, 233, 262, 313, 316, 318, 339, 342, 349, 371, 375, 377.
Dungan, Clement, 292, 303, 305, 340, 341, 349, 355, 400.
Dungan, Jeremiah, 350, 354.
Dungan, John, 350.
Dungan, Thomas, 350, 396.
Dungan, William, 20, 58, 59, 91, 103, 169, 191, 202, 266, 272, 273, 283, 400, 403, 413.
Dunk, Andrew, 88, 188.
Dunken, see Duncan.
Duplovie, John, 130, 131, 139, 142, 149, 162, 172, 176, 224.
Duplovies, see Duplovie.
Duplovis, see Duplovie.
Dure, Thomas, 305, 398.

Eastbourn, John, 179, 328, 357, 362, 394, 396.
Eire, Mary, 87, 186.
Eldridge, Jonathan, 140, 145, 226, 229.
Eliott, William, 283.
Ellet, see Ellot.
Ellis, Hugh, 378.
Ellot, Ann, 134, 246.
Ellot, Andrew, 42, 88, 93, 134, 193, 210, 211, 230, 239, 246, 253, 255, 272, 283, 295, 344, 358, 368, 371, 375, 377, 398.
Ellot, John, 415.
Ellot, William, 214, 215, 217, 230, 239, 371, 376, 377.
Elly, see Ely.
Ely, Joshua, 84, 87, 186, 192.
Ely, Joshua, Junior, 186.
Ely, Joshua, Senior, 87.
Embley, William, 145, 146, 230, 231, 232, 325, 365.
Empson, 172.
Empson, Cornelius, 130, 131, 145, 146, 149, 162, 176, 231, 232, 236, 242, 260.
England, Joseph, 150, 249.
English, 341, 363.
English, Joane, 63.
English, Joseph, 13, 86, 90, 93, 97, 100, 128, 163, 186, 190, 191, 193, 197, 199, 205, 210, 240, 262, 290, 318, 323, 331, 333, 349.
English, Joseph, Junior, 44.
English, Joseph, Senior, 20, 57, 63.

Evan, see Evans.
Evans, David, 86, 186.
Evans, Edward, 318.
Evans, William, 138, 145, 149, 227, 231, 235.

Fairman, Robert, 318.
Faireman, Thomas, 291, 296, 318, 350, 372.
Farrington, Joseph, 125, 127, 131, 133, 134, 136, 137, 237, 238, 242, 245, 246, 247, 248.
Feild, Benjamin, 309.
Fenbank, Ellenor, 33.
Ferries, Zachariah, 394.
Fisher, George, 390, 392.
Fisher, William, 113, 114, 115, 118, 120, 125, 211, 212, 213, 214, 215, 217, 218, 223.
Fleckney, John, 98, 197.
Fletcher, Benjamin, 300.
Flower, Henry, 116, 216, 352.
Forest, Walter, 149, 215, 236.
Forest, Widow, 277.
Foster, Allen, 328, 372.
Foster, Mary, 372.
Fowler, William, 57.
Fox, James, 368.
Fox, Thomas, 102, 125, 126, 146, 201, 232, 233, 236, 238.
Freeborn, Gideon, 304.
Frezey, Joseph, 67.
Fuller, John, 142, 224.
Furnas, John, 98, 198.

Gabitas, William, 93.
Gardiner, Daniel, 151, 283, 303, 399.
Gardiner, Thomas, 347, 351, 357, 358, 361, 363, 377, 382, 388, 389, 393.
Gardner, see Gardiner.
Garner, Daniel, 134.
George the Negro, 94, 95, 99, 102, 104, 194, 195, 198.
Gibbs, Elizabeth, 41.
Gibbs, John, 108, 206, 281.
Gilbart, see Gilbert.
Gilbert, John, 158, 169, 180, 256, 266, 277, 283, 301, 312, 313, 328, 341, 344, 355, 362, 375.
Gilbert, Joseph, 362, 363, 376.
Glave, George, 38, 60, 67.

Grant, Neel, 325.
Gray, John, 55, 56, 57.
Gray als Tatham, John, 160, 258, 348, 351, 357, 360, 363, 377, 382, 385, 388.
Grayham, James, 68, 69, 70.
Greaves, Jane, 19.
Green, 363.
Green, John, 26, 292.
Green, Katherine, 292.
Green, Rachel, 177, 273, 318, 323, 331, 333, 349.
Green, Thomas, 26, 75, 106, 147, 177, 204, 233, 273, 279, 292, 318, 323, 331, 333, 349.
Greenland, Doctor, 180, 276.
Greenland, Henry, 173, 175, 271, 273.
Griffith, John, 313, 314, 361.
Groesbeck, Jacob, 330.
Growdon, Joseph, 32, 75, 81, 82, 83, 84, 90, 93, 101, 102, 103, 104, 107, 111, 112, 119, 130, 133, 138, 139, 141, 146, 147, 149, 151, 152, 155, 156, 157, 159, 160, 161, 162, 163, 164, 167, 171, 172, 176, 178, 181, 182, 190, 193, 200, 201, 202, 203, 204, 205, 209, 210, 219, 227, 228, 231, 232, 233, 235, 236, 237, 242, 245, 250, 251, 253, 254, 255, 257, 258, 259, 260, 261, 262, 264, 269, 270, 288, 295, 296, 298, 299, 302, 304, 305, 313, 314, 315, 316, 318, 321, 325, 326, 328, 330, 338, 342, 348, 351, 357, 358, 363, 373, 374, 377, 382, 385, 388, 391, 393, 397, 398, 402, 404, 405, 407, 408, 409, 411, 413, 414, 415, 416.
Grub, Henry, 82, 400.

Hagath, James, 391.
Hague, William, 40, 41.
Hall, Jacob, 26, 27, 28, 29, 32, 33, 37, 70, 75, 84, 92, 95, 151, 164, 192, 195, 239, 250, 262.
Hall, Joseph, 72, 73.
Hall, Robert, 41, 42, 49, 121, 124, 269.
Hancock, Edward, 97, 197, 200.
Hardin, Thomas, 109, 158, 182, 207, 214, 215, 217, 256, 276, 295, 370, 382, 394.
Harding, Nathaniel, 210.

Harding, Thomas, 116, 149, 216, 236.
Hardman, Abraham, 331.
Harrison, James, 9, 15, 16, 31, 40, 42, 48, 50, 71, 74, 75, 112, 117, 210, 217.
Harrison, John, 309, 334, 387.
Harvey, Matthias, 310, 323, 375.
Harvie, see Harvey.
Hawkins, 268.
Hawkins, Ann, 113, 211.
Hawkins, Daniel, 83, 91, 107, 192, 205.
Hawkins, Jeffery, 41, 50, 51, 79, 80, 83, 91, 210, 367.
Hawkins, John, 146, 232, 233.
Hawkins, Roger, 39, 40, 41, 59, 66, 95, 99, 195, 198.
Hayhurst, William, 102, 110, 124, 149, 230, 236, 316, 349, 370, 372, 373, 384, 393, 397.
Hayworth, James, 387.
Hayworth, Mary, 387.
Headley, John, 370.
Hearst, William, 201, 223, 238.
Heath, Andrew, 32, 132, 134, 206, 210, 222, 230, 243, 245, 247, 255, 278, 299, 321, 331, 336, 341, 342, 343, 344, 345, 394.
Heathcoate, George, 297, 312.
Hearth, And, 282, 287.
Heaton, James, 285, 287, 289, 290, 292, 391.
Heaton, Robert, 42, 47, 49, 57, 66, 75, 85, 86, 88, 91, 116, 117, 150, 163, 168, 170, 184, 188, 191, 216, 217, 265, 267, 287, 288, 299, 313, 328, 340, 341, 342, 346, 349, 356, 358, 362, 370, 379, 383, 387.
Heaton, Robert, Junior, 291, 310, 408, 413.
Heats, Andrew, 246.
Hedley, Richard, 10.
Heesem, see Heesum.
Heesome, see Heesum.
Henbery, Joseph, 172, 246, 344.
Henbry, see Henbery.
Henry, Joseph, 134.
Herrote, George, 10.
Hewett, John, 274.
Hewit, 178.
Hickman, Eliza, 75.
Hill, James, 94, 154, 194, 253.

Hill, John, 20.
Hill, Josias, 163, 168, 266, 415.
Hinksonte, see Hinkstone.
Hinkstone, Abel, 102, 201, 396, 414.
Hodson, Thomas, 375.
Holden, Joseph, 130, 131, 138, 139, 140, 142, 145, 146, 149, 162, 175, 224, 227, 228, 229, 231, 232, 236, 242, 261, 270, 296, 298.
Holden's Case, 176.
Holgat, Robert, 47.
Hollinshead, John, 148.
Hollinshead, Joseph, 32, 33, 78, 94, 95, 194, 195, 235.
Holm, see Holme.
Holme, Thomas, 33, 47, 67, 68, 69, 70, 73.
Holmes, see Holme.
Holt, Martin, 22, 24.
Hoops, Daniel, 309.
Hoops, Joshua, 25, 29, 80, 123, 128, 130, 140, 147, 163, 171, 182, 205, 214, 222, 230, 233, 239, 240, 242, 245, 253, 268, 276, 295, 298, 299, 303, 306, 309, 313, 316, 327, 339, 340, 341, 349, 356, 358, 370, 371, 376, 377, 394, 397, 398, 415, 416.
Horner, John, 50, 287, 309, 378, 383, 387, 389.
Hoste, William, 278.
Hough, Francis, 29, 30, 49, 57, 71, 90, 91, 191.
Hough, John, 58, 93, 193, 205, 238, 269, 280, 283, 299, 303, 358, 371, 375, 376.
Hough, Richard, 41, 47, 88, 100, 123, 157, 168, 171, 188, 199, 210, 222, 255, 265, 267, 268, 285, 286, 288, 291, 293, 295, 297, 300, 301, 302, 304, 309, 310, 313, 316, 323, 325, 330, 338, 342, 345, 348, 352, 358, 366, 368, 370, 372, 373, 378, 380, 381, 385, 397, 414, 415.
Hough, Samuel, 33, 94, 95, 194, 195, 307, 322, 339, 357, 396.
Houghton, John, 276.
Houghtons, 180.
Houle, Job, 103, 107, 177, 179, 202, 203, 205, 274, 378.
Howard, William, 299.
Howel, Philip, 350.
Hudelston, see Hudlestone.
Hudleston, see Hudlestone.

Hudlestone, Henry, 102, 161, 163, 201, 214, 215, 217, 238, 259, 278, 279, 299, 313, 321, 328, 356, 371, 375, 377, 393, 394, 403, 413.
Hudlestone, Valentine, 324.
Hudson, Thomas, 151, 164, 250, 262, 309, 310, 322, 325, 334, 344, 373, 375, 415.
Huff, Joan, 83, 84, 91, 95, 191, 195.
Huff, Micheal, 42, 44, 45, 47, 57.
Hughes, William, 305.
Hull, Jo:, 79.
Hunlock, Edward, 127, 135, 154, 238, 246, 252, 253, 347, 351, 373, 374, 390, 399, 400.
Hunloke, see Hunlock.
Huntley, William, 384, 388, 389, 400.
Hutchins, Thomas, 111, 209, 220.
Hutchinson, George, 154, 155, 252, 253.
Hycock, William, 20, 25.

J—Claws, 177.
Jackson, Epharm, 36.
Jacob, James, 350.
James II, King, 55, 66, 78, 81, 83, 86, 90, 92, 93, 101, 280.
Janney, Abel, 287, 310, 394, 398.
Jamey, Jacob, 76, 77, 171, 267, 281, 353, 358, 360.
Jamey, Joseph, 399, 401.
Janney, Thomas, 9, 11, 12, 15, 23, 25, 31, 40, 46, 48, 49, 56, 66, 71, 81, 123, 126, 129, 130, 132, 133, 138, 139, 140, 157, 159, 161, 171, 198, 222, 228, 230, 237, 241, 242, 243, 255, 259, 268, 291, 357, 358, 360, 394, 397, 398.
Janney, Thomas, Junior, 304.
Janney, Thomas, Senior, 94, 99, 96.
Jeffs, Mary, 187.
Jeffs, Robert, 96, 196.
Jenings, Peter, 125, 126, 236, 238.
Jenings, Samuel, 181, 367.
Jenks, Andrew, 115.
Jennings, see Jenings.
Jenner, Thomas, 296.
Jerrome, Samuel, 316, 317, 319, 320, 321, 345.
John, 181.
Johnson, see Jonson.
Jolly, James, 401, 402.

Jones, Benjamin, 88, 109, 127, 188, 189, 207, 239.
Jones, Daniel, 66, 346.
Jones, Francis, 286.
Jones, Griffith, 33, 82.
Jones, John, 93, 132, 138, 139, 142, 145, 176, 224, 227, 228, 231, 394.
Jones, Joseph, 394.
Jonson, 158.
Jonson, Brighta, 166, 181, 182, 263, 296.
Jonson, Claws, 10, 20, 112, 166, 210, 263, 270, 277, 298, 299, 313, 330.
Jonson, Derrick, 128, 129, 182, 240, 277.
Jonson, Elizabeth, 181, 182, 296.
Jonson, John, 157, 256, 299.
Jonson, Katherine, 296.
Joseph, 409.
Jonson als Clawson, Derrick, 165, 166, 181, 263.
Jonson, Derrick's Case, 175.

Kan, Matts [Matthias Keen], 296.
Kelly, Paterick, 100, 198.
Kenerley, William, 309.
King, the, 185, 190, 192, 193, 200, 203, 284, 286, 288, 289, 295, 302, 308.
King James II, 280.
King, Thomas, 147, 148, 233, 234, 235.
King, William, 304.
King and Queen, 111, 123, 126, 138, 152, 157, 161, 162, 163, 166, 173, 180, 209, 222, 227, 237, 244, 251, 255, 259, 260, 261, 264, 271, 273, 275, 276, 277, 278, 279, 280, 281, 283.
Kirkbride, Joseph, 82, 91, 158, 168, 182, 191, 245, 255, 257, 265, 268, 276, 291, 295, 301, 304, 306, 311, 315, 325, 328, 340, 341, 352, 356, 362, 364, 369, 370, 375, 381, 383, 387, 389, 398.
Kirkbridge, see Kirkbride.
Kirkham, James, 345.
Kirl, see Kirle.
Kirle, see Cearll.
Kirle, Joseph, 326.
Kirle, Julian, 379.
Kirle, Thomas, 112, 134, 211, 246,

303, 339, 341, 342, 343, 344, 349, 356, 394, 397.
Knight, Joseph, 53, 55, 150, 249.
Knight, Katherin, 21.
Knight, Thomas, 325, 358.

L, Wm., 184.
Lacy, Thomas, 178, 179, 275, 277, 280.
Lambert, Thomas, 97, 197, 365.
Lancaster, Edward, 99, 198.
Lane, Edward, 166, 181, 203, 298, 299.
Langhorn, Grace, 109, 175, 207, 318, 355, 398.
Langhorn, Jeremiah, 299, 307, 318, 328, 339, 342, 349, 358, 371, 375, 377, 397, 398.
Langhorn, Thomas, 75, 78.
Large, Joseph, 292, 293, 377.
Lavally, Lewis, 279.
Lawrence, William, 309, 415.
Leacy, see Lacy.
Lee, John, 126, 127, 143, 225, 230, 237, 238, 244.
Lee, Martha, 143, 225.
Lee, Rachel, 143, 225.
Lees, John, 132, 133.
Lilly, David, 82.
Linck, Denis, 163, 261.
Linstone, Denis, 159, 160, 258.
Litgraine, Roger, 172.
Lloyd, David, 78, 90, 190, 361.
Lloyd, Thomas, 33, 73.
Looker, Wm., 67, 84.
Lovet, Ed:, 20, 41.
Lovet, Edmund, 32, 76, 77, 168, 169, 171, 233, 245, 265, 266, 267, 269, 289, 291, 304, 312, 313, 316, 323, 324, 328, 344, 353, 358, 359, 401.
Loyke, Hance, 296.
Lucas, Edward, 158, 169, 173, 174, 256, 266, 271, 289, 291, 337, 340, 341, 353, 358, 359, 370, 397.
Lucas, Elizabeth, 38, 337.
Lucas, Giles, 337, 349, 376.
Lucas, Robert, 3, 10, 34, 40, 41, 63, 329, 337.
Lucas, Widow, 268, 303, 306.
Luff, Edward, 97, 197.
Luinn, Joseph, 20.
Lundy, Richard, 25, 37, 67, 68, 72,

82, 86, 88, 90, 98, 112, 174, 186, 188, 190, 197, 210, 214, 215, 217, 238, 272.
Lyon, Jane, 16.

Man, Abraham, 25.
Man, Elizabeth, 25.
Manarte, Ellenor, 220.
Marg, see Margerum.
Margorm, see Margerum.
Margerum, Henry, 20, 22, 25, 41, 42, 79, 80, 86, 88, 97, 98, 116, 148, 186, 188, 197, 211, 216, 233, 235, 238, 255, 256, 279, 281, 289, 291, 295, 299, 307, 316, 336, 353, 358, 359, 363, 370.
Marjerum, see Margerum.
Marjoron, see Margerum.
Markham, Captain, 118, 218.
Markham, William, 213, 218, 289, 318.
March, see Marsh.
Marle, Thomas, 93.
Marsh, Hugh, 103, 105, 132, 134, 136, 139, 146, 147, 163, 168, 179, 202, 227, 228, 229, 232, 234, 244, 245, 247, 255, 266, 275.
Marsh, Robert, 24, 132, 134, 136, 147, 163, 179, 234, 244, 245, 247.
Marsh, Samuel, 179.
Marshall, James, 98.
Martin, George, 66.
Martin, John, 95, 195.
Masley, Moses, 204, 332.
Mathews, Thomas, 22, 24.
Matthews, Margret, 299.
Mayos, Edward, 326, 355.
Merriot, see Merriott.
Merriott, Isaac, 316, 317, 320, 368.
Milcome, Ann, 7, 18, 19, 21.
Milcome, Widow, 11.
Miles, Abigaile, 360.
Millar, see Miller.
Millard, Thomas, 82, 92, 93, 97, 98, 99, 100, 103, 104, 193, 197, 199, 202.
Millenor, see Milner.
Miller, Joseph, 80, 93, 100, 280.
Miller, Mathew, 141, 143, 224, 231.
Mills, James, 346.
Milner, Joseph, 11, 12, 20, 36, 58, 79, 80, 91, 121, 132, 133, 168, 171, 182, 186, 191, 193, 199, 205, 210,

221, 233, 238, 244, 265, 267, 276,
278, 279, 285, 301, 310, 312, 313,
323, 328, 334, 340, 341, 353, 356,
358, 359.
Milner, Rachel, 58, 59.
Milner, Ralph, 53, 55, 58, 59, 70.
Milnor, see Milner.
Moon, see Moone.
Moone, James, 76, 77, 86, 88, 94,
98, 158, 186, 188, 194, 197, 210,
256, 272, 287, 289, 291, 313, 316,
339, 358, 359.
Moone, James, Junior, 157, 194,
255, 307, 308, 401.
Moone, James, Senior, 157, 255,
279, 307.
Moone, Joan, 287.
Moore, Edmund, 107, 205.
Moore, Nicholas, 27, 28, 45, 46.
More, see Moore.
Morgan, Anthony, 168, 266, 415.
Morow, Peter, 279.
Morris, Israel, 346.
Morris, John, 372.
Morton, William, 30, 79.
Murfen, see Murfey.
Murfey, Rodger, 279, 280.
Murfeyn, see Murfey.
Murfyn, John, 280.
Musgrave, Thomas, 311, 324.
Myers, Will, 404.

Naylor, John, 88, 92, 127, 128, 188,
205, 239, 240, 296, 394, 403, 413.
Negro (George), 107, 201, 202.
Negro Will, 399.
Neild, John, 11, 12, 132, 244, 296,
299, 342.
Newell, Stephen, 102, 104, 107, 176,
177, 201, 202, 203, 205, 238, 273,
283, 305, 306, 307, 308, 313, 322,
327, 344.
Newell, Elizabeth, 307.
Nicholls, see Nichols.
Nichols, Elias, 59, 87, 186, 329,
366, 367, 380, 381, 382, 383, 386.
Nichols, John, 59, 75, 172, 173,
187, 270, 329, 366, 367, 380, 381,
382, 383, 386.
Nichols, William, 166, 167, 264
265.
Noble, 363.
Noble, Richard, 15, 25, 61, 106,

204, 318, 323, 331, 332, 333, 341,
349, 379, 384.
Norris, Isaac, 319, 320, 366, 381,
383, 385, 386, 388.
Nowel, see Newell.

Oldale, Samuel, 326, 345, 347, 351,
358, 361, 363, 364, 377, 382, 388,
389, 393, 416.
Oldfeild, John, 91, 92, 192, 193.
Oldfield, see Oldfeild.
Oldham, Jonathan, 378, 382.
Otter, John, 9, 10, 15, 19, 23, 24, 31,
40, 46, 49, 66, 73, 112, 151, 153,
210, 250, 257, 304.
Otter, Justice, 10, 24.
Overton, Hannah, 80.
Overton, Samuel, 7, 8, 26, 27, 28,
29, 47, 58, 76, 77, 162, 260.
Owen, John, 87, 186.
Oxley, Ann, 84, 183.

Page, Isaac, 178, 275.
Palmer, John, 42, 79, 80, 93, 182,
193, 205, 210, 230, 276, 280, 283,
289, 291, 295, 313, 316, 339, 342,
358, 384, 397, 398.
Pamar, see Palmer.
Parker, Lawrence, 150, 249.
Parker, Philip, 107, 205.
Parsely, see Purslone.
Partington, Isaac, 57.
Paul, Joseph, 326.
Pawlin, Henry, 71, 72, 79, 80, 169,
184, 238, 266, 312, 391, 397.
Paxson, Henry, 25, 49, 70, 71, 72,
75, 86, 93, 105, 106, 109, 114,
182, 186, 193, 204, 207, 230, 239,
245, 276, 278, 280, 338, 340, 358,
360.
Paxson, James, 20, 67, 68, 86, 88,
98, 158, 165, 168, 182, 186, 188,
197, 204, 205, 214, 238, 245, 253,
255, 256, 265, 276, 278, 280, 295,
306, 346, 352, 363, 393,
Paxson, William, 20, 43, 47, 58,
85, 152, 184, 214, 215, 217, 233,
239, 245, 253, 255, 272, 278, 295,
298, 306, 318, 346, 349, 358, 371,
373, 375, 376, 377, 393, 416.
Paxston, see Paxson.
Paxton, see Paxson.
Pearce, Richard, 399.

Pearson, Edward, 269, 289, 291.
Pearson, Enoch, 377.
Pearson, Lawrence, 377.
Peart, Mary, 350.
Peart, Thomas, 350.
Peas, William, 71, 72.
Pegg, Elizabeth, 164, 262.
Peirce, Thomas, 131, 133, 135, 136, 152, 272.
Pellexon, Jacob, 25.
Pemberton, Phenihas, 414, 415.
Pemberton, Phineas, 297, 300, 301, 302, 304, 305, 307, 309, 311, 313, 314, 315, 316, 318, 323, 324, 325, 326, 328, 330, 331, 333, 337, 345, 349, 355, 358, 366, 370, 373, 378, 379, 380, 382, 391, 397, 398.
Pemberton, Phinehas, 9, 10, 11, 15, 19, 23, 25, 32, 34, 37, 41, 42, 45, 47, 50, 56, 59, 66, 71, 73, 74, 75, 78, 81, 83, 86, 88, 90, 92, 93, 101, 105, 111, 121, 123, 126, 128, 130, 133, 138, 140, 152, 157, 159, 160, 161, 162, 163, 167, 171, 172, 173, 174, 176, 178, 181, 182, 185, 189, 190, 192, 193, 200, 203, 209, 218, 221, 222, 227, 230, 237, 240, 241, 242, 243, 244, 245, 246, 247, 251, 255, 259, 260, 261, 262, 264, 268, 270, 271, 274, 286, 287, 288, 290, 291, 292, 293, 295.
Penn, William, 9, 15, 19, 23, 31, 46, 56, 66, 71, 74, 78, 81, 83, 86, 90, 92, 93, 101, 105, 110, 111, 120, 123, 126, 133, 138, 154, 157, 161, 163, 166, 173, 176, 180, 182, 185, 190, 192, 193, 200, 203, 209, 213, 220, 227, 237, 245, 251, 255, 259, 260, 261, 264, 271, 273, 284, 286, 288, 289, 295, 297, 302, 304, 308, 315, 316, 323, 329, 338, 345, 348, 358, 369, 384, 390, 397, 401, 413, 414.
Penquoit, John, 84, 98, 179, 180, 183, 197, 233, 277, 397.
Philips, George, 159, 160, 161, 162, 163, 169, 257, 258, 259, 261, 266.
Philips, Thomas, 36.
Pickring, Charles, 34, 35, 36, 41, 48, 66, 101, 103, 200, 201.
Pickring, William, 84, 183.
Pidcock, John, 55, 57, 58, 68, 112, 133, 135, 136, 143, 144, 147, 148,
149, 152, 187, 191, 203, 225, 233, 234, 235, 236, 237, 243, 244, 246, 247, 279, 281, 299, 347, 351, 371, 372, 373, 377, 393, 399.
Plumley, James, 350, 360, 372, 399, 403, 413.
Plumley, John, 354, 360. ,
Plumley, William, 71, 72, 105, 179, 204.
Pointer, Henry, 41, 75, 76, 89, 91, 122, 138, 190, 191, 210, 221, 227, 233, 245, 253, 278, 279, 283, 394.
Pointr, see Pointer.
Pomferet, Walter, 4, 5, 6, 11, 16, 21, 183, 324, 350, 353, 358, 359, 390, 400.
Powel, David, 33, 43, 324, 325, 327, 331, 338, 344.
Pownal, Ellenor, 29, 30, 49.
Pownal, Ruben, 149, 158, 169, 171, 236, 256, 266, 267, 279, 283, 285, 289, 291, 310, 316, 349, 371, 376, 377.
Pownd, John, 279, 280.
Poyntar, see Pointer.
Poynter, see Pointer.
Preistcorin, Thomas, 109, 207.
Presmall, Robert, 71.
Prothera, Evan, 168, 266.
Prudence the negro, 177.
Purley, see Purslone.
Pursley, see Purslone.
Purslone, John, 19, 25, 58, 75, 82, 112, 115, 118, 147, 163, 165, 181, 210, 213, 215, 218, 233, 278, 280.
Pursly, see Purslone.
Pursone, see Purslone.

Queen Mary, 110.

Radclif, Mary, 140, 230.
Rakestraw, William, 286, 290, 293, 297, 308.
Rambo, Peter, 177, 270.
Randel, Nicholas, 188.
Randle, Nicholas, 117, 212, 217.
Randol, George, 355, 356, 362.
Randol, Nicholas, 350, 394.
Randolph, see Randulph.
Randulph, Nicholas, 88, 183, 188, 278.
Rawle, Francis, 396.
Read, Anne, 323.

Read, Charles, 323.
Reale, William, 102, 201.
Redman, John, 86, 186.
Revel, 129, 136, 241.
Revel, Thomas, 97, 105, 108, 110, 111, 118, 119, 122, 132, 133, 136, 151, 153, 154, 157, 200, 204, 207, 208, 209, 213, 219, 220, 243, 245, 253, 351.
Revell, see Revel.
Revell case, 175.
Richards, 172.
Richards, John, 180.
Richards, Philip, 130, 131, 139, 140, 142, 149, 162, 176, 224, 229, 242, 260.
Richards, Philip's case, 236.
Richardson, John, 132, 276, 394.
Richardson, Joyce, 394.
Richardson, Samuel, 415.
Ridgway, Elizabeth, 38, 75.
Ridgway, Richard, 20, 42, 50, 57, 59, 67, 68, 75, 76, 79, 80, 82, 88, 90, 93, 96, 102, 105, 107, 147, 164, 188, 191, 193, 196, 201, 204, 205, 210, 234, 263, 399.
Robeson, Andrew, 66.
Robinson, Paterick, 139, 142, 224, 227, 228, 229.
Rogers, Thomas, 94, 99, 194, 198, 255, 283, 306, 334.
Rogrs, see Rogers.
Roles, Mary, 178, 179, 275, 277, 280.
Roles, William, 144, 226.
Rose, 147.
Rose, Pilocarpus, 135, 143, 149, 225, 233, 234, 236, 247.
Rose, Samuel, 114.
Rosell, see Rossill.
Rossill, Francis, 47, 79, 80, 86, 93, 98, 103, 112, 119, 141, 143, 151, 152, 153, 154, 174, 182, 186, 191, 193, 197, 210, 219, 224, 231, 250, 252, 276, 278, 280, 283, 293, 338.
Rouse case, 184.
Rouse case agt Biles, 84.
Rouse, Simon, 67, 69, 70, 85, 184.
Rowland, John, 25, 33, 59, 75, 76, 100, 106, 130, 141, 158, 163, 168, 199, 204, 205, 230, 242, 245, 257, 262, 265, 268, 272, 283, 291, 304,
313, 318, 319, 324, 327, 331, 339, 348, 352, 363, 370, 391.
Rowland, Priscilla, 324.
Rowland, Thomas, 20, 33, 76, 77, 94, 98, 103, 121, 124, 194, 197, 202, 221, 223.
Rumford, John, 415.
Rush, Francis, 409.
Rush, John, 91, 92, 192.

Salter, Hannah, 33, 73.
Sands, Stephen, 67, 68, 98, 197, 306, 374, 376, 391.
Sanford, William, 14, 15, 32.
Saterthwait, Joseph, 376.
Scafe, see Scaife.
Scaife, Jonathan, 25, 32, 42, 75, 163, 182, 230, 238, 253, 269, 276, 280, 283, 285, 289, 291, 295, 298, 299, 301, 303, 308, 309, 310, 312, 316, 323, 324, 344, 345, 346, 348, 358, 370, 375, 391, 393, 415.
Sraife, Mary, 285, 289, 292.
Scarborough, John, 339, 340, 341, 364, 365, 373, 377, 379, 382, 388, 389, 391, 392, 393, 394, 400, 415.
Scarborough, John (of London), 394.
Scot, John, 391.
Scot, Roger, 91, 191.
Scot, Thomas, 141, 231.
Searle, Francis, 233, 234, 325, 328, 357, 396.
Searle, Francis's Wife, 147.
Searle, Joan, 148, 233.
Shackhars, see Stackhouse.
Shallow, Gabriel, 88, 188.
Shaw, John, 318, 326, 353, 358, 359, 379, 390, 392.
Shippen, Edwaid, 351.
Shippey, J., 122.
Shippey, James, 116.
Shippey, John, 111, 115, 144, 145, 146, 209, 215, 216, 220, 225, 232.
Siddall, Henry, 106, 107, 204, 205, 206.
Siddall, John, 291, 297, 312, 394, 396, 397, 398, 400.
Sidwell, Ralph, 8, 9, 10, 251.
Skeane, Mary, 83, 84, 183.
Smalwood, 184.
Smalwood, Joseph, 306, 346, 350, 362, 365, 379, 382, 388, 389, 391.

Smalwood, Randulph, 57, 58, 59, 70, 84.
Smith, Charles, 416.
Smith, Daniel, 346.
Smith, Edward, 7, 10, 315.
Smith, John, 68, 92, 131, 135, 136, 173, 193, 238, 243, 246, 289, 291, 306, 310, 311, 314, 318, 333, 339, 370, 397.
Smith, Samuel, 7, 377, 391.
Smith, William, 82, 280, 295, 318, 326, 328, 345, 349, 370, 372, 397.
Snowdon, Christopher, 156, 158, 255, 257, 347, 351, 357, 361, 363, 377, 382, 388, 389, 393.
Snowdon, John, 284, 285, 295, 306, 316, 366, 376, 377, 391, 394.
Spencer's Children, 73.
Spencer, James, 79.
Stacey, Mahlon, 86, 186, 329, 364, 367, 380, 383, 386, 388.
Stackhous, see Stackhouse.
Stackhouse, John, 290, 316, 353, 358, 360.
Stackhouse, Thomas, 25, 41, 59, 67, 68, 79, 91, 163, 165, 176, 186, 191, 214, 215, 217, 253, 255, 279, 280, 316, 340, 341, 342, 358, 397, 398.
Stackhouse, Thomas, Junior, 50, 79, 80, 86, 88, 161, 173, 186, 188, 238, 259, 277, 289, 295, 296, 325, 391, 397, 398.
Stackhouse, Thomas, Senior, 20, 47, 57, 75, 86, 88, 169, 181, 188, 206, 233, 238, 245, 266, 280, 397.
Stakehouse, see Stackhouse.
Stacy, Robert, 400.
Staniland, Mary, 86, 186.
Stanton, Edward, 50, 68.
Stanton, Edward, Junior, 67.
Stedon, John, 141, 143, 231.
Stetton, see Stotton.
Steward, Joseph, 134, 156, 157, 246, 254, 255.
Stewards, see Steward.
Stolon, John, 127.
Stone, George, 398.
Stork, John, 356.
Stotton, John, 224, 238, 393.
Surket, John, 328, 349, 358, 370, 396, 403, 413.

Sutton, James, 83, 132, 134, 206, 246, 303, 358, 396, 414.
Swafer, James, 93, 193.
Swift, Francis, 87, 187.
Swift, John, 19, 41, 76, 86, 87, 88, 92, 93, 103, 105, 106, 107, 108, 109, 116, 117, 118, 122, 125, 138, 140, 142, 145, 176, 182, 186, 187, 188, 193, 202, 204, 205, 206, 207, 208, 211, 212, 213, 217, 224, 226, 227, 229, 233, 245, 253, 276, 278, 279, 280, 282, 283, 284, 286, 287, 291, 293, 300, 302, 304, 313, 316, 320, 321, 323, 325, 345, 348, 350, 370, 372, 378, 383, 387, 391, 394, 395, 397, 401, 402, 414.
Swift, John's wife, 188.
Swift's Case, 188, 223.

Talman, John, 309.
Tatham, John, 125, 127, 131, 133, 134, 135, 136, 137, 150, 151, 155, 156, 157, 158, 159, 160, 237, 238, 242, 245, 246, 247, 248, 249, 250, 253, 254, 255, 257, 258, 350, 402, 408, 409, 410, 413, 414.
Tayler, see Taylor.
Taylor, 188.
Taylor, Christopher, 331.
Taylor, Israel, 41, 49, 56, 57, 67, 68, 69, 70, 71, 73, 83, 87, 88, 90, 91, 105, 108, 109, 110, 111, 115, 116, 118, 119, 122, 123, 124, 127, 128, 129, 130, 132, 133, 136, 141, 143, 144, 145, 146, 153, 163, 175, 178, 179, 182, 185, 187, 189, 191, 207, 208, 209, 211, 215, 216, 219, 220, 222, 223, 231, 232, 233, 240, 241, 243, 245, 247, 249, 251, 275, 280, 291, 314, 379.
Taylor, John, 184, 193.
Taylor, Joseph, 339, 379.
Taylor, William, 214, 215, 217, 245, 272, 277, 278, 299, 335.
Taylor's Case, 175.
Taylor's wife, 127, 128.
Tellner, Jacob, 25, 90, 190.
Terry, Jasper, 377.
Terry, Thomas, 98, 197, 286, 377.
Terrey, see Terry.
Test, John, 126, 160, 167, 175, 236, 238, 264.
Thakorf, see Stackhouse.

Thatcher, 175, 241, 276.
Thatcher, Amos, 172, 270.
Thatcher, Bartholomew, 128, 172.
239, 240, 270, 279, 356, 369, 383,
387, 389.
Thatcher, Joseph, 172, 270, 307,
356.
Thatcher, Richard, 49, 67, 68, 74,
75, 76, 82, 83, 85, 102, 107, 122,
127, 128, 129, 130, 134, 172, 173,
175, 177, 179, 180, 185, 201, 207,
208, 211, 218, 219, 239, 240, 249,
251, 270, 271, 273, 274, 275, 276,
282, 297, 306, 307, 329, 331, 335,
336, 337, 340, 344, 346, 349, 355,
361, 373, 384, 388, 389, 390, 394,
400.
Thatcher, Richard, Junior, 100,
101, 105, 108, 110, 115, 118, 119,
120, 123, 198, 199, 207, 213, 215,
216, 218, 219, 220.
Thatcher, Richard, Senior, 109,
207.
Thatcher's declaration, 84.
Thather, see Thatcher.
Thathar, see Thatcher.
Thacher, see Thatcher.
Thomas, 177.
Thomas, Charles, 21, 114, 115, 119,
120, 212, 215, 220, 221.
Thomas, William, 134, 222.
Thompkins, Anthony, 66, 82.
Thorn, Joseph, 309.
Thorn, Samuel, 309.
Tomkins, see Thompkins.
Tomlinson, John, 404.
Town, John, 88, 98, 188, 197, 209,
238, 296, 311, 322, 327, 331, 334,
372.
Towne, see Town.
Trevitham, see Trevithan.
Trevithan, Joseph, 138, 145, 146,
147, 149, 227, 231, 232, 233, 235,
236.
Trivithan, see Trevithan.
Turner, Robert, 112, 210.
Taunclifte, see Tunneclift.
Tunneclift, Francis, 289, 291, 307,
334, 365, 400.
Tunneclift, Thomas, 47, 57, 58, 76,
77, 80, 84, 116, 123, 126, 127,
134, 205, 211, 216, 222, 230, 237,
238, 246, 280, 281, 390, 393.

Twineing, Stephen, 288, 339, 358,
370, 397, 399.

Vandegreift, Frederick, 330, 373.
Vandegreift, Johannes, 330.
Vandegreift, Leonard, 330, 373.
Vandegreift, Nicholas, 327, 328,
357.
van Sand, Cornelius, 398.
van Sand, Garret, 398.
Venables, 346.
Venables, Elizabeth, 203.
Venables Estate, 61.
Venables, William, 61, 63, 64.
Verrier, James, 371, 372, 374, 378.
Virkirk, Barndt, 330, 340, 341,
373.
Vose, Samuel, 212, 214.

Waddy, Henry, 68.
Walen, see Waln.
Walker, Francis, 10, 20.
Walley, Shadrach, 47, 49, 75, 93,
124, 193, 230, 223, 238, 255, 278,
316, 397.
Wally, see Walley.
Walmsley, Henry, 73, 327.
Walmsley, Thomas, 73, 396.
Waln, Nicholas, 31, 41, 47, 48, 49,
62, 66, 73, 74, 75, 78, 81, 82, 83,
86, 90, 93, 101, 103, 105, 110, 111,
121,123, 126, 129, 130, 133, 138,
139, 152, 162, 163, 167, 170, 171,
174, 176, 178, 182, 185, 190, 193,
200, 202, 203, 209, 221, 222, 227,
228, 237, 241, 242, 245, 251, 260,
264, 267, 268, 269, 271, 272, 282,
290, 293, 346, 372.
Walne, see Waln.
Walter, Richard, 333.
Walters, Jonathan, 230.
Walton, Nathaniel, 340, 341.
Ward, Ralph, 296.
Warwin, 345.
Warwin, Henry, 344, 346, 347, 355,
358, 361.
Watson, John, 415.
Watson, Joseph, 244.
Webb, Elizabeth, 318.
Webb, Robert, 318.
Webstar, see Webster.
Webster, John, 149, 236, 279, 304,
305.

Webster, Peter, 325, 357, 362, 363, 379, 394, 397.
Weire, John, 325.
Wells, Edmund, 384, 385.
West, Nathaniel, 11, 16.
Wharley, Abraham, 56, 66, 71, 73, 74, 75, 78, 79, 81, 83, 84, 86, 88, 90, 93, 185, 189, 190, 193, 256.
Whearley, see Wharley.
Wheeler, Gilbert, 4, 11, 16, 18, 19, 21, 22, 23, 24, 25, 27, 28, 33, 37, 39, 40, 45, 46, 55, 56, 57, 58, 60, 68, 69, 70, 76, 77, 78, 84, 89, 95, 96, 100, 112, 116, 126, 129, 130, 131, 135, 141, 144, 148, 150, 154, 155, 156, 157, 158, 165, 167, 168, 169, 170, 189, 195, 196, 199, 209, 210, 216, 225, 230, 234, 235, 237, 241, 243, 247, 249, 252, 253, 254, 255, 257, 264, 265, 267, 277, 278, 279, 280, 281, 282, 283, 284, 285, 290, 291, 293, 297, 298, 299, 303, 307, 308, 321, 322, 327, 329, 334, 335, 338, 365, 379.
Wheeler, Martha, 18, 19, 21, 38, 77.
Wherley, see Wharley.
White, 271, 341, 363.
White, Benjamin, 371, 372.
White, Elizabeth, 295, 301, 302, 305, 307, 318, 333, 349, 353, 371, 372.
White, Francis, 180, 275, 276, 277, 316, 322, 327, 333, 347, 353, 356, 357, 359, 370, 372, 384, 385, 391, 403, 413.
White, John, 32, 75, 79, 80, 106, 147, 160, 168, 204, 230, 233, 250, 255, 258, 265, 279, 280, 310, 316, 349, 370, 371, 372.
White, John Pinck, 278.
White, Joseph, 279, 370, 372.
White, Peter, 278, 290, 295, 296, 299, 301, 302, 305, 306, 307, 318, 319, 323, 331, 333, 349, 353, 370, 371, 372, 379, 384.
White, William, 370, 372.
Whitpaine, John, 166, 167, 175, 264, 265.
Whitpaine, Zachariah, 131, 150, 243.
Whoops, see Hoops.
Whoops, Joshua, 283.
Wildman, Martin, 340.

Willard, George, 290, 318, 326, 379.
William, King, 110.
William & Mary, 152, 161, 166, 209, 251, 259, 261, 264, 273.
Williams, Duncan, 162, 261, 296, 326.
Williams, Dunk, 315, 328.
Williams, Hannah, 162.
Williams, Hugh, 87, 186.
Williams, Nicholas, 362, 363, 375, 376.
Williams, Thomas, 82, 91, 191, 278, 288.
Williams, William, 162, 261.
Willits, Hannah, 305.
Willits, Richard, 305.
Willsford, see Wilsford.
Willson, see Wilson.
Wilsford, John, 293.
Wilsford, Joseph, 102, 201.
Wilsford, Rebecca, 331.
Wilson, Elizabeth, 57.
Wlison, Richard, 90, 93, 108, 149, 158, 169, 190, 193, 206, 236, 256, 266, 281, 295, 306, 344, 377, 403, 413.
Wilson, Stephen, 280, 316, 334, 399.
Wilton, Samuel, 79.
Wms., see Williams.
Wood, James 326,
Wood, John, 40, 47, 59, 87, 93, 121, 134, 140, 144, 145, 147, 148, 193, 205, 214, 215, 217, 226, 229, 234, 239, 246, 268.
Woods, Joseph, 57, 86, 87, 95, 148, 186, 187, 195, 234, 277, 278, 279, 280, 281, 282, 283, 284, 286, 287, 291, 295, 306, 335, 339, 340, 341, 348, 350.
Wood, Mary, 87, 187.
Wood, Sarah, 87, 187.
Wood, Thomas, 79, 80, 191.
Woolf, Thomas, 20, 41, 47, 76, 77.
Woolly, see Walley.
Worral, Peter, 98, 101, 106, 108, 169, 194, 197, 200, 204, 206, 230, 266, 272, 289, 291, 292, 293, 299, 300, 302, 309, 310, 316, 349, 358, 365, 390, 393, 394, 396, 397, 398, 400.
Worrall, see Worral.
Worrilow, Elizabeth, 285.

Worrilow, John, 123, 222, 284, 285.
Worrilow, Walter, 123, 222, 284.
Wright, John, 30, 31, 39, 76.
Wright, Thomas, 16, 17.

Yardley, Enoch, 171, 267, 283, 285,
291, 293, 300, 302, 310, 313, 339,
358, 371, 375, 377, 389, 403, 413.
Yardley, Thomas, 310, 357.
Yardley, William, 9, 15, 19, 23, 31,
36, 40, 42, 46, 48, 49, 56, 57, 62,

64, 65, 66, 71, 74, 75, 78, 80, 81,
83, 86, 90, 92, 93, 100, 111, 121,
123, 124, 125, 126, 129, 130, 131,
132, 133, 134, 138, 140, 142, 143,
149, 150, 157, 159, 161, 162, 173,
185, 190, 192, 193, 199, 209, 221,
222, 223, 224, 225, 226, 227, 230,
236, 237, 241, 243, 244, 245, 247,
249, 251, 255, 259, 260.
Yates, James, 178, 272, 274, 307,
328, 340, 341, 357, 396.

GENERAL INDEX

Only one reference in kind is given for a page.

Action, *ejectione fermae* 43, 167, 264, 367, 369, 681; for cutting and carrying away grass 79; for damages 290; of covenant 16, 57, 396; of *detinue* 290; **of replevin for** oxen 52; of trover and conversion 8; continued 155, 159, 164, 192, 253, 256, 279, 297, 327, 338, 346, 360, 361, 363, 377, 382, 383, 385, 387, 388, 389, 390, 393, 400; deferred 21, 101, 257, 340, 351; referred to another court 157, 256,

Actions, entered 3, 4, 5, 6, 7, 8, 10, 11, 12, 13, 14, 16, 17, 18, 22, 23, 26, 27, 28, 29, 34, 35, 37, 39, 43, 45, 51, 52, 53, 67, 68, 70, 74, 82, 83, 84, 86, 90, 96, 97, 105, 108, 110, 111, 112, 115, 119, 125, 126, 129, 131, 132, 133, 136, 138, 139, 140, 142, 143, 144, 145, 147, 150, 152, 155, 156, 159, 160, 161, 165, 166, 167, 172, 173, 224, 225, 226, 243, 244, 249, 250, 251, 254, 259, 264, 271, 316, 318, 319, 322, 324, 325, 329, 338, 341, 344, 347, 348, 358, 363, 364, 365, 366, 367, 368, 369, 378, 383, 384, 389, 390 396; for assault and trespass 70, 105, 108, 143, 160, 243, 258, 259, 324, 325, 342, 343, 347, 351, 352, 353, 358, 361; for debt 3, 4, 5, 6, 7, 11, 13, 22, 26, 27, 28, 29, 30, 34, 39, 51, 53, 55, 56, 57, 67, 79, 90, 96, 97, 129, 138, 139, 140, 142, 145, 153, 197, 224, 227, 228, 229, 232, 234, 237, 241, 242, 243, 249, 252, 270, 279, 317, 348, 350, 378, 387, 390, 392, 395; suspended 134, 160, 245, 255, 262, 306; withdrawn 24, 28, 29, 31, 34, 40, 46,

82, 83, 84, 105, 112, 150, 151, 156, 157, 158, 167, 173, 178, 203, 204, 209, 222, 233, 238, 243, 249, 250, 258, 259, 263, 264, 274, 286, 322, 334, 358, 366, 367, 368, 382, 389.

Abuse, 182; of bench 80; of the jury 110, 208; to a Justice 83.

Abusing, 57; his father 211.

Account, of lands and males to be returned 222, 223; of lands surveyed and seated to be brought in 124, 223.

Accounting ordered 61, 64.

Accounts, deferred 300; exhibited 10, 62, 175, 176, 235, 405, 406, 407, 408, 409, 410, 411, 412, 413; to be brought in 59, 65, 287, 298; to be examined 59, 83; for wolf heads 313.

Adjournment of court during elections 41, 73.

Age of a boy adjudged by the Court 325, 399.

Agreement for service 280.

Appeals, to Provincial Circular Court granted 100, 169, 199, 246, 266, 280, 344, 413; refused 174, 272.

Appraisement 152, 163, 261, 348.

Appraisers appointed 85, 158, 184, 257, 323.

Arbitration 48, 49, 82, 104, 335, 352.

Arrest, granted 4, 5, 6, 145, 150, 173, 226, 227, 251, 271, 316, 319, 322, 329, 342, 345, 347, 365, 366, 367, 368, 369, 384, 390; made 184.

A Roman T to be worn 401, 402.

Assault, 58, 134, 356; and abuse 137; and abusing Justices 248; and attempt to rob 199; and bat-

433

tery 37, 297, 306, 330; threatened 75.

Assessors appointed 124, 312, 344.

Assistance ordered 288, 293, 337.

Attachment granted 4, 5, 6, 22, 31, 133, 142, 144, 224, 226, 243, 244, 323, 324, 364, 365, 366, 368, 378, 383, 384, 389, 390.

Attestation 260.

Advisers appointed 301.

Bail ordered 270.

Banishment from the Province 220.

Beating and abusing, his grand-child 362; his wife 346, 362; and wounding 371.

Bill of sale delivered in court 33.

Bonds, accepted 73; forfeited 81; given 20, 40, 48, 60, 80, 92, 116, 138, 154, 203, 248, 274, 275, 378; required 216, 228, 275, 277.

Bound to good behavior 20.

Breaking the peace 306, 326.

Bridge, necessity for a 306, 362, 416; to be repaired 110, 256; between Bucks and Philadelphia Counties in need of repairs 314; and road want repairs 321.

Carrying away a log 298.

Case referred to the bench 246, 427.

Certificate of being alive signed 287, 306.

Coming into court drunk 111, 210.

Commitment, 33, 100, 101, 102, 103, 110, 111, 135, 138, 162, 179, 187, 198, 201, 202, 208, 210, 227, 261, 276, 306, 330, 346, 374, 376; for murder 165; on suspicion of felony 274.

Complaint, 3, 5, 6, 7, 8, 12, 13, 14, 17, 18, 22, 23, 27, 35, 36, 37, 39, 44, 45, 49, 51, 124, 134, 162, 164, 184, 196, 210, 223, 261, 262, 278, 291, 292, 293, 312, 319, 320, 337, 340, 356, 361, 373, 391, 394, 395, 402; about wolves' heads 112; further 274.

Constables, appointed 25, 34, 59, 91, 101, 106, 112, 147, 159, 169, 191, 200, 204, 210, 233, 266, 278, 303, 327, 357, 362, 396; attested 10, 397; excused on account of

age 361; presentments 42; continued 159, 257.

Contempt of court 208.

Conveyance 57, 334.

Coroner, to be appointed 124, 223; his commission read 309; fees ordered paid 392; return of deaths 91, 127, 164, 165, 166, 191, 222, 238, 263, 312, 391.

County Clerk, to retain money in his custody 160, 161; discharged therefrom 259.

County records to be brought in 287.

County Treasurer's reports to be examined 59.

Cow sold at an outcry 339.

Cruelty to a horse 377.

Cursing 76, 81, 204, 340.

Debt, acknowledged 380, 385, 386, 398; denied 403.

Debtor to the County 313.

Declarations read 3, 7, 331, 334, 342, 350, 352, 381.

Deeds acknowledged and delivered in court 25, 33, 41, 47, 49, 50, 57, 59, 60, 63, 66, 68, 71, 73, 74, 75, 76, 81, 82, 83, 84, 85, 86, 88, 89, 90, 91, 92, 93, 94, 97, 99, 102, 103, 105, 106, 108, 110, 112, 116, 119, 123, 128, 140, 141, 148, 157, 163, 164, 168, 170, 174, 177, 178, 179, 183, 184, 186, 188, 190, 191, 193, 194, 197, 198, 201, 204, 206, 208, 210, 216, 219, 230, 231, 235, 240, 255, 262, 265, 267, 273, 279, 280, 281, 287, 288, 290, 291, 292, 299, 301, 302, 304, 305, 309, 310, 311, 312, 318, 323, 324, 325, 326, 329, 330, 331, 333, 336, 337, 339, 340, 345, 346, 349, 350, 352, 355, 356, 370, 371, 372, 373, 374, 375, 378, 379, 387, 393, 394, 398, 399, 415.

Deed of mortgage, delivered and acknowledged 9, 135, 168, 204, 266, 314, 333; refused 246; satisfied 386.

Deed of sale and mortgage 66, 202, 292.

Deed, in trust 222; of partition 295, 296; sheriff's 296.

Defamation, 57, 148, 187, 233; and scandalizing 58.

Discharge produced 247.

Discharged by the Court 11, 24, 32, 33, 67, 68, 91, 100, 102, 103, 108, 123, 129, 144, 158, 177, 179, 180, 182, 191, 192, 198, 201, 202, 206, 222, 235, 236, 241, 257, 273, 277, 278, 283, 336, 341, 355, 357, 370, 386, 393, 395.

Disclaim of attachment 286.

Ear mark, necessity for an 356.

Estreats 90, 91, 112, 116, 190, 192, 204, 208, 211, 220, 295.

Examination, 183, 231, 359; about a horse 145.

Execution, craved 374; granted 37, 81, 125, 129, 145, 152, 184, 187, 231, 236, 237, 242, 260, 287, 338, 339, 341, 356, 363, 384; ordered 122, 136, 153, 220, 374; returned 149, 297.

Extortion in ferriage 141, 230.

Evidence 86, 87, 88, 98, 107, 109, 113, 114, 115, 116, 117, 118, 119, 122, 127, 128, 146, 147, 169, 180, 188, 213, 233, 234, 239, 240, 246, 253, 276, 353, 354, 355, 372.

Fornication and bastardy 21, 178, 180, 183, 275, 277, 285, 289, 290.

Fine remitted 58.

Fined by the Court, 58, 59, 67, 68, 101, 112, 199, 204, 211, 285, 292, 295, 297, 319, 327, 330, 346, 359, 374, 377, 391; for absence 68; for abuse 80; for being a common swearer 78; for threatened assault 77; for contempt 77; for oaths and curses 76; for rude behavior 21; for scolding 77; for selling rum to the Indians 33; for slander and abuse 72.

Grand Jury, attested 57, 75, 93, 126 141, 157, 193, 206, 209, 230, 238, 255, 278, 280, 283, 295, 306, 313, 316, 325, 339, 349, 358, 370, 397, 401, 414; complaint 355.

Grand Jury presentments, 19, 20, 76, 84, 94, 95, 96, 109, 113, 114, 115, 158, 181, 185, 187, 194, 196, 207, 208, 211, 214, 216, 230, 232, 238, 240, 242, 256, 280, 285, 287, 298, 299, 306, 314, 321, 326, 327, 328, 340, 341, 356, 362, 371, 375, 376, 401, 414, 416; for murder 181; attested 276; no presentments 278; return Ignoramus 109.

Guardian appointed 16.

Highway in an intolerable condition 362.

Housebreaking 113, 211.

Illegal proceedings of a jury 359.

Indentures drawn and sealed 62.

Judgment, acknowledged 282; approved 240; confirmed 329, 382.

Judgment given, by the Court 10, 47, 58, 69, 70, 72, 77, 78, 80, 82, 85, 86, 87, 88, 96, 99, 102, 109, 110, 115, 119, 120, 122, 128, 136, 139, 140, 141, 146, 148, 149, 153, 154, 155, 157, 160, 174, 185, 186, 187, 188, 198, 201 207, 208, 219, 220, 227, 228, 229, 231, 232, 235, 240, 241, 247, 248, 251, 252, 256, 258, 272, 286, 290, 292, 293, 300, 306, 307, 320, 325, 333, 335, 341, 350, 360, 361, 374, 376, 377, 380, 381, 382, 385, 386, 387, 392, 395, 399, 401; by default 41, 130, 148, 196, 234.

Judgment requested 379.

Jurors fined for non-attendance 391.

Jury submits to the Court 359.

Justices commissions read 75, 93, 101, 181, 193, 200, 345.

Justices to meet 292, 294, 299.

Keeping ordinary without a license 415.

Killing a colt 106.

Land to be laid out for a County Prison 11.

Laws of the last Assembly read 93, 193, 385.

Letters of attorney, acknowledged 84, 85, 184, 185, 373; allowed 344; certified 379; proven 394; signed and sealed 9.

Letters read 168, 404.

Levying of fines and forfeitures 90, 190.

License to keep an ordinary 326, 329.

List of fines and forfeitures sent to the Governor's Secretary 85.

Maintenance, of way 306; of wife 340.

Men named to view fences 42.

Message from the Assembly 123, 222.

Money taken from 'a negro secured 107.

Necessity for a court house near the middle of the County 415; for a ferry 321; for an Ear Mark 356; for a house of entertainment 362.

New table to be made 278.

No court held 92, 111, 203, 222, 236, 249, 284.

Non-suit 76, 91, 103, 151, 155, 191, 201, 253, 256, 286, 289, 390, 392, 400.

Notice not to pay quit rents 112, 210.

Official, deficiency 401; neglect 362.

Orders by the Court, 10, 20, 25, 62, 97, 104, 112, 160, 163, 164, 202, 205, 206, 208, 210, 223, 228, 266, 278, 287, 288, 292, 293, 298, 299, 300   301, 308, 311, 312, 319, 328, 345, 352, 363, 370, 374; payment for orphans 15.

Orphans placed 62, 64, 65.

Overseers of the Highways, appointed 25, 91, 109, 149, 158, 169, 191, 207, 236, 256, 266, 278, 303, 304, 327, 356, 396; continued 81; to summon the inhabitants 370.

Patents 56, 97, 197.

Payment time extended 11.

Payment ordered for attendance in Council and Assembly 314, 315.

Payment ordered for disbursements in building the court house 314.

Payment, ordered by a Justice of the Peace 366; for services of a negro 379.

Payment promised 320.

Peacemakers appointed 25, 59.

Petition for a town to be laid out 321.

Petition, read 345; concerning a boy 60; rejected 334; for relief 299, 308; for restoration of

goods 312; for a road deferred 315.

Petit Jury, attested 57, 58, 67, 68, 76, 77, 79, 80, 86, 88, 197, 214, 215, 218, 219, 233, 235, 245, 253, 265, 279, 289, 291, 299, 340, 341, 342, 371, 375, 377, 400, 403, 413; not agreed 108; returned 108, 216.

Petit Jury returned by the Sheriff 31, 98, 168, 186, 187, 188, 205, 207, 232, 234, 239, 245, 246, 247, 253, 265, 272, 289, 291, 299, 307, 340, 341, 342, 353, 371, 375, 377, 400, 403.

Presentment from Philadelphia County 24.

Private session of court 42, 281.

Proclamations from the Governor read, against vice 153, 252; about the Scoth 385; for apprehending pirates, privateers and sea rovers 345.

Promise of repairs 370.

Rails ordered for the Court House 277.

Receipt produced 404.

Recognizances, 104, 105, 123, 148, 170, 177, 188, 235, 251, 267, 297, 307, 308, 313, 336, 337, 344, 350, 358, 359, 362, 363, 377, 413; continued 152; forfeited 91, 192, 220, 280, 306.

Recommendation to keep an ordinary 388.

Reconveyance 334.

Refusal to pay fees 218.

Register to be appointed 223.

Release, delivered 73, 82; from fine 289.

Release from imprisonment ordered 70.

Repairs to Court House ordered 337.

Replevin granted 344, 347.

Requests, for an attorney 231; an audit of accounts 351; for examination of a witness to a will 205; for deferment of trial 200; for pay for Council and Assemblymen 121; for a Register of Wills 108, 206; for payment for services 221; for respite of action 238. trial 127, 131; for sale of land 294, 296; for suspension of judgment 122, trial 164; for termination of bond 288.

Restoration of goods ordered 312.

Roads, necessity for 96, 109, 196, 256, 298, 328, 356, 362, 376, 401, 414, 416; to be laid out 10, 41, 49, 100, 170, 198, 267, 281, 293, 299, 328, 363, 394; returns on 285, 379, 397, 398; fenced up 24, 32; laid out 302, 303; not laid out well 41; neglect of 298; petitions for 124, 223, 315, 379; payment for laying out 382; view of ordered 49; to be repaired 78, 110, 185, 208, 256.

Robbing of a colt 113.

Runaways 401; searched 159, 257.

Satisfaction acknowledged 61, 128, 149, 199, 220, 236, 240, 308, 388,

Search ordered by the Court 165.

Security, entered 333; ordered for orphan's estate 42.

Selling, beer by unlawful measure 362; without a license 211; his wife 336; liquors illegally 116, 211, 216; rum to the Indians 32, 33, 37, 60, 77, without a license 321; a servant 273.

Servitude, 161, 169; ordered 11, 16, 235, 258; extended by the Court 401, 402; petition concerning 266.

Setting fire to the tail of a horse 377.

Sheriff fined 360.

Sheriff's returns 3, 4, 6, 7, 9, 17, 21, 23, 26, 28, 29, 30, 35, 38, 40, 45, 46, 51, 53, 55, 92, 125, 126, 128, 130, 131, 132, 133, 142, 143, 144, 145, 150, 152, 162, 167, 172, 173, 184, 192, 196, 223, 224, 225, 226, 236, 237, 240, 241, 243, 244, 249, 250, 251, 254, 270, 271, 316, 319, 322, 323, 324, 329, 338, 339, 342, 345, 347, 348, 349, 365, 367, 369, 383, 384, 390.

Sheriff's sale ordered 16.

Slander 18, 150.

Sold at an outcry 339.

Speaking an untruth 319.

Special court granted 275.

Stealing, a mare 113, 116, 179; a mare and colt 275; a colt 283; clothing 195; half a hide of leather 113, 212, 215; a heifer 239; a hog 213, 218, 219; the Governor's mare 118, 122, 212, 216, 218; turkeys etc. 194.

Stopping passage by the river side 256.

Striking a blow 356.

Subpoenas 26, 30.

Summonses granted 8, 9, 12, 13, 15, 17, 19, 23, 26, 27, 28, 29, 30, 35, 36, 38, 39, 40, 45, 46, 51, 53, 55, 63, 126, 131, 132, 143, 144, 145, 152, 155, 156, 160, 161, 167, 172, 173, 177, 225, 226, 236, 237, 243, 244, 249, 250, 254, 255, 258, 259, 271, 322, 338, 347, 348, 358, 364, 367, 369, 384, 387, 390.

Supposed murder 263.

Surveys and returns to be perfected 69.

Suspects examined 166.

Swearing, 20, 21, 24, 75, 116, 216, 327, 346; and cursing 340.

Taking, forcibly a colt 213, 218; goods from a chest 306, from a house by felonious entry 375; horses 361, 401, 416; a sow 341.

Tax, arrears to be collected 89, 97, 292, 321; book to be brought into Court 300; collectors accountable to the Court 269, accounts 88, 189, 300, 329, 355, ordered to pay money 69, 308, 312, appointed 121, 221, 301, 319; collection ordered 130, 190, 196; necessity for a 113, 114, 214, 298, 327, 356; ordered to be raised 121, 159, 171, 211, 221, 257, 269, 281, 282.

Telling a lie in Court 207.

To be whipt 21, 59, 120, 160, 180, 198, 219, 220, 221, 258, 279, 401, 402.

To wear a Roman T 401, 402.

Townships, the County to be divided into 130, 137, 171; necessity to divide the county into 211, 240; division into ordered 242, 248; division made 268.

Unlawful, cattle 3; swine 256.

Verdict 307.

Warrant, granted 340, 366, 367, 368; for a negro 177.

Weights and Measures 131, 240, 242, 285.

Whipping, see to be whipt.

Will, to be kept by the Clerk of Court 128, 240; to be sent to the Governor 331; and inventory read 332.

Witnesses, 134, 186, 188, 194, 195, 197, 198, 205, 212, 213, 214, 215, 217, 218, 219, 227, 232, 239, 335, 344, 354; to a will 107.

Writ for a jury 8, 9, 17, 27, 28, 30.

www.ingramcontent.com/pod-product-compliance
Lightning Source LLC
Chambersburg PA
CBHW021843020426
42334CB00013B/164